THE NAZI
ANCESTRAL
PROOF

THE NAZI ANCESTRAL PROOF

Genealogy, Racial Science, and the Final Solution

Eric Ehrenreich

Indiana University Press

Bloomington and Indianapolis

This book is a publication of

Indiana University Press
601 North Morton Street
Bloomington, IN 47404-3797 USA

http://iupress.indiana.edu

Telephone orders	800-842-6796
Fax orders	812-855-7931
Orders by e-mail	iuporder@indiana.edu

The paper used in this publication meets the minimum requirements of American National
Standard for Information Sciences—Permanence of Paper for Printed Library Materials, ANSI
Z39.48-1984.

Manufactured in the United States of America

Library of Congress Cataloging-in-Publication Data

Ehrenreich, Eric.
  The Nazi ancestral proof : genealogy, racial science, and the final solution / Eric Ehrenreich.
    p. cm.
  Includes bibliographical references and index.
  ISBN-13: 978-0-253-34945-3 (cloth : alk. paper) 1. National socialism and genealogy. 2.
Eugenics—Government policy—Germany—History—20th century. 3. Race discrimination—
Germany—History—20th century. 4. Germany—Politics and government—1933–1945. 5.
Germany—Politics and government—1918–1933. I. Title.
  DD256.7.E335 2007
  940.53'1811—dc22
                                                                            2007010547

1 2 3 4 5   12 11 10 09 08 07

Book design: David Alcorn, Alcorn Publication Design

For my parents William Ehrenreich ז"ל
and Edith Ehrenreich,
and my daughter
Ariel Gill-Ehrenreich.

Contents

Acknowledgments

I AM INDEBTED TO MANY PERSONS without whose help this book simply would not have been possible. It is a pleasure to be able to thank them here. First and foremost, I would like to express my gratitude to David Sorkin who was an invaluable source of advice and support during my work on this book. David exemplifies all the best qualities of a scholar, and I can only hope that this work lives up to the high standard that he sets. I am also indebted to Rudy Koshar, Stanley Payne, and Laird Boswell for helping me to learn about the historian's craft.

I needed an extended stay in Germany to do the research underlying this work. For that opportunity, I would like to thank both the German Fulbright Commission and the Berlin Program for Advanced German and European Studies. In particular, my appreciation to Natascha Hoffmeyer and Karin Goihl who were not only my liaisons with those two programs, but also became friends; to Gisela Bock and Wolfgang Wipperman both for their research advice and for allowing me to participate in their seminars at the Free University in Berlin; and to Volkmar Weiß who provided me with extensive support at the Saxon State Archives as well as much good counsel. Dianne Schulle generously allowed me to see her manuscript on a closely related topic prior to publication, for which I am most grateful.

The staff at the German Federal Archives was always helpful and efficient. In addition, I was very fortunate to do my research there at the same time as a number of first-rate scholars, who also happened to be great people to "hang out" with, most notably Christof Morrissey, Greg Eghigian, Greg Witkowski, and Thomas Pegelow. Thomas Bach provided both invaluable feedback on my ideas and bitingly funny observations on everything else. I am especially indebted to Caroline Fricke who not only helped me in just about everything, but also happens to be a wonderful person.

On my return from Germany, John Tortorice and the University of Wisconsin's History Department's Mosse Program provided me with the opportunity to dedicate myself to the intimidating task of putting my research into some sort of coherent form. My friend and colleague at UW-Madison, Sharon Elise Cline, read portions of the work and provided helpful feedback. I am deeply indebted to Christopher Browning who, although he did not know me, kindly gave generously of his time and profound expertise to read and comment on my manuscript.

A fellowship at the United States Holocaust Memorial Museum's Center for Advanced Holocaust Studies provided me with the opportunity to refine my manuscript. While there, I received valuable comments and assistance from many persons, including Jürgen Matthäus, Severin Hochberg, Joseph White, Vicki Caron, Gregory Weeks, Carole Fink, John Roth, and Regula Ludi.

Aaron Gillette provided both sound advice and moral support in the effort to find a publisher. Many thanks to Lee Ann Sandweiss for suggesting that I send my manuscript to Indiana University Press, as well as to Janet Rabinowitch for all her help in the publishing process. All of the staff at IUP have been friendly and helpful.

I have saved my most important thank-yous for last. I am indebted beyond calculation to my parents, William and Edith Ehrenreich, not least for being exemplars of honesty and integrity. I have tried my best to incorporate those values into this work. And although she is still too young to understand how much she helps me, I would like to thank my lovely, funny daughter, Ariel Gill-Ehrenreich.

Introduction

In the first third of the twentieth century, Germany was arguably the most technologically sophisticated and scientifically advanced nation in the world. Long acclaimed as "the land of poets and thinkers," it had also developed within the European traditions of Christianity and the Enlightenment, with their respective emphases on love and reason. How could such a nation have produced the Third Reich, possibly the most murderous society in history?

The answer seems to lie in the racist ideology that informed the Nazi worldview. This ideology claimed that distinct human races exist, each with specific, hereditarily based physical, mental, and spiritual characteristics. It also asserted that some races are more valuable than others. If true, the exploitation of inferior beings was no violation of the Christian doctrine to love one's neighbors. Such beings were no more one's neighbors than are the other lower primates, or in the case of the Jews, bacilli. What of the Enlightenment value of reason? Was it reasonable to believe that humankind is divided into distinct races of differing value? The widely asserted claim that "National Socialism is applied biology" is paradigmatic of the Nazi response to this question. It implied that racist doctrine had been proven correct with scientific means. And who could reasonably argue against governmental policies mandated by the laws of nature?

On assuming power in 1933, the Nazi regime rapidly and thoroughly institutionalized this racial scientific ideology, with virtually no opposition from either individuals or institutions. Why? To answer this question, the present study analyzes two related historical phenomena. One is institutionalized genealogical practice in Imperial Germany (1871–1918) and the Weimar Republic (1919–1933).[1] While seemingly innocuous, genealogical practice in these periods formed the backbone of the second focus of this study, the Nazi-era "ancestral proof [*Abstammungsnachweis*]" or "Aryan proof [*Ariernachweis*]." This was the method of proving "racial acceptability" in the Third Reich for the purposes of the multiplicity of racial laws implemented between 1933 and 1945. During those twelve years, the vast majority of the German population probably made such a proof.

The ancestral proof's proponents almost always rationalized their assertions with an ideological subset of racial scientific ideology: racist eugenics. This held that only some races are "hereditarily compatible." At a minimum, the mixing of persons of incompatible races weakened the cultural abilities of the more "advanced" race. Advocates of the Nazi racial laws claimed the legislation was designed to prevent such biological and cultural damage. Due to the significant historical continuities between pre-1933 genealogical practice and the Nazi ancestral proof, comparing the two provides insight into the growth and functioning of racial scientific ideas in Germany in the first half of the twentieth century.

Chapter 1 of this study assesses racial scientific theory on its merits. Examining such claims as they were expressed both before and during the Third Reich, it demonstrates that they were clearly based on ambiguous empirical evidence and tenuous logic. No one, for example, could define "racial" categories in any meaningful way. Even worse from the Nazi perspective, no one could identify a racial marker for Jews. Throughout the book, additional examples of the widespread confusion engendered by attempts to put racial theory into practice further illustrate the irrational foundation of racial scientific claims. While there is no single definition for *scientific,* well before the turn of the twentieth century logical consistency and a clearly defined empirical research method constituted the basic tools of most German scientists, including those in the natural sciences. Thus, evaluated on its merits, the claim of scientific proof for racist ideas was far from compelling. Why, then, were the Nazis so successful in claiming the opposite?

This book argues that the reason behind this acceptance was that a great many Germans *wanted* to believe that racist ideas had been scientifically proven. Such concepts supported policies that many Germans perceived as beneficial to them. The idea of racial superiority obviously rationalized exploitation of "inferiors" for economic and political gain. However, the concept of racial kinship also provided a powerful counter-ideology for the important segments of the German population who felt increasingly threatened by socialist and liberal ideologies. Thus, if racist ideas were true, they either justified personal gain or allowed one to avoid feeling the need to challenge, and thus face the hostility, of those who were reaping such gain.

But a bare claim that race was the key factor in human relations was insufficient to *allow* many to accept it as true. It was too obviously self-serving. A more morally acceptable explanation was needed. Racial scientific thought, if true, provided just this palliative. Given the immense technological advances of the nineteenth and early twentieth centuries, scientific endorsement was very powerful. Many in the West viewed the scientific method as providing a means of arriving at the "objective truth." Accordingly, if racial scientific ideas were true, racist policies were the result of fundamental necessity, not self-serving choice. One could view the material and psychic benefits derived from promoting or acquiescing in racist policies as an effect, rather than the cause, of one's promotion or acquiescence. In reciprocal fashion, the widespread desire throughout German society either to believe racist ideas true, or to have a personally satisfactory reason not to have to question them, caused scientists and others to expend great effort in creating plausible-sounding explanations for the scientific validity of racism. It is also the reason that very few Germans sought to critically evaluate these explanations.

These phenomena did not suddenly arise during the Third Reich. Chapters 2 and 3 examine, through the prism of genealogical practice, the development of racial scientific ideology between the creation of a unified Germany in 1871 and the Nazi assumption of power in 1933. During this period, the benefits of racist ideology were already becoming increasingly obvious. By the late nineteenth century, racism of course justified German (as well as other Western) imperialism. In Germany, however, racist concepts also gained an important internal political value. During the late nineteenth and early twentieth centuries, Marxist thought increasingly threatened to rend Germany along class lines. Moreover, classic liberal ideas such as constitutionalism and parliamentarianism, whose power was on the wane in Imperial Germany, nevertheless remained factors that could potentially undermine privilege based on traditional social caste. Even political Catholicism threatened to divide Germans by religion. In contrast, racism provided a unifying doctrine for many Germans that was less fundamentally threatening than these other ideologies. A shared "German essence" transcended geography, religion, and especially class. The many proponents of this idea hoped to defuse class and other social tensions without having to make major concessions in socioeconomic status.[2] The instability during Weimar acted as a catalyst in this regard.

Thus from the 1870s, even groups not perceived as particularly *völkisch* increasingly used racial thinking to promote the idea of common ancestry among those of "German blood." These endorsements coincided with a growing body of professional racial scientific literature, often written by scientists of the highest caliber, also sanctioning such ideas. Moreover, although intellectual and political tools were increasingly available to challenge the claim that science had validated racist ideas, in Germany even prior to 1933 relatively few prominent scientists or laypersons did so. This lent the ideology a growing aura of credibility.

Genealogical literature from the late Kaiserreich and Weimar Republic also illustrates another related phenomenon important for the later legitimation of racist policies in the Third Reich: the increasing endorsement of eugenic thought. Eugenics was the attempt to regulate human breeding to increase "valuable" hereditary characteristics, such as intelligence and beauty, and decrease "harmful" ones, such as "feeblemindedness" and hereditary disease. By 1933, eugenics had a highly distinguished pedigree both in Germany and in the West as a whole. It was, however, not necessarily linked to the concept of race. Nevertheless, especially during Weimar, German proponents of racist ideas began increasingly to associate them successfully with broader strains of eugenic theory and policy. They claimed that race-mixing simply comprised another hereditary threat to the German population. Thus by the time of the Nazi assumption of power, racial scientific ideology, which provided a broadly acceptable rationalization for many racist policies, was already part of the German intellectual and cultural mainstream.

✳ ✳ ✳

Chapters 4–7 of this book describe the institutionalization of racism in Nazi Germany as viewed through the prism of the ancestral proof requirement. Essentially, they illustrate the German population's massive compliance. After 1933, of course, racist ideas were associated with even greater advantages. People involved directly or tangentially in the administration of the ancestral proof, for example, received many economic and social rewards. Amateur and professional genealogists, racial scientists, and those who controlled genealogical information, such as church officials, civil registrars, and archivists, gained increased funding and prestige. But the direct benefits of a racist institutional apparatus extended well beyond those directly involved in the ancestral proof process. As historian Neil MacMaster writes: "On a material level the immense proliferation of professional posts, the establishment and extensive funding of race laboratories, research institutes, Health Courts and the overall structures of the racial state, provided a rich opportunity for academics, lawyers, civil servants and doctors to promote their careers and to achieve upward social mobility, high status and considerable wealth."[3]

Racist ideas also provided grist for the Pan-Germanic mill. By buttressing the concept of the "biological relatedness" of all Germans, racism helped to justify imperialist objectives wherever there were substantial ethnic German populations. Even more importantly, racism rationalized the exploitation of non-German populations. Between 1933 and 1945, the Nazi regime used the concept to validate the theft of both property and labor on an extraordinary scale. Directed against Jews, this took place through the "Aryanization" of businesses and other more direct methods. After the war began, racist ideology also justified the plunder of predominantly non-Jewish but still "racially alien" populations in occupied Eastern Europe. Hitler himself noted that the "racial struggle" was allied with a battle for "oil-fields, rubber, and mineral wealth." It also involved stealing land and foodstuffs, and the reinstitution of slavery on a vast scale. Finally, Nazi racism rationalized the extraordinary brutality required to carry out theft of this magnitude.[4]

The use of racist ideology as a tool for internal social and political stability also continued during the Third Reich. This application, however, was fundamentally, if indirectly, connected to racism's use as a justification for exploitation. In order to help maintain traditional social hierarchies, while still providing collective advantages to all members of the "racial community," wealth had to be infused from outside German society. In other words, if being a "racial comrade" had been of no particular social or economic benefit, it would not have served to defuse class struggle in Nazi Germany. Eventually, plunder was necessary in order to maintain social peace within the *Volksgemeinschaft* (racial community). Racial scientific ideology, the most broadly acceptable rationalization for racist policies, became an ideological core of the Nazi state. It particularly supported the claim that the racial laws, the legal mechanism for the impoverishment and expulsion of German Jews, were necessary to ensure the continued existence of the German *Volk*—to protect family and

Fatherland from destruction by a dire hereditary threat—not as a rationalization for exploitation.

The foregoing combination of perceived benefits and broadly acceptable rationalization allowed the Nazi regime to implement the racial laws with virtually no opposition from either institutions or individuals. As chapter 4 illustrates, tens of millions of Germans were required to make an ancestral proof, yet few ever questioned its necessity. Indeed, the obligation soon became an accepted part of everyday life in the Third Reich. Its proponents quickly developed methods to "prove race" through oath, genealogical documentation, and "scientific analysis." They also created specific offices designed to ensure that the obligation was put into practice as desired. Moreover, the requirement rapidly entered into German commercial life. Authors wrote "how-to" books on the process for the public; genealogists developed, and stationery stores sold, millions of convenient, pocket-sized "ancestral passports"; and businesses gave away genealogical tables as marketing devices, much as present-day companies give away pens and calendars.

Chapters 5 and 6 study the Reich Genealogical Authority, the most important of the offices developed to implement the ancestral proof requirement. These chapters form a core body of evidence for this work and further demonstrate the large degree to which the obligation infiltrated almost every level of German society during the Third Reich. They also show that the frequent dissonance between racial scientific theory and racist practice had virtually no impact on its institutionalization. Even as Authority officials struggled to square the circle of identifying "racially alien" persons who often had no identifiable racial characteristics, no individual or institution used this struggle as an opportunity to question the necessity of the racial laws. Chapter 7 pays particular attention to the three institutional and professional groupings that most benefited from the ancestral proof: the genealogists whose practice was a primary method of proving "race"; the Protestant and Catholic churches, whose documentary holdings served as a major source for establishing "racial acceptability"; and the scientists who carried out so-called hereditary and racial scientific investigations where genealogical proof was lacking. This further illustrates both the process and its widespread acceptance. Ironically, the discussion of the scientists also provides the most detailed examples of the "unscientific" nature of efforts to determine "race," showing how these men struggled to place a scientific sheen over an incoherent process. Finally, chapter 8 further helps to explain the broad compliance with institutionalized racism by illustrating how advocates of the ancestral proof also augmented its palatability by linking it to mainstream ideological currents beyond eugenics, and to existing legal and bureaucratic practices.

✳ ✳ ✳

The successful institutionalization of policies directly associated with the multiplicity of racial laws should be distinguished from another, even more infamous, Nazi racial policy: the objective of destroying all the Jews in the world. The German government issued no law implementing this policy, and it was not primarily justified by the necessity of preventing "race-mixing." It was, rather, driven by the idea that Jews were, due to their biology, implacable enemies of non-Jews. The effort to understand how such an apparently incredible idea could have achieved such prominence and driven such dire policy choices in one of the most scientifically sophisticated societies of the twentieth century has, in fact, been the motivation for this study.

An attempted answer to this question is interwoven throughout the book. As chapters 2 and 3 demonstrate, prior to 1933 Jews were not the primary targets of racist eugenic ideology. In the Kaiserreich, and even Weimar, there was still no racial scientific consensus that Jews were a "hereditary threat" to the German *Volk*. The allegation, for example, while not absent from genealogical works, was also not consistently emphasized. But these chapters also illustrate that expressions of anti-Jewish sentiment were ongoing throughout these periods. As with the promotion of eugenic ideas, this was not necessarily linked to the concept of *race*. Similarly, when genealogists did link *Jews* and *race,* they were not necessarily being antisemitic. The claim that Jews were, as a whole, "racially *different*" than German non-Jews (as, for example, many southern Europeans were said to be) was not the same as the claim that they were "racially *alien*" (as was almost universally claimed for "colored" persons) and thus a hereditary threat. Nevertheless, the foregoing circumstances prepared the ground for the Nazi ideologues.

As the chapters on Nazi Germany illustrate, upon assuming power the Nazi regime began promoting racist eugenic doctrine on a massive scale. But there was one important new conceptual development: the constantly repeated allegation that Jews were "racially alien." While this claim did not have the same venerable pedigree of other racial scientific ideas, by this time it was not blatantly incredible. It followed decades of agitation by eugenicists regarding "hidden hereditary threats," growing claims that "race-mixing" constituted a hereditary threat, widespread claims that Jewish and non-Jewish Germans were at least "racially different," and a centuries-long tradition of hostility to Jews for "nonracial" reasons. Thus by 1933, the Nazi allegation that Jews were indisputably "racially alien" and posed a "hereditary health" threat to non-Jewish Germans was not a great ideological stretch for most Germans.

But again, this racial scientific doctrine as developed up to 1933 was not the primary ideological force driving the "Final Solution." Even the most radical interpretations of racial scientific ideology held only that Jews were one among the many peoples who were "racially alien," and thus should not be "mixed" with. No "reputable" racial scientist had until then claimed that science had verified Jews were a discrete "race," hereditarily programmed to destroy non-Jews. While mainstream racial scientific ideology did not rationalize the Final Solution, this book's last chapter argues that it was nevertheless essential in creating the social conditions for the development and then implementation of genocidal policies. First, by generating a wide social consensus for brutal anti-Jewish actions, the ideology created an atmosphere in which Jews became social pariahs and thus easy targets. Second, although this vast consensus was in fact built on a rationalization that could have been shown to be questionable, no one questioned it. This signaled to the Nazi leadership that their brutal policies did not have to be based on a logically coherent ideology, and encouraged the development of ever more radical policies based on increasingly far-fetched ideas. Finally, proponents of anti-Jewish measures progressively conflated the idea of a Jewish "*Volk,*" composed of a variety of "racially alien" elements, and a Jewish "race," bearing particular "Jewish racial characteristics." Racial scientific verbiage thus helped camouflage the blatant irrationality of the idea that Jews are inherently evil. If "Jewish racial traits" included "malevolence," then that malice was presumably scientifically proven to be hereditary. In such case, one could reasonably wish to destroy all Jews.

Abbreviations

A-E	Abstammungs-Erhebungen (Ancestral Inquiries)
AfRuG	*Archiv für Rassen- und Gesellschaftsbiologie* (*Archive for Racial and Social Biology*)
AfS	Amtes für Sippenforschung der NSDAP (Nazi Party Office for Kinship Research)
ArchfS	*Archiv für Sippenforschung und aller verwandte Gebiete* (*Archive for Kinship Research and All Related Fields*)
ASS	*Allgemeines Suchblatt für Sippenforscher* (General Search Sheet for Kinship Researchers)
BDC	Berlin Document Center
BfdK	Beauftragte für das Kirchenbuchwesen bei der Kanzlei der Deutschen Evangelischen Kirche (German Evangelical Church Chancellery's Representative for Church Book Activities)
DH	*Der Deutsche Herold* (*The German Herald*)
DZfG	Deutsche Zentralstelle für Genealogie, Leipzig (German Central Office for Genealogy)
EDDA	*Eisernes Buch deutschen Adels deutscher Art* (*Iron Book of German Nobles of German Type*)
Erl.	Erlass (Decree)
FamB	*Familiengeschichtliche Bibliographie* (*Family History Bibliography*)
FB	*Familiengeschichtliche Blätter* (*Family History Gazette*)
FSV	*Familie, Sippe, Volk*
GAfS	Gauamt für Sippenforschung (Gau Office for Kinship Research)
GSA-W	Gausippenamt Wien (Gau Kinship Office Vienna)
KfRuF	*Korrespondenz für Rasseforschung und Familienkunde* (*Correspondence for Race Research and Family Studies*)
MbliV	*Ministerialblatt für die Preußische innere Verwaltung* (*Ministerial Gazette for the Prussian Internal Administration*)
MdR	*Mitteilungen des Roland* (*News of the Roland*)
MdZ	*Mitteilungen der Zentralstelle für deutsche Personen- und Familiengeschichte* (*News of the Central Office for German Personal and Family History*)
RdErl.	Runderlass (general decree)

RfS	Reichsstelle für Sippenforschung (Reich Office for Kinship Research)
RGBl	*Reichsgesetzblatt (Reich Legal Gazette)*
RMBliV	*Ministerialblatt des Reichs- und Preußischen Ministeriums des Innern (Ministerial Gazette of the Reich and Prussian Ministry of the Interior)*
RMdI	Reichsministerium des Innern (Reich Ministry of the Interior)
RMfWEuV	Reichsministerium für Wissenschaft, Erziehung und Volksbildung (Reich Ministry for Science, Education, and Volk Education)
RPA	Rassenpolitischesamt des NSDAP (Racial Policy Office)
RSA	Reichssippenamt (Reich Kinship Office)
RSH	Reichsverband der Sippenforscher und Heraldiker e.V. (Reich Association of Kinship Researchers and Heraldists)
RSW	Reichsvereins für Sippenforschung und Wappenkunde e.V. (Reich Association for Kinship Research and Heraldry)
RuPrMdI	Reichs- und Preussische Ministerium des Innern (Reich and Prussian Ministry of the Interior)
SfR	Sachverständige für Rasseforschung beim Reichsministerium des Innern (Interior Ministry Expert for Racial Research)
StAZ	*Zeitschrift für Standesamtswesen (Journal for Civil Registry Practice)*
VBS	Vereinigung der Berufssippenforscher e.V. (Union of Professional Kinship Researchers)
VfS	Verlag für Standesamtswesen (Publisher for Civil Registry Practice)
VSV	Volksbund der deutschen sippenkundlichen Vereine, e.V. (Volk Federation of German Kinship Studies Societies)

THE NAZI
ANCESTRAL
PROOF

1 | Racial Science

A hair's breadth division . . . separates faith from science.
—Max Weber

THE PRIMARY BASIS ON WHICH THE NAZI REGIME justified imposing the ancestral proof requirement on virtually the entire population of the Reich was as a public health measure. As will be shown repeatedly throughout this work, proponents of the racial laws most frequently explained them as necessary to prevent infiltration of damaging, "alien-type" (*Artfremd*) hereditary traits into the German *Volksgemeinschaft*. Again, according to these advocates, scientists had shown that distinct human races exist and that each of these races exhibits specific hereditarily based physical, mental, and spiritual characteristics. The varieties of human culture were thus directly connected to racially grounded abilities and predispositions, and only some of these races were "hereditarily compatible." At a minimum, the mixing of persons of incompatible race weakened the cultural abilities of the more advanced race.[1] Advocates of these laws thus claimed that they were designed to prevent such biological and cultural damage, and also asserted that Jews, being "racially alien," were the most direct threat in this regard.[2]

Did, however, "the scientific verdict of hereditary and racial research" actually seem to support these laws as their proponents repeatedly claimed?[3] By the early twentieth century, German science was highly sophisticated. Between 1904 and 1937, Germany was the world leader in Nobel Prize recipients, having garnered thirty-eight.[4] Einstein had already propounded his special theory of relativity by 1905. Soon thereafter, Einstein, Max Planck, and other German physicists developed the theory of quantum mechanics. While the life sciences had not yet demonstrated intellectual breakthroughs of this magnitude, life scientists were aware of, admired, and consciously followed the same methodology as the physical scientists. Already in the late nineteenth century, Rudolf Virchow, the leading German pathologist of the time, claimed as follows: "We [natural scientists] have unity of method. We are looking for the laws of human development, being, and activity with the same means."[5] The most important German textbook on genetics and eugenics in the 1920s and 1930s contained an entire section on methodology. It noted that "physics and chemistry . . . are held up before the biologists as the exemplars of exact research," and claimed that genetics, like the physical sciences, is based on "precise data" obtained from "numerous measurements" and is ultimately "based on experiment."[6]

This adherence to certain basic principles was understandable. As Planck stated during a 1935 speech at the Kaiser Wilhelm Society (KWS), Germany's most prestigious scientific organization, whatever the ultimate nature of reality, it proves most useful and productive for the scientist to stipulate a causal, real, outer world.[7] Founded in 1911 and disbanded in 1945, the KWS throughout its existence produced at least twenty-one Nobel Prize winners as members—including Planck and Einstein, and also including several winners in the fields of physiology and medicine.[8] The anthropologist Eugen Fischer and hereditary pathologist Otmar Freiherr von Verschuer, who became avid supporters of Nazi racial policy, also both directed the Kaiser Wilhelm Institute for Anthropology, Human Genetics, and Eugenics in Berlin-Dahlem.

German scientists at the time clearly understood a "scientifically valid" theory to be based on carefully gathered data that was logically interpreted and susceptible to experimental verification. The ultimate failure of the "German physics" and "German mathematics" movements in Nazi Germany, which sought to trump logical reasoning with racial ideology, further attest to the widespread consensus as to what constituted a "scientifically valid" assertion.[9] Indeed, this understanding was widespread throughout German society. Even Nazi propaganda pamphlets (when possible) attacked opposing views by claiming such views contradicted experimental findings.[10]

Racial Science Prior to 1933

Racial scientific claims rarely if ever fulfilled the widely recognized criteria for scientific validity. In 1926, the aforementioned geneticist Otmar von Verschuer gave a standard contemporary definition of "race":

> in the anthropological sense, races are defined as an extended group of humans who, through the possession of certain hereditary capacities [*Erbanlagen*] for physical and mental features are differentiated from other humans. Race is a biological concept, something innate, unchangeable.[11]

Such a definition, however, was highly problematic from a scientific perspective: the cutoff point for a "racial grouping" was highly arbitrary. At one end of the spectrum, an extended family could be seen as constituting a "race" since its members possess certain hereditary capacities differentiating them from other humans. At the other end of the spectrum, by the nineteenth century there was a general consensus that humankind was divided into a variety of major racial groupings. But the nature of these was highly disputed. In the early twentieth century, for example, the most prominent German racial scientists argued over the existence of a Falisch race—tall and blond, but unlike the so-called Nordic race, directly descended from Cro-Magnon man and thus neither slender in build, nor narrow-skulled.[12]

This lack of precision for the key classificatory basis of pre-1933 racial science was one reason that the second core theory—the alleged racial origin of mentality and culture—was also problematic as "science." This claim is key to racist thought. Even the most die-hard racists admitted that hatred based on appearance alone is irrational. Behavior, though, is rightfully subject to approval or disapproval, and in regard to groups of humans, collective behavior is referred to as culture. According to racist thought, if a culture is debased, primitive, or otherwise inferior, then by definition so is the race that produces that culture. If, however, there is no precise racial grouping to study, one cannot scientifically determine whether culture is racially based. To which group of people does the culture "belong"? This notion alone put into question the basic racist presumption of the biological basis of culture.

Even assuming, however, that particular racial groups could be precisely identified, there was still no proof that culture is biologically based. The major evidence for this assertion was the fact that people who look similar physically are often associated with particular cultures.[13] But this is no more proof that the culture developed out of the particular biology of a people with certain physical characteristics than it is proof that the culture developed out of those people's responses to their environment. In other words, such correlations neither prove nor disprove the link between heredity and culture. Until the hypothesis was tested and validated by experiment, for example determining somehow whether one "race" was capable of "bearing the culture" of another "race," there was no scientific basis to claim that culture was based on nature rather than nurture.[14] Given this state of affairs, the widespread racial scientific assertion that the mixing of "incompatible races" caused damage to the "peculiar excellencies" of each race was also without scientific validity.[15]

Nowhere were the inconsistencies and contradictions of racial science clearer than with regard to "racial-scientific" pronouncements regarding "Jews." Prior to 1933, most prominent German racial scientists had decided that, at least to some degree, Jews were racially different from "Germans." The consensus was that Jews, like Germans, were a *Volk* and not a race: a group of persons composed of a similar mixture of "compatible races," sharing a common culture. The German mixture of races, however, was said to be European (usually Nordic, Falisch, Mediterranean, Alpine, Dinaric, and/or East Baltic); the Jewish mixture primarily Asiatic (Near Eastern and Oriental). Proponents of this idea could point to supporting empirical data. Rudolf Virchow's massive anthropological survey, published in 1886, showed that approximately 50 percent of non-Jewish schoolchildren in Germany had blond hair and blue eyes, while only 20 percent of Jewish pupils had such coloration. Thus, on average, there were physical differences between Jew and non-Jew, perhaps indicating an increased likelihood of more recent arrival in Europe for the ancestors of any particular Jew.

This belief about the Jews' racial status was nevertheless highly problematic from a scientific perspective. It proved impossible ever to determine whether any particular person was Jewish based on physical characteristics alone. Jews shared neither a single physical attribute, nor a conglomeration of attributes. Nor was there any common physical property that all Jews lacked but was found in neighboring, non-Jewish populations. In fact, a disconcerting number of Jews seemed to have particularly "European" physical characteristics, such as blond hair and blue eyes, while a discomfiting number of non-Jews seemed to have "typically Jewish physical characteristics," including dark features and a "Jewish" nose.[16]

Research into other areas of biology also failed to help differentiate the Jews. For example, German blood-group researchers had shown that

> Western Europe seemed to be the homeland of the great group A race. Far to the east lay the source of group B, and along Germany's eastern frontier the Nordic race repelled the Asiatic influx with a steep rise in the frequency of group A. As [surgeon, bacteriologist, and prominent blood-group researcher Paul] Steffan said, the typically Asiatic distribution of the blood groups persisted almost unchanged right up to the east bank of the Oder.

Yet in Germany, "the proportion of groups A and B among Jews and the rest of the population in a given city differed very little. In Berlin, they even differed in the wrong direction."[17] Thus a "Jew" could be physically identical to an "Aryan"— tall, blond, blue-eyed, "Roman-nosed," with blood type A—and vice versa. In what sense, then, could *Jewish* constitute a racial category? Contemporaries raised this question. In his work *The Racial Characteristics of the Jews,* for example, published in Germany in 1913, the American anthropologist Maurice Fishberg made available the results of his anthropological study of three thousand Jewish inhabitants in Europe, Asia, Africa, and America. He, too, concluded that there was no physical marker for Jews, and also noted the dissociation between physical stereotype and ancestral relation to Judaism.[18]

In response, many racial scientists posited that Jewish culture, not physical characteristics, pointed up the primary racial difference. The biological difference between Jews and non-Jews lay in mental and spiritual characteristics. But this was also problematic as "science." First, while physical characteristics may be measured relatively easily, mental, and especially spiritual, characteristics are difficult or impossible to measure.[19] Thus, prior to the Nazi period, racial scientists failed to achieve a consensus on the nature of Jewish mental and spiritual characteristics. The best argument was simply to cite the unproven assertion that there were "average" Jewish psychic characteristics that existed in various degrees in any individual Jew.[20]

An even more difficult problem existed, however. If two individuals exhibited distinct cultural characteristics, but were physically similar, on what basis could one conclude that the cultural differences were hereditary? An inability to answer this question might be viewed as an undermining of the major racist presumption under which the scientists labored: the genetic basis of culture. Thus, before the Nazi era, one German contemporary noted as follows:

> Racial research is not a matter of pure descriptive natural science. It is not a struggle of theories fought out by scholars with purely scientific means. Rather it is about a doctrine that is accepted or rejected with the total pathos of faith. . . .[21]

And in other parts of the industrialized world, scientists increasingly contested the validity of the Nazi's claim that science had irrefutably proven the link between race and culture.[22] In sum, given the ambiguous evidence, prior to 1933 "science" clearly had not proven the theory underlying the Nazi racial laws, especially with reference to its anti-Jewish aspects.

Racial Science after 1933

Some Nazi ideologues were aware of the apparent flaws in the racist argument. A 1933 bibliography of racial-scientific writings, for example, commissioned by the Interior Ministry's racial expert, listed several works by the American anthropologist Fishberg under the category "Racial Studies of the Jewish *Volk*." Failure to refute such antiracist arguments would presumably undermine Nazi claims to scientific support for their racial laws. Moreover, despite extensive research after 1933 into the racial composition of Europeans in general, and of the German-speaking populations in particular, German racial scientists achieved no breakthrough in identifying any individual person's "racial makeup." A 1938 article in a leading racial-scientific journal noted this, albeit in guarded language: "the nature of [racial science] never allows a statement about the distribution of racial characteristics within any given portion of a presently living *Volk* with absolute numerical certainty."[23] And in a 1944 article, the geneticist Verschuer clearly acknowledged the continuing difficulty in proving that mental characteristics are inherited. He wrote: "We cannot expect otherwise given the present [level of] knowledge; the [hereditary] regulations of the psychic area are too manifold."[24] Again, this would seem to have undercut the proclaimed scientific basis of the racial laws.

With regard to Jews in particular, a 1938 article by Verschuer on the "Racial-Biology of the Jews" bears detailed consideration, as it sought to address the weaknesses in classifying Jews on racial lines.[25] In his article, Verschuer repeated the claim that Jews comprise a distinctive racial group composed of races foreign to those of non-Jews in Germany (137). His physical proof was that when compared to non-Jews in Germany, Jews on average were physically different: shorter in stature, having lower frequencies of blond hair and blue eyes, and showing higher incidences of flat feet. Verschuer acknowledged, however, that this information was of no help in identifying individuals with Jewish ancestry:

> A . . . single characteristic by which one can identify Jews with absolute certainty is not known. . . . All individual characteristics of the German racial groups are also found in individual Jews and the infrequent appearance of characteristics that are typical for Jews in persons of German ancestry still do not prove with certainty a Jewish admixture in the ancestry. . . . (138)

Verschuer, however, still insisted that Jews be driven from German society. He demanded this not because they would otherwise lower the average height, decrease the incidence of blond hair and blue eyes, and increase the incidence of flat feet in the overall population, but rather because they would bring in destructive Jewish psychic characteristics.

According to Verschuer, Jews suffered a greater incidence of mental illness. As proof, he noted that the frequency of Jewish suicide, while traditionally lower than that of non-Jews, was now higher. While Verschuer noted that some attributed this to the loss of community following emancipation (he did not mention present Nazi policies), he claimed that "only persons [already] psychopathically and neurotically minded to a certain degree would react in such a way to this type of change in external conditions" (148). Moreover, wrote Verschuer, Jews have no connection with nature, no ability for selfless love, and no sense of reverence. This was apparently self-evident as he cited no evidence to justify his remarks.

Regarding the Jews' alleged hereditary ability to maintain uniform psychic properties without consistent physical properties, Verschuer maintained that they achieved this through self-imposed reproductive policies that selected mates on the basis of mental rather than bodily characteristics. "It is diversely proven," he wrote (without citation of such proof), "that the longstanding Jewish tendency to trade, for example, is not due to historical external pressure but rather to inner aptitude" (150). Jews pick marriage partners on such basis, thus selecting for the tendency. Moreover, the "pure-formal logic" ability of the Jews, the cause of their inability to be in touch with nature, feel selfless love, or have a sense of reverence, leads to the same sort of professions, also leading to natural selection in this regard. Converts to Judaism, wrote Verschuer, probably converted because they already had hereditary affinity to Jewish psychic values, thereby only strengthening these "Jewish" mental racial characteristics. In essence, Jews were a mental "race." Jews who looked "Nordic," for example, nevertheless had the same psyche as Jews who appeared "Asiatic."

Verschuer's argument was, in fact, demonstrably circular. He was arguing: (1) that psychic characteristics are hereditary, and are genetically independent of physical characteristics; (2) this is proved by the Jews—a group of humans (apparently the only one) with diverse physical, but uniform mental, properties; (3) the Jews are, thus, by definition a "racial group" (i.e., they share a particular hereditary characteristic not common to other human groups); since (4) psychic characteristics are hereditary and may be transmitted independently of physical characteristics. Moreover, Verschuer's argument was based on the unproven assumption that,

Figure 1. Otmar von Verschuer, hereditary pathologist and racial scientist, ca. 1930.
Courtesy of the Library and Archives of the Max Planck Society.

whether environmentally or biologically based, Jews had uniform psychic characteristics. And, as he himself noted, his theory had no predictive value. It did not bring
the world any closer to that day when one would be able to state with certainty
whether a particular individual was or was not a Jew. Given Verschuer's expertise in
genetics, and his obvious knowledge of the difficulty in proving the hereditary basis

of mental characteristics, this was an especially strained and clearly "unscientific" argument.

Noting that Verschuer's analysis was logically flawed, however, is not the same as saying that his basic argument about the Jews' racial status was wrong. It is only to say his reasoning did not support that argument. In 1938, Eugen Fischer, the most prominent German anthropologist of his time, wrote a different type of argument in support of the foregoing racial picture of the Jews. Fischer wrote that "we instinctively feel" the physical, and especially mental, differences between Jew and European.[26] Unlike Verschuer's argument, Fischer's could not be shown to be logically inconsistent. But it was also clearly not a "scientific" argument.

In fact, in the Nazi era, as before, individuals could only be identified as Jews based on indisputably nonhereditary characteristics (e.g., self-identification as Jews). However, a major difference was that without any new evidence, racial scientists nevertheless began to speak of "Jewish psychic characteristics" as established, uniform, and genetically based. Indeed, after 1933 there was, if anything, a decrease in the amount of actual racial-scientific research on "Jewish racial characteristics." This stood in striking contrast to the voluminous research on European racial characteristics, as well as in the face of significant research on the characteristics of non-Jewish, non-Europeans.[27]

The reason for the paucity of research on Jews seems clear: such studies would have undermined the asserted "scientific" basis for the racial laws. This is demonstrated by one of the very rare racial scientific studies of Jews published during the Nazi era. In 1942, Dr. Elfriede Fliethmann, an assistant in the Race and Ethnic Science Section of the Institute for German Eastern-Work in Kraków, published a report on her study of 565 Jews in Tarnów, Poland. Fliethmann interviewed and took detailed head and body measurements of her subjects. She noted that physically, in comparison with "Viennese Jews," the Jews of Tarnów more frequently exhibited "components of the European races, especially the Alpine-East Baltic . . . [while] the Near Eastern-Oriental [component] was not infrequently strongly hidden." Indeed, Fliethmann wrote that the population did not look "typically Jewish" and that "their racial appearance did not allow their recognition as such."

Nor did the Jews of Tarnów appear particularly "Jewish" demographically. Of the 296 persons employed, 130 were tailors, 69 were salespersons, and the remainder were either shoemakers, plumbers, bakers, painters, furriers, clerical employees, in the free professions, or day laborers (103). About 10 percent were illiterate, while the majority (about 65%) had been educated through elementary school (*Volksschule*). Approximately 5 percent of the men and 10 percent of the women had attended secondary school (*Gymnasium*) (101). Nevertheless, according to Fliethmann, the (often strongly hidden) Near Eastern racial component still caused "an alien-type impression": primarily due to the population's "strong . . . business sense and unscrupulousness," comparable to that of "the Armenians." Typically, Fliethmann could do no more than assert the existence of a biologically based psychic unity in an otherwise physically and demographically diverse population. She concluded that it was "for racial-psychology to get to the bottom of the cause and origin of these findings."[28]

The Problem of Definition

Identifying individual's "racial composition" during the Nazi era required usable definitions of "*Aryan*" and "*German or related blood*," or conversely "*non-Aryan*" and "*Jew*." In a variety of ways, the attempts to do this also indicated the falsehood of claims to scientific legitimacy for the racial laws.

Apparently the initial such legal definition appeared in April 1933, as part of the first regulations implementing the Law for the Reestablishment of the Professional Civil Service (Civil Service Law).[29] This denoted a "non-Aryan" as a person "who is descended from non-Aryan, especially Jewish parents or grandparents. This premise especially obtains if one parent or grandparent was of Jewish faith."[30] This definition obviously used religious affiliation to define racial status. Proponents of the racial laws, aware of the seeming discrepancy in using religion as a surrogate for race, often stated that this was simply a legal presumption based on the paucity of intermarriage between Jews and non-Jews prior to Jewish emancipation. Thus it was implicitly acknowledged that a few "nonracial Jews" (presumably those who had converted to Judaism after emancipation) might be lumped in with "racial Jews."[31] Less explicable, however, was the fact that authorities either did not assign a racial presumption to membership in the Moslem faith, or assumed the exact opposite. In May 1938, for example, the German consulate in Istanbul asked the German Foreign Office for guidance as to whether "members of the Krimchak confession are to be viewed as members of the Jewish race, or whether they are Muslims and, as such, Aryans."[32] Indeed, in September 1943 Hitler specifically decreed that Muslim "Germans" may remain party members, just as could persons of "Christian confession."[33]

Providing an affirmative definition of *Aryan* posed additional theoretical and political problems, both of which could also be construed as undermining the asserted scientific basis for racial policy. In July 1933, for example, Hans Seel, an Interior Ministry official, asked Achim Gercke (1902–1997), then the ministry's racial expert, how he would reconcile the "Aryan paragraph" in the Civil Service Law with the following definition of *Aryan* by Albert Gorter, another prominent ministry official:

> The Aryans (also Indo-Germans, Japhetiten) are one of the three branches of the Caucasian (white race); they are divided into the western (European), that is the German, Roman, Greek, Slav, Lett, Celt [and] Albanesen, and the eastern (Asiatic) Aryans, that is the Indian (Hindu) and Iranian (Persian, Afghan, Armenian, Georgian, Kurd). Non-Aryans are therefore:
> 1. the members of the two other races, namely the Mongolian (yellow) and the Negroid (black) races;

2. the members of the other two branches of the Caucasian race, namely the Semites (Jews, Arabs) and Hamites (Berbers). The Finns and Hungarians belong to the Mongolian race; but it is hardly the intention of the law to treat them as non-Aryans. Thus . . . the non-Jewish members of all European *Volk* are Aryans. . . .[34]

This definition of *Aryan* was clearly unacceptable. Not only did it include large numbers of non-European peoples such as Kurds and Afghans, but it also made the racial laws seem to be based on political expedience rather than science. Gercke replied that he would use the definition of *Aryan* established by the Expert Advisor for Population and Racial Policy (*Sachverständigenbeirats für Bevölkerungs- und Rassenpolitik*): "An Aryan is one who is tribally related (*stammverwandte*) to German blood. An Aryan is the descendant of a *Volk* domiciled in Europe in a closed tribal settlement (*Volkstumssiedlung*) since recorded history."[35] This definition managed to include Finns and Hungarians, and exclude Kurds and Afghans. Why this definition was more scientifically accurate, however, Gercke did not say.

The lack of uniformity of terms that were used to define racial acceptability also reflected the imprecision of the concept. Thus, while the Civil Service Law sought to differentiate between "Aryans" and "non-Aryans," the Entailed Farm Law (*Erbhofgesetz*), also from 1933, discriminated between those with and without "German or tribally similar [*stammesgleich*] blood."[36] While early court decisions indicated that the two concepts had the same meaning, the meaning itself was not made explicit.[37] In 1935, the Nuremberg Laws established a new term for racially acceptable origin: *German or related blood.* This remained the standard wording in legal documents until the end of World War II. Nevertheless, even experts continued to use the term *Aryan* well after 1935.[38]

In any event, changing *Aryan* to *German or related blood* did nothing to clarify who was racially acceptable and who was not. The "racial status" of Finns, Hungarians, and other Eastern Europeans, for example, was in constant flux during the Nazi era. In October 1934, while evaluating the naturalization of a Hungarian citizen, the Interior Ministry informed the Saxon State Chancellery in Dresden that not all Hungarians were "non-Aryans." According to the Interior Ministry, Hungarians are "tribally alien" (*fremdstämmig*) but not necessarily "blood alien" (*fremdblütig*)—two additional terms adding to the definitional confusion.[39] On the other hand, a 1934 brochure from the series *Family, Race, Volk in the National Socialist State* simply stated that the Magyars (which it did not define) were Aryans.[40] Four years later, a major commentary to the Nuremberg Laws likewise baldly stated that "the overwhelming majority" of present day Finns and Hungarians were of Aryan blood.[41] Yet the following year an article in the *Journal for Racial Science,* on the "Racial Diagnosis of the Hungarians," noted that "opinions on [t]he racial condition of the Hungarians are still very divided."[42] In 1942, Hitler decreed that the Finns, at least, were definitely "racially related Germanic neighboring peoples."[43] There is no indication, however, that this determination was based on new racial-scientific findings. And as late as 1943, no less than four agencies became involved in a dispute over whether a private first-class should receive permission to marry a Hungarian woman. They debated whether the woman was, as initially determined, "German-blooded (Aryan)."[44]

Such arbitrariness and imprecision in classification could also be construed as an indication of the "unscientific" nature of the theory undergirding the racial laws. Nazi "racial experts," however, sought to address this problem. A standard explanation was that: "[o]ne cannot pose the question to which race this or that *Volk* belongs but rather, one can only correctly ask to which race this or that individual member of a *Volk* belongs."[45] Thus, as early as October 1934, in relation to the case of the Hungarian citizen, the Interior Ministry informed the Saxon State Chancellery that racial decisions, for Hungarians at least, needed to be made on an individual basis.[46] Similarly, a November 1940 decree of the office of Hitler's deputy for party affairs held that no party member, or member of a party organization, could marry a person who had at least two grandparents who were members of the Czech, Polish, or Magyar "*Volk* groups" without permission of the regional party official (*Gauleiter*).[47] Indeed, even with regard to "Gypsies," another expert, writing in 1941, noted that while they "cannot be seen in their totality as [German or] related-type blood," nevertheless, "[t]o the degree persons of German or related blood appear amongst vagrants living the Gypsy lifestyle, they are to make an ancestral proof."[48]

Yet, in direct contradiction to that policy, racial laws invariably treated "*Jewish*" as if it were a pure race despite the Jews' "racial-scientific" status as a *Volk*. The Nuremberg Laws, for example, distinguished between persons of "German or related blood" and "Jews." This foreclosed the possibility of a person with three or more "Jewish" grandparents from proving their individual "racial makeup." A 1941 work on the ancestral proof indicated that "[t]hose of foreign race, in first place the Jews and Negroes, are excluded from the concept of German or related blood." The author's explanation for this apparent disregard of racial-scientific findings was that the Jewish *Volk* was composed of "foreign races."[49] But this directly contradicted the assertion that one could only determine an individual's racial composition by examining the individual, not through his *Volk* affiliation.

Even assuming, however, that by definition all "Jews" were a racial threat to Germans, the question as to how much "Jewish blood" an individual could carry without comprising a threat to German racial health remained a vexing one. Such an issue could also be construed as calling the "scientific" basis of the racial laws into question. This was a seemingly urgent problem for proponents of the racial laws, as it appeared possible that many millions of "Germans" had some degree of "Jewish" blood. In his 1913 work, for example, the American anthropologist Fishberg had noted that significant numbers of non-Jews must have some Jewish ancestry. According to his calculation, without large-scale assimilation the number of presently living Jews should have been on the order of 36 million, rather than just 12 million.[50] Likewise, in April 1936, a Prof. Dr. Felix Jentzsch sent the "racial expert" Hans Günther a report titled

"How Does One Best Research the Magnitude and Type of German-Jewish Mixing (Bastardization)?" According to this report, there had been 80,000–85,000 marriages between Jews and non-Jews in Germany between 1870 and 1930. This would suggest that there were about 130,000–160,000 quarter-Jews, and 170,000–180,000 half-Jews stemming from such marriages. Moreover, in the eighteenth century, there were about twenty Jewish conversions per year in the German lands. This figure rose to about fifty per year in 1800–1840, and to about one hundred annually between 1840 and 1870. For each eighteenth-century conversion, there were probably 150 living descendants. Accordingly, there would presently be about 500,000 Germans descended from such ancestors. If one went back to the seventeenth century, or to the Reformation period (Luther, for example, converted about three hundred Jews), it became obvious that there were many millions of Germans who had some Jewish ancestry (e.g., 1/64).[51] On being presented with this essay, Kurt Mayer, the head of the Interior Ministry's race authority, confirmed that present work limited only to Jews who had been baptized around the year 1800 indicated how large a group the descendants of these Jews represented.[52]

Part of the response to this analysis of a potentially large "racial problem" was a rational debate over the best way to find the descendants of converted Jews. Jentzsch proposed first identifying baptized Jews and then tracing their descendents.[53] Assuming that a Jew was of "purely Jewish race," with this process one could then observe if the descendents had "Jewish characteristics," and if so, whether the percentage of such characteristics corresponded with percentage of "Jewish blood." Although this process seemed quite logical, Mayer criticized the plan as unfeasible since many conversions of Jews who lived in Germany had occurred outside Germany. Moreover, many German conversion records had been destroyed. Accordingly, many *Mischlinge* (racially mixed individuals) would still need to be identified by tracing back their ancestors.[54] Jentzsch's other response to the "problem," however, was his assertion that in any event, the cited calculation of numbers of Jewish descendants cannot be correct because (1) the ancestors of Jewish converts may have, on a "purely instinctive" basis, married other *Mischlinge*, which would strongly reduce the introduction of Jewish blood, and (2) as popular belief (*Volksmund*) has it, perhaps such mixed marriages are less fruitful than other marriages.[55] Such blatant speculation could also be seen as an indication of the nonscientific nature of Nazi racial policy.

Inconsistent determinations on whether members of sects practicing different forms of Judaism, primarily the Turkic-language speaking Karaites and Krimchaks, were "racial Jews," further underscored the lack of coherence and thus the unscientific nature of the theory underlying the racial laws. A May 1938 expert report from the Foreign University of Berlin's Russia Institute, for example, did not reach a definitive conclusion. Nonetheless, the report strongly implied that the Karaites were "racial Jews," based on a mixture of cultural evidence. Prior to the October Revolution, the report noted, the Karaites primarily concerned themselves with trade "and typically Jewish crafts" such as jewelry making, shoemaking, and tailoring. Although Karaites do not recognize the authority of the Talmud, they claimed to stem from Jews. Thus, due to their "extremely strong familial seclusion . . . a strong mixing of the Karaites with Tatars or Russians is not to be accepted."[56] A 1939 expert report from Prof. Dr. Lothar Loeffler of the University of Königsberg's Racial Biological Institute was less circumspect. The Karaites, he wrote, liked to portray themselves as "opponents of the Jews," but "[i]n fact, it has now turned out that they are a camouflaged Jewish organization that earlier was supposed to ease the then politically obstructed way for the Jews to [St.] Petersburg. . . . Therefore, absent proof to the contrary, it is to be assumed that any such sects contain racially foreign blood."[57]

However, an undated report in a Party Racial Policy Office file (probably also from 1939) reviewed blood-group studies, as well as other literature, and concluded that the Karaites are a racially Turkish ethnic group that should not be treated as Jewish.[58] Apparently not satisfied with this report, as late as 1945 the Racial Policy Office was still trying to determine the status of the Karaites. In March of that year, Dr. Walter Gross, the Office's head, sent the Party Chancellery several reports.[59] One from about June 1942 was called "Interim Position on the Karaite Question." It claimed that the only anthropological study on the Karaites (concerned with 130 persons in Galicia), conducted by the Italian Anthropologist Corrado Gini, found the Karaites to be of "Armenian-type ancestry." Moreover, according to this report there was a "racial psychological indication" that indicates that Karaites are not Jews: the Lithuanian Prince Witold used them as border guards. "[I]t is inconceivable," stated the report, "to view a Jewish population as carriers of a solid soldierly tradition." Nevertheless, they must be viewed as of "foreign race"—*Turkotataren*—and "marriages between Germans and Karaites are to be prevented." An August 1944 report from a Prof. R. A. Jirku in Bonn, however, indicated that it was still not clear whether the Karaites were originally Jews who had broken away due to opposition to "Talmud-Jewry" or were originally non-Semites who had converted to Judaism and "took on Jewish characteristics through marriage with Jews." Such incoherence regarding the Karaites could also be considered indicative of an inability to determine "race," and, more specifically, "Jewish racial characteristics."

In sum, the theory on which the ancestral proof requirement and racial laws were based was riddled with contradictions. In actual practice, the only consistency was found in the claim that Jews and other "non-Europeans" were a racial threat. Clearly, powerful intellectual tools were available to contemporaries who wanted to argue against Nazi claims of scientific support for their racist, and especially antisemitic, ideology and policies. Despite this possibility, however, such intellectual confrontation did not occur. Part of the reason for this state of affairs relates to the ways in which racist eugenic ideology developed in Germany prior to the Nazi period. This is the subject of the next two chapters.

2 | The Origins of Racist Eugenics in Imperial Germany

GERMANY'S QUICK INDUSTRIALIZATION in the late nineteenth and early twentieth centuries caused profound changes in German society. Germans became citizens of a newly unified and increasingly wealthy world power. But industrialization, in addition to creating wealth and might, also caused great social instability. The demand for labor encouraged massive migration to urban centers. This, in turn, caused traditional ways of life to unravel, encouraged new forms of mass politics, and led to a heightened pace of cultural experimentation. Many Germans, especially outside the new and rapidly expanding working classes, disliked and feared these changes.[1]

The politics of the Kaiserreich reflected the unease of the times. Following German unification in 1871, Germany's "Iron Chancellor," Otto von Bismarck, maintained power through uneasy coalitions of liberal and conservative political parties. He instituted repressive measures against Catholics and outlawed the *Sozialdemokratische Partei Deutschlands* (*SPD*), Germany's socialist party, from 1878 to 1890. After Bismarck's fall in 1890, a frequently uncomfortable alliance between well-heeled agrarians and industrialists dominated the German political arena. This coalition was based in large part on a common fear of socialism, as well as on distaste for liberals and Catholics. Yet despite the discord wrought by industrialization, few Germans of this period were prepared to renounce its accompanying benefits. Rather, many hoped that two of the primary motors of industrialization—science and technology—would help to solve the associated problems.[2]

During this same period, a revolution in the biological sciences also took place. Scientists in the industrialized West provided stunning new insights into the origin and propagation of life. Published in 1859, Charles Darwin's *The Origin of Species,* with its concept of evolution through a competitive process of "natural selection," was the most important manifestation of this. Soon after the *Origin*'s release, in an effort better to understand and control their societies, intellectuals in the West began applying Darwin's insights to the functioning of human civilization. This so-called "Social Darwinism" averred that competing human groups, like the various plant and animal species, were also engaged in a struggle for the "survival of the fittest." This belief became widespread throughout the West, and was appropriated by a variety of advocates across political and socioeconomic lines. For those seeking to maintain the social and political status quo, the laws of nature justified the dominance of elites, whether social, economic, or racial. For those hoping to change the status quo, "evolution" promised that a change in the oppressive social order would occur in accordance with the laws of nature. The various advocates of Social Darwinism thus disputed its implications.

They also disagreed as to whether these struggles were essentially based on class, nationality, or race, although these categories frequently overlapped. Not uncommonly, for example, proponents of Social Darwinism equated "class" with group-based hereditary characteristics—that is, "race." In any event, it is worth noting that because many persons associated "Darwinism" with "scientific," social-Darwinist concepts were legitimized by the great prestige accorded "science" across class and social boundaries. Also noteworthy is the fact that while this intellectual trend was common throughout the industrialized West, some scholars have argued that Darwinism touched a more responsive cultural chord in Germany than in any other society.[3]

Growing information about the hereditary nature of many characteristics (especially the rediscovery of Mendel's laws of hereditary inheritance) was another important aspect of the "biological revolution." The increasing interest in eugenics in the late nineteenth and early twentieth centuries was related to this knowledge and was often also connected with efforts at social control. Following the publication of Darwin's *Origin,* the English scientist Francis Galton postulated the basic idea of eugenics: humans could and should regulate their own breeding so as to increase "valuable" hereditary characteristics and decrease "harmful" ones. This concept had clear social-Darwinist applications. "Positive" eugenics was a tool to strengthen the favored social group by preserving or even improving its "human material." "Negative" eugenics was a means to weaken disfavored social groups by inhibiting their propagation. Like Social Darwinism, eugenics also struck a particularly responsive chord in the German lands. Germany, for example, was home to the first journal dedicated to the subject, the *Archiv für Rassen- und Gesellschaftsbiologie* (*Archive for Racial and Social Biology*), which began publication in 1904. Likewise, the first professional eugenics organization, the *Gesellschaft für Rassenhygiene* (Society for Racial Hygiene), was organized in Germany in 1905.[4]

While popular, the new discipline of eugenics was not a model of either conceptual or methodological precision. Notwithstanding advances in genetics, the hereditary nature of many characteristics was still unknown. Nor was the mechanism of hereditary transference understood. Moreover, the common belief of many eugenicists, that most hereditary characteristics could be quickly bred into or out of a population, was wrong. Eugenicists also frequently disagreed about which traits were "valuable" and which not, especially as related to appearance and "character." Nevertheless, many influential persons, including large numbers of scientists, still viewed eugenics as a "scientific" discipline. This lent the field great legitimacy. And at its core, eugenics was more than mere pseudo-science. Some genetic characteristics were universally viewed as "valuable," such as lack of disease, and some diseases were clearly hereditarily transferable.

The idea of distinct human races dated from at least the eighteenth century. Races were understood to be population groups distinguished from each other by biologically innate physical and mental characteristics. The use of this idea to justify exploitation or unequal distribution of opportunity and material resources began concurrently. The phenomena gained increasing acceptance during the late nineteenth and early twentieth centuries as academics and others began developing anthropological, genetic, and social-Darwinist ideas related to race. Out of these developed the basic concept of racist eugenics: "science" had shown that in order to avoid hereditary and cultural damage "incompatible races" should not mix. "Science," in fact, had shown no such thing. Yet many in Western societies had strong incentives to believe that this was true. They needed to perceive both the existence and the importance of "racial" differences in order to justify exploitation, as well as to use racism as a tool to foster internal political stability.

One significant reason that racist eugenic ideology proved an effective rationalization for Nazi racist policies was because, to a large degree, most of the intellectual strands comprising the ideology had already achieved mainstream status in German society in the decades prior to the Third Reich. Pre-Nazi genealogical literature shows that through a variety of means, proponents of racist ideas alleged, with little contradiction, that they were "scientifically proven." The literature also elucidates how this growing acceptance of racist ideas was bound with the ever-growing respect for "science." The legitimation of racist ideas was also intertwined with the German middle and upper classes' increasing sense of political, economic, and social crisis. In order to clarify the context in which racial scientific ideas arose and later flourished, however, it is necessary to grasp a basic overview of the growth and popularization of genealogical practice in Germany, as well as to have an understanding of the socioeconomic backgrounds and cultural and political orientations of the most influential persons in the field.

Growth of Genealogical Practice in Imperial Germany

> It may be asked if different people and different stories in any section of the book would have created or suggested another kind of country. I think not: the train has many coaches, and different classes, but it passes through the same landscape.
>
> —V. S. Naipaul [5]

Interest in family origins is, of course, a universal phenomenon. In forms varying from the basic to the comparatively complex, it is found in all nations and periods. In the German-speaking lands, printed ancestral tables first appeared in the early medieval period, tracing the families of the ruling elites: the Merovingians (sixth century), Carolingians (eighth century), and Saxons (tenth century). In the later medieval period, powerful noble families, as well as families of kings and emperors, also commissioned such tables. Slowly, however, the practice spread to non-noble groups, the first of these probably appearing in the fourteenth century. By the sixteenth century, genealogy had become part of the professional historical curriculum in certain German universities, and genealogies were being produced for the families of well-known scholars. Yet through this period, the commoners commissioning them were leading public figures. Over the next centuries, the practice of researching a family's genealogy continued gradually to diffuse more widely to include pastors, jurists, teachers, and historians.

The field of genealogical research in Germany, however, expanded particularly quickly in the late nineteenth and early twentieth centuries.[6] One aspect of the profound changes occurring in Imperial German society was the popularization of formerly elite cultural practices. This reflected the rapidly growing influence of the socioeconomic classes beyond the aristocracy.[7] In this vein, genealogical research in Germany began to spread across class boundaries on an important scale as members of various strata of the German middle class, and even some workers and peasants, increasingly sought to memorialize their own family histories.

One of the most significant milestones in this popularization occurred in 1869, when Stephan Kekule von Stradonowitz (1863–1933), a private instructor in Berlin, founded the Herold, the first national German genealogical society. In 1889 the Herold began producing a highly successful series called the *Genealogisches Handbuches bürgerlicher Familien* (*Genealogical Handbook of Bourgeois Families*) which, as its name indicates, contained the genealogical tables of prominent, non-noble families and served as a counterpart to the aristocratic *Gotha*.[8] In 1870, the heraldist and numismatist Ernst Hartmann von Franzenschuld (1840–1884) founded the second genealogical society to orient itself to genealogists throughout German-speaking lands, the *Heraldisch-Genealogischen Gesellschaft* (Heraldic-Genealogical Society) *Adler* in Vienna.[9] Until the twentieth century, the Herold and Adler remained the only such organizations.[10]

Just after the turn of the century, however, three of the most important organizations with a national scope appeared. In 1902, the secondary-school instructor Hermann Unbescheid (1847–1915) founded the Roland, a "Saxon Provincial Association for Family Research." Initially a regional organization, over time the Roland was to grow into one of Germany's most influential genealogical societies, as well as the largest. In 1904, attorney Bernhard Koerner (1875–1952) broke away from the Roland to found the *Verein für deutsch-völkische Sippenkunde* (Society for Völkisch German Kinship Studies), soon renamed the German Roland. Until the Third Reich, the German Roland was the only prominent genealogical society that was overtly racist and antisemitic. While always a small organization (in 1924, for example, it had approximately five hundred members) as will be seen, its influence far exceeded these numbers.

Also in 1902, engineer Johann Ueltzen-Barkhausen (1867–1937) and attorney Hans Breymann (1873–1958) established the *Zentralstelle für Deutsche Personen- und*

Familiengeschichte e. V. (Center for German Personal and Family History), in Leipzig. The Zentralstelle soon became the most important of all German genealogical societies, and the genealogists associated with its "Leipzig circle" were among the most outstanding in the first half of the twentieth century. In 1911, for example, Ernst Devrient (1873–1948), then the head archivist of the Zentralstelle, published the highly influential *Familienforschung (Family Research)*, while Friedrich Wecken (1875–1946), its next archivist (1913–1925), was author of the popular *Taschenbuch für Familiengeschichtsforschung (Pocketbook of Family History Research).*[11]

Besides an increase in the number of national genealogical organizations in early twentieth-century Germany, of which those mentioned were only the most prominent, a great number of more localized genealogical societies also appeared, primarily based on region or family name. Some of the major genealogical organizations, such as the Roland and Zentralstelle, also established regional branches. In addition to this increase in private genealogical associations, government entities also established genealogical offices. In Dresden, in 1911, for example, the Saxon Interior Ministry created the *Sächsische Stiftung für Familienforschung* (Saxon Foundation for Family Research); it was commissioned to perform genealogical research and heraldry verification.

An increase in the number of genealogical journals during the Kaiserreich also illustrates the growing popularity of the practice. At least nine periodicals with national circulation were established between 1870 and 1918, including the Herold's *Deutsche Herold (German Herald;* 1870), the Zentralstelle's *Familiengeschichtliche Blätter (Family History Gazette;* 1910), the German Roland's *Mitteilungen des Deutschen Roland (News of the German Roland;* 1913), and the Roland's *Mitteilungen des Roland (News of the Roland;* 1916).[12] The first regional journal, *Heraldische Mitteilungen (Heraldic Announcements)*, which was published in Hanover, appeared in 1890. At least five more regional journals also began publication between 1904 and 1918, and in Austria, an additional two journals appeared in 1871 and 1885.[13] Moreover, two publishing houses primarily centering on genealogy also developed during this period. The first, the Starke Company, had actually preceded the unification of Germany. Opening in 1847, and initially concentrated on aristocratic concerns, Starke was widely known for publishing the *Gotha,* the major registry of noble genealogies. By the early twentieth century, however, it had expanded its catalog to accommodate the widening interest in genealogy in other strata of German society. In 1910, in Leipzig, Oswald Spohr (1888–1970) began Degener & Co., a "specialized publishing house for family and heraldic works," whose catalogs featured a plethora of materials targeted to non-nobles.[14]

The expanding institutionalization of genealogy in education in this period also demonstrated the practice's growing influence and popularization within German society. In the nineteenth century, the celebrated historian Leopold von Ranke had called for a critically reliable genealogy to support his attempt to create a complete German Imperial history of the middle ages. By the early twentieth century, however, genealogy had become an independent subject in several German universities.[15]

Moreover, a number of eminent genealogists enthusiastically sought to educate others in the practice. In 1910, for example, the Zentralstelle's Ernst Devrient gave courses on "the science of family history" in the University of Leipzig's Institute for Cultural and Universal History that, according to the Herold's journal, were increasingly well attended. The following year, the *German Herald* reported that the respected psychiatrist Robert Sommer (1864–1937) would soon be offering a new course on "scientific genealogy."[16]

The widening tendency, beginning in the late nineteenth century, to call genealogy "family research" and then "kinship research [*Sippenforschung*]" also indicated the popularization of the subject.[17] Every German was part of a family or "clan" and thus was entitled to undertake genealogical research. The increasing variety of practitioners and fields of interest also reflected the expansion of genealogical research into ever-wider socioeconomic strata. In Vienna, in 1913, for example, Paul Diamant and Max Grunwald established the first German-Jewish genealogical journal, the *Archiv für jüdische Familienforschung (Archive for Jewish Family Research)*.[18] Beginning in the second half of the nineteenth century, prominent Germans' increasing attention to, and romanticization of, peasant life also contributed to genealogy's growing popularity, and in Imperial Germany, folklorists and others began to assemble histories of peasant families and villages into so-called *Ortsfamilienbücher*.[19]

Socioeconomic Background of Genealogists in Imperial Germany

Providing a detailed overview of the socioeconomic background of those who were interested in genealogy is a complex matter beyond the scope of this work. For the purposes of this study, however, a review of the backgrounds of the founders, editorial boards, writers, and (where possible to ascertain) readers of the journals of Imperial Germany's three most important genealogical organizations— the Zentralstelle's *Family History Gazette,* the Roland's *News of the Roland,* and the Herold's *German Herald*—provides a good basis for a general assessment. Although these organizations were all headquartered in northeastern Germany, their journals had a national readership, and the Roland and Zentralstelle also had local branches throughout the country.[20] The Roland's journal, however, did not begin publication until 1916, only two years before Imperial Germany's collapse. Thus this analysis is based primarily on the *Family History Gazette* and the *German Herald*.

Otto von Dassel, a noble, founded the *Family History Gazette* in 1903. On von Dassel's death in 1908, another aristocrat, Freiherr von Rodde, purchased it. In 1910, however, the Zentralstelle took over the *Gazette*'s publication and non-nobles increasingly attained influential positions within the journal's institutional apparatus. These men, however, were all of the educated, upper middle class (*Bildungsbürgertum*). For example, Devrient (the Zentralstelle's first archivist) and Wecken (its second) both held doctorates. Eduard Heydenreich, another leading Zentralstelle figure, was a professor (Dr. phil.) and government official (*Oberregierungsrat*). Karl Förster, founder of what was to become the important genealogical institution *Deutsche Ahnengemeinschaft, e. V.* (German Ancestral Community), and who also briefly worked with the Zentralstelle, was a lawyer and provincial court director. Concurrently, however, Adolf Freiherr von Schönberg, another noble, maintained the position of deputy director. Thus, to the end of the Imperial period, the *Family History Gazette*'s executive staff was a mixture of men of noble and, primarily, upper-middle-class status. The *Gazette*'s contributors during this period were of the same socioeconomic status.

Until the late 1920s, the *Gazette* listed the titles and professions of its owners, editors, and contributors. Determining the socioeconomic status of its readers is more difficult. It seems fair, however, to presume a high affinity between the two groups based on mutual interest. Moreover, there is direct, albeit limited, evidence within the pages of the *Gazette* to support this presumption. During World War I, for example, the *Gazette* printed a series of "Fatherland Tables of Honor," listing Zentralstelle members who had received the Iron Cross or were killed in action.[21] The great majority of those listed were also nobles or members of the educated middle class (e.g., holders of doctorates), and almost all were officers. This social composition thus probably offers a fair representation of the Zentralstelle's members, and thus probably reflects the *Gazette*'s readership accurately as well.

The *German Herald,* the organization's monthly that began publication in 1869, started to list its contributors by title and occupation in its third volume (1872). As with the *Family History Gazette,* these writers were both nobles and members of the educated middle class, but unlike the *Gazette,* aristocrats initially clearly predominated. In 1872, for example, twenty-three of thirty contributors were titled. By 1880, however, noble preponderance had ended: only fourteen of twenty-nine contributors were aristocrats. Indeed, henceforth, almost to the *German Herald's* last edition in 1934, aristocrats generally averaged between approximately one-third and one-half of contributors. Kekule, the Herold's most influential member until his death in 1933, was, nonetheless, from a noble family. He was also a professor and private instructor. Kekule thus exemplified in his own person the Herold's primary socioeconomic orientations.

Unlike the Zentralstelle and Herold, the Roland represented an almost entirely upper-middle-class perspective. Established in 1902, there were no nobles among its fifteen founders. They were, rather, almost all members of the *Bildungsbürgertum:* professors, lawyers, doctors, and government bureaucrats, though the membership also included a factory director. The Roland's first director, Unbescheid, was a secondary-school instructor, while the subsequent director (1915–1918) was a medical doctor. While, again, the Roland's journal *News of the Roland* did not begin publication until 1916, and did not list contributors' professions until 1921 (as will be seen in the next chapter), from 1921 on they were overwhelmingly upper-middle-class. This was almost certainly the case as well in the last years of Imperial Germany.

Generally speaking, then, in this period the *Bildungsburgertum* was becoming increasingly involved in institutionalized genealogical life, but, as shown in the cases of the Herold and Zentralstelle, there continued to be important involvement by aristocrats. In other words, while there was growing socioeconomic diversity in genealogical practice, the leadership of the major societies continued to consist primarily of "elites." This socioeconomic structure, in turn, helps to explain the types of political and cultural views expressed in the journals.

The Journals' Political and Cultural Orientations in Imperial Germany

During the Kaiserreich, Germany's leading genealogists expressed a variety of political opinions, though rarely within the pages of their journals. Ottokar Lorenz (1832–1904), the main proponent of "scientific" genealogy (discussed below), lost his full professorship in history at the University of Vienna in 1887 after he had alienated prominent persons through his liberal politics and conversion to Protestantism. The other outstanding genealogist, Stephan Kekule, founder of the Herold, consistently associated himself with conservative political movements. Despite differing political opinions among genealogical practitioners, however, a primary motivation for interest in tracing family history in Imperial Germany seems to have been a desire for stability and order: for a feeling of "rootedness." Thus, political differences in some areas aside, the leading genealogical journals nevertheless showed significant overlap in other political and, especially, cultural values.

Politically, prior to 1918 persons interested in genealogy "almost without exception had belonged to the non-socialist camp."[22] Culturally, traditional values manifested themselves in a variety of ways on the pages of all of these journals. In the 1915 edition of the predominantly upper-middle-class *Family History Gazette*, for example, an article on the importance of family history in the context of world war, urged readers to be steadfast by reminding them of the hardships their families went through in the Thirty Years' War.[23] While ardent nationalism in 1915 was certainly not confined to cultural conservatives, glancing backward 250 years for inspiration to fight World War I did have a conservative ring.[24]

The journals' iconography also signaled their culturally traditional orientations. From inception through the Nazi period, the cover page of the *German Herald* featured a medieval herald while the *News of the Roland*'s featured a knight in armor standing before a coat of arms. The *Family History Gazette*'s initial covers also featured medieval icons—again a knight in armor and several coats of arms—although this illustration was discontinued in 1911. Moreover, all of the journals used the old-style German script. In their contents, both the *Family History Gazette* and the *German Herald* evinced a keen interest in the nobility and its concerns, also a traditional "cultural value." The *Gazette*'s first issue, for example, promoted creation of a "New German Noble Lexicon." By contrast, the *News of the Roland*, oriented to the middle class, had little to say about the aristocracy. In any event, genealogical practice, with its emphasis on the past and tradition, was almost by definition culturally conservative.

Figure 2. Cover, *The German Herald,* 1877.
From the Library of Congress.

Whether because of or despite this orientation, all three journals evinced keen awareness of the increasing influence of the "lower" classes—that is, whatever classes the editors and contributors perceived as beneath them—in Imperial Germany. And, for the most part, these journals sought to accommodate rather than resist the process. The very title of the Zentralstelle's journal illustrates this. Although its founder was a noble, he nevertheless named his periodical *Familiengeschichtliche Blätter. Zeitschrift zur Förderung der Familiengeschichtsforschung für Adel und Bürgerstand* (*Family History Gazette: Journal for the Advancement of Family History for Nobles and Burghers*), making it clear that he sought a middle-class, as well as noble, readership. The title did not, however, mention the working class. After gaining control of the *Gazette* in 1910, however, the Zentralstelle, while initially continuing to issue the journal without any other major revision in format or content, immediately dropped the phrase "for Nobles and Burghers" from the title. Indeed, the Zentralstelle's own full organizational name emphasized "Central Office for *German* Personal and Family History," without class distinction. By implication, the family histories of all Germans were worthy of research.

The primary reason for this tendency to accommodation by leading genealogists was likely their hope that they could thereby instill their own values into "other classes" as a force for unity and order in a rapidly changing society. The principal methods by which they attempted this were through the related exhortations to use genealogical practice to appreciate traditional family life, and to understand Germans' common heritage. An 1893 *German Herald* article, for example, urged Herold members to work to spread "the sense for family" from their own domestic circles to "middle-class families where," according to the article, "the prejudice exists that genealogy is either 'child's play' or 'must be left to the nobility'."[25] This was a typical call for the promotion of genealogy as a tool for the selling of traditional family values.

From early on, the journals linked this encouragement of a "sense for family" through genealogical practice to the quest to instill feelings of unity into wider population circles. Thus an 1888 *German Herald* article—also throwing sentiment against the working class into the measure—claimed: "It is a happy sign of the present that, apart from the efforts of certain parties to destroy and deride family life and the historical sense of the *Volk*, on the other side the nobility and bourgeois notably strive to demonstrate [through genealogical practice] the honorable origins of the generations. . . ." The *Family History Gazette's* motto, set forth in its first edition (1903), revealed a similar belief, although framed in more inclusive language: "It is lovely to seek the traces of the family line; the ancestral tree is to the individual what the history of the fatherland is to the entire *Volk*."[26]

While not overtly racist, this promotion of "German unity" based on a perception of shared heritage was conceptually ambiguous and, in fact, quite compatible with racist ideology. Genealogy was, after all, primarily the process of determining biological connections between individuals. Yet calls for unity based on shared biological heritage were not the same as calls for the biological purification of the

German *Volk,* later the core rationalization for the racial laws and the ancestral proof. It was also in this historical period, however, that a multifaceted process began—also evident in the pages of genealogical journals—that prepared many readers to promote aggressive racist policies in the Third Reich, and many others to acquiesce in that promotion. This was the rise of racist eugenic ideology.

"Scientific Genealogy" and Racist Eugenics

Racist eugenic ideology developed out of three related intellectual currents—hereditary science, eugenics, and racial science—articles on all three of which increasingly appeared in genealogical literature well before the Nazis assumed power. On the one hand, such interest, at least in hereditary science and eugenics, did not necessarily imply that any particular genealogist was sympathetic to racist thought. Nor were those genealogists who did promote racist ideas inevitably interested in providing "scientific" foundations. On the other hand, genealogical literature shows that due to the great prestige associated with the label *science,* in order to legitimize racism, its proponents frequently, and increasingly successfully, sought to associate their ideas with that appellation.

Genealogy and Hereditary Science

The oldest method of human genetics is genealogical research.[27]

Given the stature of *science* in the late nineteenth and early twentieth centuries, it is not surprising that genealogists sought to prove the "scientific importance" of their field. Prior to the turn of the twentieth century, Germany's two most influential genealogists, Lorenz and Kekule, were also, not coincidentally, the most prominent champions of "scientific" genealogy. They aimed to promote the practice as a tool for studying not just the social, political, and cultural histories of families, but also their natural history, in particular the tracing of hereditary characteristics.[28] Thus by 1894, Kekule had defined genealogy as the study of lineages and their origins, reproduction, and spread.[29] Lorenz's seminal 1898 work, *Lehrbuch der gesammten wissenschaftlichen Genealogie (Manual of Complete Scientific Genealogy),* had an entire chapter on reproduction and heredity. Their emphases gained increasingly wide currency in genealogical circles. By the turn of the century, Lorenz and Kekule were only the most conspicuous champions among a growing group of genealogists who insisted on the "scientific" importance of genealogical research. Devrient's influential *Family Research* (1911), for example, stated "genealogy now steps in the closest relationship with natural science." Following Lorenz's example, one of his six chapters was on "Problems of Genetics."[30]

Indeed, among the generation of genealogists following Lorenz, it became almost a cliché to credit him with changing genealogy from a "helping science" of political history (merely tracing the lineages of important persons) to a "border science" between natural and cultural history (tracing the hereditary path of culturally important individuals).[31] As Kekule, who straddled the first and second generations, stated in 1919: "Until the appearance of Lorenz's handbook, the *Stammtafel* [a genealogical table showing an individual's descendants] was everything . . . since Lorenz's handbook found a wide audience, the *Ahnentafel* [a table showing an individual's ancestors] is everything."[32] The reasoning was that a *Stammtafel* traced only the male offspring, following the family name. It therefore had no value in tracing hereditary relationships.[33] In the same year, Kekule described genealogy as "part of hereditary science."[34]

Genealogical journals, too, began increasingly to emphasize the scientific value of the field. In the late Kaiserreich, articles appeared with such titles as "Goal and Task of Scientific Genealogy" (1900), "Genealogy as Science" (1906), and the "Social Scientific Significance of Genealogy" (1910).[35] Other journal pieces discussed how genealogical tables could be used to trace hereditary inheritance (1912, 1916, 1917) or study the biology of twins (1917).[36] Indeed, the connection between genealogical practice and hereditary science became so clear in many genealogists' minds that the journals regularly featured articles and book reviews on the subject of heredity that did not even mention a direct connection with genealogy.[37]

Heredity also became a popular topic in local genealogical discussion groups, the so-called *genealogical evenings*. Genealogists likewise promoted public courses and lectures on the subject.[38] After the turn of the century, scientists and scientific journals also increasingly discussed the importance of genealogy for hereditary research. A 1904 article in the eugenic journal *Archive for Racial and Social Biology,* for example, discussed the significance of the ancestral table for this field, while a 1912 article in the same journal contained a "historical overview on medical-genealogical activities of individual researchers."[39] The psychiatrists Wilhelm Strohmayer and Robert Sommer, and the anthropologist Walter Scheidt were particularly assertive in emphasizing genealogy's value to their own fields, as well as to hereditary research in general.[40] Thus when, ten years into the Third Reich, a leading genealogist wrote that "[t]he significance of an investigation of descendants lies, above all, in the task of following the path of genetic material [*Erbgutes*]," he was not stating anything that had not already been said many times in previous decades.[41]

Genealogy and Eugenics

In addition to the fact that genetics was considered to be the primary link between genealogy and "science," and the fact that this link enhanced genealogical practice's prestige, there were a number of other reasons why many German genealogists in the Kaiserreich were fascinated by hereditary science. For one, it could play a concrete role in the practice of genealogy. A genealogist, for instance, could use blood groups to establish lineage by identifying the fathers of illegitimate children.[42] Nevertheless, as noted by a speaker during festivities honoring the Roland's thirtieth

anniversary in 1932, "the most decisive ground" for the increased interest in hereditary science was racial hygiene, the common German term for eugenics.[43]

Articles on eugenics did not actually become an important aspect of the journals'
contents until the interwar period, likely due to the fact that eugenics did not gain
an institutional base in Germany until just after the turn of the twentieth century.
Yet despite the relative paucity of articles on the subject in Imperial Germany, from
the very time in which these eugenic organizations were founded, important genealogists and genealogical institutions began directly affiliating with them. Indeed,
genealogists took part in their development. In 1905, for example, several genealogists helped found the Society for Racial Hygiene, while the Zentralstelle became an
"institutional member."[44] In the three journals studied here, the first articles mentioning eugenics followed some few years later. One of the earliest was in the *German
Herald,* in 1912 informing its readers that the Herold had received an invitation to
the Congress for Eugenics in London.[45] The same year, a *Family History Gazette* article on genealogy and the international hygiene exhibit in Dresden expressed concern
not only that genealogists become familiar with hereditary science, which would
assist them in tracing lineage, but also that genealogy be properly used in the practice of "racial-hygiene."[46]

Again, given their predominant socioeconomic statuses, prominent German
genealogists' interest in eugenics probably stemmed primarily from their concerns
with social stability; they hoped that eugenics would help them to create a society
in which their own social station was maintained and their own values propagated.
The fact that these people became increasingly interested in eugenics in Imperial
Germany, however, clearly did not ineluctably lead them later to comply with racist eugenic policies in Nazi Germany. Many leading scientific genealogical works of
the period had no racist content.[47] On the other hand, as will be seen in the next
section, others did. Moreover, the interest in nonracist eugenics in itself helped to
prepare the ground for later acceptance of Nazi racist eugenic policies by promoting
ideas with "dual use." As will be seen in the following chapter, these nonracist continuities were much more pronounced in the interwar period, but many had their
origins in the Kaiserreich.

One such intellectual continuity between Imperial-era, nonracist eugenic ideology and Nazi racial policy, for example, was the emphasis on heredity over environment in determining human capacity and character. This was an indispensable idea
for racist eugenics: "racial characteristics," hereditary by definition, were claimed to
be one of the most, if not the most, important determinants of an individual's nature.
This concept first appeared in genealogical circles no later than 1886 when a *German
Herald* article, praising Darwin, asserted that the "derivation of human perfection . . .
comes from heredity," and further claimed that this concept was recognized throughout history by persons "without distinction of race, belief, ratio of [head] length and
width [*Längen-* and *Breitengrade*], etc. . . ."[48] This idea continued to be repeated in the
later Kaiserreich. In a 1917 *German Herald* review of the psychiatrist Sommer's book,

Frederick the Great from the Standpoint of Genetics, for instance, Kekule praised the attempt to determine "through which hereditary path or blood lines the great king arrived at his mental ability and literary talent."[49] Kekule did not acknowledge that environmental factors could have played any role.

In addition to stressing the importance of heredity in human ability, the genealogical journals also began to advocate eugenic policies similar to those actually implemented in Nazi Germany. As early as 1912, the *German Herald* printed at least two articles calling for the "prohibition of marriage of defective persons" or their sterilization. One of these articles further noted that "gentleness and compassion are out of place with them."[50] Both the idea of prohibiting "hereditarily dangerous" procreation, and the use of brutal means to achieve this, were, of course, basic components of both Nazi nonracist and racist eugenic policy. While these phenomena were rare in the Kaiserreich and did not approach mainstream status in the genealogical literature until the interwar period, they did begin the process of familiarization necessary to achieve their later implementation.

Genealogy and Racial Science

By the late nineteenth century, many Germans—like other Westerners—were aware of the benefits of racist ideology in conjunction with the acquisition of colonial empire. The "inferiority" of the colonized people justified their exploitation.[51] Thus, many advocates of German imperialism used racist ideas to justify German rule in Africa, Asia, and even Eastern Europe.[52] During the same period, eugenics was widely considered "scientifically valid." Proponents of racism thus gained legitimacy for their ideas, in large part, to the degree to which they successfully equated "racial characteristics" with either "valuable" or "harmful" hereditary characteristics. This "scientificization" of racism was important not because it served a eugenically useful purpose—there was no proof that it did—but rather because it helped to legitimize other racist policies that were clearly of material and political benefit.

Nazi racist eugenic polices were simply the culmination of this trend. The idea that science had proven there are distinct biological races with hereditarily based physical and mental abilities and predispositions; that mixing of "incompatible" races is "unhealthy"; and that "Jews" comprise the greatest threat in this regard were relatively uncommon in genealogical literature prior to the interwar period. Nevertheless, one can still trace the origins of all of these concepts in that literature. This, too, helped prepare the ground for their flowering in later decades.

Prominent genealogical works of Imperial Germany often took as established the idea that "biological races" of humanity existed. In his *Family Research* (1911), for instance, Devrient sought to illustrate hereditary dominance and recessiveness with what he called "true racial characteristics." Claiming that "racial crosses lead to mixed forms," he stated that when such children breed only among themselves, "without provision of pure blood, the original [racial] forms return."[53] This statement was not in itself racist, as it did not discuss the nature of "racial characteristics," much less their relative value. Nonetheless, it did contain a key assumption of racist eugenics: the existence of "pure-blooded human races."

The journals generally assumed the superiority of Western culture, but this assumption was not necessarily racist either. An 1898 *German Herald* article, for example, describing a speech by Kekule on genealogy as science, noted his discussion of the "marriage forms of the natural and half-cultured peoples."[54] According to the description, however, Kekule made no connection between these peoples' lack of "whole-culture" and their "race." On the other hand, in Imperial Germany some journal articles also began occasionally asserting, or at least implying, scientific proof that the existence of superior and inferior cultures was tied to race. One of the earliest examples was a 1915 *Family History Gazette* book review of Theodore Arldt's *The History of Derivation of the Primates and Development of the Human Races.*[55] The reviewer wrote that at present it was not possible finally to evaluate Arldt's thesis that the various human races arose from different primates. The idea that there were distinct human lineages, however, was clearly grist for the racist mill.

Likewise, the overt claim that "race-mixing" causes hereditary damage was rare. Yet interest was taken in such "mixing." An article in the 1917 *German Herald,* for example, averred that a recent marriage between a Prince Georg von Battenberg and Countess Nada Torby was especially noteworthy as Torby brings "a by no means insignificant addition of African blood into this genealogically notable marriage! . . . The Negro admixture is unmistakable in all pictures of the poet."[56] It also listed "Turkish baptisms" in 1916 and 1918.[57] Taken out of context, these items could be viewed as nothing more than interesting trivia. In view, however, of other articles dealing with "race"—and as will be seen, especially regarding Jews—in the genealogical journals, they had more ominous implications.

The prevalence of antisemitic thought in Germany before 1933 is well documented.[58] The particular idea of Jews as a "biological threat," however, also had deep roots prior to the Nazi era. Indeed, it actually preceded the "golden age" of racial science, which began in the late nineteenth century. Already in 1814, for example, the German nationalist Ernst Moritz Arndt had written that Jews should not be allowed to enter Germany "because they are a thoroughly foreign *Volk* and because I wish to preserve as much as possible the purity of the German tribes from alien-type elements."[59] More than one hundred years later, "racial scientists" repeated this justification almost verbatim, adding only the claim that science had proven this assertion.

It was during the Kaiserreich, however, that racist ideas made their first prominent appearance as a tool in internal German politics, and their use was directly linked with antisemitic thought. In the late nineteenth century, specifically antisemitic political parties arose in Germany and Austria, and actually attained significant political power in Vienna. Otherwise ranging across the political spectrum, and borrowing ideas from both right and left, these parties were nevertheless united in their claims that "Jews" were the cause of Germany and Austria's problems.

Frequently, such parties also claimed that this was due to Jews' negative racial characteristics. "Racial purification" from Jews was necessary in order to solve these problems.[60] While the claim that science had proven this statement was not always overt, it was implied in the very claim that the "Jewish problem" was a "racial problem." Not coincidentally, this was also the period in which racial antisemitic ideas were first popularized in Germany through widely read political tracts, such as Wilhelm Marr's *Victory of Jewry over Germandom* (1879) and Theodore Fritsch's *Antisemitic Catechism* (1896), and influential philosophical works, including Houston Stewart Chamberlain's *Foundations of the Nineteenth Century* (1899).[61]

This growth of racial antisemitism in the Kaiserreich was reflected in the pages of genealogical journals. There was little in the way of a developed racist eugenic ideology. Moreover, for the most part, genealogists' calls for German social unification, and discussions of race, also remained distinct. Yet racial antisemitism did become more common. The unabashedly antisemitic *News of the German Roland,* which began publication in 1913, was awash in such thought. Yet the journal's editor, Bernhard Koerner, was occasionally also allowed to spread these ideas in the more mainstream genealogical journals. In the course of a 1910 *German Herald* book review, for example, Koerner asked rhetorically: "When will the time come that the Germans recognize their strength and not need to wait for the black-locked Oriental . . . ?"[62]

More common than such overtly hostile racial antisemitism in Imperial-era German genealogical journals, however, were subtler assertions that Jews were "racially" foreign. That this "racial difference" posed a threat was not always openly stated, but was often implicit. One of the earliest instances of its expression was an 1893 *German Herald* book review critiquing the anonymously authored *Ennobled Jewish Families,* published by the *völkisch* Kyffhäuser press in Salzburg, Austria.[63] Calling the text an "interesting little work [that] exhibits to us alphabetically and rather completely the ennobled non-Aryans," the reviewer nevertheless claimed that the book was "strident" and lacking in "scientific cachet." This review is notable not only in its acceptance of the assertion that Jews are "non-Aryans," and, therefore, racially different, but also that its sole criticism was directed against the book's "nonscientific" tone. In another early example, in 1889 the *German Herald* reviewed another edition of *Ennobled Jewish Families.* Quoting the author's belief that his work "is not an uninterested contribution to the most burning question of the day, the Jewish question," the *German Herald* criticized the book for its lack of completeness, its many mistakes, as well as its "fantastical digressions and conjectures."[64] The article, however, did not question the assertion that "the Jewish question" was indeed "the most burning . . . of the day."

Articles containing racial antisemitism continued occasionally to appear in genealogical journals throughout the era. In the 1912 *Family History Gazette,* for instance, Devrient reviewed the book *Jewish Baptisms,* in which economist Werner Sombart, and others, debated both the assimilability of Jews into German society and the viability of Zionism.[65] Devrient was critical of the lack of consensus and argued that only the investigation of a great number of genealogical tables of Jewish communities could lead to an answer to these questions. Thus, while this review was not overtly antisemitic, it legitimated questions about of the assimilability of Jews into German society, thereby implicitly questioning their status as Germans. Moreover, the "racial basis" of "Jewishness" was tacitly argued by noting the necessity to "reveal" baptized Jews through genealogical tables.

Overall, however, during the Kaiserreich, overtly racist antisemitic articles appeared only infrequently in the journals besides the *völkisch News of the German Roland*. But this literature nevertheless contained another manifestation of racial antisemitism. This was the aforementioned practice of "unmasking" individuals or families with Jewish ancestry, revealing those who themselves, or whose ancestors, had converted. By its very nature, this practice implied that "Jewishness" was biologically based and foreshadowed one of the Nazi Genealogical Authority's main tasks. The *News of the German Roland,* early on, naturally dedicated itself to identifying so-called camouflaged Jews. Also not surprisingly, no later than 1911, the *German Book of Lineages,* edited by the German Roland's Koerner, also began to identify persons with Jewish ancestry by writing their names in Latin, rather than in the usual Gothic script, or by adding two commas.[66] But the *German Herald,* the most conservative of the "mainstream" genealogical journals, also early on engaged in the same task. Possibly the first such effort was an 1890 article titled "The Oldest Jewish Ennoblements in Lithuania."[67] While not overtly antisemitic, this article nevertheless noted that the descendants of some ennobled Jews "later attempted to veil [*verschleiern*] their Jewish ancestry," implying that they were trying to disguise some sort of hereditary flaw. Similarly, in 1907, one *German Herald* article, unremarkably by Koerner, listed without further comment four pages of "Jewish family names . . . newly chosen in Prussia in 1812," while another published a list of such names in Kanton Calvörde in 1808.[68]

Occasionally, the *German Herald* gave a direct explanation of the necessity for "outing" persons with Jewish ancestry. A 1917 article, for instance, written by a pastor, and innocuously entitled "Family Studies in Newspapers," detailed a dispute over the racist author Houston Stewart Chamberlain's accusation that Professor Lujo Brentano came from an "Italian-Asian Minor *Mischling* family, the forerunner of the Jewish dissolution" and that "in all members of this family known to him [i.e., Chamberlain], the oriental type was extraordinarily pronounced."[69] Brentano had responded by sending Chamberlain a genealogical tree going back to 1530 showing no Jewish ancestry. The *German Herald* article's commentary on this situation was to praise Brentano's use of genealogical methods to settle this controversy: "The family researcher knows that it is a question of racial mixing here, that this question can only be decided with the help of an ancestral table, that this is formulated as far as possible, and then it is demonstrated for each person in the table whether they belong to one race or another." The article also noted *völkisch* novelist Artur Dinter's (1876–1948) claim that Brentano had a Jewish ancestor in the "eighth row" (i.e., seven generations back). Dinter, wrote the *German Herald,* "correctly understands the value of the ancestral table," but did not prove his point because he could not show that Jews had Italian names in the fourteenth and fifteenth centuries (which, the *German Herald* claimed, would have been "an important discovery"). Nor had Dinter proven that Brentano "had no drop of Indogermanic, let alone German blood in his veins." Even the journal *Semigotha,* noted the *German Herald* reviewer, "which loses no opportunity to prove Jewish blood in German families," had asserted nothing of the sort over Brentano. Nevertheless, the *German Herald* argued:

> one can only agree wholeheartedly with what Dinter says over maintaining purity of the races and over the danger threatening us Germans from race-mixing. But in [Brentano's] case, it is a matter of proof whether in the veins of certain persons racially foreign blood flows or not. But this is a scientific question and can only be answered scientifically. . . .[70]

In this article, written sixteen years before the Nazi assumption of power, the conservative, but not *völkisch,* genealogical journal *German Herald* was sounding very much like the later Reich Genealogical Authority. It is also interesting to note that this dispute was widely covered in the press of that time (e.g., in the *Frankfurter Zeitung, Deutsche Tageszeitung,* and *Unabhängige Nationale Korrespodnenz*), indicating the German public's familiarity, well before the Third Reich, with the argument for the necessity of proving one's "race" for hereditary health purposes, as well as the allegation that Jews were "racially un-German."

Perhaps more surprisingly, the less conservative *Family History Gazette* also early on embraced the practice of identifying baptized Jews, and for reasons similar to the *German Herald.* In a 1912 *Gazette* critique of the book *German Jewish Names,* dedicated to identifying such names, the reviewer agreed with the book's author that one must combat the desire of many Jewish families to obscure their ethnicity (*Volksangehörigkeit*) in an attempt to integrate into wider society.[71] The *Gazette* reviewer's only criticism was aimed at the author's failure adequately to identify Jewish names in order to achieve this goal, admittedly a major flaw in such a work. Occasionally, that journal also directly "uncovered" Jewish baptisms. Possibly the first such effort was a 1915 description of a 1706 Jewish baptism.[72]

It is important not to overemphasize the prevalence of racial scientific thought in the pages of Imperial-era German genealogical works. During this period, for example, the *German Herald* was at least as interested in identifying "counterfeit German nobles"—persons representing themselves to be nobles who were not—as in identifying persons with Jewish ancestry.[73] Yet, it is also important not to underestimate its prevalence. Aside from overt sanction of racism and, especially, racial antisemitism, other, and more subtle, aspects of endorsement also occurred in this period. Genealogists not known as enthusiastic proponents of racist views nevertheless indirectly lent prestige to such expression. They recommended books and associated with organizations that promoted the ideas, or simply failed to contradict them when espoused in their journals. Koerner, founder of the blatantly antisemitic German Roland, provides a good example. Despite his well-known views on race and Jews, in 1900 Koerner was made editor of the highly prestigious *German Book of Lineages*. He was also, concurrently, an ongoing contributor to the *German Herald*. Moreover, by 1914, the German Roland had become a corporate member of the Zentralstelle, and in 1918 Koerner was elected to the Zentralstelle's twelve-man board.[74] Even without express approval of Koerner's racism, these occurrences were all forms of tacit sanction.

In sum, in Imperial Germany participation in genealogical practice increasingly expanded across socioeconomic barriers. This reflected the wider trend in German society of formerly elite cultural practices beginning to transcend class lines. In "genealogical life," however, the traditional social elites still clearly held the balance of power. But they were struggling to maintain it in German society as a whole. The feeling of insecurity this engendered created an increasing amenability to racist ideas, which, among other things, supported attempts to maintain the status quo through exhortations of unity based on shared "heritage." While a refined eugenic rationalization for racism had not yet appeared in the pages of Imperial German genealogical journals, it was clearly developing, and was primarily directed at supporting racist attacks on Jews. In this regard, however, the main concern of leading genealogists was not the spread of racism, but that this racism appear "reasonable," that is, scientifically sanctioned. As will now be seen, such a superficially scientific, racist eugenic framework matured during the Weimar Republic, and concurrently achieved mainstream status.

3 | The Spread of Racist Eugenics in Weimar

During the Weimar era, traditional social and political barriers increasingly broke down in Germany. This collapse was exemplified by the promulgation of a democratic constitution, the hitherto unprecedented power of the Social Democratic and Catholic Center parties, and the growing role of women in public life.[1] In the cultural sphere, some formerly elite practices such as dueling began to disappear. Others, including genealogical practice, continued to spread with even greater rapidity throughout German society.

Despite genealogy's increasing popularization in Weimar, the socioeconomic status of leading German genealogists remained much the same as it had been: the educated middle-class and nobility. Now, however, with the growing turmoil of their times, these men grew increasingly worried. The Weimar Republic arose out of Germany's unconditional defeat in World War I. Numerous Germans therefore associated the new regime with both the abortive communist revolutions in 1918–1919 and the humiliation of the Treaty of Versailles. While many supported the fledgling republic to at least some degree, a significant number of others sought to undermine it. Expanding political democratization and cultural experimentation were often countered by strident right-wing reaction. Economic disaster in the form of hyperinflation and then depression contributed to the feeling of crisis. This, in turn, led to widening political polarization and radicalization on both the left and right.

Many leading genealogists increasingly viewed "science" as at least a partial solution to these growing problems: cleansing society through eugenic means. For others, the solution was to increasingly stress the underlying unity of all "Germans" in the hope of diffusing social tensions. And many began to perceive a connection between these two remedies: claims of the biological unity of all Germans and the necessity for a "racial cleansing" of German society multiplied in the genealogical literature during this period. Indeed, virtually all of the elements of Nazi racist eugenic ideology appeared in the genealogical writing of those years, helping to explain the ease with which that regime institutionalized racist policies after 1933.

Growth of Weimar Genealogical Practice and Changing Socioeconomic Backgrounds

During the Weimar Republic, all major regions of Germany saw the growth or creation of genealogical societies and related journals.[2] In 1920, for example, the Roland had approximately 600 members throughout Germany; in 1930, it had close to 3,000. With some 288 members in its first year (1904), by 1924 the Zentralstelle numbered more than 1,800. In 1920, German civil registrars also created their own national organization, the Reich Federation of German Civil Registrars. While not, strictly speaking, a genealogical society, the Federation published an organ, the *Journal for Civil Registry Practice* (*Zeitschrift für Standesamtswesen*), from 1921, and evinced great interest in genealogy, regularly featuring articles on the practice. Because the Federation was by far the largest "genealogical society" (with about 50,000 members in 1925) and because of its quasi-governmental standing (its journal was an official organ for many national and regional government pronouncements), this study also uses that journal to evaluate German genealogical practice in the Weimar era. Located in northeast Germany, as were the three other genealogical organizations studied in detail, the Federation's journal also had national distribution. Moreover, like the Roland and Zentralstelle, the Federation had local branches throughout Germany.

In addition to this expansion of existing national genealogical societies in the Weimar era, by the 1920s there were also hundreds of so-called "family associations [*Familienverbände*]" in Germany. Moreover, between 1918 and 1938, more than fifty local study groups arose. Likewise, between 1919 and 1932, at least eight more periodicals with national circulation appeared, as did at least nineteen new regional journals. In Austria, an additional three journals appeared prior to that country's incorporation into Nazi Germany in 1938. By 1924, hundreds of family associations were publishing newsletters for their members.[3] The spread of genealogical organizations and journals also occurred in German-speaking areas outside Germany and Austria. In 1926, for instance, Dr. Franz Josef Umlauft established the Central Office for Sudeten-German Family Research in Czechoslovakia. By 1928, it distributed a broadsheet of the same name to "over a thousand clients."[4]

While Starke and Degener still remained the two primary specialty publishing houses, both the Reich Federation of German Civil Registrars and especially the Zentralstelle also increasingly published genealogical related works in Weimar. Nonspecialty firms, too, began to issue such works. In 1928, the Herold's journal, the *German Herald,* expressed pleasure that the "famous, popular, and beloved" Reclams Universal-Bibliotech had begun publishing an introductory brochure on genealogy.[5] The growth in the size of the *Family History Bibliography* (*Familiengeschichtliche Bibliographie*), which, from 1837 on listed the most prominent German genealogical publications, gives a fair indication of the dramatic increase in demand for such works, and thus interest in genealogy, after World War I. Between 1897 and 1899, the *Bibliography* totaled roughly nineteen pages per year. Between 1900 and 1920, it averaged about twenty-four pages. By 1929 alone, however, its peak year, it was 204 pages long.

During Weimar, sub-areas of genealogical interest also continued to expand. The interest in peasant genealogy became especially pronounced. Publishers released books on peasant family research; articles on peasants appeared more frequently in genealogical journals; and volunteers began to catalog regional church books into so-called *Ortssippenbücher*, outlining familial relationships of entire villages.[6] Although the first German-Jewish genealogical association did not survive World War I, in 1924, the ophthalmologist Arthur Czellitzer (1871–1942) established a successor in Berlin, the Society for Jewish Family Research.[7] Nevertheless, despite genealogy's increasing popularization, the interest in "blue blood" also remained a significant aspect of the practice.[8]

The major changes in German society in the interwar period were, for the most part, not reflected in the composition of the genealogical journals' editors and contributors. The Zentralstelle's leadership remained much the same, although Johannes Hohlfeld (1888–1950) became director in 1927. Hohlfeld, however, held a doctorate. An analysis of the *Family History Gazette*'s contributors during this period indicates that they, too, were almost exclusively either nobles or members of the educated middle class, although with increasing predominance of the latter.[9] As already noted, there was likely a similarity between the socioeconomic composition of contributors and readers during World War I. There seems little reason to doubt that a general correlation continued in this sphere into the 1920s, and even into the 1930s. Also, as already has been shown, the social composition of the *German Herald*'s editors, contributors, and presumably readers also remained much the same during the Weimar years.

The overwhelmingly middle-class orientation of the Roland demonstrated but minimal change in the socioeconomic composition of its leadership. In 1918, a high government official and a district court director became its codirectors. On the former's death in 1920, an assistant at the Saxon Foundation for Family Research replaced him. In 1922, however, a merchant became head, and was the first member of the "moneyed," as opposed to educated, middle class to attain the position. Yet in 1930, a retired state's attorney replaced him.[10] Thus the Roland's leadership in the interwar period remained thoroughly upper middle class, and predominantly of the educated.

The Roland's journal began listing its contributors' professions in 1921. The majority of these men were also of the educated middle class: they were members of the free professions and upper-level government bureaucrats. There were, however, also a number of less prestigious occupations listed: tradesman, librarian, postal director, and goldsmith. Nine had *von* in their names, indicating noble lineage. This overwhelmingly upper-middle-class composition remained the norm until 1932, when contributors began to increasingly include more lower-middle-class occupations, such as elementary schoolteacher, post office worker, photographer, and technician. In 1919, the *News of the Roland* also began publishing an ongoing list of new Roland members, stating their professions. Although a number of titled persons joined, this roster was also overwhelmingly upper-middle-class through 1933. But the number of persons who could be construed as "lower-middle-class" or even "worker" did expand, including such occupations as lithographer, foreman, engraver, watchmaker, optician, furnace manager, actor, soap maker, and gardener. There was a clear trend of expanding socioeconomic status among the Roland's membership.

The primary class affiliation of persons associated with the Reich Federation of German Civil Registrars is the easiest to determine. The *Journal for Civil Registry Practice* was always, naturally enough, primarily edited, written by, and geared towards civil registrars. These were predominantly lower- to middle-level government officials and thus overwhelmingly from the lower middle class. Accordingly, the establishment and growth of this new "genealogical organization" also represented the continuing expansion of genealogical practice across socioeconomic lines in the Weimar Era. Most of the *Journal's* editors, however, including Friedrich Knost, an attorney and later Genealogical Authority official, tended to be of the educated upper middle class. In sum, while the socioeconomic status of the members of at least some of these genealogical organizations increasingly widened in the 1920s and 1930s, that of the organizations' leaders appears to have remained relatively unaltered.

Political and Cultural Orientations in Weimar: From Family Values to Racial Unity

Despite the traumas of the Weimar era, as in the Kaiserreich overt expression of political opinion remained rare in the four journals studied. They also continued to reflect differing political views. The editors of the *German Herald,* for instance, were clearly hostile to the republic. In 1919, they cautiously requested that due to "the doubtlessly differing opinions of its readers . . . no position be taken either for or against the . . . new imperial colors of black-red-gold." By 1926, however, they printed an article opining that the "new state form" can choose any colors it wants for the imperial flag, "but [black-red-gold] has no historical basis." Such disdain for the Weimar colors was a clear indication of hostility to the republic. A 1930 *Journal for Civil Registry Practice* article, on the other hand, stated that it would be "the greatest folly to call for the dissolution of parliamentarianism through a dictator." The text continued: "Not the system, but rather our attitude towards it, is wrong. . . ."[11] And, in 1934, when Genealogical Authority director Achim Gercke was seeking assistance in his struggle to "coordinate" a resistant Zentralstelle into his national genealogical umbrella organization, he "smeared" Hohlfeld, then the Zentralstelle's head, by noting that Hohlfeld had earlier been a member of the left-liberal "State Party [Staatspartei] . . . and therefore always had an anti-National Socialist position."[12]

Yet the antisocialist orientation of the leading genealogists remained constant beyond 1918. In the first edition of his popular *Pocketbook* (1919), for example, the Zentralstelle's archivist, Friedrich Wecken, claimed with regard to the working class: "Its oldest components arise from the subjugated prisoners of war of alien tribes or on the crime, vice, and distress-riddled members of the typical tribe. . . ."[13] In the second and third editions (1922, 1924), he repeated these words verbatim. Likewise, a 1924 *German Herald* book review asserted that socialism, through a "stab in the back, and leadership of the rabble, pauperized our *Volk*." A 1932 *News of the Roland* article by a pastor claimed that "Americanism and Bolshevism lack history and do not correspond to the German essence."[14]

Genealogists' traditional cultural values also continued to manifest themselves in Weimar. In 1928, for example, Zentralstelle director Hohlfeld noted that family research was not just an individual practice, but also a national task: it served to promote German family life against modern immorality.[15] Similarly, the 1927 *Family History Gazette* began a subhead in its table of contents, called *Ständische* genealogy. The use of *Stand* or "estate" conjured up a medieval flavor favored by many cultural conservatives.[16] The continuing interest in nobility during the Weimar years also reflected this cultural conservatism. As late as 1928, the *Family History Gazette* published an impassioned plea for preservation of noble lineages in northern Europe.[17] The *German Herald*'s concern with the nobility was even more pronounced. A 1924 book review, for instance, asserted that the "the aristocratic worldview is the precondition for all progress."[18] On the other hand, neither of the more middle-class-oriented *News of the Roland* or *Journal for Civil Registry Practice* had much to say about aristocrats, though the *Roland*'s cover also featured a medieval knight. The civil registrars' journal was, unlike the purely genealogical journals, concerned above all with legal and other practical aspects of civil registry work. But this work also tended, by its very nature, to promote traditional values. In fact, apart from an increase in discussions about the relationship between "scientific" topics and genealogical practice, the four journals' conservative sociocultural content stayed much the same, not only through Weimar, but through the Nazi era as well.

As in Imperial Germany, during Weimar the leading genealogists continued to seek to accommodate the increasing influence of those they perceived as "below" them in the social hierarchy by calling for the spread of the practice to those groups. In 1919, the *German Herald* urged its readers to fight the "still widely spread misbelief that family research is . . . only of value for the nobility. . . ." Ten years later, an article in the *Journal for Civil Registry Practice* claimed that family studies was not only for "noble, famous, rich, [or] politically and economically leading families," but for all families.[19] Leading genealogists also consciously sought to address potential audiences in the ways most likely to reach them. A *Family History Gazette* book review in 1928, for instance, noted that "one brings a Catholic women's society into contact [with genealogy] in a different manner than a workers' education society, an adult school class [*Volkschulklasse*] differently than a university lecture."[20]

The Weimar era began with outbreaks of actual class warfare in Berlin, Munich, and elsewhere. Political and social unrest loomed throughout much of the period. Thus, calls for German unity based on both a "sense for family" and a common heritage greatly increased in all four journals during the interwar years. In a typical example, the *Journal for Civil Registry Practice* claimed in 1927 that "genealogical research gives one the understanding of how he . . . is bound with Heimat and Volk. . . ."[21] In addition to increasing in frequency, however, these exhortations were also often more strident in tone, a trend also evident in all four journals. A *German Herald* review in 1920 of two books on adult education centers (*Volkshochschule*), for example, praised the movement: "that wants to awaken the sense for German history and study of the Heimat. All family research is based on the love of the past and ancestors, which the coarse materialism of our time ridicules. Now, however, a countermovement has arisen in all circles of the Volk. . . ." The same year, the *Family History Gazette* bemoaned that Germany stood at the gate of a "deep black future." All was not lost, however, as the *Gazette* claimed that its genealogical work served the "national rebirth" of the German people by instilling a love of *Volk* and history. Likewise, an article in the *Journal for Civil Registry Practice* in 1926 claimed that because of the civil registrars' close connection to the past, the registrars could help reduce the present "mutual internal estrangement" through knowledge of "our forefathers." A 1932 speech by the Roland's head asserted the importance of genealogy for the reconstruction of the *Volk*.[22]

Again, while not overtly racist, this promotion of German unity based on perception of shared heritage was conceptually ambiguous. A 1927 article in the civil registrars' journal, for example, exhorted its readers to encourage the giving of "good German forenames" to children for the purpose of "reawakening the German essence."[23] Although "the German essence" was not defined in this piece, especially in the Weimar period German genealogists' growing emphasis on Germans' "shared heritage" appeared in conjunction with a large increase in articles devoted to "race." Thus even if not overtly stated, there was an implication that shared heritage included shared biology. The concept of *Volksgemeinschaft* increasingly took on connotations of "racial community." Moreover, some articles were quite explicit in this regard. An article in the *Journal for Civil Registry Practice* in 1922, for instance, using rhetoric that could easily have come from the Nazi period, stated that "the German, son of the intellectually richest land . . . is a member of the great family of the tribe [*Stamm*] and Volk, not on the basis of constitutional law fictions, but rather by virtue of the blood of the same ancestors . . . that circles in him and all truly born *Volksgenossen*."[24]

These ideas were not limited to the genealogical journals studied in this work. A book dedicated to explicating the meaning of the word *völkisch*, for instance, noted in 1927 the "natural" relation between the family and the *Volksgemeinschaft*: the family was "the natural heart of the Volk-essence [*Volkstum*], required through unity of blood. . . ."[25] Likewise, in 1931, Karl Förster, the founder of the German Ancestral

Community, wrote that its collection of genealogical information served to show "the rooting in blood of each German . . . we are a people, a great German family, bound to each other through blood ties."[26] Accordingly, when in 1933, the Nazi Genealogical Authority official Karl Fahrenhorst stated that "German genealogical research is research of the German *Volk*," he was merely repeating an idea that was already well established in Weimar, in cultural circles well beyond the radical right. Many genealogists' promotions of *German* as a biological concept in the interwar period, even without being overtly racist, were nevertheless quite compatible with the Nazi conception of a "racial community."

"Scientific Genealogy" and Racist Eugenics in Weimar

The sense of crisis during the interwar period, which caused many genealogists increasingly to stress "German unity," was also a factor in their growing attention to hereditary science, and especially to eugenics. Proper breeding, it was felt, would improve society. Also during this period, parallels between nonracist eugenics and later Nazi racial policies become increasingly apparent. Genealogists' endorsements of new and often harsh measures to deal with the "hereditary dangers" threatening Germany began to escalate. Other factors of continuing importance in this growing interest in hereditary science and eugenics included the fact that association with a "scientific" enterprise simply afforded genealogists more prestige, as well as inherent interest in genetics.

Genealogy, Heredity Science, and Eugenics

During the Weimar years, popular books on genealogical practice, such as Friedrich Wecken's *Pocketbook,* continued to contain entire chapters on hereditary science, while the emphasis on the scientific value of genealogical practice increased.[27] As in the Kaiserreich, the journals also regularly featured articles and book reviews on the subject of heredity that did not even mention a direct connection with genealogy, and to purchase such books for their libraries.[28] Similarly, the titles of genealogical works increasingly contained the words *science* and *biology*. In 1920, for instance, the *Family History Gazette*'s subtitle became *Monatschrift für die gesamte deutsche wissenschaftliche Genealogie* (*Monthly for Complete German Scientific Genealogy*). Moreover, during the Weimar period, at least two new journals that expressly combined genealogical practice and biology appeared: the *Zeitschrift für kulturgeschichtliche und biologische Familienkunde* (*Journal for Cultural-Historical and Biological Family Studies;* 1924) and the *Archiv für Sippenforschung und aller verwandte Gebiete* (*Archive for Kinship Research and All Related Fields;* 1928). The latter noted in its first issue that "related fields" included not only heraldry, but also "natural and social science."[29] In fact, a specific section on "Biological Genealogy" appeared for the first time in the 1927–1930 edition of the *Family History Bibliography,* the standard bibliography of genealogical works, and showed a fairly steady increase in the number of entries during the remainder of Weimar.

According to an historian of German genealogy, by "the [nineteen] twenties, there was [also] scarcely a single genealogical group in Germany that at some time did not have a lecture evening on this theme [i.e., the heredity nature of intellectual and corporal characteristics]." Genealogists also continued to promote courses and lectures on the subject.[30] To be sure, even in the Weimar era not all genealogists' scientific interests were centered on heredity. In 1925, for instance, Friedrich von Klocke favorably reviewed two books on sociology, claiming that because genealogy is considered a social science, genealogists should acquaint themselves with sociological ideas.[31] Nevertheless, the overwhelming scientific interest of most genealogists in this period remained focused on hereditary inheritance.

As with other concepts related to racist eugenic ideology and the Nazi era ancestral proof, the growing social instability in Weimar was also a probable factor behind the increasing interest in eugenics. Following World War I, the journals began more frequently to report on meetings of eugenic organizations and congresses, reviewing the contents of eugenic journals, and emphasizing the importance of the field and its ties to genealogy. A *Family History Gazette* article in 1922, for instance, stressed the ability of genealogy to serve medical and biological sciences by evaluating "human data" and thus to advance the interest of the broad "national essence [*Volkstums*]."[32]

The journals also began routinely, and positively, reviewing books on eugenics. A *German Herald* discussion in 1926 of anthropologist and eugenicist Walter Scheidt's *Family Book,* for example, claimed that it contained everything one needed to know "if he wants to form his life according to the biological grounds demanded by his existence."[33] The affiliations between genealogists and eugenics organizations also grew. Thus in 1923, officials from a variety of government ministries in Berlin invited the Zentralstelle's Hans Breymann, among others, to discuss the creation of a National Institute for Human Genetics and Population Science.[34] Similarly, Edwin Krutina (1888–1953), head of the Reich Federation of German Civil Registrars, was also on the board of the German Federation for *Volk* Regeneration and Genetics. Created in 1926, and partially financed by the Civil Registrars' Federation, this organization was dedicated to spreading eugenic ideas to all Germans.[35]

A more systematic way to illustrate genealogists' growing interest in eugenics is to evaluate the topic's position in the *Journal for Civil Registry Practice*. Because of its wide circulation, middle-of-the-road political tendencies, and close connection with local, state, and national government entities, the journal closely reflected the interests of "mainstream" genealogical practitioners in the approximately twelve years before the Nazi assumption of power. During its first three years of publication (1921–1923), the journal did not contain a single article dealing specifically with eugenics. This changed, however, in 1924, when it featured at least three such articles. By the following year, it had at least seven. Moreover, other articles in 1925, while not specifically on eugenics, discussed the concept favorably in passing.[36]

Additionally, of the eight lectures presented at the Professional Training Week for Civil Registrars in that year, two dealt specifically with "racial hygiene." Likewise, the Congress of the Reich Federation of German Civil Registrars in 1925 also featured three speakers on racial hygiene, including the prominent geneticist Erwin Baur.[37] Also in 1925, in order to assist the civil registry workers in their increasingly important task of offering hereditary advice, the Federation began publishing eugenicist Carl von Behr-Pinnow's *The Future of the Human Race: Foundations and Demands of Genetics (Die Zukunft der menschlichen Rasse: Grundlagen und Forderungen d. Vererbungslehre)*. This eugenic work, the *Journal for Civil Registry Practice* noted, was easier to understand than the difficult standard work, the so-called Baur-Fischer-Lenz.[38] Thus within four years of initial publication, eugenics had gained an important place in the German civil registrars' professional organization. Their journal's concentration on eugenics continued into the Third Reich.

While all the genealogical journals increasingly featured material related to eugenics, each—not surprisingly—had its own "spin" on the topic. For example, a 1917 article in the more aristocratically oriented *German Herald* emphasized that data from the Berlin Society for Racial Hygiene showed that "the nobility marches at the peak of all German families with the number of casualties [*heldenopfer*]" in the war.[39] Yet, whatever their individual emphases, the foregoing journals clearly illustrate a trend of growing interest in eugenics among genealogists. It should also be noted, however, that not every prominent genealogist was entirely smitten with the increasing stress on the connection between genealogical practice and eugenics. In a *News of the Roland* article in 1929, for example, Klocke, ever the voice for moderation, warned against the conceptual blurring of genealogy (*Familienkunde*) and eugenics, which he termed "family policy [*Familienpolitik*]." Yet even Klocke claimed that genealogy was also the foundation for policies to strengthen the Volk "through selection, the prevention of damaging [hereditary] poison, and higher breeding."[40]

Eugenic ideas were not inherently racist. However, even when race was not mentioned as a hereditary threat, many ideas compatible with racist eugenic ideology became more prominent during the Weimar era. The most fundamental of these, and one that was often either implicit or explicit in many books and articles on eugenics, was the idea that an invisible hereditary danger posed a significant threat to the future of the German Volk. An article in the *Journal for Civil Registry Practice* in 1931, for example, warned that carriers of "pathologic genetic capacities" could appear "completely healthy," because the pathology is in the "germ cells."[41] Likewise, in a radio speech in September 1932, the civil registrars' leader Krutina warned that "hereditary biology had established that certain [hereditary] diseases . . . can be reproduced in such a way that they appear in children without appearing in the parents."[42] The basic idea that a hereditary threat could be passed on through the generations without outward manifestation was, of course, true. Nevertheless, the concept provided at least a partial pedigree for the later quest to seek out and destroy the allegedly often invisible hereditary threat posed by the "racially alien." For example, a September 1935 Interior

Ministry report outlining the basis for the Nuremberg Laws claimed that any admixture of "Jewish characteristics" into the German population, even without further infusion, could still reappear after "many generations."[43]

As with many other concepts related to racist eugenic ideology, the claim that nature trumped nurture also appeared more frequently during the Weimar period.[44] An article in the *News of the Roland* in 1923, for example, claimed that "the best German Kinship periodical, *Nachrichten der Familien Hornschuch* [*News of the Hornschuch Family*]" showed that despite holding totally different professions and political affiliations, everyone in the Hornschuch kinship group played a musical instrument. "This family gift is a classic example of the heredity and growth of a talent," continued the article, seemingly oblivious to the idea that simply growing up in a musically oriented family might also play some role.[45] By the end of the Weimar era, these claims had also grown in stridency. An article in the *Journal for Civil Registry Practice* by the eugenicist Behr-Pinnow claimed in 1928 that "Zytologie and Mendelism" had rendered laughable the concept of the equality of all men. Likewise, in the 1931 edition, Konrad Dürre, editor of the *völkisch* journal *Türner,* railed against the "biologically false teaching of the equality of humanity."[46]

This extreme stress on heredity was not without its critics. A 1924 *German Herald* review praised the book *Sozialbiologie* for giving "blood" its "due place, without forgetting environment." Similarly, the 1930 *Family History Gazette* criticized the book *Genetics and Hereditary Health Care* for, among other things, an overemphasis on genetics, at the expense of environmental factors.[47] These voices were, however, in the minority and they became rarer yet in the Nazi era. Thus in 1938, when Genealogical Authority official Arthur Schultze-Naumburg asserted in the institution's journal *Familie, Sippe, Volk,* that racial science had shown the falsehood of "the belief in the equality of everyone who had a human face," he was not saying anything new, or even extraordinary. He was simply repeating an idea that had already become mainstream, at least in genealogical circles, during Weimar.[48]

In addition to conceptual continuities, there were also policy connections. One was the gathering and centralizing of biological data on the entire German population for eugenic purposes. A 1925 *News of the Roland* article, for example, discussed coordinating family and genealogical registers, and proposed introducing a health passport (*Gesundheitspaß*) that would contain hereditary information.[49] Given, however, the high potential increase in importance for civil registrars in conjunction with such proposals, the *Journal for Civil Registry Practice* was, of all the genealogical journals, their most enthusiastic promoter. During Weimar, articles promoted making "health passports" mandatory (1926); asked civil registrars to help prevent the propagation of "low-value [*unterwertig*] individuals" while encouraging the propagation of "valuable personalities" through the creation of "so-called eugenic registers" (1928); and called for the gathering of genealogical information on the entire population by state authorities to determine whether a marriage was hereditarily advisable (1930).[50] All of these ideas pointed the direction to later Nazi racial policies.

The Ahnenpass in particular, which became a popular method of making the ancestral proof, had pre-Nazi progenitors in two Weimar-era booklets that civil registrars promoted for recording genealogical information. In the early 1920s, the Civil Registrars Federation introduced the *Einheitsfamilienstammbuch*. Like the Ahnenpass, this was essentially a genealogical table in booklet form, one that the Federation hoped would become standardized throughout Germany.[51] While a desired result of this booklet was to have all genealogical information contained in one document, many civil registrars also viewed it as a tool for promoting eugenic ideals. Articles in the *Journal for Civil Registry Practice* claimed that through the *Einheitsfamilienstammbuch*, "hereditary science receives new impulses" (1922), described it as "a good means of advertising the goals of eugenics" (1929), and claimed that "it can awaken the sense for racial-hygiene . . . in the young peasants" (1931).[52] Moreover, the *Journal* in 1928 not only noted that the "careful management of . . . the *Familienstammbuch*" could play a role in instituting eugenic policies by cataloging lineages, but also noted that the authorities had recognized the booklet's importance by giving it status as legal proof of what was contained in the actual genealogical documents.[53] Both features were to become primary elements of the Ahnenpass.

In 1931, the civil registrars' organization also began promoting a similar booklet, but one with a more overtly eugenic purpose. This *Urkundenbuch der Kindheit* (*Infancy Document Book*) was created in association with the Kaiser Wilhelm Institute for Anthropology in Berlin and was designed to record physical information about newborn infants. In 1932, the *Journal for Civil Registry Practice* called for civil registrars well schooled in eugenics to engage in the "closest work with . . . the district medical doctors to secure eugenic lists" for marriage counseling and hereditary research. It advised that this practice should begin with "obligatory introduction of hereditary health papers [*Erbgesundheitsbogen*] for all students of all classes," and claimed that the *Infancy Document Book* marked a good start.[54] The civil registrars were, in fact, fairly successful in promoting this booklet. In late 1931 and 1932, it was quickly endorsed, and its use was encouraged, by the Prussian Welfare and Interior Ministries, the Justice Ministries in Baden and Württemberg, the Interior Ministries in Saxony and Braunschweig, and the governments of Anhalt, Schamburg-Lippe, Lippe, Dessau, Hamburg, Oldenburg, and the Saar region. In the first six months of its existence, the civil registrars distributed more than fifteen thousand copies. By late 1932, an advertisement in their journal claimed that "75 percent more births are recorded in the *Infancy Document Book* than were last year."[55] While none of the foregoing genealogical eugenic documentation referred to "race" as a hereditary health factor to be considered, the intellectual and policy continuities with the ancestral proof—the comprehensive gathering of biological data for use in combating a hereditary threat to the *Volk*—are obvious.

Genealogical literature varied in regard to the means approved for engendering public compliance with such eugenic measures. Some called only for mild enforcement methods. In the 1922 *Journal for Civil Registry Practice*, for example, a high-ranking civil registrar promoted the issuing of "health brochures" to the public to promote the goal that "only healthy persons will unite in marriage."[56] Increasingly, however, authors called for more brutal policies, anticipating those later implemented under the Nazi regime. The first edition of Wecken's *Pocketbook* (1919), in its discussion of "hereditary hygiene," stated that this should include "forbidding marriage or sterilization" of people with genetic illnesses. Articles in the civil registrars' *Journal* also called for the legal prevention of marriages between the hereditarily valuable and the inferior.[57] And again, these calls rose in both frequency and stridency in the years just prior to the Nazi assumption of power. A 1929 *Journal* piece, for example, called for the "extermination [*Ausmerzung*]" of the "reproductively unsuited."[58] Hence, in this way as well, in the years prior to the Nazi assumption of power, genealogical journals were already sounding very much like proponents of the Nazi "hereditary health" laws.

There was little criticism of such ideas in the pages of the journals. While there was also no uniformity of opinion, debate generally centered not on *whether*, but to *which* degree the state should impose itself on the lives of the "hereditarily ill." Thus, an article in the *Family History Gazette* in 1924 criticized the attempt by a Dr. Gerhard Boeters, in Zwickau, to have legislation passed allowing the sterilization of persons allegedly comprising "life unworthy of life."[59] Boeters, stated the article, confused personal, hereditary, and congenital sicknesses. Such a law, it continued, required further research before it could achieve its purposes. Thus the *Gazette* piece did not oppose sterilization in principle, but only as promoted by Boeters. Similarly, in 1928, the prominent genealogist Wilhelm Karl Prinz von Isenburg (1903–1956) wrote: "The killing of living beings who, according to the opinion of certain people, are damaging in some respect, has still not helped to create its intended effect in the world."[60] Although Isenburg opposed the killing of such persons, he nevertheless called for their separation from society.

The calls for harsh policies directed against the "hereditarily ill," by men of great social distinction, varied in the degrees of brutality they endorsed. Nevertheless, even their conditional support helped to normalize the idea that the greater good required cruelty to certain classes of hereditarily "destructive" individuals. This support also prepared the ground for the acceptance of later government-sanctioned mistreatment of Jews and other "racial aliens." And it should be noted that even after the Nazi assumption of power, and even in a journal like *Familie, Sippe, Volk* (which was controlled by the Genealogical Authority), articles on eugenics continued to be published without overt racist content, although they were often harsh in their assessment of the "hereditarily ill" or the "culturally incapable."[61] These two forms of eugenic thought and policy existed in tandem both before and during the Third Reich.

Before 1933, however, nonracist eugenics had the more credible pedigree: it was indisputable that certain illnesses were hereditary. Proponents of racist eugenics gained legitimacy primarily by blurring the differences between the two. Contemporaries were aware of these attempts. In 1931, for example, the head of the Society for Jewish Family Research asked his predominantly Jewish readers not automatically to discount eugenic thought even though it was often combined with the "ominous concept of 'race'."[62] The way this combination occurred in the pages of genealogical journals during the Weimar years is the subject of the next section.

Racist Eugenics

In the interwar period, discussion of the importance of "race" and the dangers of "race-mixing," rare in Imperial Germany, increased substantially in genealogical literature. Discussions of the "Jewish racial problem" continued much as before. Moreover (as later happened regularly in the Nazi era), during Weimar, in the effort to legitimize racist thought, its advocates began to consistently claim that it was "scientific." Again, the majority of leading genealogists did not overtly endorse racism themselves. But they generally failed to critique such ideas when they increasingly appeared in the genealogical literature—except when the claims appeared to be "unscientific." And again, this provided an implicit endorsement. By helping to make racist ideas sound plausible, these factors all played a vital role in creating widespread acquiescence to institutionalized racism in the Third Reich.

Genealogy and Racial Purity

> It is curious that the origin of the word *race,* the Gothic *reisza* or split, line . . . already had a biological sense; it meant the blood-line, the series of generations following one another.
> —*JOURNAL FOR VOLK REGENERATION AND GENETICS,* 1926[63]

By the time the Nazis assumed power, virtually all of the basic components of their racist eugenic theory had already appeared in Weimar-era genealogical journals: "science" had proven the existence of distinct human races, the dependency of culture on race, and the necessity of preventing mixing with the "racially alien." To a lesser degree, "science" also suggested that Jews posed the greatest threat in this regard. The journals had already also endorsed some of the specific racist eugenic policies later implemented by the Nazis. In other words, racist eugenic thought had already spread widely within German society by 1933.

While racism was definitely on the ascendant in the interwar period, assessing its existence and its level in genealogical works of the period is not a straightforward task. This is because the terminology was ambiguous. The first edition of Wecken's *Pocketbook* (1919), for example, discusses the Mendelian laws of hereditary inheritance and uses the terms *bastard* and *race* in relation to breeding lines of mice and slugs, rather than humans.[64] In most genealogical literature, of course, authors clearly used *race* in reference to human beings. But even then the meaning of the word was usually vague. An article in the *Journal for Civil Registry Practice* in 1923 called for medical approval to marry, yet buttressed these demands by saying "we need only to think of antiquity when one sought, more so than today, the ennoblement of his race."[65] In this context, it was unclear whether by *race* the author meant family, tribe, *Volk*, race (in the anthropological sense), or mankind. Likewise, a *Journal* review in 1927 of a special edition of the journal *Kultur und Leben* (*Culture and Life*), devoted to Sudeten Germans, noted in passing that one section was on "Racial Care and Racial Poisoning."[66] Again, the use of *race* was ambiguous: "racial poisoning" could refer to hereditary illness, the influx of "racially alien blood," or both.

Even when an author delimited the term *race* in some way, the ambiguity was rarely eliminated. A 1917 *German Herald* review of the book *Racial Hygiene and Reproductive Hygiene (Eugenics),* for instance, claimed to be talking about "race" in the sense of a "continually living *Volks*-body [*dauernd lebende Völkskorper*]" rather than the so-called "system races,"—the specific, anthropologically defined races. This, of course, left open to question the "racial composition" of the "*Volks*-body." Similarly, a 1924 *German Herald* review of anthropologist Walter Scheidt's *Introduction to Natural Scientific Family Studies* noted that Scheidt, later a "racial expert" for the Genealogical Authority, promoted the idea that the "existence of a race is actual, real, like the existence of genetic capacities." However, he did not define the term.[67]

Often writers used other words with an expressed or implied biological connotation, but usually without much further clarity. An article in the *Journal for Civil Registry Practice in* 1925 claimed that *Volk* was predominantly a biological concept, but nevertheless failed to define its parameters. Likewise, a piece by a civil registrar in 1926 claimed that "locality [*Heimat*], family, tribe [*Stamm*] and *Volk*: the concepts fuse into unity. . . ."[68] However, the author did not indicate which families and tribes were included within the *Volk*. Similarly, writers sometimes highlighted the term *German* in conjunction with "race." But this usually just added to the conceptual confusion. In the 1926 *Journal,* for example, an author called for "health certificates" before marriage for "the preservation of the German race," but did not define "German race." In the 1929 *Journal,* the same writer similarly argued the necessity of eugenic counseling for couples in order to create a "healthy German race."[69] While, again, "German race" was not defined, within the context of this article the author made clear that "healthy" meant the "extermination" of "low-value, sick and reproductively unsuited elements." He did not mention mixture with the "racially alien" as a threat.

A 1923 *News of the Roland* article, on the other hand, claimed that based on the anthropological and genetic work of Hans Günther, the Baur-Fischer-Lenz, and Walter Scheidt, "[i]n the next hundred years one will arrive at a conscious German race."[70] While this assertion implied the inclusion of some "racial types" and the exclusion of others, again, it did not clarify which "types" were involved. A 1928 *News of the Roland* review of a book on "cultural and racial history" did directly describe the "racial" basis of *German*. It noted the book's contention that the "Germans" were not racially pure or predominantly Nordic, but rather a mixture of the Nordic and Dalic [*Dalisch*] "races."[71] This, however, was likely still confusing to many readers as *Dalic* was not one of the more frequently cited "racial components" of the German *Volk*. Nor did the article note that race's identifying characteristics.

The 1930 *Family History Gazette* reviewed K. Saller's *The Fehmaraner: An Anthropological Investigation from East Holstein,* volume four in the multivolume *Deutsche Rassenkunde* (*German Racial Studies*) series edited by Germany's leading anthropologist, Eugen Fischer. The piece noted that Saller provided a detailed physiological description of the two major reproductive communities (*Fortpflanzungsgem einschaften*) of the area.[72] The word *race* was absent from the review. A 1931 *News of the Roland* review of the previous book in the series, however, described the series itself as a "representation . . . of the race-related [*rassenmäßige*] condition of the population that speaks German and creates German culture," while a 1932 review of the book called it a "cultural-biological description of a population."[73] Based on these varied descriptions, a reader could well be confused about the meaning of *race*. Indeed, a 1932 *Family History Gazette* article was concerned not only with the dangers of mixing between the so-called anthropological races, but also the dangers of increased "nervous and corporeal degeneration" caused by mixing between persons of the same "race" but different "ancestrally established genealogical groups."[74] After reading this, one could be left wondering about the difference between a *race* and the latter grouping.

Various authors' utilization of the word *blood* threw additional uncertainty into the picture. Sometimes the author clearly meant biological affinity. A 1927 *News of the Roland* article celebrated the appearance of the first "German-Bohemian" edition of the journal as crossing "the border to [our] blood-related German brothers in Czechoslovakia," while in the 1927 *Journal for Civil Registry Practice* the *völkisch* author Ludwig Finckh claimed the existence of one hundred million Germans "according to blood."[75] Other times, however, use of "blood" was more indeterminate. A 1922 *Journal* article, for example, described the "charm" of investigating the "Saxon-Thuringian-Frank-Slav blood admixture [*Bluteinschlag*] in Upper Silesia." Did the author mean the mixing of different races in the biological sense, the mixing of different cultural groups, or did he think that these were fundamentally the same thing? Moreover, a book such as Otto von Forst de Battaglia's *The Secret of the Blood* was, according to a 1932 *News of the Roland* review, concerned with the "significance of heredity" in general, not with "race" in particular.[76]

In any event, as the foregoing articles attest, whatever genealogists thought the words *race* and *blood* meant, and whether or not they believed in a racial hierarchy, especially beginning in the Weimar era, they exhibited a growing interest in the concept of *human races*. This interest was also expressed in other ways. In 1924, for example, the *Journal for Civil Registry Practice*'s index had, for the first time, a heading for Racial Science and Racial Hygiene (with three entries). While *racial hygiene* did not necessarily indicate anything more than eugenics, *racial science* clearly referred to the study of biological "races." Likewise, the journals promoted lectures with racial themes, published information about "racial scientifically" themed journals such as the *Archive for Racial and Social Biology,* and informed their readers of institutional efforts in racial studies.[77] Not surprisingly, the journals also asserted the importance of using genealogy, in conjunction with other sciences, in determining "racial questions." A 1927 *Family History Gazette* article, for example, was titled "On the Co-work of Family Studies and Anthropology in Racial Questions."[78] Thus in the Weimar era, interest in, and discussion of, *race,* a key element of racist eugenic ideology, significantly increased in genealogical journals.

The line between promoting the idea that distinct biological races existed and asserting that they were of differing "value" was extremely thin. According to a 1931 *Journal for Civil Registry Practice* article, "each race has its good qualities and faults." Moreover, continued the article, "[b]iologically observed one to another, each race is completely equal to the other."[79] Yet dyed-in-the-wool racism was usually not far below the surface of even seemingly neutral statements. To the author just mentioned, for example, the person of Nordic "race" was the "true spiritual man," a quality unequaled by other "races." The faults of the Nordic race were "courage even unto pointless death" and "fear of marriage." Such faults likely would have paled in comparison to those the author would have ascribed to other "races."

German or European cultural superiority was, in fact, a recurring theme in the genealogical journals. But this presumption was not always tied to "biology." For instance, a 1924 *Journal for Civil Registry Practice* article asserted that genealogical organizations showed "the invincibility of German *Volk*-strength and German *Volk*-essence . . . a *Volk* born of the earth and competent to the core . . . ," while a 1926 article waxed poetic over "German diligence, German order, German thoroughness, [and] German love of *Volk* and Fatherland." Neither article, however, asserted that these favorable qualities were related to German "racial" composition.[80] Likewise, the presumption of cultural inferiority in others was also not always tied to "race." In the 1927 *Journal,* for example, a Reich Justice Ministry official wrote an article about the "problems" inherent in marriages between German women and foreigners.[81] Often enough, wrote the official, the men are nationals of "half-civilized nations that stand a greater or lesser distance from the European cultural circle." He further described such marriages as a "deep wound to the German *Volk* body [*Volkskörper*]." Yet, while cultural bigotry was clear, the author did not link cultural superiority to race, at least not directly. Given the context in which such articles appeared, however, it was easy for readers to make such a connection.

Yet, as with so many other continuities with the Nazi era, overt claims of racial superiority also became increasingly pronounced in the journals. Thus a 1919 *Family History Gazette* article claimed that the most current anthropological research had "demonstrated the significance of light-skinned humans for all cultures and, with this, its preservation for the future of a *Volk*." Likewise, a 1926 *News of the Roland* article recommending eugenicist Behr-Pinnow's *The Future of the Human Race,* noted that it showed the "special mental qualities of the Nordic race. . . ." A 1927 *Journal for Civil Registry Practice* article asserted that "the brain of the Phymäenmanns in Central Africa is closer to that of the manlike apes the orangutan and the gorilla than it is to that of the Nordic man. . . ."[82] The genealogical societies also promoted the idea of racial inequality by purchasing racist works for their libraries. In 1929, for example, the Roland's library obtained W. His's *On the Natural Inequality of Humans.*[83]

The line between an interest in preventing "race-mixing" and racism was also paper-thin. The former was sometimes described as necessary to prevent the loss of the "peculiar excellencies" of each race, neither of which supposedly was inherently better. On the other hand, appearing as they did in German genealogical journals, calls for preventing "race-mixing" virtually always came from members of a "race" that enjoyed, or sought, some (nonbiological) advantage over members of another "race." This indicated that such demands were not based on a fundamental belief in the equality of the "races." Indeed, the aversion to "race-mixing" was increasingly justified expressly on claims of racial superiority. Articles in all four journals warned that such mixing would destroy German culture.[84] Given these concerns, specific instances of admixture of "alien blood" in individual families continued to be worthy of note. The 1927 *Family History Gazette,* for example, pointed out the presence of "Indian blood" in the Witte family due to the late-eighteenth-century marriage of Magdalena Marie Luise, whose maternal grandmother was an Indian, and medical doctor Gabriel Wilhelm Witte. Such articles also appeared in other journals.[85] Even though this type of piece usually did not mention the "dangers" of "race-mixing," it is likely that many readers would have understood this as the basic need driving the quest to discover and publicize such occurrences.

Besides containing racist eugenic ideas identical to those of the Nazis, suggestions for similar policies based on those ideas also appeared in genealogical journals during the Weimar Republic. The 1925 *Journal for Civil Registry Practice* called for the creation of eugenic divisions in the civil registries to help insure the "improvement of the hereditary capacity of our *Volk,*" and for the recording back "four to six generations," of "family history and biological records" at the civil registry offices. In addition to preventing hereditary defects, another stated reason for this practice was to maintain the predominance of the Nordic element in the "German racial mixture."[86] Similarly, an article in the 1931 *Journal* argued that the *Einheitsfamilienstammbuch* should record racial as well as hereditary data as "[o]nly both types of registration united allow scientific use of the material in the interest of raising offspring who are thoroughly useful for human society."[87] Anticipating the Nuremberg Laws by sixteen years, in 1919 Friedrich Wecken, then the *Family History Gazette's* editor, enthusiastically reviewed (stating, "Buy!") Friedrich Siebert's *The Völkisch Quality of Racial-Hygiene,* which promoted a law to take away the citizenship of the "un-German, racially alien."[88]

Racial Antisemitism

As with other precursive elements of the racial laws and ancestral proof, racial antisemitism increasingly appeared in genealogical literature after 1918. In 1921, for example, the *German Herald* favorably reviewed the anonymously written *The World War in Light of Natural Scientific Historical Views*. This contained a chapter entitled "Racial Instinct," discussing, inter alia, "the instinct in the Germans" in relation to "the Jewish problem."[89] Other articles warned against the immigration to Germany of "Semites" from the East (1924); cautioned against "race-mixing," which was said to include "the Jewish question" (1924); contrasted the nobility of Nordic contributions to art and culture with "Jewish" Expressionism (1927); noted that a "*völkisch*-racist" genealogical society sought to exclude "Semitic . . . hereditary material" (1929); and warned that breeding between "indo-Germans" and Jews leads to a decrease in fertility for both physical and social reasons (1932).[90] Given the relative prevalence of racial antisemitism in the Kaiserreich, however, its growth during the Weimar years was less dramatic than was the growth of more generalized racist rhetoric.

The practice of "exposing" people with Jewish ancestry (as with others of "alien blood") also continued in Weimar. In 1931, the *Family History Gazette* published a ten-page list of Jewish baptisms and expressly requested that readers "send us further opportune findings regarding baptisms and weddings of those of foreign race." It promised to credit by name those who provided such information.[91] Occasionally the journals also published in-depth articles on this "outing" process. If the racist motivations behind the *Family History Gazette*'s efforts in this regard were not already clear, a 1919 article by professional genealogist Werner Konstantin von Arnswaldt made them explicit: "in regard to blood and racial-mixing, it may be valuable to establish which families that now have completely German family names are of Jewish origin."[92] Similarly, in 1928, the *German Herald* published an article by Otto Fischer, a pastor, titled "Evangelical Pastors of Jewish Ancestry."[93] Fischer wrote that he had been inspired by an article in the paper for the prominent Jewish organization, the Central Association of German Citizens of Jewish Faith, which had bemoaned ongoing attempts to identify the "many" pastors with Jewish ancestry. He also noted that his inquiries about the number of such pastors were refused due to fear that the findings could be used by antisemites. Apparently having no such fear, Fischer ascertained for himself several pastors who "carried Jewish blood," and then listed the names of six in Brandenburg. He also noted that he had found "two others who were, with a probability bordering on certainty, of Jewish ancestry through the grandmother, even though documentary proof cannot yet be brought." This last sentence anticipated the Nazi-era ancestral decision both in its use of language of probability and its reliance on documentary proof. Both gave it a "scientific," disinterested patina.

With the introduction of the ancestral proof in Nazi Germany, the pace of uncovering Jewish baptisms of course greatly accelerated. But the Nazi effort did not only represent a general social and cultural continuity. It also constituted a direct succession. In 1928, Achim Gercke, the first head of the Genealogical Authority, but then at the University of Göttingen, began to publish a series of volumes seeking to identify all "Jews," "part-Jews" and faculty married to such persons in a particular university or university department. Between 1928 and 1932, eight volumes appeared, all entitled *The Jewish Influence and the German Universities.*[94] In conjunction with this effort, Gercke also established an Archive for Racial Statistics of Professional Groups, based on the extensive collection of genealogical information in his Alien Origin Registry. In 1932, this organization became the National Socialist Information Office of the NSDAP Reich Executive (NS-Auskunftsstelle bei der Reichsleitung der NSDAP), the direct precursor of the Nazi Genealogical Authority.

Of course, along with the increase in racial antisemitism in genealogical journals in the years preceding the Third Reich, traditional antisemitic discourse continued as well. The 1925 *Family History Gazette,* for example, offered the story of a Jewish man who underwent five baptisms in the early eighteenth century (evangelical, reform, evangelical, catholic, and again evangelical). The author noted that "the Jew" did not undergo these conversions for spiritual reasons, but rather because the money he received from his godparents [*Patengelder*] was "good business" (he reportedly had received 130 Thaler and 22 Groschen just for the first baptism).[95] Yet this statement was not overtly racist as it did not directly tie negative views of Jews to biologically based criteria. These more traditional expressions of ethnic bigotry, however, appeared much less commonly during Weimar than did racially oriented attacks.

Implicit Endorsement of Racism

Even in the interwar period, racist thought constituted a substantive core, rather than an area of peripheral interest, for only one major genealogical society: the German Roland. Although such ideas became more prominent during the 1920s and early 1930s, they still represented only a relatively minimal portion of copy in the genealogical journals. Moreover, positive reviews of racist works such as the *Eisernes Buch deutschen Adels deutscher Art* or *EDDA (Iron Book of German Nobility of German Type)*, a series of noble genealogical tables certified as having no "racially impure" admixture that began in 1919–1920, or Hans Günther's *Racial Studies,* existed side by side with positive reviews of books written by Jews on Jewish participation in the Leipzig fair in the early modern period, on the history of Jewish family names, or on Jewish family history.[96] On the other hand, simply counting page space devoted to racist ideas incorrectly minimizes the degree to which these journals, and their underlying organizations, assisted in the spread of such thought.

The growing, if limited, incidence of racist ideas in genealogical literature was not the only factor important in creating a social atmosphere in which racism could later be quickly institutionalized on a large scale. A number of more indirect means assisted in this process by functioning as sources of implicit endorsement. One such factor was the growing use of the word *Sippenforschung* in place of *Familienforschung* (i.e., "kinship" rather than "family" research) to denote genealogical practice. An archaic Germanic word, *Sippe* specifically indicated "consanguinity" and had connotations of "race"—that is, a biological tie extending beyond that of the immediate or extended family, but excluding those of "different blood."[97] In 1920, for instance, in one of his first public speeches, Hitler referred in the same sentence to Jews as both a "foreign race" and a *Sippe*.[98] While first gaining prominence in the late nineteenth century, use of the word increased especially rapidly in the 1920s and often became a type of "code" indicating *völkisch* sympathies. In 1928, for example, the editors of the *Journal for Cultural-Historical and Biological Family Studies* changed its name to the *Archive for Kinship (Sippe) Research and All Related Fields*.[99]

Another way in which genealogists implicitly promoted racist eugenics specifically during the Weimar era was by conveying the idea that racial and nonracial "hereditary threats" had been proven to the same degree of scientific validity. A 1917 *German Herald* book review, for example, stated that "race" should be treated as any other "valuable" or "harmful" genetic characteristic. A 1924 *Journal for Civil Registry Practice* article called on civil registrars to take leadership positions in the "racial-hygienic *Volk*-movement" to prevent both the breeding of the physically inferior and the disappearance of the "Nordic race" in Germany. The following year's edition called for "biological recording" at the civil registry offices of both nonracial and "racial" hereditary characteristics. This would conserve the "valuable hereditary characteristics" of both humanity and "the individual races." Articles in all of the other journals studied conveyed the same idea, as did civil registrars in their promotion of the *Einheitsfamilienstammbuch*.[100]

The most frequent (and subtle) way in which Weimar-era genealogical journals equated the scientific validity of racial and nonracial "eugenic threats" was by placing works on both subjects side by side, without any differentiation, in book reviews, indexes, and bibliographies. All of these eugenic works, in turn, were usually dignified in the same manner by being placed in the same category as general works on hereditary science. In 1926, for example, a new section called *Hereditary and Racial Studies; Biology* was added to the *News of the Roland*'s regular feature listing new additions to the Roland's library. This is noteworthy, first, in that the section combined "hereditary" and "racial" studies in its name, implicitly equating the scientific legitimacy of the two. Moreover, while not all of the eighteen new books listed in this category endorsed racist ideas, four were by the racial supremacist Hans Günther, and others were by racist ideologues such as L. F. Clauß.[101] Similarly, both the *Family History Gazette* and *News of the Roland* featured reviews of the journal *Archive for Racial and Social Biology* whose very title managed to conflate "race" and "social-biology." The line between racist and nonracist eugenics, not to mention science and pseudo-science, was also thin, and the journals consistently helped to blur it.

Such equation of racist and nonracist thought was by no means limited to the four journals most closely examined in this study. A *Biological Genealogy* section of the *Family History Bibliography,* the general bibliography for German genealogical works, first appeared in 1927. Of the thirty-two entries in that year alone, three were written by Günther; one each by professors Fritz Kern (Bonn) and Franz Schütz (Berlin), both authors of overtly racist works; and seven by later, Nazi-era "racial experts": Eugen Fischer (three), Walter Scheidt (three), and Rudolf Polland (one). Again, not all of these books and articles necessarily contained racist content. But many of their authors clearly sympathized with racist ideas, and the editors of the *Bibliography* implicitly legitimized their views by categorizing them with less tendentious, more clearly "scientific," works.

Another common way in which genealogists implicitly promoted racist ideas in the interwar period was simply through association with well-known racists and their organizations. The *völkisch* genealogist Hans Friedrich von Ehrenkrook and *völkisch* author (and medical doctor) Ludwig Finckh were Roland members. Finckh also joined the Zentralstelle, as did the völkisch author Banniza von Bazan, and Nazi leaders Walter Darré and Falk Ruttke.[102] Finckh was also a "corresponding member" of the Herold. Conversely, Karl Förster, founder of the genealogical organization German Ancestral Community, was an honorary member of the racist and stridently antisemitic German Roland.[103]

These associations extended beyond the immediate world of the genealogical societies. In May 1927, for example, Carl von Behr-Pinnow, an avowed racial supremacist, was a featured speaker at the annual meeting of the German Federation for *Volk* Regeneration and Genetics, which was closely affiliated with the Reich Federation of German Civil Registrars.[104] Also present at this meeting were officials from the Welfare Ministry (*Volkswohlfahrtsministerium*) and the National Health Office (*Reichsgesundheitsamtes*), the Berlin publisher Alfred Metzner, representatives of the Civil Registrars' Federation, and the *völkisch* publicist Konrad Dürre. Thus, at this single meeting there was significant cross-affiliation at one and the same time between genealogists, proponents of both racist and nonracist eugenics, and high-ranking government officials. Such fraternization signaled, at a minimum, that racist ideas were not anathema to the leadership of the mainstream genealogical societies.

But these genealogists' implicit encouragement of racist eugenic ideas went much deeper than simply associating with the persons who promoted them. They also accorded these people respect and power. In 1922, for example, Hans Friedrich von Ehrenkrook, one of Koerner's German Roland colleagues, was elected to a leadership position at the Zentralstelle.[105] Similarly, in 1921, the *Journal for Civil Registry Practice* cited the German Roland as one of the seven most important genealogical societies in the country (actually ranking it second, after the Zentralstelle).[106] A 1927 *News of the Roland* review likewise referred to the German Roland as the Roland's "younger brother," claiming that while the Roland and the German Roland "struggled over theory," both shared the "same love of fatherland and *Volk*."[107] The journals also frequently praised the *German Book of Lineages* without mentioning its editor Koerner's racism and antisemitism.[108] And even when they did mention this, it was often without further comment.

In like manner, prominent genealogical organizations also actively embraced Ludwig Finckh, the well-known proponent of racist eugenics. Finckh was not only an occasional contributor to both the civil registrars' journal and the *News of the Roland;* both editorial boards as well as their affiliated organizations also treated him with great respect. A *News of the Roland* article in 1926, for example, recounting the festivities surrounding Finckh's fiftieth birthday (in which the Roland participated), and referred to him as the "effective *Volk*-based [*Volkstumlich*] author . . . who carrie[s] biologically . . . grounded family and ancestral research to wide circles of the German *Volk*."[109] While these genealogical organizations did not necessarily emphasize Finckh's racist views, none seems to have viewed them as any sort of impediment. Moreover, the *Journal for Civil Registry Practice* also regularly featured articles by the *völkisch* eugenicist Behr-Pinnow and the *völkisch* publicist Dürre. Different genealogical journals did the same for other proponents of racist ideas.[110]

Leading genealogists also treated with respect the racist *Iron Book of German Nobility of German Type* (*EDDA*). A *German Herald* review in 1925, for example, did not mention the *EDDA*'s basic racist premise, but described how well the book was produced and encouraged its purchase to enable "further publication of such volumes." A *News of the Roland* review, the next year on the other hand, actually noted that only persons who could prove pure "ario-Germanic or equivalent stock" back to the fifth generation could appear in this work. But the review provided no further comment.[111] By 1929, however, both journals openly embraced the *EDDA*'s racism. That year, the *German Herald* stated that "joyful pride should be taken in [the most recent *EDDA* genealogical tables] from the racial-biological point of view as well as the purely genealogical." Two *News of the Roland* reviews similarly praised the *EDDA*'s "goal of a racial-biological selection of the members" which, it was noted, meant keeping out "blood of alien type."[112]

"Racial scientist" Hans Günther's blatantly racist works reveal yet another way in which prominent genealogists implicitly endorsed racism: they were widely, and generally positively, referenced in the mainstream journals.[113] The journals also sanctioned Günther's views by promoting talks "based on [his] masterly racial works. . . ."[114] The 1931 *News of the Roland* applauded Günther's appointment to a professorship in the University at Jena, stating that "thanks to Günther's work ever more *Volksgenossen* have had their eyes opened to human racial ties."[115] The journals also endorsed other racist eugenic works, such as the Baur-Fischer-Lenz, either with or without mention of their racist agendas. In addition, they heaped praise on the Munich-based Lehmann publishing house. Lehmann released many nonracist eugenic, as well as purely medical and scientific works. But it also published a good deal of overtly racist eugenic literature, most notably Günther's corpus.[116]

Despite the large amount of implicit endorsement, clearly not all persons interested in genealogy, or even in the connections between genealogy and eugenics, sympathized with racist ideas. Moreover, of those that did, the degree of sympathy varied. Indeed there was, albeit rarely, some censure of racism in the pages of genealogical works. A 1921 *News of the Roland* review of five books dealing with swastikas and runes, for example, criticized one of these books for representing the "Aryo-germanic" movement which "substitutes zeal for argument." In order to "prevent further confusion," it advised making a "sharp distinction between the content that the present German *völkisch,* antisemitic, Young German, and other circles place in their new insignia [i.e. the swastika] and the unshakeable view into the history of this ancient means of expression of many human lineages." Similarly, in 1922, the genealogist Klocke disparaged Koerner's "Aryan-Armanic" racism as a "guide to nonsense and absurdity," while a 1923 *News of the Roland* book review censured Koerner's "hair-raising dilettantism." Likewise, a 1931 *Roland* review of the latest edition of eugenicist Fritz Lenz's *Human Selection and Racial Hygiene* (the second volume of the renowned Baur-Fischer-Lenz) claimed a "clear division line between Lenz and the racial madness of Günther."[117]

More often than not, however, such criticism served as a case of praising with faint damnation. Lenz, for example, was obviously still an advocate for the notion of racial supremacy, even if the Nordicist element was toned down. Likewise, in the 1922 *Family History Gazette,* in the same edition in which he criticized Koerner's racist "nonsense," Klocke also provided a list of his own articles dealing with "generational studies" and genetics. These had appeared in such publications as the *German Herald* (1898, 1900, 1910), the *Neue Preussische Kreuz Zeitung* (1904), the *Grenzboten* (1906, 1907), the *Archive for Racial and Social Biology* (1911, 1913), and the *Richard Wagner Yearbook* (1907), all of which openly promoted racism and/or antisemitism to some degree. This indicated that Klocke was not condemning racism as such, but rather was attacking "nonsensical" or "nonscientific" racism. In the same vein, a 1929 *News of the Roland* review of Wilhelm Schmidt's *Rasse und Volk* (*Race and* Volk) praised the work as clearly explaining "the racial question," which, it noted, although now acceptable "salon talk," nevertheless remains subject to much "senseless . . . half-knowledge." "[F]ormerly happy marriages," continued the review, "were destroyed when the husband discovered Eastern [*Ostisch*] features in his wife. . . ."[118] The implication was, of course, that destruction of such a marriage would not be senseless if the husband had discovered "Negro" features in his wife.

Zentralstelle leader Hohlfeld's reactions to increasing racist antisemitism in German genealogical practice provide a good example of the ways in which a prominent genealogist, not known for either his racist or antisemitic views, nevertheless endorsed the intensifying radicalism of such ideas. Already in 1924, during a Zentralstelle board meeting, some of Koerner's followers had demanded that the society's journal, the *Family History Gazette,* speak out against "Jewish influence." Hohlfeld responded that it "lies completely outside of our task to take a position in our organ on Jewry.”[119] Thus rather than dispute the validity of Koerner's position, Hohlfeld simply elided the subject, implicitly sanctioning it. Similarly, in a 1924 article, Hohlfeld decried attempts to mix *völkisch* politics with science. This would, he wrote, “damage both.” He continued that, accordingly, no genealogical society could justifiably exclude “all Jews and other racially foreign persons.” Again, it is notable that Hohlfeld not only endorsed the idea that Jews were “racially foreign” (a fact Koerner's *German Roland* noted with satisfaction), but also tacitly acknowledged that in the field of politics, at least, their exclusion was debatable.[120]

By 1930 at the latest, however, Hohlfeld began to openly espouse antisemitic stereotypes, if not to completely embrace racist antisemitic ideology. In the *Family History Gazette* that year, he reviewed the second edition of Heinrich Kurtzig's *East German Jewry: Tradition of a Family*, the author's family chronicle.[121] Critical of the book's “highly anecdotal style,” Hohlfeld claimed that the tone was representative of a particularly Jewish form of literature. The chief value of the book, continued Hohlfeld, was in the way in which it showed that members of the family retained their “Eastern conception of life” no matter where they went in the world. This apparently included even Uncle Alexander, who began his career as a Talmud teacher but died in 1846 as a Protestant bishop. Hohlfeld was now clearly flirting with racist antisemitism. Yet he remained “moderate.” Earlier that same year, he had also reviewed several books on racial science, including Günther's *Racial Studies of the Jewish Volk (Rassenkunde des jüdischen Volkes)* which he criticized as lacking methodological merit.[122]

By the Nazi period, however, Hohlfeld openly embraced a Günther-style racist antisemitism. In the 1939 *Gazette,* for example, he wrote an apology regarding a series of articles from the previous year's edition on “Jewish Baptisms and Jewish-Christian Families in East Prussia.”[123] He noted that the author of those articles, Gerhard Kessler, had done his research long before the Nazi assumption of power. Thus, according to Hohlfeld, when Kessler had written of Jewish-Christian marriages as “confessional mixed-marriages [*Mischehe*],” the reader should understand that the *Gazette* was in no way supporting the idea that a marriage between a Protestant and Catholic was of the same character as a Jewish-Christian marriage any more than would be a marriage between classes, or a marriage between different peoples (*Völker*) of the same race.[124] Such a view, wrote Hohlfeld, only served to cloud the problem of “race-mixing.” Kessler, he continued, although in favor of keeping the race pure, and thus opposed to such marriages, was still under the influence of the idea that “all men are God's children.” He therefore saw the children of such marriages as without fault (*unverschuldet*). Kessler, wrote Hohlfeld, did not understand that purification of the race is not possible without racial struggle. With some tact then, Hohlfeld subtly endorsed policies that might hurt such children.

In sum, German genealogical practice in the first third of the twentieth century, and especially after World War I, must be seen in the context of great social upheaval. In an attempt to reduce social tensions, and to preserve their own socioeconomic prerogatives, prominent genealogists began promoting "scientific" ideas that demonstrated social, cultural, and intellectual continuities with the theory of the later racial laws. The great concern of leading genealogists of this period was not that racist thought was being promulgated in their fora, but rather the promotion of racist thought that did not appear "scientific." Thus many scoffed at Koerner's Ario-Germanic "nonsense" and still supported "rational" racist policies, or favorably contrasted the *EDDA's* "goal of a racial-biological selection of . . . members," to "the uncritical sensationalism of the *'Semigotha'*. . . ."[125]

By the Weimar period, this attitude likely reflected much conventional thought, at least in middle- and upper-class German society. For example, just as the genealogical journals exhibited a propensity to depict *Jew* as a "racial" category, the seventh edition of *Meyer's Lexikon,* the standard German reference work, published in 1927, contained an *Anthropological and Ethnographic* section under the entry *Jews.* Moreover, the anthropological description was almost identical to that set forth in Günther's *Racial Studies of the Jewish Volk:* a "predominantly Near Eastern/Oriental racial mix." Indeed, Günther's work was one of the sources listed for the entry. While not as hostile as its "authority," the lexicon stated as fact that Jews exhibit such racially based characteristics as "business sense, cleverness, aversion to physical work[,]" and an "exceptional ambivalence of their essence."[126]

While reaching its apogee under the Nazi regime, the concern with "racial threats," and the use of genealogical methods to identify a person's "race" were already mainstream in genealogical circles, and beyond, in the pre-Nazi period. With regard to the journals themselves, even calling the Nazi era an *apogee* is a misnomer. In the *News of the Roland,* for example, the first two years of the Third Reich saw annual peaks of 18 percent and then 31 percent of primary articles and book reviews featuring racist, antisemitic and eugenic topics, or some combination thereof. But after that, the average yearly percentage of such articles was only slightly higher (7%) than in the Weimar period (5.7%). By 1941, in fact, articles in the *Family History Gazette* dealing with such topics were almost absent. Traditional fields of genealogical concern took precedence: tracing the lineages of particular families, and the families of particular regions. Yet if, during the Nazi era, the genealogical journals continued to devote only a relatively small amount of page space to racist eugenics, they remained tenacious in their willingness to do this. "Jewish baptisms," for example, continued to appear in the *Gazette* until its very last edition in 1944.[127]

By the time Nazis and their accomplices began instituting racist policies, and the ancestral proof in particular, most of the components of racist eugenic ideas already appeared conventional to anyone acquainted with genealogical literature, and likely to many others. As we will now see in the following chapters, this led to a very rapid and thorough institutionalization of racist policies in the Third Reich. This occurred despite the fact that contradictions between claims to scientific legitimacy and incoherence in both theory and practice repeatedly surfaced.

4 | Making the Ancestral Proof in Nazi Germany

THE NAZI REGIME IMPOSED THE ANCESTRAL PROOF REQUIREMENT on a massive scale. During the twelve years of the Third Reich, state and Party authorities together issued approximately two thousand statutes, ordinances, and regulations establishing legal rights on the basis of "racial" status.[1] Those falling under the provision of one or another of these laws had to prove their racial acceptability through an ancestral proof. In most cases, this was simply a confirmation that one had no Jewish ancestors within a certain number of generations. In rare cases, one also had to prove that one's ancestors, while demonstrably not Jewish, were nevertheless also not otherwise "racially alien." While in theory straightforward, in implementation this process proved to be complicated. Yet despite the massive number of people affected, and the often complex, time-consuming, and expensive obligation, there was virtually no opposition to the ancestral proof in principle. This, along with the rapid incorporation of the requirement into commercial life, further illustrates the amenability of German society to institutionalized racism.

Number of Persons Affected by the Ancestral Proof

> In due course, all *Volksgenosse* [racial comrades] will be placed in the position of having to show proof of their ancestry. For many racial comrades, it is of vital importance to be able to show this proof as quickly as possible.
> —GERMAN CIVIL REGISTRARS' INSTRUCTIONS, 1939[2]

A brief overview of only the major laws and regulations to which the ancestral proof was linked illustrates the magnitude of the number of persons who were affected by this requirement, probably the vast majority of the population in the Third Reich, approximately 60 million persons in 1933. The articles of the Nazi Party are the earliest important example. Promulgated in 1920, they provided that only persons of "pure Aryan descent [*rein arischer Abkunft*]" could become party members.[3] A member's spouse also had to be "racially pure." Indeed, a party member could not even be indirectly related by marriage to a "non-Aryan." He could not, for example, marry the widow or divorcee of a Jewish man.[4] Approximately 8.5 million persons joined the Nazi Party from its inception in 1919 until its demise in 1945.[5] Thus party members and their spouses alone constituted a substantial number of persons who had to make an ancestral proof.

Additionally, all persons who belonged to a party-affiliated organization (*Gliederung*), such as the SA, SS, Hitler Youth, and Students', Professors', and Women's Federations, even if not a party member, also had to be of "pure Aryan descent."[6] At their highpoints, the Women's Federation, the SA, and the Hitler Youth alone had, respectively, about 2.3 million, 4.2 million, and 8.7 million members. While there was likely considerable overlap between party members, their wives, and membership in party-affiliated organizations, on balance it is certain that many millions of additional persons made an ancestral proof based on membership in a party "section" alone. The Hitler Youth's millions of members, for example, were too young to join the party.[7]

The Civil Service Law was the first major law requiring persons without party affiliation to prove their racial acceptability. Promulgated less than two months after the Nazi assumption of power, Article 3(1) of the law provided: "Officials, who are of non-Aryan descent, are to be retired; honorary officials are to be dismissed from office." This law applied "to the Reich, provinces [*Länder*], local authorities, and public corporations, and affected the entire corps of public officials, and, to some extent, the dependents of deceased officials—equivalent to millions of cases. . . ."[8] The nationwide census of May 17, 1939 provides a more precise indication of the number of persons affected by the Civil Service Law: 4,737,962.[9] The actual number of persons affected by the ancestral proof requirement pursuant to this law, however, was much higher. The number excludes persons who became civil servants subsequent to May 1939, as well as those already removed from civil service jobs due to "racial unsuitability." Moreover, civil servants also had to prove their spouse's "racial suitability."[10] Again, there was certainly some overlap between persons who had to make an ancestral proof for purposes of the Civil Service Law and those who had to do so for other reasons. Nevertheless, this law undoubtedly caused significant additional numbers of Germans to make an ancestral proof.

The May 1935 Military Law also required many millions of persons to make the proof. It stated: "A Jew cannot perform active military service . . . [and] Jewish *Mischlinge* (part-Jews) cannot become superiors in the Wehrmacht." Thus after the promulgation of this law, every person entering German military service had to prove their lack (or extent) of Jewish ancestry. Often, soldiers' wives also needed to be "racially pure." By the end of May 1944, approximately 12.4 million men had been drafted into the Wehrmacht.[11] Again, of course, this number must be discounted by any overlap with other categories. Nevertheless, the additional numbers of persons required to make an ancestral proof under this law also probably ran into the millions.

At the Nuremberg Party rally of September 15, 1935, Hitler introduced the so-called Nuremberg Laws, which included the Law for Protection of German Blood and German Honor (Blood Protection Law).[12] Among other features, this law pro-hibited a person of "German or related blood" from marrying a "Jew," and, with cer-tain exceptions, a "*Mischling*." Accordingly, after this law was promulgated, all per-sons seeking to marry had to provide an ancestral proof.[13] Between 1936 and 1943, there were 4,806,117 marriages in the Reich.[14] Since both spouses had to prove their racial suitability, this required an additional 9,612,239 persons to provide an ances-tral proof—again less any overlap with the other categories. Finally, the Reich Work Law of September 9, 1939, which required young persons of both sexes to perform several months of state work, paralleled the Military Law. It provided: "(1) Jews are not permitted to engage in Reich work service. (2) Jewish *Mischlinge* cannot become superiors in the Reich Work Service."[15] This likely required the provision of many additional ancestral proofs.

The foregoing laws, however, are only those that in themselves had an impact upon many millions of persons. A profusion of laws and decrees affecting virtually every aspect of life likely caused additional millions of Germans to seek an ancestral proof. In April 1933, for example, the first in a series of laws seeking to purify the educational system racially was passed. Between 1934 and the first semester of 1944, college matriculations alone exceeded one million.[16] In professional and commercial life, many other persons were likely required to provide an ancestral proof. As an example, by the early 1930s, those seeking to practice law, medicine, pharmacology, tax advising, editorial work, or even voluntary work in the fields of social insurance and public care had to prove "racial acceptability."[17] Later, determining whether a business would be "Aryanized" due to "non-Aryan" ownership also required provi-sion of the owner's ancestral proof. These laws eventually affected tens of thousands of persons, at least some of whom must not have fallen into any earlier category.

Laws affecting various aspects of family life imposed the ancestral proof require-ment on still more people. Persons seeking a "marriage loan" had to make such a proof, as did parents seeking state-funded child support payments. Nor could a child be adopted or placed into foster care without a determination of his or her "racial composition." Moreover, according to an April 1938 law, state's attorneys could con-test the legitimacy or acknowledgment of a child if it was in the public interest, which was defined to include cases in which the child might have been "racially alien." One also needed an ancestral proof to change one's name.[18]

In due course, the regime extended the racial laws to the newly annexed por-tions of the Reich (e.g. Austria, the Sudetenland, and portions of Poland) causing additional millions of people to be affected by the ancestral proof requirement.[19] One seeking naturalization as a Reich citizen also needed a proof of racial suitability, as did persons attempting to claim status as "ethnic Germans [*Volksdeutschen*]" pur-suant to Nazi resettlement policies.[20] The various anti-Jewish laws probably caused additional, significant numbers of people to attempt to obtain an ancestral proof showing that they were not "Jews." Thus for example, as a consequence of the law of 1938 requiring persons defined as Jews to take the names "Israel" or "Sara," many sought to prove that they were not "Jewish" despite Jewish-sounding names. In other cases, the government sought to prove that people with names that did not sound Jewish were actually Jewish.[21]

A variety of contemporary sources attest to the pervasiveness of the ancestral proof requirement in Nazi society. A 1936 article in the genealogical journal *Familie, Sippe, Volk,* for example, noted that "at this time, . . . due to the [need for proof of] Aryan ancestry, large circles of our *Volk* are engaged in, voluntarily or not, the ABCs of their ancestral . . . relations." A 1938 wholesaler's advertisement for a "mini-Ahnenpass" (an ancestral proof related document) claimed that the "small Aryan proof" (discussed below) is required "for a very large circle of clients." And, in 1940, Dr. Bernard Lösener of the Interior Ministry, author of an official commentary on the racial laws, stated that the many laws requiring "proof of German-blooded ancestry . . . have had the consequence that the majority of Germans have already produced such a proof."[22] By 1943, a commentator on the Nazi eugenic laws confirmed that "there is scarcely a German today who will not be required to obtain the proof of his ancestry at least once in life."[23] It is probably not an overstatement to say that by 1945, aside from the very old and the very young, virtually every Reich citizen, or would-be citizen, had made an ancestral proof at one time or another.

Legal Requirements and Document Acquisition

> [T]he National Socialist legislator does not pass a law today and then change it tomorrow. Rather, when he passes a law, it must stand for centuries, corresponding to the demands and needs of the German *Volk*.[24]
>
> —Kurt Mayer, Director of the Reich
> Genealogical Authority, 1936

Between 1933 and 1945, the rules and regulations regarding the making of the ancestral proof underwent continuous additions and revisions. At any given time, both the ancestral degree to which a person had to make the proof, and the method of proof, varied according to applicable law, the particular authority enforcing the law, and the availability of evidence. A document of the Reich Genealogical Authority from about 1936 listed the extant ways of making an ancestral proof:

1. Small [*Klein*] ancestral proof;
2. Large [*Gross*] ancestral proof;
3. Decision on Ancestry [*Abstammungsbescheid*];
4. Decision of Acceptability [*Unbedenklichkeitsbescheid*];
5. Ahnenpass;
6. Certification of Ancestry [*Bescheinigungen über Abstammung*]; and
7. Decision Board [*Spruchkammer*].[25]

Most of the tools for making the ancestral proof were not new, most basically genea-logical research. But the underlying goal, the attempt to "racially cleanse" a society, was fundamentally something that had never been done before. Thus creation of the regulatory framework to facilitate that process was often a matter of trial and error.

The authorities invested much effort into making the ancestral proof procedure both efficient and acceptable. They sought methods that would identify as effectively as possible the "racially alien elements" living within the body of the German *Volk*. At the same time, they also made significant efforts not to alienate either the bulk of the German population or the institutions on which they relied to carry out the process, with duties so burdensome as to induce opposition. Yet no element of the procedure seems to have been influenced by any official concern that the *reason* for the ancestral proof—the "racial cleansing" of the German *Volk*, primarily through the identifica-tion and expulsion of Jews—appeared questionable to anyone. In fact, the require-ment quickly became a "normal" element of German public life in this period.

For Nazi Party members, who had to be of "pure Aryan descent," the ances-tral proof obligation began well before the assumption of power. They were duty bound to report an "alien blood admixture" in their own, or their spouse's, lineage. Such a report would, ostensibly, not lead to an expulsion from the party, unless the information had been known for a long time and withheld.[26] Yet without a verifica-tion mechanism, one might question to what degree members voluntarily complied. During the 1920s, the usual evidentiary process, then variously known as an "ances-tral proof [*Ahnenprobe*]," "profession of Aryan blood [*arischen Blutbekenntnis*]," or "proof of German blood [*Nachweis der Deutschblütigkeit*]," consisted primarily of a simple declaration.[27] At the end of 1931, the party leadership established the afore-mentioned National Socialist Information Office to determine the racial qualifica-tions of potential members by checking their names against its "alien-origin index [*fremdstämmigen Kartei*]."[28] This check, however, could have affected only a minor-ity of party members as the office had only four employees at the time, and limited access to relevant information. In fact, its chief task appears to have been to smear party enemies by exposing their "non-Aryan" ancestry.[29]

Serious party verification of members' racial background did not actually begin until the Nazi assumption of power, when significant resources became available. Even then, however, the actual degree of proof that was required varied according to a member's political responsibility and, as will be seen, generally decreased over time. In 1934, for example, only Nazi political leaders (*politische Leiter der* NSDAP [the Nazi Party]) and their spouses had to show lack of "racially alien" ancestry back to all direct ancestors who had been alive on January 1, 1800.[30] Known as the "large ancestral proof," this call for information meant that if an ancestor had been born on January 1, 1800, or later, then that person's parents also needed to be "proven." The stated reason for the date 1800 was that the start of Jewish emancipation occurred around 1805, and the incidence of intermarriage increased thereafter.[31] A person typically made the proof by providing the authorities with genealogical documents showing that none of the ancestors of specified degree had been part of a Jewish religious community. A successful proof led to a "formal decision on origin."[32] Other party members were to make a so-called small ancestral proof, requiring verification only through the grandparents.

At any given time, the ancestral proof requirements for members of party-affiliated organizations varied. Thus, for example, in 1939 a member of the Nazi Doctors' Federation (*NS-Ärtzebund*) had to provide the same ancestral proof as a party member; a member of the Nazi Teachers' Federation (*NS-Lehrerbund*) had to make an ancestral proof according to the Civil Service Law requirements; and a member of the German Workers' Front (*Deutsche Arbeitsfront*) had to find ancestral proof per the requirements of the Nuremberg Laws. Members of the SS had to make their own, more stringent ancestral proof, sometimes going back to all relatives alive in 1750.[33]

For nonparty members, the ancestral proof requirement began in earnest with the passage of the Civil Service Law in April 1933. This led to a great outpouring of implementing regulations by government agencies, as well as wide compliance by various officials in seeing that their employees made the obligatory proof. A random sampling of the files of the Reich Genealogical Authority, for example, shows that these authorities ranged from Reich ministries to local government administrations.[34] The Genealogical Authority, itself, required its employees to make the proof.[35]

At least officially, many Germans besides party leaders had to make a "large" ancestral proof, including farmers claiming an "entailed farm [*Erbhof*]," postsecondary students, and members of certain professions. But the small ancestral proof was much more common. Additional laws and regulations propounded between 1933 and 1938 required, among others, prospective civil servants, notaries, lawyers and other legal advisors, tax advisors, doctors, veterinarians, dentists, superiors in the military and Reich Work Service, engineers, surveyors, students, health care workers, members of the Reich Cultural Chamber [*Kulturkammer*], and editors to make this.[36]

Despite the plethora of regulations requiring either a "small" or "large" ancestral proof," in 1936 the author of a popular book on genealogical research noted that "[u]ntil now, the key method of official proof of Aryan ancestry is essentially still use of religious confession and one's own declaration."[37] Thus, during the Third Reich, in actual practice the great majority of Germans likely made an ancestral proof less rigorous than even the "small" version. The authorities in fact soon began to vary the strictness with which they enforced the ancestral proof regulations. Pursuant to the Civil Service Law, for example, all affected employees in the Prussian Interior Ministry were ostensibly required to make a "small ancestral proof." The ministry did require all such persons to fill out a questionnaire on ancestry. Yet by the summer of 1934, it was already differentiating the degree of thoroughness by which it verified these documents. For all employees at the higher levels of service, even where there was no ostensible reason to doubt origin, the personnel division sent the questionnaire to the Reich Genealogical Authority, which checked it for accuracy. For the lower and middle levels of the service, however, the personnel division only passed the questionnaire on to the Genealogical Authority if there was some indication of "non-Aryanness." Moreover, in cases of illegitimately born employees, at the lower and middle levels of the service, if there was no direct suspicion of "non-Aryan" origin, the ministry presumed the employee to be "Aryan." At the higher levels of service, however, it presumed the opposite. An official explained the reason for these differences as insuring that the leadership was as "racially pure" as possible while not antagonizing the bulk of employees with overly burdensome investigations.[38]

In this vein, in addition to simply varying the level of scrutiny aimed at persons who were nominally to be treated in the same manner, the authorities soon also began decreasing the overall strictness with which the ancestral proof requirement was applied. In March 1935, for example, the Education Ministry decreed that the birth and marriage certificates of an employee's parents were alone sufficient for the proof. Only if there was "well-founded doubt regarding . . . the religion of [the employee's] ancestors" were further documents to be demanded.[39] By 1937, a sworn declaration alone that one was not Jewish sufficed as an ancestral proof for at least some persons affected by the Civil Service Law. By 1939 at the latest, all public employees without high-level civil servant status could make an ancestral proof by oath, stating that they understood the "concept of Jew" and that they were unaware of any evidence indicating they might be a Jew.[40]

This easing of the ancestral proof requirement seems to have affected most other racial laws as well. For instance, per the Nuremberg Laws, every person seeking to be married had to show "racial status." The Interior Ministry, however, quickly issued an implementing regulation stating that for such an ancestral proof, a person needed only to provide their own and their parents' birth certificates, and make a sworn statement, given to the best of their knowledge, on the race and religion of their grandparents. Again, the reason for this was to eliminate "unnecessary difficulties" for the "vast majority of the German *Volk* which is of German or related blood."[41] The party itself also quickly eased the burden on most members (or more accurately continued to refrain from applying the full measure of requirements). As previously noted, for example, in 1934, only "political leaders" had to make the "large ancestral proof." By October 1935, an Interior Ministry decree noted that the "great majority of [party] members will only be required to bring the [full] proof [of Aryan ancestry] at a later time."[42] Frequently, in cases for which there was difficulty obtaining documents but there was no reason to suspect "alien blood" in any ancestor living within the statutory period, the proper authorities, both state and party, could issue a so-called decision of acceptability. This form typically stated: "There is no reason not to presume that the named party is of German or related blood in the sense of the first ordinances to the Reich Citizenship Law of November 14, 1935. . . ."[43]

An additional reason for the continued lowering of the ancestral proof evidentiary bar was incomplete compliance. In August 1936, for example, more than three years after the promulgation of the Civil Service Law, Interior Minister Wilhelm

Frick issued a secret decree to upper-level administrators, ordering provision of the prescribed (since 1933) questionnaire on the ancestry of the spouses of all civil servants who had not yet filled it out. Not long afterward, the ministry simply lowered the standard for making at least an initial ancestral proof, asking only that affected civil servants make a declaration that neither they nor their wives "are descended from Jewish parents or grandparents." That the "Aryanization" of the civil service was not proceeding with the desired efficiency even in the spring of 1937 is evidenced by SS leader Heinrich Himmler's seemingly redundant May 1937 order, requiring all public employees and their wives to prove their racial purity either through birth and marriage certificates or through an expert report from the Reich Genealogical Authority.[44]

Another informal factor that likely eased the burden of making the ancestral proof is the probability that superiors often exercised significant discretion in deciding on whether to investigate an employee's "racial purity." Thus, for example, in June 1937 a police official (*Haupt Wachtmeister*) submitted a "notification of marriage" that indicated his wife's father had been born out of wedlock. His agency drafted a letter to the Genealogical Authority asking for an official ancestral decision, but this letter was apparently never sent. A note from the police chief, typed on the back, stated: "according to the regulations, on the basis of records produced, absent proof to the contrary it is not to be assumed that [his] wife . . . is not German or related blood."[45]

War conditions and the concomitant decrease in resources substantially sped up the reduction of ancestral proof evidentiary requirements. In September 1939, the Interior Ministry decreed that when persons applying for German citizenship were also military volunteers, and additionally had difficulty in obtaining documentation, the ancestral proof could be made simply on the declaration of the applicant that there were no circumstances known to him speaking against the "German-blooded ancestry" of his parents or grandparents.[46] The authorities also eased the evidentiary requirements for ethnic Germans who sought Reich citizenship, in particular for those willing to join the military.[47] As the war continued, so did the easing of the evidentiary burden. In March 1941, the Interior Ministry decreed that employees in the low and middle levels of the civil service were to delay documentation of their ancestral proof until the end of the war. By 1943, the military demanded a small ancestral proof only on appointment or promotion to officer status, and prior to marriage for "long-serving, active soldiers." By July 1944, "until later," an oath that neither one nor one's spouse had Jewish parents or grandparents was sufficient for "admission to the medical examinations."[48]

The party, too, eased up the evidentiary requirements of the ancestral proof due to the war, usually also with the stated proviso that complete proof would be made after the war.[49] By 1943, for instance, both the party and its affiliated organizations demanded a documentary (small) ancestral proof only "in special cases." These included the naming of political leaders by the Führer or a Gauleiter, admission of candidates to the Adolf-Hitler or Reich Schools, and marriages of members of elite Nazi organizations (*Ordensjunker, Nachwuchsführer*) and the heads of party schools (*Stammführer der Ordensburgen*). Even the SS by this time usually demanded only a small ancestral proof.[50]

Despite the many, and growing, exceptions to making a full documentary ancestral proof, and the often great efforts to comply made by those who were required to do so, numerous cases arose where a person could not, or claimed to be unable to, make the required specific proof. In general, difficulties could arise due to personal inability to carry out the necessary genealogical research, a lack of access to documents, or because conditions of origin made such research impossible (adoption, change of name, illegitimate birth, foundling status, etc.). In the first case, one could hire professional help (more on this below). Moreover, in the second and third cases, the general presumption was that such person was "racially acceptable," often resulting in issuance of a decision of acceptability. When, however, a grandparent or great-grandparent had a Jewish-sounding name, or other circumstances indicated that there was a Jewish or other "racially alien" person in the lineage, the authorities often undertook further investigation. In addition, even if a party member had a "clean" genealogical table, if he nevertheless had a "racially alien" appearance, then he also had to submit to further investigation of his origin.[51]

Early on, the authorities developed an administrative tool for such situations: the "ancestral decision," a determination of "racial composition" issued by a duly empowered agency. Who and what constituted such an expert was a subject of continuous political struggle. But the primary authorities for making the ancestral decision were always the Reich and other genealogical authorities whose work will be discussed in detail in following chapters.

✳ ✳ ✳

While the majority of Germans probably made an ancestral proof by oath, the "standard" method for showing "racial acceptability" was through production of birth, baptismal, and marriage certificates of one's ancestors in order to verify their religion. Because so many were actually required to make the proof this way, from 1933 on a massive demand for genealogical documentation developed. The great majority of these documents came from either the civil registries or church books.[52] When, however, documentary evidence was unavailable from either of these two sources, other material could be used, such as courts of law, inhabitant registry offices, clinics and hospitals, city halls, schools, military registers, tax lists, and other government offices.[53]

German society quickly reacted to this new and colossal need for genealogical documentation. The responsible governmental authorities rapidly established detailed regulatory schemes relating to document acquisition, copying, certification of authenticity, and translation (where necessary).[54] The bulk of regulations, however, concentrated on the matter of the fees to be charged for these services. In June 1934, the Interior Ministry initially decreed that "documents and official attestations sought and granted for the purpose of the proof of Aryan ancestry are free of charge." Civil registrars and pastoral officials, however, soon began to complain about the massive, uncompensated increase in work for them caused by the ancestral proof. In early April 1935, the Interior Ministry responded by decreeing that documents were only free when the ancestral proof was required for official purposes or when the applicant was unable to pay.[55] Later that month, the Office of the Führer's Secretary, in conjunction with the Interior Ministry, instituted a standard fee of RM 0.60 for the provision of each documentary excerpt. This was for the express purpose of allowing the document providers to hire additional staff to meet the growing demand.[56] But fees also significantly affected those who had to make the proof. A cost of RM 100 for a single "large ancestral proof" was common.[57] Because of their powerful impact both on those making the ancestral proof and on those providing the genealogical records, the question of fees remained among the most regulated aspects of the process.[58]

But the authorities also needed to control many other aspects of obtaining genealogical documents. Acquiring them from foreign countries often presented a whole host of difficulties. An Interior Ministry decree of September 1935, for example, warned that because "the understanding of the necessity of the racial decision is only just beginning to be grasped abroad," there were often long delays in the provision of these documents from outside Germany.[59] Thus, prior to the war, the Interior Ministry implemented special regulations for obtaining documents from various countries, as well as from newly created political entities such as the German Protectorate in Bohemia and Moravia. Likewise, the Foreign Office printed informational brochures on obtaining documents from specific countries.[60] Moreover, in an effort to staunch the flow of hard currency out of Germany, in November 1938 the Interior Ministry limited acquisition of documents outside of Germany to only those cases where there was "well-founded" doubt over a person's "German-blooded" ancestry. In January 1939, the Party Chancellery did essentially the same thing for party purposes.[61]

War conditions substantially reduced the availability of genealogical documents both from abroad and later from within Germany. In March 1940, for example, the Party Chancellery informed party offices that, for the time being, no documents for the "large" ancestral proof could be obtained from the newly annexed Gaue Danzig–West Prussia and Wartheland.[62] By 1942, church authorities could at their own discretion decide whether to allow access to "bomb-protected" documents. By 1943, they generally provided no documents from church books dating before 1830. Moreover, if the church books could only be secured in such a way that provision of documentation was impossible, then no provision was required at all and the applicant was advised to seek an official decision on ancestry from the Reich Genealogical Authority.[63]

Another ongoing concern for the authorities was the fact that many individuals had to make an ancestral proof multiple times. This put an additional burden on both the individual and the document providers. In response, as early as October 1934, the Interior and Finance Ministries jointly decreed that a person who had already provided his "proof of Aryan ancestry" in his capacity as a party officeholder did not need to do so again for purposes of holding municipal office.[64] Redundancy, nevertheless, remained an ongoing concern of the authorities. They continued to issue multiple regulations seeking to combat this, with only limited success.[65] Thus in 1940, Dr. Bernard Lösener of the Interior Ministry was still complaining that many Germans "have to bring the same proof twice or even more often."[66]

There was, however, one notable success in the battle against redundancy. This was due, however, not to government effort but to private initiative. In the years 1933–1934, the Reich Federation of German Civil Registrars developed the Ahnenpass. Again, basically a genealogical table in the form of a passport-sized document, the Ahnenpass holder would fill out the required information (most importantly religion) to the required ancestral degree. He or she would then have the person responsible for the genealogical documents containing this information—usually a civil registrar or church-book official—certify its authenticity with an official stamp. Subsequently, the holder could produce his or her Ahnenpass as an ancestral proof, rather than having to provide certified copies of genealogical documents on each required occasion.

Governmental authorities soon recognized the value of the Ahnenpass. In 1935 and 1936, the Interior Ministry noted that it would relieve "a superfluous and, in the long run, unbearable burden on the civil registrars and church book officials. . . ." They also heavily promoted its use. In June 1936, for example, the military high command ordered that the Ahnenpass be used to the widest extent possible in the armed services. The following month, the Office of the Führer's Secretary decreed that a valid Ahnenpass sufficed as ancestral proof for party purposes as well.[67]

The detailed regulatory scheme that arose around the Ahnenpass was designed to further lighten the burden on both the authorities and the *Volksgenosse*. Thus, for example, the Interior Ministry ruled that an Ahnenpass could be certified on the basis of another validly certified one containing the same ancestral information (usually for a full sibling). But the regulators also sought to ensure that each entry was certified on the basis of an original document in order to prevent mistakes or intentional misrepresentations. The ministry thus allowed certification of an entry only on the basis of an original document, or proper civil registry or church-book entry; set a limit on the age of certified excerpts from church books that civil registrars could use as the basis for an Ahnenpass entry; and required civil registrars and church-book officials to determine the genealogical relationships between the individuals entered in the Ahnenpass in order to insure that persons whose names were spelled differently were nevertheless biologically related.[68] Yet even with the Ahnenpass, redundancy remained a problem due to widespread confusion over its acceptability. The Interior Ministry was forced to continue issuing decrees regarding use of an Ahnenpass in relation to the various racial laws that the government enforced.[69]

Another response to the intense demand for genealogical documentation during the Third Reich was the appearance of a variety of governmental and quasi-governmental institutions dedicated to facilitating the provision of such information. It is difficult to establish the overall organizational structure of these entities, which were governed by a variety of authorities and were inconsistently named. Nevertheless, they arose across the length and breadth of the Reich and in many parts of Nazi-occupied Europe. The party, for example, created at least twenty-three so-called Gau Kinship Offices (*Gausippenamter*), regional genealogical authorities. Some, like the Viennese office, appear to have been dedicated primarily to making ancestral decisions rather than to gathering, organizing, and providing genealogical information. Others, like the office in Posen, were primarily entities that provided genealogical information.[70] On a lower administrative level, *Kreisleitung* and other party administrative units created so-called *Sippenauskunft* and *Sippenforschungsstelle*. These gathered both church books and non-church-related genealogical documents for purposes of the ancestral proof.[71] Party offices also released brochures and other informational materials to help in the ancestral proof process.[72]

Civil authorities developed similar agencies. The Interior Ministry of the Protectorate of Bohemia and Moravia, for example, had a "Post for Purchasing Ancestral Proofs" in Prague, the General Government administration in Kraków had a "Document Obtaining Agency," and the Reich Commissioner for the East had an "Officer for Kinship Research" in Riga.[73] Within the Reich, provincial administrations established at least eight so-called Provincial Kinship Offices (*Landessippenamt*) and thirty-eight Kreis Kinship Offices (*Kreissippenamter*). City administrators in Gau Wartheland created seven City Kinship Offices (*Stadtsippenamte*).[74] A variety of other civil entities arose as well. In 1934, for example, the Hessian Provincial Administration (*Landesregierung*) opened a State Office for the Organization of Church Books (*staatliche Stelle für die Verzettelung der Kirchenbücher in Hessen*) as a division of the Hessian State Archive in Darmstadt.[75] Numerous other state archives, such as the City and Reich Gau Archive in Vienna, created their own "family research divisions."[76] Likewise, civil registries throughout Germany established Advisory Offices for Family Studies and Kinship Research (*Beratungsstelle für Familienkunde und Sippenforschung*). Finally, at least twenty-six hybrid state-church entities called *Sippenkanzlei* also developed.[77] All of these institutions, however, developed primarily to facilitate the acquisition of genealogical documentation. The main sources for these documents remained the thousands of civil registries and church-book offices throughout Germany and elsewhere in Europe.

In sum, the degree of regulation of genealogical documentation shows both how widespread the ancestral proof obligation was, and how seriously the authorities took it. Indeed, the authorities were requiring individuals to make these proofs well into the last months of the war.[78] Moreover, no regulatory authority ever questioned the necessity of, much less evinced an intention to do away with, the requirement. To the contrary, despite reductions in the stringency of the proof, they consistently extended the number of persons who had to make it in some form. Almost every decrease in strictness was justified on the basis of practical difficulties, primarily related to cost. Most regulations easing the ancestral proof burden also indicated that at a later date when more resources would become available, a full documentary ancestral proof would be required. The speed with which these regulations were implemented and the variety of institutions that arose to facilitate document acquisition indicates further that the ancestral proof requirement, in principle, was acceptable to large swaths of the German population. Essentially, the proponents of the racial laws had to walk a fine line between applying them vigorously enough that they appeared to have an important purpose, yet not so forcefully as to cause widespread discontent, or to seriously contribute to actual problems ranging from loss of hard currency to carrying on the war effort. At no point, however, did the authorities seem to worry about whether the population thought the requirement "made sense."

The Ancestral Proof and Commercial Life

> No *Volksgenosse* without an officially certified Ahnenpass!
> —Advertisement, National-Verlag "Westfalia"[79]

The institutionalization of the ancestral proof requirement also led to the increasingly rapid commercialization of genealogical practice in Germany. After 1933, the number of books and articles published on the subject grew exponentially, as did a variety of commercially produced genealogical tables. The Ahnenpass spawned its own cottage industry. Moreover, a new profession made its debut: the state-licensed kinship researcher (*Berufssippenforscher*). Indeed, even businesses that had no fundamental connection to genealogy used the increasing interest in the subject as a marketing tool. This rapid commercial embrace of the ancestral proof further illustrates the degree to which the requirement infiltrated German life during the Third Reich, and demonstrates the swift "normalization" of institutionalized racism.

The racial laws proved a boon for the authors and publishers of works on genealogy. For the years 1931–1932, for example, the *Family History Bibliography*, the standard bibliographic work in the field, listed publication of 14 significant, new, general genealogical works. In 1933 alone, however, there were 26; in 1934, 66; in 1936–37, 89; and between 1938 and 1945, 116. Similarly, while between 1909 and 1945 the specialized genealogical publishing house Metzner released 50 "occasional publications and small brochures," 38 were from the period 1933–1945. Likewise, the Starke publishing house's catalog literally doubled in size between the 1933 and 1937 editions.[80]

This post-1933 genealogical boom included increasing publication of regional guidebooks designed to assist in the acquisition of genealogical documents, and the production of inexpensive "how-to" brochures such as the *Practical Course for Family Researchers (Praktikum für Familienforscher)*.[81] New genealogical broadsheets and journals, including the Genealogical Authority's *Allgemeines Suchblatt für Sippenforscher* (*General Search Sheet for Kinship Researchers*) and *Familie, Sippe, Volk,* did not just represent an increase in publications related to genealogy. They also provided increased marketing opportunities for such standard works as Friedrich Wecken's *ABC for Kinship Researchers: Main Points in Family History Research,* and various works from the Zentralstelle's catalog.[82] Additionally, nonspecialty newspapers and magazines increasingly published articles on genealogical research.[83]

A significant portion of such post-1933 genealogical works directly related to the ancestral proof. These were "how-to" books produced specifically for the requirement, such as Wecken's *The Ancestral Table as Proof of German Ancestry,* a sixteen-page instructional booklet on making the "Aryan blood-proof [*arische Blutnachweis*]." By 1934, this inexpensive brochure was in its seventh edition.[84] Similar "how to" books included such titles as *How Do I Find My Ancestors? A Guide to Quick Proof of One's Aryan Ancestry* and *Determination and Proof of Ancestry: Systematic Description.*[85] There was also a substantial literature on genealogical research that did not refer specifically to the ancestral proof in its titles, but nevertheless was aimed at those seeking to make the proof.[86]

A December 1939 article in the journal *Correspondence for Race Research and Family Studies* remarked on the "great number of different Ahnenpässe" for sale.[87] Indeed, the Ahnenpass meant big business for publishers. As early as 1933, Degener & Co. began selling Dr. Alfred Eydt's "Racial and Health Passport" as a means of proving "full racial value."[88] The *Family History Bibliography,* however, did not note the first versions of an actual Ahnenpass until 1934. It listed two more versions in 1935; eleven in 1936 and 1937, including a special "mini" version, called an *Ahnenspiegel,* for those persons who only needed to make the "small" ancestral proof; and thirteen more between 1938 and 1945, including special editions for such diverse groups as married couples and ethnic Germans in Romania.[89] The foregoing, however, was not an exhaustive list of *Ahnenpässe* styles. The Nazi Party Central Publishing House, for example, sold at least one additional version, as well as the *Ahnenbuch der deutschen Familie* (German Family Ancestral Book), which also contained an Ahnenpass. The Starke publishing firm sold an item called "My Kinship Group and I" (*Ich und meine Sippe*), which it advertised as "the life and Ahnenpass for each German."[90] In early 1943, alone, the civil registrars' publishing house sold at least four different types of "Ahnenpass," as well as an "*Ahnenspiegel*" and "*Ahnenpaßbriefe*"—other versions of "mini-*Ahnenpässe*."[91] It also sold supplementary inserts to extend the capacity of its various types of Ahnenpass, "Sammelmappe" to protect them, a supplement for adding information on the "most important hereditary and genealogical (*sippenkundlich*) information on one's ancestors," and several styles of genealogical tables that it marketed as useful for making the large and small ancestral proof.[92]

Advertisements proclaimed that *Ahnenpässe* were "available in every bookstore."[93] While I could not ascertain the exact number printed and sold, it was easily in the millions. Correspondence from the spring of 1941 gives some indication of the

Figure 3. Cover, Ahnenpass.
From the United States Holocaust Memorial Museum.

size of this business. In April of that year, the Nationalverlag "Westfalia" complained to the Genealogical Authority that its stock of *Ahnenpässe,* sold in approximately 20,000 different bookstores and stationery stores throughout Germany, was almost sold out. The Nationalverlag now wanted to print between 150,000 and 200,000 new Ahnenpässe with space for thirty-one entries, and an additional 50,000 with

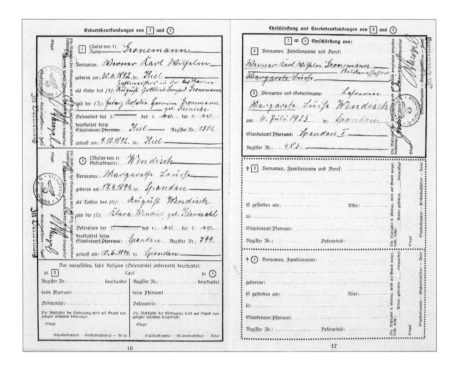

Figure 4. Inside, Ahnenpass.
From the United States Holocaust Memorial Museum.

space for sixty-three entries. Its printers, however, were having difficulty obtaining paper. In a follow-up letter that fall, the publisher informed the Genealogical Authority that while, subsequent to its first letter, it had received some paper, this was sufficient only for the printing of 40,000 *Ahnenpässe,* covering sales for only about four weeks.[94]

Extrapolating these figures would yield well over 2,240,000 *Ahnenpässe* sold per year by the Nationalverlag alone. During the Third Reich, however, at least seventeen different publishing firms printed and sold them. Certainly not all companies printed *Ahnenpässe* in these numbers, and it is unlikely that the Nationalverlag itself sold these amounts every year, perhaps not even in 1941. Nevertheless, to put the numbers in context, it is worthy of note that the Nationalverlag was probably not the largest producer of *Ahnenpässe*. The civil registrar's publishing house, which began selling them in 1934, likely held this position. By 1937, this publisher was already printing the 31st edition of its standard Ahnenpass, and by the following year, the 136th edition. Taking all of the foregoing into account, total sales of *Ahnenpässe* in the millions is almost certain, and in the tens of millions is probable.

Not surprisingly, this lucrative business could lead to fierce competition. In 1937, the company RNK Papier- und Schreibwaren, GMBH in Berlin was producing a product called "Firnhaber's Little Ahnenpass" (named after the designer).

This passport-sized document unfolded into a full genealogical table that could be viewed all at once, rather than requiring turning pages as with the standard Ahnenpass. RNK sent high-ranking Nazi official Martin Bormann an exemplar, and Bormann wrote back that he thought this product was "especially suited for officials, [white-collar] employees, and workers in public service." RNK then began to print on their Ahnenpass that it was "officially examined and designated by decree of the Reichs Chancellery as 'especially suited for officials, [white-collar] employees and workers in public service.'"[95]

This use of Bormann's endorsement led to a quick response from the civil registrars' publishing house. In January 1938, it asked Bormann to put an end to this "doubtless misuse" of his letter and complained that RNK had taken the "name, concept, and method" of the Ahnenpass from it. Soon, RNK released a four-page advertisement directed at retail outlets, which again prominently made the claim. Moreover, this advertisement, in addition to printing the Bormann letter in full, also included endorsements from the president of the Reich Music Chamber, the head of the Racial Policy Office in Gau Silesia, and from the well-known and widely respected genealogist Erich Wasmannsdorf, all praising its practicality and inexpensive cost.

The civil registrars' publishing house immediately fired off another letter to Bormann, informing him of this "misuse of a private writing" of the Reichs Chancellery for purposes of "economic competition." It complained that buyers and retailers got the impression that the Firnhaber Ahnenpass had some special, official recommendation when, in fact, other publishers had already created essentially the same low-cost Ahnenpässe ("for example the 'Ahnenbrief' published by us"). Bormann ordered Firnhaber to stop the advertisement and to remove all such items from commerce. Firnhaber responded that he would obey, but also asked Bormann to see the complaint for what it really was: "a competitive maneuver." Indeed, the civil registrars' publishing house advertised its own Ahnenpass as "*The* Ahnenpass," recommended by the Interior Ministry and other "authoritative agencies of the party and state."

This episode shows that like the producers of any other product in a market economy, the producers of products designed to prove racial purity fought for market share. Moreover, the advertising that encouraged purchase of this product indicates the aura of "normalcy" that surrounded the practice of providing ancestral proof. In Nazi Germany, the Ahnenpass was bought and sold like any other consumer commodity. And the huge numbers of Ahnenpässe sold is further evidence of the degree to which the ancestral proof requirement infiltrated German life during the Third Reich.

The growth of the profession of state-licensed kinship researcher was another manifestation of both the quick acceptance and the normalization of the ancestral proof obligation in Nazi Germany. Professional genealogical practice was obviously not unheard-of prior to the Third Reich. By 1926 at the latest, practitioners had created an Association of Professional Genealogists (*Interessengemeinschaft der Berufsgenealogen*).[96] Nevertheless, it is probable that very few genealogists earned a livelihood in this manner. This changed after 1933 when the practice turned into something of a growth industry. Genealogical documents became *the* way to make the ancestral proof, and a burgeoning demand developed for expert services in obtaining them. Moreover, as genealogical practice became professionalized, it took on the trappings of a typical business, also adding an aura of "normality" to the new requirement.

The immediate reason for this quick professionalization was the fact that there was good money to be made. Fees of RM 200, equivalent to the monthly wage of a low-level office worker, for the research leading to a "small ancestral proof" were not uncommon.[97] But the fee could even be much higher. One genealogist, for example, charged a wealthy client RM 1,000 for "expenses in establishing the ancestry of the parents of [his] deceased father."[98] Of course, most clients paid more modest sums.[99]

One Genealogical Authority file contains several hundred pages of correspondence from the genealogist Kurt von Staszewski, from the years 1937–1939, and provides a detailed view of professional genealogical practice in the Third Reich. During this period, Staszewski operated a business called the Society for Family Research in East and West Prussia, e.V. He charged a standard fee of RM 1.50 per hour, plus costs. Estimating Staszewski's actual income from these documents is difficult. A typical client, a government builder (*Regierungsbaumeister*) in Hanover, paid him RM 143.60 for his services. On the other hand, a customs worker informed Staszewski that he could pay a maximum of RM 30 as his income was only RM 200 per month. For RM 24.75, Staszewski located all but one needed document and advised the client to place an ad in the monthly *General Search Sheet for Kinship Researchers* to find the last one. What is clear, however, is that in those years at least business was good for Staszewski. In a 1938 letter he complained of "continuing overwork."[100]

Increasing income was accompanied by growing prestige. Professional kinship researchers often acted in the role of client advocates in the ancestral proof process. In 1939, for instance, Staszewski threatened to report the parish office in Germau, East Prussia, to the Genealogical Authority for charging for an unrequested marriage certificate. In another case, the Genealogical Authority advised the anthropological expert Josef Wastl "to direct the summons for the investigation of the examinee to the kinship researcher . . . Karl F[.] . . . who represents the examinee in this ancestry case. . . ." Examinees also hired genealogists specifically to contest the authorities' determinations of their "racial" status.[101]

As Staszewski also illustrates, in the Nazi era professional genealogists opened businesses throughout German-speaking Europe. They carried such names as "Expert Bureau for Extended Family Research," "Family Research Institute," "Workplace for Sudeten German Family Research," "Research Help," and "Institute for Extended Family Research."[102] They also began to market their services extensively, using stamps and letterhead indicating their professional status, and often advertising their areas of expertise. They also began using titles incorporating the initials of the licensing organization such as "Extended Family Researcher (VBS)" or "(RSH)," and devised important-sounding appellations such as "Authorized Agent for the Central Office for Church Book Research and Ancestral Proof for the Catholic Pastoral Offices for Bamberg and Stegaurach."[103] Genealogists also advertised widely in popular journals and newspapers. A contemporary noted, for example, that "genealogists are doing a grand business. There are advertisements . . . daily. . . . 'We provide you with every kind of document and evidence.'"[104]

Distribution of brochures, postcards, and flyers constituted another advertising method. One genealogist, for example, provided potential customers with flyers outlining the relevant requirements of the Aryan Proof and the Ahnenpass, topped with his name, address, and telephone number, and a warning that reprinting of the flyer was prohibited. Another distributed a postcard picturing a family tree and the inscription: "Blood and soil / holy inheritance / we are appointed and obliged / to maintain and protect it."[105] As with any professional enterprise, genealogists also developed sophisticated "boilerplate" contracts setting out exact services to be provided, costs, client authorizations to access and copy all necessary documents, warnings that final costs could be higher, and disclaimers of guaranteed success.[106] This advertising was a normal response to market forces created by the ancestral proof. It was also an additional force for, and aspect of, the "normalization" of institutionalized racism.

Given the growth of this profession, the Genealogical Authority files contain numerous requests from individuals for information on how to become a professional genealogist. In fact, however, while there was indeed significant expansion in professional practice during the Third Reich, even at its peak it still did not provide a living wage for many people. By 1941, for example, the Reich Association of Kinship Researchers and Heraldists had issued only 620 licenses.[107] Moreover, even given the fact that there were also many unlicensed persons doing genealogical work for money, the post-1933 numbers appear large only in comparison with those from before 1933. Beginning in 1934, the licensing organizations repeatedly informed would-be professional genealogists that the market was saturated.[108] Yet the contemporary perception of a large market for genealogical services, as well as the substantial growth in relative terms of such a profession, also indicate the importance of genealogy in Nazi Germany, the ease with which the topic became a normal part of German life, and the widespread acceptability of racist policy. After all, every professional genealogist, licensed or otherwise, as well as the many would-be professional genealogists must have been aware that such a livelihood, as stated in the forward to the Reich Association of Kinship Researchers and Heraldists' membership register, was dependent on their ability "to help the German *Volksgenosse* with the proof of German-bloodedness."[109]

The rapid acceptance and normalization of the ancestral proof requirement was further reflected in the fact that diverse businesses embraced genealogy as a marketing tool. An Interior Ministry circular from 1937, for instance, noted that "savings banks, [commercial] banks, private insurance companies, and similar businesses feel compelled to give free genealogical tables to their customers for advertisement purposes."[110] Banks were particularly amenable to this advertising method. As a German Savings Bank Press flyer (probably from 1936) marketing such tables stated: "The genealogical table is a document that has today achieved special importance for each family. It is especially suited for a savings advertisement. In contrast to other advertising means, it is a medium that represents memorialization not for a specific term or a short time frame, but for many years, indeed in most cases generations. . . ."[111] This marketing practice, however, was not limited to banks and insurance companies. The Genealogical Authority files also contain genealogical tables distributed by a metalworking firm and a shoe factory.[112]

While clearly reflecting the infiltration of the ancestral proof requirement into German society, these free tables also reflected a variety of approaches to the racism underlying the upsurge in interest in genealogy. The City Savings Bank in Haynau in Silesia represented one extreme. It provided customers with a swastika-bedecked, blank genealogical table containing two quotations: the first encouraged savings; the second, quoting *Mein Kampf,* encouraged racial purity.[113] Other tables, however, encouraged both savings and, less explicitly, the honoring of the "stream of blood" or even just "the forefathers."[114]

The spontaneity of this commercial trend is shown by the fact that many regime officials were not pleased. In October 1936, for example, the Genealogical Authority's director complained to the Interior Ministry that genealogy was becoming an "industrial product." This, they claimed, debased the practice by combining it with "purely material things." And the Interior Ministry later noted that this advertising method, by "flooding of the market" with cheap brochures on genealogical research, was hurting the business of the old specialized publishers in the field of kinship research. It was also causing "incalculable" damage to the practice in its "ideal aspects." In response, the ministry ordered all such undertakings to be reported to the Genealogical Authority, which would advise the perpetrators to desist.[115]

In sum, Germans quickly incorporated the ancestral proof requirement into commercial life. This, in turn, indicates that a great deal of German society was receptive to its implementation despite the fact that the racial laws were based on questionable "science," required tens of millions of Germans to make an ancestral proof, often in itself a complicated and frustrating process, and led to results that were clearly grievous for certain persons. The next chapters further illustrate this through a detailed examination of the office in Nazi Germany most closely associated with the ancestral proof requirement: the Reich Genealogical Authority.

5 | The Reich Genealogical Authority and Its Tasks

The Reich Genealogical Authority has been established in the course of carrying out the German racial laws.
— CHRISTIAN ULRICH FREIHERR VON ULMENSTEIN, *DER ABSTAMMUNGSNACHWEIS*, 1941, p. 13

W HILE ONLY A SMALL OFFICE (or, more accurately, a succession of two small offices), the Reich Genealogical Authority's files provide great insight into the institutionalization of racism in Nazi Germany. The ancestral proof process was the office's raison d'être: its primary task was to determine a person's "racial composition" when that was in question, and its officials consistently stated that the maintenance of the German *Volk's* "racial purity" was the underlying rationale for nearly all of their work.[1] Authority officials also repeatedly declared "Jews" to be the main threat to German racial purity. In 1935, for example, Authority official Wilhelm Jahn gave this explanation of his office's mission: "the fact that Jewish blood in particular has won an ominous influence in German space in the last hundred years requires the establishment of the racial inventory of the German *Volk*, the extermination of alien blood and its influence, and the keeping of it away in the future."[2] The Authority's leadership also viewed the office's other principal tasks—the preservation and organization of genealogical records, the regulation of genealogical practice, and the provision of advice and education in the fields of race and genealogy—primarily as components of the larger race-purification task.[3] In the course of its work, the Authority interacted with a great many elements of German society, whether categorized on the basis of ethnicity, class, profession, religion, or geography. While no single set of records can provide a comprehensive view of the ancestral proof process, the Authority's records probably come as close as possible.

Brief Institutional History

The civil servant is the custodian of the welfare of the state and the people; he is the guardian in the Platonic sense. . . . Genuine and truthful in his whole outlook, abjuring weakness, hostile to the counterfeit, German, not fashionable—in short, Existence not Appearance.
—H. MÜLLER, *OFFICIALDOM AND NATIONAL SOCIALISM*, 1931[4]

Created in late 1931, the National Socialist Information Office was the first genealogical authority of the Nazi Party. In April 1933, however, directly on the heels of the Nazi assumption of power, the Interior Ministry quickly established its own counterpart: the Interior Ministry Expert for Racial Research. It appointed Achim Gercke, the Party Information Office director, to head this office as well.[5] Administratively, the two offices were distinct. The National Socialist Information Office was a party entity: funded by the party, to carry out party business, and headed by a party official (*Amtsleiter*). The Interior Ministry agency, on the other hand, was part of the civil government: funded by, and located within, the ministry, dedicated to enforcing civil law, and headed by a high-ranking civil servant (*Oberregierungsrat*). For all intents and purposes, however, the offices performed virtually the same tasks in the same manner. Moreover, both always had the same director, and were located at the same Berlin address.[6]

During the course of the Third Reich, the two offices underwent several name changes. In October 1934, the Party Chancellery changed the Party Information Office's name to the Office for Kinship Research, a title it retained until it was disbanded in 1945. In March 1935, the Interior Ministry renamed its office the Reich Office for Kinship Research. In November 1940, it again changed the name—to the Reich Kinship Office—in anticipation of pending legislation (a *Sippengesetz* or kinship law), which in fact was never actually implemented.[7] Because, however, the state and party organizations overlapped in so many respects, I collectively refer to both as the Reich Genealogical Authority.

The Authority had two directors over the course of its existence. Gercke, the first, lasted only until March 1935.[8] Unpopular, Gercke's political and personal enemies engaged in a variety of intrigues to bring about his downfall. In January 1935, for example, Gercke wrote an indignant letter to an SS officer, claiming that an SS man was spreading the rumor that for a few thousand marks Gercke would produce a "proof of Aryanness" for a "non-Aryan."[9] In fact, Gercke was a hard-liner on racial questions, consistently arguing for minimal exclusion from the racial laws' provisions.[10] In any event, Gercke was removed on another pretext. The Gestapo soon accused him of homosexuality, and the party leadership stripped him of his office and expelled him on March 18, 1935.[11] The same day, SS Captain Kurt Mayer (1903–1945) became the Genealogical Authority's new leader and remained in this position until his suicide at the end of World War II. Prior to taking over the Authority, Mayer had served as divisional head and specialist for racial questions on the staff of the Reichsführer-SS.[12]

Both the state and the Party Genealogical Authority entries were divided into several departments: one administrative office and others corresponding to each of the Authority's main tasks. Department names and organization changed, as did specific responsibilities and staffing. But the divisions of the Genealogical Authority's state branch in September 1934 give a fair idea of its general structure throughout its existence. At that time, apart from the administrative office, it had departments

Figure 5. Achim Gercke, first director of the Reich Genealogical Authority, 1933.
Courtesy of the German Federal Archives, Koblenz.

for overseeing the practice of genealogy; for gathering, organizing, and protecting genealogical documents; and for making decisions on race.[13] The party branch of the Genealogical Authority was similarly constituted.[14]

The central place of racial decisions in the Authority's work was reflected in the allocation of resources to that task. In April 1939, for example, of its 142 employees, 60 percent worked directly at finding the "racially-alien": 67 in Division I (reviewing ancestral proof submissions) and 18 in Division IV (maintaining databases on the "racially alien"). Another 18 percent (26 employees) worked for Division III (the

Figure 6. Kurt Mayer, second director of the Reich Genealogical Authority, date unknown. The map Mayer is pointing to is titled "Racial Distribution in Europe and Its Border Areas." Courtesy of the German Federal Archives, Koblenz.

related field of document protection) and the remaining 21 percent (30 employees) worked for Division Z (administration).[15] This allocation of labor remained essentially the same until 1945, although with some later increase in "document protection" at the expense of racial determinations. This was due to the growing need to guard the papers from bombing attacks in the latter part of the war.[16]

I found no documents clearly setting forth the categories of cases on which the Genealogical Authority worked. A 1936 report, however, provides some insight. According to this report, the division then making racial determinations (Department II), had 5,172 files in process, but its 13 employees were not working them at the same pace. This led to a call for a partition of files based on expertise, rather than an alphabetical breakdown. The proposed categories and numbers of workers for these "ancestry cases" were as follows: Interior Ministry (1 employee); military and work service (2); various agencies (*Behörden*) (2); adoptive children (2); examinees with Russian ancestors (1); Jews and *Mischlinge* (3); artists (1); and "various ancestral matters" (1).[17] While this allocation undoubtedly changed over time—likely increasing for military cases, for example—it probably still provides a fair picture of the Genealogical Authority's relative degree of attention to different areas.

Early on, the Interior Ministry granted the Authority broad power in the field of "race determination." In July 1933, it deemed the Authority the sole entity allowed to perform "racial certifications (*Gutachten*)" for purposes of the Civil Service Law. In October 1934, it proclaimed the Genealogical Authority sole arbiter in determining race in all doubtful civil cases.[18] Yet, despite this ostensibly expansive conveyance of authority, the Interior Ministry nevertheless subsequently issued numerous laws and decrees reiterating the Authority's jurisdiction in specific instances—for example, for doctors seeking permission to work with public medical clinics (*Krankenkassen;* 1934), in cases of possible "alien-type, non-Jewish blood admixture" (1935), in all doubtful cases related to the Nuremberg Laws (1935), in all questions relating to paternity (1937), in doubtful cases by applicants for name changes (1938), and for the Entailed Farm Law that prohibited sales to "non-Aryans" (1939). It also recommended use of the Authority by the military.[19] Moreover, the Genealogical Authority frequently claimed jurisdiction to render ancestral decisions on persons whose ancestors lived in Russia, arguing that it was extremely difficult to obtain genealogical records from the USSR and that the Authority needed to act as a mediator.[20]

In fact, the legislative framework under which the Genealogical Authority operated became so redundant that later decrees sometimes repeated earlier specific competencies that were already given to it.[21] This duplication indicates that the racial laws and the bureaucratic framework for implementing them remained ill-defined throughout the Nazi period. It also shows that the Authority's "sole right" to determine "race" was never firmly established with regard to competing institutions and organizations such as party regional authorities (Gau and Kreisleitung), the party's Racial Policy Office, and even the civil courts. There was, for example, often much overlap between lawsuits seeking to establish paternity and the ancestral proof process. Individuals frequently saw a lawsuit as an alternate way to gain a more favorable ancestral decision.[22] Moreover, when the courts were incapable of making a decision (as when a party was missing), the Authority also sometimes became involved.[23] Because, however, there were no clear jurisdictional lines in cases to determine race, sometimes those cases became mired in procedural quagmires.[24] In light of this jurisdictional uncertainty, both the Genealogical Authority and the Interior Ministry fought an ongoing battle to guard the Authority's "sole" authority to make ultimate decisions on individuals' racial classification. Thus even as late as 1941, the Interior Ministry was complaining that the highest civil administrator (*Reichsstatthalter*) in Posen had proposed that the Ethnic German Central Office (*Volksdeutsche Mittelstelle*) make racial decisions for Baltic Germans entering the civil service, thereby trespassing on Authority turf.[25]

The original National Socialist Information Office was quite small, consisting of Gercke and three others. Later, despite its own increasingly broad if sometimes unclear competencies, the Genealogical Authority remained relatively small. In 1937, it had a budget of RM 598,000. By 1944 this had increased only to RM 811,350.[26] In December 1934, it had 64 employees. Two years later, it had more than doubled in size to 130, and reached its greatest size in April 1939, with 142 employees. While later documents indicate a higher number—165 in January 1940, for example—in reality, many of these persons were doing military service. Indeed, a loss of workers to the military became an ongoing concern for Authority officials.[27] In any event, over the course of its existence it appears to have employed about 362 persons in total.[28]

Yet even before the loss of manpower due to the war—indeed from its very start—the Genealogical Authority's leadership claimed it was overburdened. By August 1933, Gercke was already asking the Interior Minister for increased funding to meet the rising workload. A year later, he was still complaining that large numbers of files were not being worked on.[29] In October 1934, the Interior Ministry responded with a decree authorizing governmental authorities to seek an Authority ancestral decision only in cases in which there was "well-founded doubt" regarding Aryan origin. As a further screening measure, the government agency itself, not the individual whose race was at issue, was required to make the request.[30] Thus, paradoxically, while Authority officials sought ultimate authority to make final decisions on "race," due to scarcity of resources they also sought to delegate the initial decision as much as possible.

Notwithstanding this delegation of authority, Authority officials continued to complain of overwork. In a memo (probably from April 1935), Mayer stated that in the previous month 1,500 applications for racial certification had been submitted, and presently the Authority's state branch (i.e., the Reich Office for Kinship Research) had to work on the naturalization of 9,000 Austrian refugees and 35,000 incomplete ancestral proof cases for Berlin bureaucrats.[31] In a March 1936 speech to civil registrars, Mayer claimed that his office was getting 2,200 requests for decisions per month, and asked his audience to try to communicate to the public that the Authority was not the place to turn for advice on the ancestral proof.[32] Again responding to these complaints, in July 1936 the Interior Ministry decreed that only when all possible alternative methods for determining race had been exhausted could the Genealogical Authority's services be used.[33] Despite these efforts, however, Authority officials continued to complain of overwork. Both the Authority and the Interior Ministry continued trying to ease its workload.[34]

Besides causing manpower loss, the changing tide of the war also considerably disrupted Genealogical Authority operations in other ways. By January 1944, bomb damage to the main office on Schiffbauerdamm forced the Authority to divide its offices between Schiffbauerdamm and a branch office on Oranienburgerstrasse (the former office of the Jewish archives).[35] By May 1944, the main office was totally destroyed. Nevertheless, Departments I ("alien origin") and Z (administration) remained in Berlin because it was thought that "they must be easily accessible for the Gau and provincial kinship offices. . . ." Indeed, many Authority officials carried out their duties as best they could until the bitter end.[36]

The Genealogical Authority files support the view of Nazi Germany as a polycracy: numerous agencies, without clear lines of authority, competed with each other for increased power. The Authority itself was in a constant state of tension between the maintenance and delegation of its authority. Yet despite the ongoing conflict over questions of power and resources, in no instance did I note in any other institution's dealings with the Genealogical Authority even a hint of doubt as to the propriety of the ancestral proof requirement.[37] Again, all—whether party, state, or private—acted as if having to prove one's racial suitability was a completely natural practice.

The Reich Genealogical Authority's Tasks

In addition to making formal racial decisions (see chapter 6), the Genealogical Authority's other primary tasks were gathering, evaluating, and preserving genealogically important documents; regulating the practice of genealogy; and advising and educating in the field of genealogy and race. All of these duties related to the greater goal of "racially purifying" German society. While carrying them out, the Authority was in constant contact with party and government authorities (both civil and military) at all levels (local, regional and national). It also interacted with individuals from every part of the Reich and, after 1939, the occupied territories. In addition, the Authority was heavily involved in helping other entities, both state and party, make ancestral decisions themselves—on employees, inductees, and hosts of others—as well as acting as the "institution of last resort" for difficult cases. These relations provide further insight into the extent to which the ancestral proof requirement permeated German society during the Third Reich, and the reactions of Germans to it.

Gathering, Preserving, and Evaluating Documents

> . . . a further task of the [Reich Genealogical Authority is] the securing of materials that are necessary for the investigation of the genealogical, demographic and blood-related history of the German *Volk*. . . . it is impossible for the National Socialist state to carry out its population policy if it does not immediately preserve this material.
>
> —KURT MAYER, 1936[38]

Due to the importance of genealogical information for determining "race," the Nazi state quickly took steps to gain control of this material. In his letter accepting the Genealogical Authority's directorship in April 1933, Gercke already set forth his intent to make the office the central repository for all genealogically important documents.[39] Both the Interior Ministry and the Office of Hitler's Deputy for Party Affairs (later Party Secretary) consistently thereafter supported the Authority's efforts in this regard, albeit with varying success. As early as July 1933, the Interior Ministry issued a decree requiring the protection of genealogical documents. In July 1935, it ordered all persons and organizations holding genealogically valuable materials to turn them over, or at least identify them, to the state, by way of Authority-approved archives and individual researchers. Apparently, however, compliance was spotty. In February 1936, the Interior Ministry ordered conformity with its July 1933 decree.[40]

With regard to the church books in particular, in his letter of acceptance Gercke claimed that pursuant to the civil registry law of 1876, they "belong completely to the church. . . ." On the other hand, he asserted "the contents belong to the state, and examination must be possible at all times."[41] The same year, the Genealogical Authority began to systematically gather and copy them. In July 1936, it officially announced its intention to photocopy, "without exception," all church books up to the time of the beginning of the civil registries if they did not already exist in duplicate.[42] To facilitate this process, in spring 1938, the Authority requested that the churches provide an alphabetic listing of all church books, and the Party Chancellery ordered its offices to assist the Authority in all these efforts.[43] Both the Racial Policy Office, and the *Reichsnährstand* (the Nazi agricultural organization headed by Walter Darré) in conjunction with the National Socialist Teachers' Federation, also became involved in church-book cataloging, although the Authority often viewed the latter agency more as a competitor than a collaborator.[44] Government archivists, too, provided information on the location and condition of church books.[45] The Authority in turn provided money directly to both Catholic and Protestant churches for use in church-book preservation. Toward the end of the war, many of the Authority's activities were devoted to saving the church books from destruction.[46] Nevertheless, as will be seen, control of these books was to become perhaps the most contested aspect of the Authority's mission.

Efforts to preserve and control genealogical data extended well beyond the church books. The Authority, with the help of the Gestapo, among others, also sought to obtain materials ranging from collections of address registration cards (*Einwohnermeldekarten*), to military archival material, to private genealogical collections.[47] In order to preserve ethnic German archival sources outside the Reich, the Authority also worked with numerous state, church and party agencies, including the Reich Commissioner for the Strengthening of Germandom (*Reichskommissar für die Festigung des deutschen Volkstums*), the Reich Archive, the Transportation Ministry, the Foreign Office, the Lutheran Church Archives, the Provincial Kinship Office for Eastern German Returnees (*Landessippenstelle, Sippenamt für ostdeutsche Rückwanderer*), and the Ethnic German Central Office (*Volksdeutsche Mittelstelle*).[48] It also maintained a considerable degree of control over genealogical material through its authority in relation to the many newly created state offices established to gather, organize, and preserve genealogical documents: the so-called (local) kinship offices (often simply already existing civil registry offices), provincial kinship offices, and *Sippenkanzelei*.[49] In 1933, the Authority also took over the database of at least one major German genealogical society, moving the German Ancestral Community's Ancestral Lineage Card File of the German People to Berlin. It thereafter administered it as one of its own departments.[50]

For obvious reasons, the Genealogical Authority was particularly keen on obtaining genealogical information relating to Jews. Shortly after Mayer took over the Authority, in an undated memo justifying his request for additional personnel, he wrote: "I consider it an imperative expenditure for the blood-related work of my agency to secure through photocopies the collections of all Jewish archives in Germany. . . . our alien-origin card file centers on this and is thereby to be further extended . . . in the interests of the final solution to the Jewish and *Mischling* question. . . ."[51] In order to carry this out, as well as to obtain genealogical information on Jews in other ways, the Authority worked with the Security Police (including the Gestapo), the SS Security Service (*Sicherheitsdienst*), various state offices, professional and amateur genealogists, and the churches, as well as the Reich Union of Jews in Germany (*Reichsvereinigung der Juden in Deutschland*).[52] In 1933, for example, Gercke's assistant Rudolf Kummer began a bibliographical project attempting to list all sources on the "Jewish question." He received hundreds of responses, many extensive, from city and town officials, to his requests for "sources on the history of the Jews in Germany . . . especially for the eighteenth and nineteenth centuries."[53] In 1939, the Authority simply turned the Jewish communal archive on Oranienburgerstrasse in Berlin into one of its own branches.[54] Again, while the Authority worked with a plethora of institutions in the task of regulating genealogical documents, no one questioned the fact that all of this work was intended primarily to help enforce the racial laws.

Regulation and Promotion of Genealogical Practice

Management of genealogical research constituted another primary means of state control over access to, and use of, genealogical materials. Much of this power quickly fell to the Genealogical Authority. In July 1933, the Interior Ministry officially acknowledged it as the chief regulatory agency in this field. The following month, the ministry ruled that only genealogists officially recognized by the Authority could examine the civil registries.[55] Soon thereafter, the Authority began issuing permits for this purpose: 1,827 between August 1933 and December 1934 alone.[56]

The permit application process required provision of detailed political and personal information that the Genealogical Authority utilized to weed out racial and political undesirables. The obligatory genealogical table of one applicant, for example, a party member and teacher from the Hanseatic city of Stralsund, revealed that one of his maternal great-grandfathers was Jewish. In 1938, the Authority referred the case to the NSDAP Supreme Party Court (*Oberste Parteigericht*).[57] Following issuance of such a permit, the Authority continued to exert control over individual genealogists by requiring them to file quarterly or biannual "activity reports" in order to renew their permits. Most such reports discussed the genealogist's personal research, and problems with access to, or maintenance of, genealogical sources. This provided the Authority with further information on genealogical materials.

The regime, through the Genealogical Authority, also sought to control genealogists through political "coordination" of German genealogical societies. The first such attempt occurred in March 10, 1934, when Gercke founded the Reich Association of Kinship Researchers and Heraldists (Reichsverband der Sippenforscher und Heraldiker e.V.). He intended it to act as the central body for all German genealogical associations. The Reich Association was, in fact, the single organization that the Nazi Party initially recognized in the field of genealogical research. By 1935, it numbered about two thousand groups and as many individual members, organized into twenty-one local affiliates (*Landesverein*).[58] In March 1935, however, Mayer, as new Genealogical Authority director, dissolved all connections between the Authority and the Reich Association. Two months later, Mayer founded the *Volk* Federation of German Kinship Studies Societies (VSV), a new umbrella organization directed by him and subsidized by the Authority.[59]

The Volk Federation was less centralized than its predecessor had been. For example, rather than directly issuing a permit allowing the holder to research genealogical sources for purposes other than his or her own family history, the Genealogical Authority now provided an authorization stamp on each genealogical society's personal membership card. Nevertheless, the Authority still required all significant genealogical groups to register with the Volk Federation. In fact, by August 1936, Mayer reported at a conference of the German Foreign Institute that "almost all existing genealogical societies had joined." By March 1937, approximately ten thousand genealogists were members. After the Anschluss in 1938, Austrian genealogical associations also came under the Authority's oversight.[60]

In December 1935, the Genealogical Authority, in conjunction with professional genealogists, also created the Union of Professional Kinship Researchers (*Vereinigung der Berufssippenforscher e.V.*). For RM 8 per year, Union members received a special permit giving them exclusive access to archives, museums, and various collections. To become a member, applicants were required to provide proof of genealogical expertise through attestation by existing members, a public archive, or a recognized genealogical society. A recommendation from the local Nazi official (*Ortsgruppenleiter*) was also strongly advised. Documents showing a potential member's "racial purity" were also necessary, and members had to file a biannual "activity report."[61] From November 1936 on, Karl Themel headed the Union. In 1939, the Union expanded into the Reich Association of Kinship Researchers and Heraldists.[62]

The Genealogical Authority also enforced the "ethical" practice of the profession. In a speech he gave in March 1936, Mayer justified government control of genealogical practice, in part because his office had access to criminal records. This factor allowed it to identify "unethical businessmen" during the application process and thereafter refuse them permits. In addition, the Authority published hortatory articles in its sponsored journals denouncing unprincipled behavior. In a 1937 editorial, for example, it criticized the overcharging for genealogical research and documents in response to the "Law for the Registering of Sects and

Israelite Communities.[63] The Genealogical Authority/Union of Professional Kinship Researchers also answered queries from government authorities, private institutions, and members of the public, informing them whether a particular genealogist or research firm was registered with them.[64]

As part of its enforcement function, the Authority and its affiliated genealogical organizations accepted complaints regarding dishonest practice from the public, genealogists, and other institutions. In a typical complaint, in June 1937 the genealogist Dr. E. von Behrens, in Bromberg, Poland, informed the Authority that another genealogist, Stadtmüller, was not paying him for Polish documents he had acquired on behalf of one of Stadtmüller's clients who needed to make an ancestral proof.[65] When the Genealogical Authority deemed such complaints sufficiently grave, it would issue warnings to government agencies not to use a particular genealogist's services, threaten legal action, revoke a permit, ask the Gestapo to investigate, or even take a genealogist to court.[66] It also sought to prevent genealogists from misrepresenting their credentials, especially when they implied or stated an unwarranted connection with the Authority.[67]

A well-documented Authority investigation that began in June 1939 provides insight both into this regulatory function as well as into the nature of professional genealogical practice in the Nazi era.[68] In that month, the Nazi newspaper *Völkischer Beobachter*'s Vienna office sent the Authority a copy of the following advertisement from an April 1939 edition of another newspaper, the *Neuen Wiener Tageblatt:*

> Aryan Proof fast and inexpensive through the Institute for Kinship Research Vienna ... Procurement of entire documents both domestically and from all countries of the world—Duplication of *Ahnenpässe* and genealogical tables—Research in all pastoral, state, community and military [illegible]—Officially valid document translation in all languages (Ferdinand Burkowski, admitted as professional genealogist by the director of the Reich Office for Kinship Research, Berlin)

The *Beobachter* claimed that the advertisement had also appeared in other local newspapers and questioned Burkowski's claim of endorsement from the Authority. In response, the Authority informed Arthur Schultze-Naumburg, then head of its Vienna branch, that the ad was factually incorrect: Burkowski had applied to, but had not yet been accepted in the Union of Professional Kinship Researchers. The Authority was also apparently concerned that the name of the business was uncomfortably close to its own name. Schultze-Naumburg then contacted the Gestapo, which in turn demanded that Burkowski liquidate his business. In September of that year, however, Schultze-Naumburg informed the Authority that the liquidation had been postponed in order to prevent economic harm to Burkowski's partner, SS Lieutenant Zimmerman, who was now running the business. Moreover, Zimmerman had changed the business's name to Agency for Document Procurement, no longer mimicking the name of the Genealogical Authority.

This did not end the problems, however. A month later, the German Foreign Office in Zagreb warned German authorities in various countries that the Agency for Document Procurement had failed to pay for documents it had received from the Foreign Office for ancestral proof purposes and advised, in the future, only sending documents if payment were received upon delivery. Moreover, in January 1940, a businessman complained to the Genealogical Authority that Burkowski refused to pay RM 715.70 that he owed for two typewriters. Schultze-Naumburg again ordered the business to close.

In September 1941, however, it was still operating. SS Lieutenant Zimmerman wrote Schultze-Naumburg that the reason for the earlier difficulties lay in the fact that a man named Seidlinger had been running the business while Zimmerman had been doing military service. Despite specific orders, Seidlinger did not liquidate the business in the summer of 1940, did not stop taking new business, and did not pay taxes or insurance. Moreover, wrote Zimmerman, Seidlinger had allegedly "misused the office to obtain Aryan documents for a Jew" and was now in prison. "Through this," wrote Zimmerman, "I am completely ruined. On the day my office is completely closed I will at the same time put aside my profession as genealogist. . . ." As this story shows, people of questionable moral fiber were drawn to the practice in the hope of making quick money. Moreover, the Genealogical Authority's overseeing of professional genealogical practice was in fact haphazard, and the Authority was ready to give ethical leeway to ideological allies. Not least (concerns about ethical and legal problems aside), the great variety of institutions and individuals involved, from government ministries to typewriter salesmen, all behaved as if proving one's "racial suitability" was a perfectly normal function.

The Authority not only regulated genealogical research, but also heavily promoted the practice. It was itself a significant employer of genealogists. In addition, it farmed work out to professional genealogists for such tasks as the organization of genealogical records, the identification of baptized Jews and other "racially alien" elements, and even for expert reports on the "racial status" of particular ethnic groups.[69] The Authority also assisted professional genealogists by providing them with advice on the legal intricacies of the ancestral proof requirement and on obtaining documents.[70] It promoted the use of professional genealogists by others as well. Books on the ancestral proof by Authority officials Knost and Ulmenstein, as well as the Authority's journal *Familie, Sippe, Volk*, advised using professionals to obtain hard-to-find documents.[71] In addition, the Genealogical Authority/Union of Professional Kinship Researchers also frequently recommended professional genealogists in response to specific requests for research help from government and party authorities, and members of the public. Sometimes it also recommended particular genealogists or simply transferred the request for help to that genealogist.[72]

To further assist professional genealogists, the Authority provided official attestations to help them gain a variety of scarce benefits, such as passports and gasoline rations.[73] In August 1941, for example, it sent Prof. Dr. Otto Rosenhainer of the

Berlin business Family Studies Research Service an attestation testifying to the necessity of his travel to the General Government in order to establish the "ancestry of [his client] the French industrialist Lucien R."[74] Attestations from late in the war testified to the importance of a particular genealogist's work for the war effort, typically reading as follows: "the activities of the professional genealogist . . . are to be viewed as important for the war effort when they involve the obtaining of documents for the ancestral proof of members of the military, for marriage, naturalization, inscription in the German *Volkslist* [the list of "ethnic Germans" used by the SS and Interior Ministry in "Germanizing" former Polish territory] and similar goals."[75]

The Genealogical Authority also both controlled and promoted genealogical practice through the publication of its two journals. In January 1935, the Authority's umbrella group, the Reich Association for Kinship Research and Heraldry, began issuing *Familie, Sippe, Volk.* Modeled after a traditional genealogical journal, it regularly published features of interest to all genealogists, as well as more ideologically oriented articles. In 1937, the Authority took over the journal directly, and Authority official Wilhelm Jahn became editor. In January 1936, the second iteration of an Authority-controlled genealogical umbrella group, now called the Volk Federation of German Kinship Studies Societies, took charge of a broadsheet entitled *Praktische Forschungshilfe* (Practical Research Help), which printed genealogists' research queries on particular persons or families, and claimed to reach an audience of approximately fourteen thousand.[76] In March 1937, the Authority/Volk Federation replaced that paper with its own *General Search Sheet for Kinship Researchers,* which continued to provide a forum for research inquiries and practical "genealogical news" concerning, for example, the location and preservation of genealogically valuable materials.[77] While such functions were typical for a genealogical broadsheet, there was no doubt that the *General Search Sheet* was the regime's organ. Its first edition, for instance, warned readers that the *Semigotha,* an effort to expose nobles with Jewish ancestry published in three volumes in 1912–1914, was unreliable due to use of unverifiable sources.[78]

Advice and Education

It is essential today to again bring to the consciousness of the German *Volk,* down to the last person, the significance of one's own blood for German culture and the prestige of the state, to arouse an appreciation of the racial-political demands actualized in the Nuremberg Laws and, in this connection, to cultivate blood-aware kinship studies. This will allow the proof of German-blooded ancestry to become an easy and self-evident duty.

—*Familie, Sippe, Volk,* 1936[79]

Many of the Reich Genealogical Authority's officials viewed part of their mandate as educating Germans, and German institutions, on the necessity, implementation, and functioning of the racial laws. Thus, one of Gercke's first acts on becoming Authority director was to order compilation of a bibliography dealing with racial science and the "Jewish question." In May 1933, he obtained, for a three-month period, the services of State Librarian Dr. Rudolf Kummer of the Bavarian State Ministry for Instruction and Education. The result was *Race in Literature*.[80]

Others recognized the Genealogical Authority's expertise in the field of race. High-level policy makers included Gercke in their meetings on racial legislation. In December 1934, for example, he attended such a meeting at the NSDAP Supreme Party Court in Munich, held to determine the Party's fundamental position on "racial policy." In addition to Gercke, the participants included such Nazi luminaries as Gerhard Wagner, head of the Nazi Doctor's Union; Walter Buch, Party Supreme Court Judge; Walter Gross, head of the Racial Policy Office; and Karl Brandt, General Commissioner for Medical and Health Service, and later a key figure in implementing the "T-4" program under which thousands of disabled Germans were "euthanized."[81] The Authority also advised other branches of the Interior Ministry. In 1935, for instance, Dr. Jur. Falk Ruttke, managing director of the Ministry's Reich Committee for Volk Health Service, wrote to the Authority, asking for information that he could include in his lectures on Hereditary Care in German Legislation at Berlin University, and Race and Law at the German University for Politics.[82]

Interior Ministry and other officials also sought the Authority's advice on such discrete racial issues as "whether or not pure racial-Turks are to be viewed as Aryans," and, conversely, whether children with mixed German-Samoan or Dutch-Indian parentage were "non-Aryan."[83] The Party's Racial Policy Office not only sought the Genealogical Authority's view on the racial status of Karaites, but requested other informational services as well, such as references to books relating to Jewish origin, and party documents on defining "Aryan ancestry."[84] It asked the Authority for its views on individual cases, such as the status of a civil registrar who was a party member but nevertheless had authorized the marriage of an Aryan and a Jew, or the naturalization of a Romanian woman whose child was half-Jewish.[85] The Genealogical Authority was also heavily involved in the provision of guidance, proper forms, and actual ancestral decisions to the large variety of new offices in Nazi Germany that arose to help implement the ancestral proof process. These included personnel offices in the various party districts, as well as the numerous governmental and quasi-governmental genealogical offices.[86]

As "racial expert" for the Interior Ministry, Gercke reviewed drafts of laws regarding racial definitions and designations.[87] In addition, Authority officials were seriously immersed in drafting prospective laws directed toward the creation of a central genealogical authority with broad, clearly defined powers. In an early memorandum on this subject (from 1933 or 1934), Gercke laid out both the basic purpose and structure. Claiming that race was just as important as "military defense" (*Wehr*) for the *Volk's* "self-preservation," he argued for creation of an independent agency that, in conjunction with a "national membership law [*Reichsangehörigkeitsgesetz*]," would lead to racial separation by helping to identify Jews and other non-Aryans. This institution would also increase knowledge about race in the population, and would create a union of all race and genealogical researchers.[88]

Although the Genealogical Authority came to perform many of these tasks, it never achieved independence from the Interior Ministry. This was not for lack of effort. After Gercke was replaced, the Genealogical Authority produced several more drafts of laws of similar intent.[89] And in March 1936, Mayer told an assemblage of civil registry officials that a Kinship Office Law was coming.[90] In fact, no such law ever took effect. Yet other ideas promoted by the Authority in its draft laws were later implemented in the new Civil Registry Law (*Personenstandsgesetz*) of November 1937. This directed, for example, that the civil registries create a "family book" that would clearly show the biological relationships among all members of a family, as well as their ancestors and descendants. The Authority estimated that through this requirement, "in about thirty years the racial classification of the majority of all persons living in the Reich will be clear," simplifying the proof of "German-blooded ancestry" for each *Volksgenosse*.[91]

On a more mundane level, through a variety of activities, Authority officials continually educated and advised individuals and institutions not directly implicated in enforcing the racial laws on the necessity and functioning of those laws. It counseled government administrators, church authorities, soldiers and private citizens on the intricacies of rules related to the ancestral proof, their duties under the various racial laws, and even answered specific questions related to individual genealogical research.[92] Even the SS, which, through its Race and Settlement Office (Rasse- und Siedlungsamt, later Rasse- und Siedlungshauptamt) made its own official ancestral decisions for its members and their spouses, occasionally referred individuals to the Authority for help in genealogical research.[93]

In fact, the files of the Genealogical Authority contain hundreds of letters from "ordinary" Germans that did not directly concern an Authority case, but nevertheless requested some sort of help. I reviewed about five hundred of these letters scattered throughout disparate files, covering the years 1935–1945. They came from every major geographic region of the Reich, from Königsberg in the northeast, to Freiburg in the southwest; from Schleswig near the border with Denmark, to Innsbruck near the Italian border; from Aachen to Zittau. Moreover, they roughly corresponded to the population densities of the Reich, with by far the largest number coming from Berlin (sixty-five), but other major cities also fairly heavily represented, including Hamburg (twenty-two), Leipzig (eight), and Stettin (six).[94]

The approximately two hundred correspondents for whom I could determine a profession fell into the following generalized categories: government service other than education (thirty-four), soldiers (twenty-seven), applied sciences (twenty), education (eighteen), business (eleven), "workers" (eleven), health care (nine), work for the Nazi Party in some capacity (six), law (four), and self-identified "genealogists [*Sippenforscher*]" (six). In addition, there were thirteen correspondents who had the title "Dr.," but whose profession was unclear from the letters. There was also a smattering of other professions, such as pastor, singer, and accountant. Again, while this is not a scientific sampling, the list nevertheless indicates the wide variety of the writers' professions. These letters thus provide insight into how a great variety of ordinary Germans viewed the Genealogical Authority's work, especially in regard to the ancestral proof process.

Why, then, did these people write? Many sought advice on genealogical research in general, on making the ancestral proof in particular, on related help in matters such as translation of documents, or on the specific requirements of the racial laws.[95] A few, who had some pull, sought direct favors. In September 1934, for example, Viktor Brack, a Nazi official in Munich, asked Gercke to immediately send the "Aryan note [*Arierschein*]" for his daughter, who needed it for permission to continue in her gymnastics course.[96] As with genealogists, many laymen also wrote the Genealogical Authority to complain. The costs associated with the ancestral proof were often a sore spot. A man in Essen, for example, wrote to ask whether it was correct for a genealogist to charge him RM 30 to obtain two documents about his bride.[97] Other complaints were more unique. A young woman griped to the Interior Ministry that the Kaiser Wilhelm Institute for Anthropology had refused her request for a hereditary investigation because the Authority had not referred her. The Authority, however, refused to make such a referral because her paternity question involved deciding between two "Aryan" men. While, continued the woman, she understood why taking cases directly was problematic—possible "misuse by Jewish *Mischlinge*"—she also wanted to be able to use the "newest scientific achievements" in her case as well.[98]

All of these letters confirm the impression that "ordinary Germans" behaved as if the ancestral proof requirement was valid. This is underscored by the fact that the regime was not averse to the airing of complaints about the mechanics of the process. Indeed, in an article that appeared in *Familie, Sippe, Volk* in 1938, on women and genealogical research, the author was allowed to describe the cause of "90 percent of the 'kinship research'" presently done by most Germans as the "more or less annoying 'Aryan proof'."[99] Despite the "annoyance" of the ancestral proof, however, correspondence from ordinary Germans, as well as the Authority's regulatory interactions with a great variety of institutions, indicate that virtually no one questioned the requirement's fundamental necessity.

6 | The Reich Genealogical Authority and the Ancestral Proof

ALL OF THE GENEALOGICAL AUTHORITY'S FUNCTIONS described up to this point centered on the concept of racial purity. But the so-called ancestral decision—an official determination of race, valid as a full-fledged ancestral proof—was the Authority's raison d'être.[1] In the course of its existence, it probably produced more than 160,000. The Authority based most of these decisions on genealogical evidence, but also used other evidentiary sources, most notably so-called biological investigations (*erb- und rassenkundliche Untersuchung*).

In the process of making so many ancestral decisions, the Reich and other genealogical authorities developed a great variety of standardized procedures and forms: from initiating the process to appealing the final decision to billing the examinee. They also established official language for several possible outcomes of an ancestral decision, depending both on ancestry and applicable law. An examinee could be one of the following:

- "German-blooded and Aryan" (with variations depending on whether it was a "normal case," or involved a foundling or Jewish adoptive parents);
- "German-blooded" (with variations for "Married to a Jew or Jewish-*Mischling*");
- "Valid as German-blooded" (with variations for "a Jewish great-great-grand-parent," "a Jewish great-grandparent," or a biological investigation);
- "Second-degree *Mischling* and non-Aryan" (with variations for the "normal case" and "half-Jewish father");
- "First-degree *Mischling* and non-Aryan" (with variations for the "normal case," "Jewish father," and "a Jewish and a Mosaic [German-blooded (Jewish by religion, not race)] grandparent"); and
- "Jew and non-Aryan" (with variations for "Half-Jew who belongs to the Jewish religious community," "Half-Jew married to a Jew," "Three-quarter Jew," and "Full-Jew").[2]

Other variations included "Alien-blooded," "Alien-blooded *Mischling*," and "Jewish-non-European *Mischling*."[3]

Despite its other tasks, the Genealogical Authority's main reason for contact with public and party agencies was also in relation to its primary mission of making

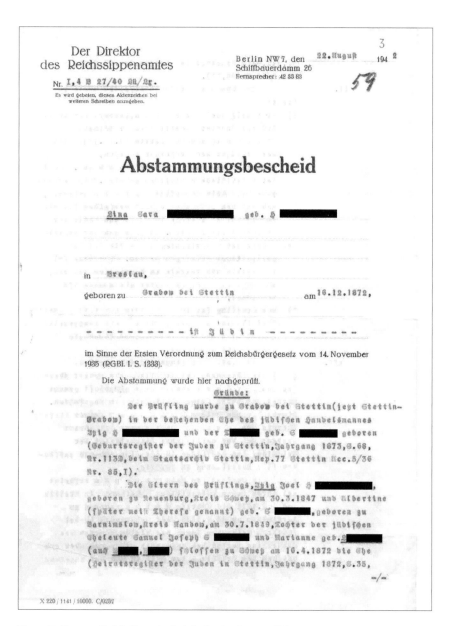

Figure 7. Excerpt, Reich Genealogical Authority Ancestral Decision.
Courtesy of the German Federal Archives, Berlin-Lichterfelde.

ancestral decisions. For this, the Authority needed a constant stream of documents. Beyond the churches, government institutions were the primary sources for these materials. Moreover, once any of the various genealogical authorities made an ancestral decision, it invariably informed a variety of civil, military, and party officials of the outcome. These included the Gestapo, which tracked the whereabouts of such persons; the draft board; the local work office, which controlled labor induction; the local housing office, which regulated living accommodations; the tax authorities; the local police, which insured that examinees who received a negative ancestral decision "complied with the conditions prescribed for Jews"; and *Reichsstatthalter,* the highest civilian officials, which established the voting lists.[4] Such informing insured that racially unacceptable persons, and their property, would be properly dealt with in due course.

Per regulation, examinees usually came before the Reich Genealogical Authority on referral from some other organization. While the Authority files frequently do not indicate the particular agency requesting an ancestral decision, or the trigger for the request, most often the requests seem to have been from government employers; marriage, adoption, and naturalization authorities; and the military in regard to marriage and promotion.[5] Legal officials frequently referred cases, especially in family law matters, as well. Various Nazi authorities were, of course, another prime source of ancestral decision requests for candidates to the party or related institutions. Those regulating the arts seem to have been especially prone to seek ancestral decisions about their members.[6] In sum, requesting institutions covered the institutional gamut from the Nazi Racial Policy Office, to regional welfare offices, to the Viennese municipal administration, which in April 1940 wrote the Authority that it needed a quick decision on the racial status of a recently deceased composer because of "present negotiations with the widow over the eventual assumption of the musical estate. . . ."[7] The Authority also acted in conjunction with the Reich Chancellery regarding decisions on the "legal equation [*Gleichstellung*]" of "non-German-blooded" persons as "German-blooded."

Although the Authority tried to discourage the practice, individuals also often directly approached it seeking an ancestral decision. The wife of a medical doctor from the Sudetenland, for example, instituted the process so that her husband could remain in Germany to work. So, too, did a man having difficulty making the ancestral proof required to obtain accident insurance from the professional organization to which he belonged. At least one man claimed to be seeking an ancestral decision out of his own "private interest."[8] Whatever the initial reason, the opening of one Authority investigation often led to further investigations. In a not atypical case, in 1935 the Rector of the Albertus University in Königsberg informed the Genealogical Authority that "doubt existed" whether a particular student was an "Aryan," and thus whether she could be a "member of the German Student Group [*Deutschen Studentenschaft*]." A month later, the Reich Committee for *Volk* Health Service asked the Authority whether the student's grandfather, a professor of law in Heidelberg, was a "full Jew." This eventually led to an investigation of the entire extended family—and their families as well.[9]

Genealogical Method

The Reich Genealogical Authority made the vast majority of its ancestral decisions using documentary evidence. The paperwork often revealed both an individual's biological ancestors and their religion, the latter of which the Authority frequently used as evidence of "race." In September 1934, director Achim Gercke explained to the Interior Ministry how the Authority carried out a standard check of racial origin for a "small ancestral proof." The examinee was to bring (1) a birth certificate, (2) the parents' marriage certificate, (3) the parents' birth (baptism) certificates, (4) the grandparents' marriage certificates, and (5) the grandparents' birth (baptism) certificates. Where birth certificates were unavailable, death certificates could be used. While the originals were preferred, when not available, indirect references to the documents in other bureaucratic entries could suffice.[10] This remained the basic method in theory.

In practice, because many persons had difficulty obtaining all of the required documents, the Genealogical Authority frequently made its decision "on the basis of the information in the required questionnaire, submitting documents or materials at hand."[11] Often in such cases, however, Authority officials chose to carry out their own in-depth investigations. Between May 1933 and March 1935, for example, the Authority received 12,579 applications for an ancestral decision, and performed 9,762 in-depth investigations. This required it to obtain vast numbers of documents; Gercke estimated ten to forty per case.[12] During the investigation of the wife of a noted sculptor that was more detailed than usual, but by no means extraordinary, the Authority, in the seven months between November 1936 and May 1937, sought documents from four different Berlin civil registry offices, the Berlin Courts, the Berlin City Archive, the cemetery administration in Prenzlauerberg, the Prussian State Archives (*Geheimnis Staatsarchiv*), the Erfurt civil registry office and police, the Lutheran Church Book Office of Berlin, six Lutheran pastoral offices (Alte Garnisonkirche Berlin, Garnisonkirche Potsdam, Nowawes b. Potsdam, Erfurth, Dovotheank, and Geldern), the Catholic pastoral office in Erfurt, the Archbishop's Diocesan Archive in Breslau, the national Jewish archives (*Gesamtarchiv der Juden in Deutschland*), and the Israelite Religious Congregation in Breslau.[13] Because the Authority's work was so dependent on documents, the Interior Ministry soon granted it the power to obtain these at no cost.[14]

As these cases indicate, the required documents usually came from civil registries and church books, but where necessary the Authority used virtually any other documentation that might point to the biological ancestors of the person concerned, and their religion. The Authority naturally worked with a great variety of party offices to obtain such documents. But it also worked closely with many nonparty institutions. Courts and states attorneys' offices regularly sent the Authority their files, especially regarding paternity and adoption cases. The German foreign office assisted not just individual Germans, but also the Authority to obtain genealogical documents in foreign countries. After the war started, German civil occupation officials did so as well.[15] In addition, such seemingly "benign" agencies as the Reich Adoption Office and the German Red Cross provided the Authority with genealogical information.[16]

The Authority also maintained its own genealogical databases. When Gercke became director of the National Socialist Information Office in 1932, he brought his personal collection of almost 400,000 cards. This became the core of the Genealogical Authority's ever-increasing "card file [*Karteikartenbestand*]" which, during 1937 alone, grew from 904,125 to 1,033,220 pieces. The Authority also maintained a card catalog listing 30,000 to 50,000 so-called Volga Germans, ethnic Germans living in Russia.[17] Typically these cards carried such information as profession and birth, marriage, and death dates. They were organized if possible by extended family.[18]

Once in hand, genealogical evidence had to be evaluated. Thus another task related to the ancestral decision was determining the authenticity of documents. In a March 1936 speech to civil registrars, director Kurt Mayer claimed that his office was encountering numerous forged documents, both German and foreign, some going back to the Middle Ages. "Luckily," he stated, "we are . . . thoroughly educated historians," capable of identifying such forgeries.[19] In certain cases, however, the Authority also sought the help of forensic experts to determine whether documents were falsified or had been tampered with. It also sought assistance from state and pastoral offices to prevent such problems. Where Authority officials suspected machinations, they sometimes instituted police actions.[20]

Even when a document was determined genuine, its contents often had to be interpreted. With regard to foreign documents, in July 1935, the Genealogical Authority decreed that each examinee was responsible for their translation, and the work had to be certified by the Reich Translators' Organization (*Reichsfachschaft für das Dolmetscherwesen in der deutschen Rechtsfront*).[21] Authority staff also familiarized themselves with such esoteric skills as dating documents from the period of the French Revolution, which sometimes required conversion due to use of the "Revolutionary Calendar."[22]

Examinees and the Ancestral Decision

To get an idea of who examinees were, as well as the course of their ancestral decision process, I reviewed the 523 Genealogical Authority files that I found in the German Federal Archive. I also examined 145 files from the Gau Kinship Office Vienna (GSA-W). These were simply the first 145 in the alphabetically ordered collection of thousands. I am not certain how representative these cases are of the hundreds of thousands of ancestral decisions made by the Reich Genealogical Authority, the Gau Kinship Office Vienna, and other genealogical authorities. They do, however, represent every Genealogical Authority examinee file that I could find, and a random selection of Gau Kinship Office Vienna files. Thus, they likely provide a fairly accurate representation both of the types of persons who became examinees and of the conduct of the ancestral decision process. Only further research, however, can determine this with certainty.

In the one area in which it is possible to make a fairly clear determination of accuracy—the number of Genealogical Authority files opened per year—my sample (498 of 523 Authority files for which I could determine a date) does not correspond well to either the percentage of files actually opened by the Authority in most years, nor to trends of increase or decrease.[23] The age range of my samples, however, seems more representative. In 252 of the 523 Genealogical Authority files, I established both an examinee's date of birth and an approximate date on which his or her Authority investigation began, and thus the approximate age at the time of the investigation. These ages ranged between one and eighty-three. The average age was thirty-seven and the median was thirty-five. I could do the same for 132 of the 146 Gau Kinship Office Vienna files. These ages ranged between one and seventy-seven. Both the average and median ages were thirty-eight. This correspondence in ages between the two authorities indicates that this is a fair representation overall. I established gender for 495 Genealogical Authority files examinees. Approximately 57 percent were male and 43 percent female. I did the same for 148 Gau Kinship Office Vienna examinees. Approximately 59 percent were male and 41 percent female. Again, this correspondence in gender breakdown also indicates an accurate overall representation.

I determined the examinee's address for 449 of the 523 Genealogical Authority files. Almost 50 percent came from the four largest cities in the Reich: 23 percent (105) from Berlin, 20 percent (89) from Vienna, 4 percent from Hamburg, and 3 percent from Munich. The medium-sized cities of Leipzig, Dresden, Breslau, Frankfurt am Main, and Nuremberg together represented another 6 percent (29) of examinees. The remainder came from the length and breadth of the Reich: from Aalen in south central Germany to Zuckmantel in the eastern portion of the Sudetenland. The addresses thus represent a fair approximation of the geographical diversity one might expect. A few examinees lived abroad, in places ranging from Asunción to Zurich. I could also determine an examinee's address in 136 of the 146 Gau Kinship Office Vienna files. Of these, 90 percent (122) lived in Vienna. Of the 14 remaining, 7 were domiciled in other parts of Austria, 3 in Germany, and 1 each in the Sudetenland, Slovakia, Moravia, and California (!).

I established the examinee's method of livelihood for 189 of the 523 Genealogical Authority examinee files and for 82 of the 147 Gau Kinship Office Vienna files (see Table 1). In addition, 14 examinees in the Genealogical Authority files had the title *Dr., Prof. Dr.,* or *Dr. phil.* The lack of correspondence in occupational breakdown between the two offices does not allow an inference as to the actual occupational breakdown for all examinees. But clearly social elites, including their spouses, were disproportionately affected by the requirement.

Table 1. Professions of RGA and GSA-W

PROFESSION	RGA	GSA-W
Housewife	35 (18.5%)	9 (11.0%)
Lawyer	20 (10.6)	2 (2.4)
Doctor	14 (7.4)	7 (8.5)
Other health care	2 (1.1)	4 (4.9)
Higher government official	12 (6.3)	3 (3.7)
Lower government official	4 (2.1)	0
Skilled worker	15 (7.9)	1 (1.2)
Unskilled worker	6 (3.2)	7 (8.5)
Artist	11 (5.8)	7 (8.5)
Student	8 (4.2)	3 (3.7)
Military, no other profession listed	25 (13.2)	8 (9.8)
Educator or academic	6 (3.2)	2 (2.4)
Lower-level office worker	6 (3.2)	11 (13.4)
Commerce	5 (2.6)	6 (7.3)
Retail or service	1 (1.0)	4 (4.9)
Educated technical, industrial	14 (7.4)	4 (4.9)
Party worker	0	2 (2.4)
"Other"	5 (2.6)	2 (2.4)

I determined the result of the ancestral decision process for 246 Genealogical Authority examinees. For the remaining 276, no ancestral decision was ultimately made (which, in most cases, probably meant that the result was favorable for the examinee), the result is missing, or the Authority refused to make a decision. I found similar results for 103 Gau Kinship Office Vienna examinees. Regarding the other 43 examinees, again either no ancestral decision was made, the result is missing, or, in six files, the Gau Kinship Office itself stated that it had insufficient information to make an ancestral decision (see Table 2). For three Gau Kinship Office Vienna files, the decision was nonconclusive but had legal effect: "at worst Jewish *Mischling* first degree," "at worst Jewish *Mischling* second degree," and "at least Jewish *Mischling* first degree." Again, the lack of correspondence in "racial" findings between the two offices does not allow an inference as to the actual breakdown for all findings over the course of the Third Reich.

Once instituted, the ancestral decision process was rather secretive from the examinee's point of view. Genealogical Authority director Mayer instructed his low-level employees to give no information about the process, but rather to refer any questions to the research division.[24] While at least by June 1936, the Authority had

Table 2. Ancestral Proof Findings by RGA and GSA-W

Finding	RGA	GSA-W
Decision of Acceptability	46 (19%)	2 (2%)
"German-blooded," "free from foreign blood admixture," "German ancestry"	80 (33)	15 (15)
"Jewish Mischling third degree" (for party ancestral proof purposes)	0	1 (1)
"Jewish Mischling second degree"	19 (8)	11 (11)
"Jewish Mischling first degree"	60 (24)	41 (40)
"Jew"	37 (15)	25 (24)
"Alien-type Mischling second degree"	2 (>1)	1 (1)
"Alien-type Mischling first degree"	2 (>1)	2 (2)
"Jewish-alien-type Mischling first degree"	0	1 (1)
"Jewish-non-European"	0	1 (1)

established set office hours (11 A.M. to 1 P.M., Monday to Friday) at which interested persons could speak with an employee about their file, if special attention was needed, a written request was required of the applicant. Mayer also instructed his employees not to give substantive information out over the telephone.[25] Indeed the process became progressively more concealed. By December 1942, the Interior Ministry decreed that requests to view Authority files were to be denied as a matter of course. In special cases, such request could be granted, but if the file also contained a "genetic expert report [*erbbiologisch Gutachten*]" the permission of the expert was also required.[26]

Often the decision process moved relatively quickly. When, for example, in 1944, an SA Lieutenant in Untertannowitz, Moravia asked for the "establishment of the impeccable [*einwandfrei*] Aryan ancestry" of his adoptive daughter, the result was provided within three months.[27] In many cases, however, the process was, from the examinee's perspective, excruciatingly slow. In March 1940, for instance, an examinee's lawyer wrote the Authority that "the concerned parties [the examinee and the father of her child, whom she had been seeking permission to marry for over a year] were gradually losing their nerves." Ten months later, the Authority had still not rendered a decision.[28] In another case, the investigation began in November 1936, at the instigation of the Interior Ministry. Despite numerous requests from the examinee, her family, and even Nazi authorities, the investigation ended only in March 1945, when the office of the expert who was to perform a biological investigation

(Professor Abel) informed her he would not be able to do so because he had been involved in an accident."[29]

The finding of "racial unacceptability" sometimes came as a rude awakening to persons who had hitherto perceived themselves as "Aryan." The wife of master crafts-man (*Reichshandwerksmeister*) Schmidt, a "reliable early fighter" of the Nazi move-ment, for example, discovered to her surprise that she was a "half-Jew."[30] It should be noted, however, that even a finding of "Aryan" or "German-blooded" did not neces-sarily mark the end of the examinee's ordeal. In one case, after the Gau Kinship Office Vienna issued an October 1938 ancestral decision of "Aryan" on a 64-year-old Viennese woman, three low-level Nazi officials (*Zellenwalterin*) wrote the local party office in Braunhirschen that they had observed her in the hospital and "had become convinced that [the examinee] definitely gave the impression of a Jewish type." The local office then informed the regional office, whose ancestral proof expert (*Kreisbeauftragte für Sippenamt*) in turn informed the local city administrator. The regional office noted that the examinee's mother had converted to Judaism one year before the examinee's birth "without apparent reason," and, therefore, the examinee should submit to a biologi-cal investigation. As a consequence of this pressure, in October 1939 the Genealogical Authority's Vienna branch office issued the examinee a new, interim ancestral deci-sion, stating that, until promulgation of a final ancestral decision, "in the worst case, [the examinee] is to be viewed as a first-degree Jewish *Mischling*."[31] In a similar case, the putative "Aryan" father of an 18-year-old examinee wrote the Authority to complain that although it had issued an ancestral decision of "German or related blood," the SS had released his son from military service, alleging he was a Jewish-*Mischling* first degree. Subsequently, a local Nazi official in Lower Silesia wrote the Authority that he had a statement from a neighbor that she had overheard the examinee's claimed father call him "dirty Jew kid [*Judenbalg*] and evil Jewish offspring." Based on this informa-tion, the Genealogical Authority apparently reopened the boy's case, as a new biologi-cal investigation was pending at the end of the war.[32]

Other examinees were even unluckier. In September 1940, for instance, the Gau Kinship Office Vienna issued a decision of acceptability to a 23-year-old woman. Two years later, however, it received an anonymous letter from a man who identi-fied himself as an attorney and party member. He alleged that the examinee had lied about her identity to hide her full Jewish ancestry—moreover, he alleged that she was engaged in sexual relations with an "Aryan" man and, further, operated a street concession of some sort despite the fact that she suffered from a stomach ailment and was "infectious." The Gau Kinship Office reopened the investigation, verified the examinee's Jewish ancestry, and informed both the Gestapo and the agency in Vienna responsible for deporting Jews (*Abwicklungsstelle der Zentralstelle für jüdische Auswanderung*). By December 1942, the Gestapo had taken the young woman into "protective custody."[33]

Whatever the ultimate result of the process, with whatever the speed the authori-ties worked an examinee's file, whatever their age, gender, place of residence, or occupation, the Genealogical Authority and Gau Kinship Office Vienna files indicate that examinees never questioned the "scientific" premises on which the requirement was based. Yet when an unfavorable finding was likely, virtually all of them resisted in *some* way. A Genealogical Authority official commented, with some understatement, that this was "understandable since the racial classification for each German is of great significance."[34] Apparently, only a very few examinees tried to escape the process by fleeing. When they did, the genealogical authorities requested help from police officials, including the Gestapo.[35] Overt noncompliance was also extremely rare. I only saw one instance, and this did not directly involve an examinee. In May 1941, the Authority asked a possible full brother of an examinee's deceased half-brother to participate in a biological investigation. The man wrote back that the Authority must have written him by mistake as "I don't have the slightest interest in kinship research." The Authority replied that there was no mistake and that participation was not optional. The man thereafter participated.[36]

What examinees usually did was fight to obtain the most favorable result within the "system." This often included hiring a professional genealogist, an attorney, or both, as well as presenting any plausible (and frequently implausible) claim that might avert a finding of "Jewish" or other "alien-type" ancestry. At the same time, Genealogical Authority officials strove with great dedication to insure that any false claims were unsuccessful. Indeed, they eventually became exasperated by examinees' continuing efforts to disguise their ancestry. An undated Authority memorandum from about 1942 noted: "In recent years it has increasingly been observed that Jews throw doubt on the racial classification arising from civil registry documents, and also in individual cases achieve a more favorable racial classification, whether through a legal judgment or a Genealogical Authority ancestral decision." The memorandum suggested that in order "to be able to resist this Jewish attempt," the Reich Citizenship Law's first implementing regulation (holding "Jewish" a person with three or more "full racially Jewish" grandparents) should be amended by adding: "For the ancestral proof, the civil registry documents are authoritative. A counterproof is not permitted."[37] This apparently never happened. The various genealogical authorities and their examinees continued to struggle over the appropriate "racial" classification to the bitter end.

Determining Ancestors

In most cases, both the Reich and other genealogical authorities established an examinee's ancestors—usually the first step in the "race-determination" process—with birth certificates. In the vast majority of cases this sufficed to identify the biological mother. Establishing the biological father, however, could be much more difficult. This was due, in part, to the feasibility of the mother's sexual relations with more than one man during the possible conception period. As will be seen, a great many examinees claimed their biological father was not their legal father. In other instances, no legal father had ever been established.

In such cases, the Genealogical Authority used a number of methods to try to determine the biological father. Often, it simply relied upon well-established legal presumptions from the field of family law. Thus, for example, it assumed, absent proof to the contrary, that a child born to a married couple was the husband's child.[38] For a child born out of wedlock, the Authority similarly presumed that a man listed as the father on a public document (court, notary, youth welfare office, or civil registry) was the biological father, although this assumption, too, could be rebutted.[39] The Authority also checked to see if annotations containing clues to paternity appeared in a civil registry or church book. A man's payment of child support was evidence of paternity in civil law, and the Authority also viewed it as such in making an ancestral decision. Occasionally, it used witnesses' sworn statements as evidence.

Where there was more than one acknowledgment of paternity, a child could make an ancestral proof by showing that all putative fathers were "racially acceptable."[40] Where there were no indications of paternity, a child could bring a legal proceeding to establish it, or to obtain support. The Genealogical Authority usually honored these findings. For example, in one ancestral decision, the Authority cited as evidence of truth a court finding that the examinee's mother had sexual relations with the examinee's putative "Aryan" father while she was married to his legal Jewish father.[41]

When, as happened fairly often, no biological father could be determined, and there was no other evidence to indicate the contrary, the Genealogical Authority's standard presumption was that the biological father of a child born to an "Aryan" mother was also "Aryan." It presumed the opposite when the mother was Jewish. If the child was conceived "in the time preceding Jewish emancipation," this presumption was considered to "border certainty." For a conception after emancipation, the presumption could be rebutted.[42] Thus, in a case involving an appeal of a conviction of "racial shame [*Rassenschande*]," based on no more than the 62-year-old, illegitimately born examinee's claim, the Authority presumed that his father was "German-blooded" because the examinee was born in 1879, after Jewish emancipation in Germany.[43]

In cases of "foundlings," where neither biological parent could be determined, the Genealogical Authority usually relied on the civil registrars to make a judgment as to whether there was reason to believe the child was "racially alien." Only in such circumstance would it make an ancestral decision. Where biological ancestry could not be established due to inaccessibility of genealogical documents, the Authority relaxed the evidentiary rules. For example, it gave sworn declarations greater weight.[44] In fact, its official policy seems to have been to presume "Aryanness" absent an indication otherwise. As noted in an ancestral decision from 1941, which the Authority used as an exemplar: "When Jewish ancestry is not certain, the [Genealogical Authority] should not issue a decision that will place the heaviest burden on a family for all the future. . . ."[45]

Where, however, there was some suspicion of Jewish, or other "racially alien" ancestry, the Genealogical Authority was usually both thorough and relentless in its investigative efforts. In a not atypical case, an 18-year-old boy from Luneburg claimed that his father had been an American occupation soldier of German ancestry in the Rhineland after World War I. Although the Authority opened the examinee's file in September 1935, due to thorough investigation it did not issue an ancestral decision until October 1938.[46] In 1944, in another fairly typical example of Authority implacability, it insisted that the 38-year-old illegitimate daughter of a Jewish woman and the former Egyptian consul in Germany—and thus per the Authority completely "racially alien"—be treated as a "full-Jew." It did not waiver despite questioning of this policy by both the Viennese Police Chief and the Gestapo (!).[47] The Gau Kinship Office Vienna was equally relentless. Also in 1944, for instance, even after learning that a 22-year-old examinee had been deported to Auschwitz, it continued to work on his ancestral decision, as his "Aryan" girlfriend was then pregnant with their child.[48]

The most common method used by examinees to try to escape a finding of Jewish or "alien" ancestry was to argue that an ostensible "racially alien" ancestor was not really biologically related. In such cases, the examinees' mothers, putative "Aryan" fathers, and others frequently made sworn declarations on their behalf. In a typical case, the mother of a 31-year-old woman from the town of Bedburg testified that her "German-blooded" husband, not the Jewish man for whom she had worked as a maid, and who had paid child-support, was her daughter's real father.[49] Generally, however, the Genealogical Authority viewed these statements as of limited use. The assertions often could not be notarized due to the passage of time between the birth and the affidavit. More importantly, witnesses (often the examinee's close relatives) were frequently highly interested in the outcome.[50] Thus the Authority discounted the statement of the Bedburg woman's mother and held the Jewish man to be her father. Similarly, when a biological investigation concluded that it was likely that a Jewish man was the real father of a 23-year-old Schwetzingen woman, the claimed "Aryan" father, who had sworn that the examinee was his biological daughter, stated:

> The entire state of affairs [i.e., the biological investigation] is only a probability. . . . In order to set the state of affairs right, I would like especially to emphasize that I as an old party member gave a sworn declaration that Sachs [the Jewish man] . . . absolutely could not be the father of Lisolette K[.]. Is an indeterminate investigation supported only by probabilities, of more value than an oath before God and our Führer? . . .[51]

The answer was clearly "Yes."

Genealogical Authority officials had good reason to be suspicious of these declarations. The dates of many indicate that they were often made in reaction to an Authority investigation. Accordingly, examinees and declarants offered a variety of excuses for the tardiness of the "real" father in acknowledging paternity. One, for example, declared that the "Aryan" man had been very young at the time of conception and would have been forced out of his parents' house had he been named as the examinee's father. Another claimed that the "Aryan" father "could not marry [the examinee's] mother, an actress in a small city," so the examinee's legal Jewish father acknowledged her paternity out of love of her mother and the desire to protect them from shame. Another asserted that the "Aryan" father, due to his studies, had not been in a position to support a family.[52] Not all declarations supported the examinees' claim. A woman from Frankfurt am Main, for example, whose file contained a sworn declaration from a Jewish man that he *was* her father, insisted this testimony was false: "You should ask Herr N. to testify; there is nothing in life he hates more than my mother and me."[53]

Yet, depending on circumstances, sworn statements sometimes carried weight. When another examinee, a 21-year-old Nuremberg man, submitted sworn declarations of his mother that the Jewish man to whom she was married was not his real father, he was clearheaded enough to acknowledge that such "sworn declarations do not carry sufficient veracity since every mother might make such statements out of love for her child." Yet he also claimed that after two months of searching he had located his real father in Brazil. That man not only swore to the truth of the story, but also provided photos of himself together with the examinee's mother. In addition, the examinee sent a copy of the hotel guest book where his conception allegedly took place, indicating that both were present at the same time. The Genealogical Authority then ordered a biological investigation. In November 1940, it issued an ancestral decision of "German blooded."[54] Similarly, in the case of a 56-year-old Hamburg attorney, the Authority based a December 1939 ancestral decision of Jewish-*Mischling* first degree in part on the notarized statement of a friend of the examinee's Jewish mother. This statement averred that the mother, married to a Jewish man, had had an affair with a "German-blooded" gardener. The claim, however, was buttressed by the testimony of the examinee's wife who stated that his mother had told her this as well, and also that disease prevented the legal father from conceiving a child. Finally, a biological investigation at the University of Kiel did not contradict the story.[55]

In any event, Genealogical Authority officials took the position that such claims of illegitimacy were true "only in an extremely small percentage of cases. . . . The bare claim . . . that a youth or family friend or the family doctor is the true father is insufficient to trigger a biological investigation."[56] They also sought to warn their superiors about this tactic. In 1941, for example, Authority director Mayer informed the Interior Ministry that claims asserting that the illegitimate father was a professional soldier were especially common because, in contrast to "other young professional groups . . . according to the common view, this profession remained Jew-free."[57] Indeed, the general claim of illegitimacy when an ostensible ancestor was Jewish was so widespread that in November 1942, the Party Chancellery, the highest Party authority, warned its officials to be much more cautious when evaluating "Jewish *Mischlinge.*" Such people, it asserted, served in the army, attempted to be treated as if they were "German-blooded," and frequently claimed that "their real father is not the Jewish spouse of the mother, but rather a golden-blond Aryan. . . ."[58]

A less common method that examinees used to dispute Jewish ancestry was claiming to have been adopted by their Jewish parents. According to Genealogical Authority official Christian Ulrich Freiherr von Ulmenstein, this declaration "is even less likely [to be true] than the claim of a non-Jewish father due to adultery."[59] More commonly, other examinees sought to support their assertion of "non-Jewish" ancestry by taking advantage of discrepancies in genealogical records. A 70-year-old housewife in Breslau, for example, produced a genealogical document (*Meldeblatt*) showing that her tradesman father, indisputably Jewish, had been married both to a Jewish woman named Albertine and a Lutheran woman named Theresa. She claimed that Theresa, not Albertine, was her mother. Authority official Friedrich Knost noted, however, that although "Lutheran" appeared by Theresa's name in one document, "Jewish" appeared at other times. Moreover, the local Lutheran pastoral office showed neither a "Theresa" nor an "Albertine" born at the relevant time. Thus, according to Knost, it was more likely that Albertine and Theresa were the same woman: Albertine had converted and changed her name to Theresa. In August 1942, he issued an ancestral decision of "Jewess."[60] In a similar attempt, a 56-year-old Berlin housewife claimed that documents showing her parents to be Jews were unreliable because they had incorrectly left out one "l" from her father's family name, and incorrectly stated that her mother's last name was "Warsaw" when, in fact, that was the city where she was born. The Authority was not convinced and in June 1940 also declared her to be a "Jewess."[61]

The need to prove ancestry sometimes caused embarrassing dilemmas. In 1943, for instance, the Authority received a request from the Weimar Party leadership that a dying party member wished to acknowledge his paternity in a way that could be used to prove the child's "German-blooded" ancestry, but without revealing him as the father.[62] Likewise, the mother of a 20-year-old examinee, a Waffen-SS member who needed an ancestral proof to become an officer, wrote the Authority that her son did not know that the man he believed to be his biological father, was not. She requested that the Authority defer the process until the end of the war so their only son would not be reluctant to come home on leave after discovering the truth.[63]

Yet, in an interesting inversion of the moral order, it was vastly preferable to be illegitimate than Jewish. Indeed, it was better to have a prostitute for a mother than a "Jew" for a father. In 1945, for instance, the lawyer for an examinee argued to the Genealogical Authority that the mother's statement that a Jewish man was the father was entitled to no weight. "[T]he mother of the applicant," wrote the lawyer, "is an incorrigible whore [*Dirne*] and a source of infection of the most dangerous type." After describing her sexual relations with a variety of men during the conception period, he argued that only a "hereditary biological examination . . . as to whether the applicant had Jewish racial characteristics" could be determinative in such a case.[64]

Determining "Race"

The various genealogical authorities usually classified an individual as a "Jew" based on whether and when an individual, his or her spouse, and his or her ancestors were members of a Jewish religious community. Thus, when biological relationship could be established, the authorities then had to ascertain several ancestors' religious affiliations before determining an examinee's "racial composition."[65] The Nuremberg Laws, for example, defined a *Jew* as a person with three or more Jewish grandparents, or a person with two Jewish grandparents who was either married to a "Jew" or had belonged to a Jewish religious community as of the date the laws were implemented. A grandparent was by definition a "Jew" if he or she had belonged to the Jewish religious community.

However, the racial laws were inconsistent in this regard. A regulation relating to the "racial provisions" of the civil service and military laws stated that "the assumption in [those laws] that a Jew by religion [*Religionsjude*] is also a Jew by race [*Rassejude*] can be refuted."[66] Thus, some examinees sought to avoid the harsh effects of the racial laws not by disclaiming their Jewish ancestors, but rather by claiming that such ancestors were "judaized Aryans" rather than "racial Jews." In 1935, citing the foregoing regulation, the Heidelberg law professor Walter Jellinek, whose grandfather had been one of the leaders of the Viennese Jewish community, claimed that this grandfather was an "Aryan—a Bohemian deist and Israelite." This meant a Protestant who had converted to Judaism in the eighteenth century.[67] While Jellinek's argument was ultimately unsuccessful, it helped buy him enough time to survive the Third Reich.

A 57-year-old Rotenkirchen man, who came to Germany as a Russian POW in 1915, had less success with this type of argument. During a 1941 interrogation, he asserted that although he was a Jew by religion, racially he was an ethnic German since "a bit of German was spoken" in his childhood home, and "Gerschmann" was not a particularly Jewish name. In giving the man an ancestral decision of "Jew," however, Genealogical Authority official Knost noted that Yiddish was a German dialect and that "Gerschmann" was "typical for the Germanization of Hebrew names." It arose "from the Hebrew name Gerson. . . ."[68]

Other examinees attempted to use ethnic ambiguity to their advantage in the ancestral proof process. A June 1938 expert report by the Foreign University's Russian Institute noted: "It seems that the Karaites in Germany seek to avoid being treated as Jews based on their earlier special position in the Russian Empire."[69] In fact, in December 1938, the Interior Ministry decided that the Karaites did not constitute a "Jewish religious community" in the sense of the Nuremberg Laws. If necessary, any person validly claiming to be a Karaite should undergo an individual examination to see if he or she was of "German or related blood."[70] The Authority followed this decision. In 1939, the Gestapo wrote the Genealogical Authority that Himmler had ordered all Jewish citizens of the USSR to be removed from Reich territory. It then asked what to do about the assertion of a Soviet citizen, who in response to Berlin police efforts to remove her, claimed "not to belong to the Jewish race, but rather to be a Karaite." The Authority responded that she should undergo an individual examination.[71] Similarly, in 1940, Knost informed the Dessau district court that "the so-called 'Sabbath-Aryans' [probably a Christian group in the Carpathians that practiced Jewish religious customs] should, like the Karaites, have their race determined on an individual basis."[72] But this, in fact, did not resolve the confusion over the "racial" status of Karaites and similar ethnic groups. In direct contradiction to the Interior Ministry's directive, for instance, a biological investigation report from November 1939, regarding a woman who claimed to be a "Daraimen," argued that all members of Judaizing sects, "absent proof to the contrary," should be considered of "foreign racial blood. . . ."[73] In any event, as in other issues related to ancestral proof, the Authority put determination of individual Karaites' racial status on hold after the onset of the German invasion of the Soviet Union.[74]

Rather than claiming "Judaized Aryan" ancestors, other examinees argued that allegations that their ancestors were Jewish were mistaken. A Russian immigrant in Vienna named Bartel, for example, declared that he was of Mennonite ancestry. He also offered proof that there were Mennonites in Russia named "Bartel," and asserted that the Bolsheviks had destroyed his birth and baptismal certificates. The Gau Kinship Office Vienna, however, informed the requesting agency, the Vienna Economic Chamber, that the examinee had established no connection between his birthplace, Brody, and St. Petersburg, the "ancestral site of the Mennonite Bartels." The Kinship Office official continued: "the family-name Bartel appears in my Jew-index as frequently coming from the area of Brody." He also claimed that the appearance of the examinee and his sister "speaks to their full-Jewish ancestry." Moreover, the examinee's sister had married a "full-Jew" and "in this connection . . . has remained true to her blood." The official advised the requesting agency to "treat the examinee as a Jew."[75]

In practice, neither inconsistency in the racial laws nor ethnic ambiguity seems to have posed much of a problem for the various genealogical authorities. Relatively few examinees raised them as defenses. Accordingly, membership in the Jewish religious community was generally the sole criterion that officials used to find "racial Jews." Yet, in this regard, another more serious problem existed: as Genealogical Authority official Knost noted, "in individual cases, membership in the Jewish religious community [can] be unclear." The Authority claimed to resolve doubtful cases by using "objective criteria" such as participation in the ceremonies of the community, appearance of the name on a synagogue membership list, or the paying of taxes to the Jewish community without protest. "The internal attitude to the Jewish religion," wrote Knost, "is of no importance."[76]

In reality, however, the decision was often arbitrary. For example, a 56-year-old Berlin housewife, whose paternal grandparents were indisputably Jewish, claimed that she herself was no longer a member of a Jewish religious community. She had not been inscribed in a community book for many years, had held a church membership card since 1929, and had paid Protestant church taxes for the years 1927–1937. Nonetheless, the Genealogical Authority declared her to be a "Jewess." Documents in various inhabitant registry offices (*Einwohnermeldeamt*) showed some continued affiliation with the Jewish religious community.[77] Likewise, when a 70-year-old Breslau housewife asserted that she had formally left the Jewish religious community in 1912, Authority official Knost struck down this assertion. He noted that while records in the Dortmund inhabitant registry office listed her as "non-religious (*glaubenslos*)" in 1914, they showed no formal "resignation" until May 1939.[78]

Yet, in a similar case, the Authority held that despite lack of formal resignation, a 52-year-old Berlin housewife was not part of the Jewish religious community because it could not be proved that she had Jewish schooling, she was listed as "evangelical-Lutheran" or "free-thinker [*freireligiös*]" in three different inhabitant registry offices, and she declared herself "without religion" on marriage. Moreover, in this case, in direct contradiction to the Authority's self-proclaimed "objective standards," the ancestral decision listed the woman's claim that she did not feel herself to be Jewish as a factor in the decision.[79]

Another factor the Genealogical Authority sometimes looked at when trying to determine religious affiliation was an ancestor's name. Thus the Authority took particular interest in files where an examinee's grandparent was named "Sareh," or when the great-grandfather of the wife of an applicant for genealogical research permit had the Jewish-sounding name "Goldhorn."[80] Indeed, on their own initiative, persons interacting with the agency sought to explain away such names. For example, when a bookseller in Saxony with the last name Mendel applied for a genealogical research permit, he assured the Authority in 1933 that despite his name, there were no Jews in his ancestry.[81] Names could clearly be ambiguous evidence of "race." An Authority internal memorandum noted that sometimes "a name appearing in an examinee's ancestral table shows up in Jewish as well as German-blooded families" in the "alien origin registry."[82]

Some examinees, despite efforts to evade the harsh consequences of the racial laws, failed to grasp the laws' fundamentally racist, as well as antisemitic, essence. Thus in 1938, a Cypriot medical student living in Vienna obtained a letter, on church letterhead, from his Greek Orthodox pastor. The note stated: "It is hereby confirmed that A. . . . was born to Egyptians, is of Greek Orthodox religion and is Aryan." After A. allegedly fathered a child by an "Aryan" woman, the Gau Kinship Office Vienna became involved in determining the racial categorization of the child. A. produced the letter from his pastor to "prove" his German-blooded racial status. In a biological investigation instigated by the Gau Kinship Office in June 1943, however, the racial expert Dr. Pendl opined that A. was actually predominantly of the "Oriental and the Near Eastern races, [but] also with a small but discernible Negro component." Schoen of the Gau Kinship Office then asked Deputy Gauleiter Scharizer to please respond to A.'s "nonsense." Scharizer referred the case to the Gestapo, which later wrote that it had taken "measures," the nature of which were not spelled out.[83]

Personal Characteristics as a Factor in the Ancestral Decision

Individual examinees often sought to emphasize what they thought were important personal factors in an effort to gain a favorable ancestral decision, with mixed success. Whether physical, mental, or socioeconomic, such characteristics occasionally played some role in the decisions of the Reich Genealogical Authority. Yet the degree varied in individual cases, adding to the impression that the ancestral decision process was often based on arbitrary factors.

Numerous examinees argued that they or their relatives felt and acted racially acceptable. One woman in Berlin wrote the Authority that she and her son were "innocent" and "we think and feel . . . only Aryan," while another wrote that her daughter had "an impeccable German inclination." In support of their claim that their "Jewish" father was actually an "Aryan," two sisters submitted the affidavit of a man who swore that he was told the father could not be Jewish because he had had a "Christian character."[84] And after the Genealogical Authority designated the wife of a Viennese professor a "Jewess," he wrote back that its decision must be incorrect because she "lacked any Jewish racial characteristics." While a biological investigation had indicated only a "possibility" of an "Aryan" father, wrote the professor, it had failed to take into account his wife's "spiritual and dispositional aptitude . . . that arose from Aryan genetic material [*arischen Erbmasse*]." Moreover, her siblings always said she was "somewhat different."[85]

Claims to "Aryan" character mingled easily with claims to "Aryan" physique. Examinees thus frequently asked the Genealogical Authority to note the "non-Jewish" appearance of their ancestors, themselves, and their descendants. The Heidelberg law professor Jellinek, for instance, wrote the Education Ministry: "Emotionally it is impossible for me to perceive how my father could be a full Jew. Indeed his appearance was . . . not especially Jewish."[86] An attorney, drawn into an Authority investigation of his sister in 1940, claimed to "have doubt over my Jewish ancestry based on my way of life, character, and appearance." His sister, who sent photos to the Authority, earlier claimed that "no typical Jewish racial indication is to be noted in either me or my descendants. This would surely be the case with my son, if the [Jewish man] were my biological father since, with mixed marriages, the Jewish race comes through if not with the daughter, than absolutely with the grandson." Writing in May 1944 to the anthropologist who was to carry out her biological investigation, the same woman noted that the following information might be "scientifically valuable": a very experienced eye doctor (*Augendiagnostiker*) had told her "that brown-black nipples were a sure sign in women with Jewish blood." Presumably her nipples were a different color.[87] Another examinee emphasized his blue eyes, blond hair, oval face, and slim figure. He also invited a comparison between himself and his older brother who was indisputably conceived by the putative Jewish father, and "who simply differs from me in everything."[88]

In an August 1933 letter to Hitler's deputy Rudolf Hess, Genealogical Authority director Gercke stressed that his office did racial research on the basis of genealogical, not medical, science.[89] Yet in another indication of the frequent arbitrariness of the ancestral decision-making process, Authority officials—despite lack of "expertise"— often did use an examinee's physical appearance in making their decisions. Indeed, in May 1935, Mayer ordered his employees to more frequently use photographs, especially in doubtful cases. Soon the request for certified photographs became a standard part of the ancestral decision process.[90] In a case in which an examinee asserted that his illegitimate father was "Aryan," Mayer based his contrary decision partly on evidence from the examinee's paternity case (ca. 1914). There the examinee's mother had claimed his father was Jewish, and may even have been her sister's Jewish husband. But Mayer also compared photos of the examinee and his ostensible cousin, claiming that he saw "striking similarities" between the two men. This, he asserted, fundamentally confirmed his conclusion that they were actually half-brothers with the same Jewish father.[91]

As a further means of persuasion, some examinees proffered their own, or their ancestors', antisemitic credentials. When the Genealogical Authority denied one of the aforementioned examinees a biological investigation in part because her legal Jewish father had named her in his will, she responded that the dedication in the will was false. Her legal father did this, she continued, to protect the children from his business partners who were "Jews typical of their race, greedy and dishonest," and who sought to dispute her paternity so that they might seize all the property. Her legal Jewish father, she continued, had done this on the advice of a family friend, a civil registrar who, as an "Aryan and Christian, wanted to protect the Aryan, Christian child [i.e., her] from this Jewish persecution."[92] In a later letter, she stated, in closing, that she would prevail in this matter and that "after the war, the Jews will with justice be even more hated." Her brother similarly noted that he had been a member of the Nazi Party since 1933, two other Nazi organizations since 1938, and had received his "primary education in the Joachimsthalschen Secondary School in Berlin, nationally recognized as antisemitic." Likewise, a witness for two sisters swore that not only had he been told that their ostensibly Jewish father was born to non-Jews, but also testified that the father was antisemitic and "always refused Jewish renters in his house."[93] There is no indication, however, that these particular means of persuasion played much role in any Authority decision.

Examinees also sought to influence Authority decisions by citing their services to Germany. In 1944, a woman wrote that the "German-bloodedness" of her son's likely father could not be doubted since the man had been an officer in the East since 1940. Another examinee had a local Nazi official testify that she frequently contributed to the Nazi Winter Relief Fund, and that she insisted on contributing even when accused of being a Jew. Likewise, a woman in Berlin wrote an Interior Ministry official: "I have honorably gained my distinction in the great world war . . . I saved countless children from undernourishment through German, not Quaker-American, food."

The official, however, wrote Authority director Mayer that he was sending the examinee back the documents honoring her war service "since naturally they can play no role in the decision on ancestry."[94] Indeed, the Authority seemed to be above such considerations. Sometimes, however, the Interior Ministry was not. Thus, in one case, it ordered the Genealogical Authority to change a finding from first- to second-degree Jewish *Mischling* for an examinee who claimed his Jewish paternal grandfather was not his father's biological father. While the Interior Ministry noted that the record was ambiguous—especially as the examinee's father was born in 1892 in heavily Jewish Galicia—it also noted that the examinee "was severely wounded in the last war" and is "especially deserving that his ancestral process not be decided to his detriment."[95]

Examinees also frequently wrote about the huge stress the ancestral decision process put on them, presumably in the hope that sympathy would play a helpful role in the result. In 1935, Professor Jellinek laconically informed the Authority that its decision was "of considerable significance for the fate of my children." These pleas, however, often became increasingly desperate. In 1936, a woman in Berlin, seeking a "mercy exclusion" for her only son (who sought to marry an "Aryan" woman) from Hitler's Deputy for Party Affairs, wrote that her son was in a "fearful situation" waiting for his ancestral decision. "No one knows my unbearably heavy sorrow," she continued; "I can scarcely describe my mental and related health condition." In 1937, another woman, begging a contact in the Interior Ministry to continue to intercede on her behalf after an ancestral decision of first-degree Jewish *Mischling*, wrote: "Please leave me this little ray of hope. I grasp so desperately at your help."[96]

Indeed, by the summer of 1941, the pleas indicated knowledge that the ancestral decision came down to a matter of life and death. In August 1941, for example, an attorney for two sisters, one of whom was involved in a "racial shame" case for allegedly having sexual intercourse with her "Aryan" ex-husband, wrote:

> For my clients, the quickest decision over their ancestry is an existential question. As a consequence of the impediment to the further conducting of the criminal case [due to the ancestral decision process], in the meantime both have had to take [Jewish] identity cards and supplementary names [i.e., "Sara"] and must bear all the disadvantages that arise out of the legal position of Jews.[97]

In June 1942, a professional genealogist asked Dr. Fred Dubitscher, acting director of the Polyclinic for Hereditary and Racial Care in Berlin, to provide the results of his biological examination as quickly as possible as "Stuttgart police authorities had already imprisoned" his client's aunt, who was needed for the investigation. A month later, the genealogist again wrote, saying: "It would be regrettable if an examinee were evacuated in the middle of a process," and asking if Dubitscher might not have "a simple telephone conversation with the Gestapo."[98]

In April 1943, an "Aryan" woman in Breslau, who twenty years earlier had married a Jewish man and converted to Judaism, pleaded with the Genealogical

Authority to change her two children's designations from "Jew" to "Jewish-*Mischling* first degree." Her son had failed to officially leave the Jewish community prior to the official cutoff date and had now been "evacuated." Moreover, her daughter, who had left the Jewish community in time, was nevertheless still designated a "Jewess." She continued: "the fear of also losing my second child has almost broken me. . . ." The woman further explained that she had converted to Judaism on marriage to maintain peace in the household and "could not recognize twenty years ago that she had done something wrong." Moreover, in explaining her children's late attempts to leave the Jewish community, she informed the Authority that her husband, who was now "extremely ill, had shared all the good years with us and accordingly we could not now leave him alone in his misfortune."[99]

In an effort to improve their "racial" categorization, even those who received an ancestral decision less drastic than "Jew" informed the Genealogical Authority of the problems they consequently encountered. In July 1942, a Breslau teacher wrote that the local party administrative office had stopped delivery of his family's ration cards to their house because it viewed their son as a "half-Aryan." In April 1944, with her biological investigation still pending, the sculptor's wife, who had already received an ancestral decision of "First-Degree Jewish *Mischling*," asked Authority official Dr. Max Prowe to please hurry with a revised ancestral decision: her husband was dead, his work destroyed, and her house and garden had been bombed into ruins. "The worst," however, she wrote, was "to be disrespectfully treated and to be incorrectly valued as inferior." Despite the prevalence of these tales of woe, however, there is little evidence that they played any role in any genealogical authority's decisions. After one examinee's daughter wrote the Gau Kinship Office Vienna that her 71-year-old mother had died of a heart attack, an official responded that this was "very sad," but the investigation continued and she needed to send money for the further procurement and translation of documents.[100]

Socioeconomic status, however, could be important. Persons of wealth and connections had more tools available to help avoid or delay an undesirable ancestral decision. In the case of the full sisters Alice G. and Margarette K., for example, the Genealogical Authority initially decided that the evidence did not overcome the presumption that their father was a "full-Jew." This resulted in one sister's "evacuation" to the "occupied East," and probable death. However, Winifried Wagner, Richard Wagner's daughter, intervened on the other sister's behalf. The Authority then decided that the evidence actually did overcome the presumption of "full-Jew."

As previously noted, Professor Jellinek offered complex legal and factual arguments related to his ancestry, which Genealogical Authority officials were ready to dismiss out of hand.[101] Jellinek, however, must have had powerful friends within the Interior Ministry, which placed pressure on the Authority to disprove his assertions. In 1936, the Authority asked the Institute for the Study of the Jewish Question in Berlin to assess the likelihood of Jellinek's claim of Aryan ancestry. The Institute answered, essentially, "not very," especially as "it is inconceivable that a full-Aryan would been able to occupy a position" in the Jewish community comparable to that of Jellinek's grandfather. Later that year, Authority official Ulmenstein wrote the Interior Ministry that Jellinek's "methods of disavowing his ancestry confirm his racial status."[102] Yet, in order to substantiate his claims, Jellinek was eventually allowed, with the permission of the Interior Ministry but at his own cost (estimated at RM 1000), to take research trips to Vienna, Prague, and other places. A professional genealogist (Hans von Bourcy from Vienna) was chosen by the Authority to accompany him. These research trips became increasingly difficult due to the war, but the Interior Ministry allowed Jellinek to continue them as late as 1941. Although the Authority eventually issued an ancestral decision of "Jew" against him, he ultimately succeeded in buying enough time to prevent full application of the anti-Jewish measures against himself. Moreover, his four children received an ancestral decision of Jewish-*Mischling* second degree.[103]

Yet connections were no guarantee of a desired outcome. In October 1939, after receiving an ancestral decision of Jewish-*Mischling* first degree despite claiming her real father was an "Aryan" man, the previously mentioned sculptor's wife insisted on a "racial-biological investigation." She stated that she would ask Dr. Theodor Morell, Hitler's personal doctor, whom she had known for eighteen years and whose sister was her friend, to perform the process. She also noted that after the war she would also ask for the intervention of Minister Hermann Göring, a good friend of Morell, and she would not be shy about enforcing her rights.[104] Yet in April 1944, her biological investigation was still pending.

The Interior Ministry actually seems to have appointed at least two officials as intercessors before the Genealogical Authority for examinees who had some social standing. However, the results for these examinees were mixed. An official (*Ministerialrat*) named Metzner, for example, interceded before the Authority and Hitler's Deputy for Party Affairs both on behalf of the aforementioned woman who had served Germany by feeding malnourished youth during World War I, and also on behalf of a retired major.[105] The file does not indicate whether Metzner's intercession helped the former, and it did not seem to have helped the latter. In that case, Metzner asked the Authority to speed up the man's ancestral decision as that man was to return to active service. Director Mayer responded that his office was proceeding apace, but there was "strong incertitude regarding the examinee's ancestry on the side of his paternal grandparents."

Other examinees were allowed to use a police official named Steinkopff, also an adjutant to the Interior Minister, as an intercessor. Steinkopff managed to insure that one examinee received a biological investigation. This action, however, failed to exclude her putative Jewish father as her biological father. Despite Steinkopff's efforts, she received an ancestral decision of first-degree Jewish *Mischling*.[106] Similarly, a 73-year-old retired general-major who used Steinkopff to intercede on his behalf in order to be "released from the ordinances concerning Jews" was nevertheless denied "in view of his full-Jewish ancestry." This was despite the fact that the man was married to an "Aryan," had served Germany "in the field," and had received the attention of the *Reichsstatthalter* in Vienna, and of highly placed authorities in the Interior Ministry.[107] On the other hand, in a case in which the number of Jewish maternal grandparents was at issue, Steinkopff wrote the Authority that a Salzburg teacher "makes a good, and absolutely non-Jewish impression." It then changed an ancestral decision of Jewish-*Mischling* from first to second degree.[108]

One Family and the Reich Genealogical Authority

While cases involving the well-connected were atypical, often these files, due to their density, provide a broad overview of the workings of a Genealogical Authority ancestral decision. Thus this chapter closes with a detailed look at one such file, concerning the author Minni V. and her two children Wolfgang and Beate.[109] In 1916, Minni had married Johannes V. He was an early Nazi Party member, recipient of the "Golden Party Medal," author of the *völkisch* book *Vom Ich zum Wir* (*From I to Us*), and from May 1931 had been a mid-level party official. For reasons unclear from the file, in April 1935 the head of the Munich Hitler Youth asked the Genealogical Authority to investigate the "Aryan origin" of Minni and Johannes's son Wolfgang, which it promptly began to do. Two months later, Minni informed the Authority that she too needed to establish her "Aryan origin" for her further membership in the Reich German Press Union.

Within weeks, the Genealogical Authority claimed to have established through birth and marriage certificates that both of Minni's parents were Jewish. It then immediately informed the Hitler Youth that Wolfgang was "not free from Jewish blood admixture in the sense of the admission conditions of the N.S.D.A.P"; the Supreme Party Court in Munich that Johannes's wife did not meet the racial requirements for Party membership; and the Press Union that Minni was "non-Aryan within the meaning of the guidelines to the Reich Civil Service Law."

The V. family, however, was well connected. In September 1935, Dr. Kurt Jahncke, a Propaganda Ministry official, asked the Authority to conduct a biological investigation. After noting Johannes V.'s impeccable Nazi credentials, Jahncke stated that Minni had heard from a now deceased uncle that her Jewish parents had adopted her. Moreover, a Lieutenant Hermann Blank confirmed this in a sworn statement from July 1935. That month, Johannes had also sworn that Minni had told him of her French ancestry, that as a convinced antisemite he would only marry an Aryan, and that Minni's literary works, even though written before the Nazi "seizure of power," nevertheless contained the "spirit and feeling of National Socialism." This pressure was sufficient for the Genealogical Authority to reopen the investigation—now including, incidentally, research into the ancestry of Lieutenant Blank (whose parents both turned out to be Catholic). Minni, however, now also revealed that she had earlier been married to a man named Gerhard K.

In January 1936, the Authority returned twenty-five photos and seven documents to Minni under cover of a letter that informed her that it had again determined she was the daughter of her legal parents who were both Jewish. She was, accordingly, "not Aryan . . . within the meaning of the Reich Civil Service Law . . . and also . . . the Military Law of 21 May 1935." Further, her son was also "non-Aryan." Finally, since there was insufficient evidence contradicting her legal lineage, there would be no biological investigation. The Authority also relayed this information to Jahnke in the Propaganda Ministry.

Despite this decision, for reasons unclear from the file, the Genealogical Authority continued to investigate Minni's case, perhaps because the racial status of her daughter Beate was also now at issue. In March 1936, Minni had asked the Authority how she could change the name of her daughter from Beate K. to Beate V. According to this letter, in 1913 Minni had separated from her first husband, now revealed to have been Jewish, cohabitated with Johannes V., and Beate resulted from this cohabitation. Gerhard K. had died in 1915 and Minni then married Johannes.

The investigation continued very slowly. A July 1937 letter to the Authority from a Dr. Krenn of the Central Office of the Party Supreme Court questioned the veracity of Blank's declaration and noted that "[t]he external appearance of Frau V[.] in her photographs is completely non-Aryan." Krenn also did not agree that Minni's writings were "pure German and completely Aryan." Nevertheless, he still recommended that the Authority conduct a racial scientific investigation. The Authority then wrote Minni that after she sent RM 75, it would arrange for such an examination in Munich.

Minni, however, took matters into her own hands. She arranged for Professor Fabio Frassetto, director of the University of Bologna's Institute of General and Applied Anthropology, to conduct a biological investigation. In November 1937, Frassetto issued a "certification of racial diagnosis" indicating that since Minni claimed her legal parents were not her real parents, and there was no other way to determine the truth of this, "[w]e have therefore resolved the racial diagnosis strictly on the basis of the objective characteristics exhibited by the person concerned." The report continued that based on Professor Frassetto's numerous observations and measurements of, inter alia, Minni's fingers, feet, color and form of hair and eyes, form of the nose and mouth and especially head, as well as her mental characteristics, he was convinced that she was a racial mixture of the "Nordic or Subnordic" and the "Mediterranean or Mediterranoiden" races. Apparently in 1938 Johannes divorced Minni.

Minni sent Professor Frassetto's report to the Supreme Party Court which, in January 1939, forwarded it to the Genealogical Authority. That same month, Minni's daughter Beate submitted an Authority form. Referring to Frassetto's findings, Beate continued to assert that her mother was the biological child of unknown parents. Beate claimed that the Italian regime had designated the University of Bologna as the site for "clarification of racial-scientific questions" that are "undertaken there in the same way as with us." Beate also submitted sworn statements of her mother, Johannes V., Hermann Blank, Erna Stahl (Johannes V.'s sister), and

Otto V. (Johannes's brother), all supporting the contention that Johannes was her father. The next month, however, the Authority informed the Supreme Party Court that it could not base any decision on Frassetto's report because "an examination in the course of an ancestral proof must be carried out exclusively by those institutions designated by the Interior Minister." Accordingly, it stated, Minni must still be viewed as a "Jew."

The Genealogical Authority continued to slowly gather information while Minni's family and others pressed for a final decision. In August 1939, Beate wrote the Authority that she would appreciate the matter being resolved since she had two children and a third was on the way. She claimed that a comparison of her hands and Johannes's would show his paternity. In October and again in November, Wolfgang, too, asked the Authority when his mother could undergo a biological investigation. In March 1940, the local Nazi official for the neighborhood in which Beate lived also questioned the Authority about whether he was dealing with an "Aryan" or "non-Aryan."

In July 1940, the Authority informed Minni that for RM 150 the University of Munich's Anthropological Institute would perform a biological investigation of her and Beate, with Johannes participating. Two authenticated photos of Gerhard K. would also be necessary. No one in Minni's family responded to that letter, or to two follow-up letters. In March 1941, however, Beate wrote the Authority that her mother was very sick, enclosed a certification of illness, and indicated that she and Johannes were nevertheless ready for the biological investigation. In July 1941, the Repatriation Office of the Nazi Foreign Organization (*Rückwanderer-Amt, NSDAP Leitung der Auslands-Organisation*) in Berlin informed the Genealogical Authority that in May Minni had returned to Germany from Italy for the biological investigation. This letter also noted that while Minni's passport indicated that she was a "Jew," during a "state police" (presumably Gestapo) interrogation Minni claimed to be of "French ancestry and Roman Blood," and said she was only the adopted, foundling daughter of the Jewish couple. More details of Minni's story emerge from that letter. She claimed that at age eighteen she had left her parents' house and acted for several years. At twenty, she married Gerhard K. After less than two years of marriage, she met Johannes V., who she claimed fathered both her children. Beate herself was unmarried and lived off of an "inheritance from the alleged grandparents." The Repatriation Office also indicated that it, too, wanted the results of Minni's examination.

In August 1941, the Genealogical Authority finally requested the long-delayed biological investigation. The Anthropological Institute, however, did not issue its report until February 1942. In this report, Theodor Mollison, the expert, opined that Minni was the daughter of her Jewish, legal parents, and that Beate was the daughter of Gerhard K., not Johannes V., and was therefore also a "full Jew." In May, the Authority sent Minni a bill for RM 12 (RM 162 for the investigation, less 150 already paid) and in June issued three ancestral decisions: Minni and Beate were "Jewesses," and Wolfgang was a Jewish *Mischling* first degree. The Genealogical Authority then sent copies of the ancestral decisions to Minni, the Party Foreign Office, the Party Supreme Court, the Gau leadership in Munich-Upper Bavaria, and the university's anthropological institute. By form letter, it also informed the Munich city administrator of the results. Later that month, the Authority billed Minni RM 50 for the three ancestral decisions.

But the file was still not closed. In August 1942, the Interior Ministry informed Johannes that Beate and Minni's ancestral decision would be "reexamined." This was likely due to Johannes's efforts. A letter in September 1942 from the Gestapo to the State Criminal Police, Munich, noted that Johannes had requested this. The Gestapo, which asked to be kept abreast of the outcome, seems to have become involved because the father of Beate's three children, two of whom were conceived after promulgation of the Nuremberg Laws, may, as an "Aryan," have thus engaged in the crime of "racial shame." In a further effort to help his ex-wife and putative daughter, that same month Johannes also requested that Hitler himself order a reexamination of the Authority's decisions. An official in Hitler's Chancellery (*Oberbereichsleiter*) responded: "I have ordered the [RSHA—an SS office] not to initiate any measures against your divorced wife as well as your illegitimate daughter until the Interior Ministry makes its decision. . . ."

In October 1942, Johannes and his lawyer came to the Genealogical Authority offices to discuss the appeal of the ancestral decisions. They informed the agency that Minni had also instituted suit in the civil courts to contest her legitimacy. The Authority responded that the civil suit was without merit as Minni claimed to be an adopted, not an illegitimate child. Nevertheless, it again began collecting information on Minni, seeking her birth certificate and testamentary documents of "the Jewish salesman Hermann E." from the justice of the peace in Berlin-Lichterfelde. It also sought to convince the legal authorities that Minni's lawsuit was meritless, and sent copies of its ancestral decisions on Minni and Beate to the public prosecutor. The Authority again argued that the attempt by Minni to dispute her parentage should be denied since she was not an illegitimate child, but supposedly "a foundling in which case there is no place for a proceeding according to [the governing statute]." The letter continued that the expert report from the University of Bologna "was of no evidentiary value since it was the result of a pure racial scientific investigation," while the Authority's "*hereditary and* racial scientific investigation . . . fully contradicts the aforementioned assertions. . . ." (emphasis in original). In January 1943, the Authority sent the same letter to the Interior Minister. But the Authority also suspended the appeal process of its ancestral decision pending the outcome of the paternity proceedings.

The file is not clear on the final results of all the examinees' efforts, although it does indicate that they may have paid off. Not until February 14, 1945, almost ten years after the file was opened, did the Interior Ministry write the Genealogical Authority that it was in "full accord with the ancestral decisions of June 25, 1942."

With the Nazi regime near collapse, this may well indicate that Minni and her family survived the war. This single case thus not only illustrates in some detail an entire ancestral decision process from start to "finish," but also its capricious nature, especially where persons of wealth or influence were concerned. It also gives some inkling of the arbitrary character of the biological examination, which will now be examined in greater detail.

7 | Three Beneficiaries of the Ancestral Proof

THREE NONGOVERNMENTAL, NONPARTY GROUPS worked particularly closely with the Reich Genealogical Authority: the scientists who performed biological investigations for purposes of the ancestral decision; the genealogists who were not only regulated by the agency but also provided it with manpower and data; and both the Catholic and Protestant churches, which constituted a primary source of genealogical information. Research into their relationships with the Authority also provides insight both into how important sectors of German society viewed the ancestral proof requirement and how racism was institutionalized in Nazi Germany.

The Scientists and the Ancestral Proof: The Biological Investigation

> We would gladly burn a hundred if just one among them were guilty.
>
> —THIRTEENTH-CENTURY INQUISITOR IN
> *ANNALES WORMATIENSES* [1]

Genealogical Authority officials did not hesitate to use biological characteristics as *part* of their decision-making process. Yet in a significant number of cases involving such factors as illegitimacy or adoption, no genealogical or other nonscientific evidence (e.g., sworn declarations) was available to establish a person's ancestors to a "reasonable certainty." In some of these instances, however, either because circumstantial evidence indicated "non-Aryan" ancestry (including an examinee's appearance), or due to stringent requirements applicable to a particular individual, an in-depth ancestral proof still had to be made. Accordingly, in April 1934 the Interior Ministry authorized the Authority to use scientific experts to help determine "race." This procedure became known as a "hereditary and racial-scientific investigation [*erb- und rassenkundliche Untersuchung*]," which, for simplicity's sake, I refer to as a biological investigation. [2]

I could not accurately determine the percentage of Genealogical Authority examinees who underwent a biological investigation. It was, however, only a small fraction, probably just 4 percent or less. [3] Yet, despite their small numbers, these biological investigations were extraordinarily important, not only to the ancestral proof process itself, but to the Nazis' entire racist enterprise. The files show that a significant number of scientists made these investigations, including some of the most eminent natural scientists in Germany and Austria. The evidence also shows that their expert reports frequently, if inadvertently, highlighted discrepancies between accepted scientific methodology and their own "racial-scientific" processes. Indeed, the biological investigation was, of all aspects of the ancestral proof requirement, the most riddled with inconsistencies, as they often mixed sophisticated forensic evaluation with haphazard methodology and flawed logic. It therefore offered the strongest evidence that the asserted need for the ancestral proof was, despite repeated claims to the contrary, demonstrably not supported by "science." Moreover, the scientists who carried out these examinations were of all people those best placed to note and critique the unscientific nature of the ancestral proof enterprise. The Authority files, however, are devoid of any such criticism. They show, rather, enthusiastic promotion of, and participation in, the process. Thus, despite the small total performed, the biological investigations provided a stamp of scientific legitimacy that was the sine qua non for broad public acceptance of Nazi racial policy.

As the full name of the biological investigation—*"hereditary and racial-scientific examination"*—implies, the evaluation consisted of two conceptually different procedures. In the typical case—an examinee claiming that a putative Jewish father was not his or her biological father—the Genealogical Authority usually posed three questions to the investigating scientist:

1. Is it probable that the German-blooded man is the examinee's biological father?
2. Or is it more probable that the Jewish man is the biological father?
3. Does the examinee exhibit Jewish racial characteristics?[4]

The "hereditary" portion, represented by the first two questions, was essentially a paternity test: an attempt to make an ancestral proof by identifying a man, whose "race" was already known, as the examinee's biological father. The "racial" part, however, represented by the third question, was ostensibly a determination as to whether an examinee had Jewish ancestry, based on the presence or absence of "Jewish" features.

The hereditary examination usually started with a blood test to see if a possible father could be definitively excluded. These tests were, however, only of limited use. They could not confirm, but only rule out, a biological father, and could only do so if the man was physically available to provide blood.[5] In a typical case from 1940–1941, for example, the examinee, a 23-year-old woman born out of wedlock, from Schwetzingen, in southwest Germany, claimed that her real father was the "Aryan" man presently married to her mother, not the Jewish man who had initially acknowledged paternity. In response, the Authority first ordered a blood test on the possible "Aryan" father (the potential Jewish father having fled Germany some time before). The "Aryan" man proved to be blood type A. The examinee, however, had type O.

89 89

UNIVERSITÄTS-INSTITUT
FÜR ERBBIOLOGIE UND RASSENHYGIENE
DIREKTOR: PROF. DR. FRHR. V. VERSCHUER

FRANKFURT A.M. DEN 5.4.1941
HAUS DER VOLKSGESUNDHEIT, GARTENSTR. 140
FERNRUF SAMMELNUMMER 63354
NACHTRUF 63355

SPRECHSTUNDEN DER POLIKLINIK:
MO. DI. DO. FR. 9—10 UHR
DO. 18—19 UHR

TAGEBUCH NR. Li./

An
das Reichssippenamt
Berlin NW 7
Schiffbauerdamm 26

[stamp: Reichssippenamt 10. APR. 1941 Vm.]

Betr.: I^5 Blut A 1764/1550 Go/Lx.

[handwritten notation: ...RM. 159,- und 26,60... 10.4.41]

Der Aufforderung vom 7.12.1940 nachkommend, erstatte ich das erb- und rassenkundliche Gutachten über Lieselotte K███████, geb. am 28.1.1918 zu Marburg/Lahn, wohnhaft Schwetzingen, Karl Theodorstr. 17.

Die Untersuchung der beteiligten Personen, der Antragstellerin, deren Mutter Anna K███ geb. R███████, geb. am 9.6. 1896 zu Otterstadt/Krs. Speyer, wohnhaft Schwetzingen, Karl Theodorstr. 17 und des angeblichen Erzeugers, Jakob S███, geb. am 30.3.1899 zu Otterstadt, wohnhaft Heidelberg, Plöckstr. 13, fand am 22.1.1941 im Universitäts-Institut für Erbbiologie und Rassenhygiene in Frankfurt/M. statt. Ein Lichtbild des auszuschliessenden Erzeugers, des Juden Fritz Israel S███ stand für die Untersuchung nicht zur Verfügung. Auf die erst nach der erb- und rassenkundlichen Untersuchung der beteiligten Personen erfolgte Mitteilung des Reichssippenamtes über noch nachträgliche Einsendung von Lichtbildern des auszuschliessenden Erzeugers musste die Erstattung des Gutachtens hinausgeschoben werden.

Die Identität der Persönlichkeiten ergibt sich aus den hier vorgenommenen photographischen Aufnahmen, von denen je ein Abzug beigefügt wird, sowie aus den hier aufbewahrten Finger- und Handabdrücken. Ausserdem füge ich einen Durchschlag des Untersuchungsbogens bei, aus welchem die hier erhobenen Befunde zu entnehmen sind sowie eine Aufstellung für die Auswertung der Finger- und Handabdrücke.

Für die erbbiologische Vaterschaftsbestimmung ergibt sich bei den Einzelmerkmalen folgende Beurteilung:

Figure 8. Excerpt, Hereditary and Racial Scientific Investigation Report. Courtesy of the German Federal Archives, Berlin-Lichterfelde.

Because only a man with type AB blood could be definitively excluded as her father, the test was inconclusive.[6]

As was often required, the next step in an hereditary investigation was an anthropological comparison of other physical characteristics such as fingerprints; eye and hair color; skull shape; facial features such as chin, eye, mouth, ear, and nose; hands and feet; and skin pigmentation. The goal was to determine which traits came from an undisputed biological parent (again, usually the mother) and whether the others were more likely to have come from one or another possible biological father.[7] In the case of the 23-year-old Schwetzingen woman, for instance, after the blood test proved inconclusive, the Genealogical Authority ordered a full-fledged biological investigation at the University of Frankfurt's Institute for Hereditary Biology and Racial Hygiene. The Institute conducted a detailed physical comparison of the examinee, her mother, and her putative Aryan father, as well as a photo of the Jewish man.[8]

In keeping with the empirical nature of these investigations, the scientists usually framed their findings on the basis of probabilities. Thus, in a typical report, Prof. Dr. Egon Freiherr von Eickstedt of the University of Breslau's Anthropological Institute wrote: "The number of characteristics in which the examinee did not resemble either his mother or [his claimed "German-blooded" father] does not exceed the amount of dissimilarities that would be expected between the members of a biological family." The scientists also readily acknowledged that the process was not an exact science. Professor and physician Hermann Boehm, director of the Institute for Hereditary and Racial Care in Gießen, for example, wrote in one of his reports that if one is precluded from using "blood groups and blood corpuscle properties, it is generally only very rarely possible to exclude a man with certainty as the biological father of a particular child."[9] The Genealogical Authority, however, like many courts of law, took the tenable position that "a serviceable degree of probability in practical life is valid as truth."[10] Nonetheless, such investigations were often still inconclusive, not even reaching "a serviceable degree of probability." In the case of the Schwetzingen woman, for instance, the expert, Otmar Freiherr von Verschuer, determined that she and the "Aryan" man shared no physical characteristics in common, and the single photo of the Jewish man was insufficient to assist in deciding if he and the examinee shared such attributes.[11]

While of relatively recent origin, the hereditary portion of the biological investigation had been developed prior to the Nazi period, primarily to assist in the field of family law. Professor and Dr. Phil. Otto Reche, director of the University of Leipzig's Institute for Racial Science and Cultural Anthropology, performed the first such hereditary examination for a Viennese Court in 1926. Reche's Institute (1927), the Kaiser Wilhelm Institute for Anthropology (1928), and the University of Munich's Anthropological Institution (1928) thereafter made the first such examinations in Germany. The procedure quickly became standard practice in family law cases. By 1931, the highest Viennese court held that failure to make such an investigation in a paternity suit constituted legal malpractice.[12] Thus, although fairly new, by 1933 many in the scientific and legal communities already viewed a hereditary investigation as both scientifically legitimate and forensically useful.

Unlike the hereditary segment of the biological investigation, the "racial" portion—the attempt to identify "racially-alien" (usually "Jewish") ancestry based on physical and mental traits—became part of legal and administrative practice in German-speaking lands only after 1933. By its very structure, which began with the question, "Does the examinee exhibit Jewish racial characteristics?" this part of the investigation assumed the existence of such features. Because the racial and hereditary portions of the biological investigation were usually combined, and no scientist questioned the validity of the racial part, the process gained an aura of legitimacy through proximity. Due to a variety of methodological and practical problems, however, it is hard to avoid the conclusion that it was, in reality, a farce.

One such problem involved the lack of standardized descriptions of "alien" or "Jewish" characteristics. This made the search for such traits highly subjective. Indeed, different scientists described their task in different ways. A few, conforming to the "true" racial-scientific description of Jews, refrained from using the term *Jewish characteristics* altogether and claimed to be searching for the presence or absence of "Near Eastern–Oriental" racial traits.[13] Other experts maintained that they were determining whether an examinee had attributes that were "typical in Jews" or "typically Jewish."[14] Most experts, however, simply used the terms "Near Eastern/Oriental," "typically Jewish," and "Jewish racial" characteristics interchangeably. This theoretical imprecision indicated the scientists' lack of conceptual clarity. The last of the three terms also implied that there was some sort of racial "marker" particular to Jews rather than that some "racial characteristics" appeared with more frequency among Jews than non-Jews.

Whichever way the experts labeled the characteristics they were seeking to identify, they invariably faced the difficult question of just what those characteristics were. The only clear consensus was that they were "alien." This knowledge, however, was of limited assistance, and scientists were consequently left pretty much to their own devices. In a 1940 report on a middle-aged man, for example, Professor Reche observed that the examinee had curly hair and "curly hair is common with Jews!" Given the vast number of non-Jews with curly hair, and the large number of Jews with straight hair, it is not clear why Reche was excited about this. Nevertheless, he also provided a detailed description of the examinee's paternal grandparents' noses: the grandfather had a "very long, sharply bowed-out and, at the tip, under-bowed ridge, pronouncedly Jewish-like nose," while the grandmother also had "a nose which, in the way it protrudes, . . . in the build of the nostrils, and especially in the very strong curve of the lower edge of the nostrils, seems Jewish." Despite this, Reche noted that the examinee himself did not have a nose that "one could call a 'Jewish' or even a *Mischling* nose." Still, he claimed that the examinee's face, especially in "half-profile," had a definite "alien-type" appearance. Moreover, Reche claimed that the children of the examinee's sister had "more Jewish (or at least Jewish-like) characteristics than would be expected if they were only 'one-eighth Jews,'" implying that both of the examinee's paternal grandparents were probably Jews.[15] The highly subjective nature of Reche's determination of "alien" or "Jewish" characteristics is obvious: they were "alien" or "Jewish" because they looked "alien" or "Jewish" to him.

Occasionally, in making the racial determination, an expert also looked to the presence or absence of "Jewish mental characteristics." If anything, this process was an even more subjective endeavor. In a February 1942 report, for example, medical doctor and professor Theodor Mollison of the University of Munich's Anthropological Institute wrote that the examinee, a 28-year-old woman from Munich, "in the type of her manner and in her total behavior . . . makes an unmistakable Jewish impression. . . ."[16] He did not, however, specify what mannerisms and behaviors caused such impression. Similarly, in a December 1942 report, Prof. Dr. Hans Weinert of the University of Kiel's Anthropological Institute noted that, in contrast to the putative Jewish father's hasty and irascible nature, the examinee, a soldier, exhibited a quiet and cheerful nature.[17] However, Weinert did not state on what basis he had determined that haste and irascibility were particularly "Jewish" markers, and that quietness and cheerfulness were not.

The lack of standardized descriptions of "Jewish" or "alien" racial characteristics was not the only methodological problem in carrying out a "racial" investigation. There was also no consistent procedure for performing the check. The expert reports in the Genealogical Authority and Gau Kinship Office Vienna files range in length from two to twenty pages, exhibiting varying degrees of thoroughness. Some were made using comparison charts with detailed measurements while others were not. In order to justify a conclusion, some went into long treatises on topics as arcane as the racial composition of the Irish.[18] Others were simply perfunctory statements by the expert on the examinee's "racial composition." Dr. Pendl, for example, the Anthropological Expert for Hereditary and Racial Care at the Main Health and Social Office for the Gau Vienna municipal administration, routinely issued decisions consisting of little more than conclusory statements, such as that the examinee predominantly showed characteristic combinations of the "light and dark Eastern races," or was of the "Oriental and Near Eastern Races" with a small "Negro component."[19] Moreover, while Genealogical Authority officials themselves noted that "the evidentiary value of . . . anthropological investigations [based on photographs of a deceased putative father] cannot be seen as very high," some scientists, including Pendl, freely accepted such evidence.[20] Whether or not an expert considered an examinee's mental characteristics also appears to have been a decision based primarily on the expert's need to justify the conclusion. Nor was it clear just how the expert measured the mental characteristics. This lack of methodological consistency was in itself another powerful indication that the process was not "scientific." The occasional case in which full siblings received different racial diagnoses from different experts only highlighted the arbitrary nature of this portion of the biological examination.[21]

Despite the highly subjective nature of the racial examination, most of the experts seemed quite comfortable with their own ability to detect "alien or "Jewish" racial characteristics. In a report from 1941, for instance, Weinert claimed: "We can recognize a great many Jews as such."[22] Nonetheless many experts were also clearly aware that "Jews" frequently did not have "alien-type characteristics" (however defined) while "non-Jews" frequently did. In one case, for example, Dr. Pendl in Vienna noted that while "signs of alien-type blood mixture, in particular the Oriental–Near Eastern racial mix that is the essential distinguishing mark for the Jewish Volk, do not appear in [the examinee] . . . it is possible that [the alleged Jewish father] himself had no typical Jewish characteristics. . . ."[23]

This state of affairs could, of course, give the impression that the experts' finding of "alien" or "Jewish" racial characteristics had little probative value in determining whether any given individual had Jewish ancestry, or, in other words, that the racial examination was essentially worthless. In fact, Genealogical Authority officials were sometimes quite candid in this regard. A 1940 letter, for example, dealt with a case of two possible fathers, one Jewish and one "German-blooded," where only a poor picture of the Jewish man was available, and none of the "German." Authority official Eberhard Schircks wrote: "The inquiry must remain limited to a pure racial-scientific investigation of the examinee. However, according to experience, the results of such an investigation are rarely determinative in the decision in the process of establishing ancestry." And in his book on the ancestral proof process, Authority official Christian Ulrich Freiherr von Ulmenstein likewise wrote that "the assertion by others that someone appears 'typically Jewish' never suffices to require a hereditary and racial-scientific investigation" where the documentary evidence indicated no Jewish ancestry.[24]

The scientists usually dealt with this problem in one of two ways. Some simply refused to perform a biological investigation when it had to be limited to the "racial" portion.[25] Many others, however, used semantic acrobatics to obscure the dilemma. In an expert report from 1941, for instance, Weinert noted that the examinee, a low-ranking Nazi official, had no "Jewish characteristics." He then acknowledged the problem with the racial investigation, stating:

> An individual characteristic is not "Jewish" in so far as its occurrence is only to be found in Jews. The Jews are not a unified race. . . . Accordingly, a person who exhibits this or that "Jewish looking" characteristic cannot [automatically] be accused of having received that characteristic due to Jewish ancestry. He could always fall under the more or less large percentage of persons that have Jewish looking characteristics without being Jews.[26]

Yet, Weinert also claimed: "I have often already pointed out that persons who give no evidence of being 'Jewish' but come into question as Jews, hardly ever are full-Jews." He thus implied that the identification problem did not exist for "full-Jews." Similarly, in a 1942 report, Weinert again wrote that determining whether "an individual person was an Aryan or a half-Jew is always only conditionally possible" on the basis of "a pure racial-scientific evaluation," again implying that such an examination could differentiate between an "Aryan" and a "full-Jew."[27]

Such conceptual obfuscation took other forms as well. In his February 1942 investigation of Minni V. (see chapter 6), Professor Theodor Mollison wrote:

> The examinee's Jewish ancestry can in no way be excluded with high probability. Indeed, the individual features of the area around the eyes—the slight almond-shape of the lid-cleft, the highly-placed eyelids, the high upper-lid area—moreover the hanging nasal-septum, the plump lips, the receding chin, and not least the somewhat alien-type total impression caused by the face, alone do not force a finding of the examinee's Jewish ancestry.

In other words, based on her physical features, Minni may or may not have been Jewish. Mollison, however, overcame the fact that this determination was not helpful with a bit of rhetorical sleight-of-hand: "All the same," he continued, "no adequate ground exists to explain the combination of these type of features other than a Near Eastern–Oriental admixture. The posed questions are thus to be answered as follows: the examinee exhibits certain Jewish racial characteristics. . . ."[28] In other words, Mollison simply labeled the "alien impression" a "Near Eastern–Oriental admixture," which he then called "Jewish racial characteristics." The Genealogical Authority subsequently gave Minni an ancestral decision of "Jewess."[29]

In the case of the 23-year-old woman from Schwetzingen, for whom both the blood test and hereditary investigation proved inconclusive, the expert, Verschuer, did not hesitate to respond to the question of whether the examinee's "appearance displays racial characteristics that indicate a Jewish biological father." He answered that based on her individual and general physical and mental features, he could not exclude the possibility of a Jewish biological father. On the other hand, he also wrote that he would only accept that a "German-blooded" man was her biological father if that man shared hereditary characteristics with her that were not also present in the mother. Verschuer was thus saying that the examinee might well have "racial characteristics indicating a Jewish biological father," unless it could be shown that her father was not Jewish, in which case those characteristics would not indicate a Jewish father.[30] The same month, the Genealogical Authority declared that examinee a Jewish-*Mischling* First Degree.[31]

Such linguistic acrobatics were not always detrimental to an examinee. In a somewhat confused report in 1942, for example, physician Fred Dubitscher, acting director of the Berlin Polyclinic, wrote both that his examinee, a 46-year-old Heidelberg man, exhibited "no typically Jewish racial characteristics in [his] general physical characteristics" nor in his "mental behavior," but also that the man actually did have some "Jewish characteristics."[32] Even more strangely, but to the examinee's benefit, Dubitscher asserted that these Jewish characteristics were explicable as coming from the "genetic material" of the examinee's paternal grandmother, who was not alleged to be Jewish. In other words, Dubitscher was saying the man's "Jewish characteristics" came from a non-Jewish grandparent.

Similarly, in December 1942, Prof. Dr. Egon Freiherr von Eickstedt, of the University of Breslau's Anthropological Institute, commented on his subject, a 16-year-old boy from that city, whose "racial appearance" showed "swollen lids," "relatively thick nostrils," "thick lips [but] with slightly less thick lower lip," "receding chin," and "weak demeanor [*matte Blick*]." Eickstedt said that without the benefit of also examining the boy's mother and putative "Aryan" father, he would "not have been able to preclude a Jewish admixture with sufficient security." Nevertheless, Eickstedt decided on the basis of the hereditary portion of his exam that the Jewish legal father was very likely not the subject's biological father, as the Jewish man did not have the aforementioned "Jewish characteristics." Eickstedt explained this seeming paradox with a turn of phrase: the boy exhibited "pseudo-Jewish" characteristics arising out of the combination of the characteristics of his two Aryan parents.[33] The Genealogical Authority subsequently gave the boy an ancestral decision of "German or related blood." Whether, however, such verbal gymnastics helped or hurt an examinee, they were clearly an attempt to obfuscate the uselessness of the racial-scientific examination as a tool for identifying Jewish ancestry.

The experts did not limit such artful rhetoric to individual "racial-scientific" reports: it appeared in other forums as well. Some experts, like Professor Reche, served as primary apologists for the racial investigation. In September 1939, for instance, the Party Racial Policy Office's Information Service published his article "The Value of the Genetic Proof of Ancestry. An Official Position."[34] While the title of the article did not include the word *race,* its content made clear that the Racial Policy Office and the German Society for Racial Research had commissioned him to write this piece in order to challenge attitudes among legal officials against the racial investigation. Thus, before emphasizing the great role the process had to play in helping to enforce "racial-political and racial-hygienic legislation," Reche first noted the initial hostility that had existed only ten years before to the now widely accepted blood-group investigations that were used to help determine paternity. He thereby implied that the attempt to identify "Jews" by their "racial characteristics" was presently suffering from the same unjustified skepticism. At the least, such reasoning, which remained unquestioned, provided some intellectual "cover" for the scientists themselves.

Genealogical Authority officials were also sometimes prone to disingenuous descriptions of the value of the racial examination. A three-page Authority form, probably from 1935, entitled "Guidelines for the Proof of Aryan Ancestry through a Hereditary and Racial-scientific Examination," noted:

> Appearance alone cannot be used to establish with certainty whether someone is Aryan or non-Aryan. However, with a racial-scientific investigation going over several generations it is often possible to determine whether the person concerned is free

from foreign blood admixture (especially Negroid or Mongoloid) with a likelihood bordering on certainty.[35]

How this would help identify "Jewish blood," the primary "racial" concern, was not mentioned. Similarly, in his book on the ancestral proof, Genealogical Authority official Ulmenstein claimed that a pure racial investigation was of "special value" in the case where a legal Jewish grandparent was known to exist but where only a photograph of such person was available. In such a case, wrote Ulmenstein, all the living descendents would be investigated to see if "Jewish racial characteristics appeared."[36] In reality, however, Ulmenstein was simply describing the effort to see if the physical characteristics of the Jewish person appeared in the alleged descendents, and thus was referring to the hereditary portion of the biological investigation.

I saw only one instance in which someone actually spoke forthrightly in relation to the racial investigation. In July 1940, the Thuringian head of government (*Reichsstatthalter*), writing Genealogical Authority director Mayer regarding the "racial classification" of a particular examinee, expressed the view that an "an anthropological expert report" was of questionable use: "I have seen hundreds of extremely criminal full-Jews in the Buchenwald concentration camp by Weimar, who, for the most part, did not exhibit even a trace of anthropological Jewish characteristics. Frequently they were tall and blond and possessed a sharply defined 'Aryan' countenance." He also cited expert concurrence: "In the book *Jewish Villainism (Das jüdische Gaunertum)* by Herwig Hartner-Hnizdo, you can see numerous pictures of Jews that would in no way be anthropologically recognizable as Jews." This state of affairs, however, did not cause that high-ranking Nazi official to question the necessity of identifying "Jews." In instances in which there was even a question of Jewish parentage, he suggested that the examinee automatically be classified as a *Mischling,* as he maintained that "In those few cases in which the paternal father would actually not be a Jew, usually the so-called non-Jewish father is at least as bad if not worse than the Jews."[37]

Thus even a layman outside the official ancestral proof process was aware that racial-scientific investigations were virtually useless in determining Jewish ancestry. This uncertainty, however, did not seem to undermine that official's desire that "Jews" be identified and removed from society. Indeed, despite all of the methodological and theoretical flaws, which flew in the face of claims to scientific legitimacy, the men who carried out these biological investigations never overtly questioned the assumption that Jewish racial characteristics existed, or disputed the validity of the racial examination as a means of uncovering Jewish ancestry. Rather, they invariably acted as if they were performing a scientifically sound inquiry. This lent the entire Nazi racist enterprise an invaluable sheen of legitimacy. And the Genealogical Authority, for its part, routinely used the reports to make what often amounted to life-and-death decisions.

How does one explain the readiness of first-rate scientists to endorse as "scientific" a process that clearly was not? One obvious reason is that in many ways the

Nazi regime was very good for them. The endorsement of scientists was key to widespread acceptance of Nazi racial policy. Biological scientists were thus indispensable and were in a powerful position to gain prestige and resources.[38]

I did not attempt to determine how much profit, if any, accrued to the experts and their institutions specifically from performing biological investigations. In 1936, an Interior Ministry official estimated the average cost of such a probe to the examinee at RM 90, close to the average German worker's monthly income. In 1941, Ulmenstein stated that the average cost was between RM 30 and 250, but in the same year the Interior Ministry reported a price as high as RM 400.[39] Of the 169 Genealogical Authority files that I saw indicating the examinee's cost for a biological investigation—mostly from late 1939 and early 1940—the fees ranged from RM 5 (probably from either a partial bill or a subsidized procedure) to RM 604, with an average of about RM 91. While the investigations were thus certainly expensive from the examinee's perspective, in most cases, rather than being profitable for the scientists, they appear to have actually been concessions to a regime that generously supported the scientists in other ways.

Indeed, a number of scientists complained to the regime that the biological investigations were a burden to them. In November 1938, for example, Eugen Fischer, head of the Kaiser Wilhelm Institute for Anthropology, wrote the Interior Ministry that recently his organization had been receiving increasing numbers of requests for expert reports from the Genealogical Authority. Even more were to be expected. The high numbers, he claimed, constituted a "workload that cannot be maintained[.]" He added, "Despite hard work, fifty certifications remain incomplete. . . . [and] apart from these racial-certifications from the Genealogical Authority, . . . about the same number of paternity certifications from various courts also remain incomplete. . . ."[40] Other experts expressed similar sentiments.[41]

It is unlikely that these claims of being overburdened were a form of covert resistance to the process. In a letter to the Interior Ministry in November 1938, for example, Fischer expressed sorrow at the inability to accept further cases. He said he viewed the certification process as an important component of the "scientific education of our progeny," and had no desire to "discomfit" the Genealogical Authority with whom the Kaiser Wilhelm Institute for Anthropology worked "gladly and without any trouble." More telling than expressions of remorse, however, was the fact (implied by the tone of Fischer's letter) that almost invariably the scientists' requested relief for this lack of capacity was not for a reduction in the number of examinees, but for an increase in resources. Other scientists, however, were less coy. In 1940, for example, Reche complained to Dr. von Brescius, head of the Saxon Ministry for Volk Education, about the lack of qualified scientific personnel for this purpose, even though "it was certain to be expected that ever increasing numbers of courts would make use of the possibility [of using biological investigations]."[42] A letter in February 1939 from Prof. Dr. Lothar Loeffler, then director of the University of Vienna's Racial-Biological Institute, to the Curator of the Albertus University in

Königsberg was particularly aggressive. Loeffler warned that lack of resources for biological investigations could threaten the regime at its most vulnerable ideological point, the "scientifically proven" necessity to racially purify society. "[I]t is difficult to imagine," wrote Loeffler,

> the effect it will have on the further development of National Socialist jurisprudence, if the order is given that certifications may be made only in the rarest cases or only in those cases in which an official interest lies . . . the judges . . . will rebel . . . that it is an absurdity to claim for years the significance of race—including for jurisprudence—and then abandon the applicant [i.e., the judge] after he makes a legal finding on the basis of blood by stating that it is impossible to make the accompanying expert report.[43]

These scientists were clearly concerned with funding, not with the inherent worth of the racial investigation.

While social and material enrichment was obviously a factor in the scientists' compliance, it is probably insufficient in and of itself to explain the virtually complete absence of their criticism of the racial-scientific investigation in particular, and of Nazi racial policy in general. The evidence indicates that a variety of other factors also came into play. For one, the regime maintained significant control of the biological investigation process: governmental authorities determined who was qualified to perform it. In March 1936, for example, the Justice Ministry listed nine "especially suited" organizations: the Kaiser Wilhelm Institute for Anthropology, the Institute for Hereditary Health and Racial Care in Gießen, the Thuringia Provincial Office for Racial Studies in Weimar, as well as university institutes for anthropology, genetics, racial hygiene, racial biology, and racial science in Breslau, Frankfurt am Main, Hamburg, Leipzig, Königsberg, and Munich.[44] The Justice and Interior Ministries subsequently added additional authorities and institutions.[45] Even the doctors authorized to perform blood-group tests were regulated.[46] Such control may have led to the exclusion of scientists whom the authorities viewed as ideologically unreliable.

There may have been other forms of official control as well. In 1932, for example, the anthropologist Friedrich Keiter wrote an article critical of Hans F. K. Günther, a major advocate of racial supremacy, and a darling of the Nazi regime. In 1939, in what may have been an attempt to impose conformity on a recalcitrant scientist, the government forced Keiter to undergo his own racial analysis at the Kaiser Wilhelm Institute for Anthropology on the allegation that one of his grandparents was Jewish. This investigation, however, concluded that his maternal grandfather (a converted Jew) was not the real father of his mother. Keiter went on to be certified as an expert by the Interior Ministry and to become Director of the Racial Biological Institute in Würzburg in 1941–1942.[47]

Yet the Genealogical Authority files contain little evidence about the pressuring of scientists into conformity, if indeed that is what occurred in Keiter's case. In fact, there seems to have been no shortage of scientists willing to make racial-scientific investigations. Even "racial scientists" not certified by the Interior or Justice Ministries, both within and outside the Reich, regularly wrote expert reports on individuals' "racial composition."[48]

Another likely factor in the scientists' lack of criticism is that many simply felt affinity for racist thought. In 1925, for example, well before the Nazi assumption of power, professor and medical doctor Rudolf Polland, later director of the University Institute for Genetics and Racial Hygiene in Graz and a racial expert certified by the Interior Ministry, translated the German edition of the American Madison Grant's 1923 racist book *The Passing of the Great Race.* In his introduction to the translation, Polland warned that "racial degeneration also threatens our Volk in many forms," leading to a "cultureless racial chaos . . . diluting the blood of the noble races to ineffectiveness."[49] Similarly, the latter two of the three authors of the pre-Nazi Baur-Fischer-Lenz, the most important German anthropological work of its time, also later became certified racial experts. The Baur-Fischer-Lenz had embraced overtly racist sentiments, asserting that there were superior and inferior races and citing the dangers of racial mixing. It seems probable, then, that during the Nazi era at least some scientists were willing to endorse the scientifically questionable practice of identifying "Jews" by their "racial characteristics" in order to promote what they saw as the "greater good" to be gained from institutionalized racism.

Another plausible reason for many scientists' acceptance of the racial scientific investigation is that identifying individuals' "racial composition" comprised only a small portion of their work, making it easier for them to ignore their own disingenuousness in this regard. While there were exceptions (Dr. Pendl in Vienna, for example, routinely carried out pure racial investigations for the Gau Kinship Office Vienna), generally the "racial" section of the biological investigation report was no more than an addendum to the hereditary portion. Most experts thus submerged their "racial-scientific" work in more scientifically credible paternity investigations. Moreover, the direct search for Jewish and other "alien-type" ancestry was further isolated as biological investigations themselves seem to have constituted only a very small fraction of most experts' work. A six-page activity report for the Kaiser Wilhelm Institute for Anthropology for the period April 1935 through March 1936, for instance, contained only a single sentence referring to the "more than sixty expert reports on racial purity" done for the Genealogical Authority. The rest of the report detailed a large amount of work with a substantially stronger basis in traditional scientific methodology.[50] Similarly, experts' publications during the Nazi period also indicate that few devoted much time to the science of determining racial, much less "Jewish racial," characteristics. Scientists thus buried deadly nonsense within a plethora of legitimate and quasi-legitimate scientific activity, which made it easier to ignore.

Genealogists and the Ancestral Proof: A Windfall

> Now we who stand in noble service to the three fates and estab-
> lish and document the most important moments of existence of
> cultured men have strangely enough received rather little atten-
> tion and authority from our fellow-man.
> —*JOURNAL FOR CIVIL REGISTRY PRACTICE,* 1921 [51]

> Kinship research is essential for detecting racially foreign heredi-
> tary substance.
> —*FAMILIE, SIPPE, VOLK,* 1938 [52]

The importance of genealogy to the Nazi leadership was evident from the party's
earliest days. A 1920 article in its official newspaper stated:

> That each German family procures a family tree [*Stammbaum*] and ancestral table
> [*Ahnentafel*], if they still are not in possession of such, is also part of the care and
> renewal of the German soul. . . . The Germans must not come after dogs, horses, and
> cattle. Dogs and horses have family trees. Cattle are registered in herd books. This
> is the first condition to keeping the blood pure and will further yield a true Aryan
> foothold to the kinship group. [53]

In Nazi Germany, this significance became even more pronounced. Schools stressed
the central value of teaching children about genealogical research. [54] At the university
level, in 1938, Wilhelm Karl Prinz von Isenburg, a leading genealogist, became the
first Professor for Kinship and Family Research at the University of Munich. By 1943,
genealogical lectures and drills were provided at most German universities in the
faculties of philosophy, law, political science, and medicine. Many teacher-training
schools also taught such courses, and the prestigious Kaiser Wilhelm Society for scientific research established a genealogical division. [55] Journals on eugenics, such as *Volk
und Rasse,* were filled with articles on the use of genealogy to strengthen the German
Volk, while publishers released swelling numbers of books, pamphlets, and journals on the subject. [56] In 1937, the first "Village Kinship Book [*Dorfsippenbuch*]"—a
genealogical work showing the biological relationships between entire villages—was
published for the "*Ort Lauf* in Baden." [57] By 1938, such work was being undertaken
in three thousand parishes; between 1938 and 1940, thirty volumes were published. [58]
Genealogy's infiltration into German commercial life has already been discussed.
The fact that in March 1943 Ernst von d. Delsnitz became the first genealogist to be
awarded the Goethe Medal symbolized the newfound prestige of the practice. [59]

One reason for the importance of genealogy to the Nazis was, obviously, its
use as a tool for identifying the "racially alien." Contemporaries noted that after the
Nazi assumption of power, "genealogical research experienced a very strong increase"

due to the ancestral proof requirement.[60] But during the Third Reich, engagement in genealogy received impetus from other important sources as well. One was the desire to identify "racially acceptable" but "hereditarily ill" individuals. In order to provide for the "systematic cultivation of German genetic material," officials in Nazi Germany sought to create "extended family tables and card indexes" regarding persons' "genetic value." By demonstrating the existence of the same "disease" in other family members, the ancestral table helped officials determine genetic character for purposes of forced sterilization under the "Law for the Prevention of Hereditarily Ill Progeny."[61]

Genealogy was also particularly well suited for carrying out the regime's policy of stressing the underlying biological unity of the "German Volk." In 1939, for example, genealogist Erich Wentscher stated that he who traces his "blood and ancestors" is tracing his "homeland" and "thus proceeds simply and fundamentally like an animal secure in his own environment, connected to the soil that carries his being."[62] Similarly, articles in *Familie, Sippe, Volk* spoke of "homeland in the belonging of blood [*Heimat in der Blutszugehörigkeit*]" and seeing oneself "within the endless chain binding eternity with eternity."[63]

Probably the primary motivation for the use of genealogy to promote the idea of German biological unity during the Third Reich, as before, was the desire to defuse class conflict. Its sponsors intended that the recognition of common roots would advance a "racist egalitarianism" that would transcend economic and social class. Thus in Genealogical Authority director Mayer's March 1936 speech to civil registrars, he claimed that the Nazi state, with laws rooted in the "German *Volk* soul," provided legal security to all, not just to "certain classes" as had been the case in Weimar.[64] In a later article in the party journal *Ziel und Weg,* Mayer stated that one of the chief goals of the Genealogical Authority in the future would be to concentrate on raising the level of interest of workers in kinship research. "Once the worker is shown his own kinship group," Mayer wrote, "where he comes from, that he is not from a class that stands alone, but which is by blood an indivisible part of our entire *Volk,* then he will also no longer live separated from the greater community, but rather feel, from the blood, a part of the community of fate of the Germans."[65] Similarly, in his highly popular *Introduction to Practical Genealogy* (1939), Wentscher wrote that whoever comprehends the wonder of the ancestral table will recognize the "day laborer in the blood of the ruler and the ruler in the blood of the proletariat."[66] Books such as *Genealogical Research as a Guide to Volksgemeinschaft* (1935) embodied this function.[67] Even those prominent genealogists most hostile to the working class changed their tune during the Nazi era. Thus, for example, in the fifth edition of his *Pocketbook of Family History Research* (1937), another popular work, Friedrich Wecken no longer paid the bulk of his attention to the aristocracy, and removed previous derogatory comments about the working class.

The several proposed laws for creation of a central, independent genealogical authority were also partly legitimized as emphasizing the biological unity of the German *Volk.* In one memorandum supporting such a law (ca. 1934), the author argued that a *völkisch* state must be built upon the knowledge of the blood relationship of its members.[68] Similarly, the new Civil Registry Law of 1937 required creation of a "marriage and family book," with each new couple taking on a fresh page in the book. One purpose of this requirement was "to strengthen the sense of family in the individual, and the sense that he is a connected member in a long chain of generations." This, in turn, would "awaken the feeling of responsibility for the preservation of his generation and thus at the same time for the future of the German *Volk*."[69]

This conception of the value of genealogical practice was widespread throughout the Reich. An unpublished September 1943 essay by a genealogist in the Sudetenland, for example, entitled "Genealogy as a Means to Community Education," concluded: "We are all, as tribal members [*Stammesangehörige*], related to each other by blood, and as a *Volk* constitute a single, great, indivisible community of blood and fate."[70] In sum, genealogy was a powerful tool for promoting the vision not only of a racially pure, hereditarily healthy society, but also one untainted by class divisions.

Genealogy's status as an important component of Nazi ideology and policy proved to be a windfall for many involved in the practice. Anyone interested in the field, whatever their motivation, benefited in some way from the regime's interest: from increased literature on the subject, to greatly extended efforts to catalog church books, to accelerated development of the technological means to preserve documents.[71] There were also many additional individualized benefits. Because of the ancestral proof, for example, civil registrars not only gained power due to control of genealogical information, but also from their right to determine whether a "hindrance to marriage [*Ehehindernis*]" existed due to "race." It was not by chance that Interior Minister Frick's address to the 1934 convention of civil registrars and genealogists marked the first time that an active national minister had addressed such a gathering.[72] As previously shown, the commercialization and professionalization of genealogical practice also increased wealth and prestige.

Genealogists were not slow to comprehend the benefits the Nazi regime afforded them. The Genealogical Authority files contain both expressions of gratitude to the regime for finally giving genealogy its place in the sun, as well as a reveling in that status. A 1936 essay, for example, written by a Würzburg State Archive official began as follows:

> For decades, kinship research was science's Cinderella. While other branches of learning were represented by university chairs, and encouraged by the state, people dismissed us with a pitying laugh. That has now changed thanks to the regime of Adolf Hitler. Today, genealogy has tasks of state-level importance to fulfill.[73]

Similarly, in the 1939 edition of his *Introduction to Practical Genealogy*, Wentscher exulted that the practice had finally become a "true science [*Gestaltwissenschaft*]" in the nature of biology, psychology, and sociology. Others described civil registrars as the "carriers of the will of the National Socialist state," the "ruler[s] of the German kinship groups," and the "nourisher[s] of German blood."[74]

At least initially, however, relations between institutionalized genealogy and the Genealogical Authority were not entirely cordial. In early 1934, Lorenz, head of the Zentralstelle, Germany's largest genealogical society, balked at joining the Reich Association for Kinship Research and Heraldry, Authority director Gercke's new genealogical umbrella organization. The Herold, Germany's oldest genealogical society, also refused to join.[75] Yet the basis for this resistance seems to have been a personal dislike of Gercke and a reluctance to give up institutional autonomy, rather than distaste for Nazi ideology. Indeed, in early 1934, at the very time Lorenz was resisting joining the Reich Association, he also informed Gercke that the Zentralstelle had been reorganized on the "Führer principle," and that as a member of the National Socialist Party board of directors he had been named organization chair. Lorenz further noted that the head of the Collective Association for German History and Antiquity Societies, of which the Zentralstelle was a member, had since autumn 1933 been under the Nazi leadership of Prof. Dr. Willy Hoppe.[76] In any event, this conflict was short-lived. Kurt Mayer soon thereafter became head of the Herold, and then director of the Genealogical Authority. The Herold and Zentralstelle then both quickly joined Mayer's more loosely organized umbrella group, the Volk Federation of German Kinship Studies Societies.[77]

This may have been the only significant bump on the road to the Nazification of German genealogical societies. Like the Zentralstelle and Herold, during the course of the Third Reich many of Germany's most prominent genealogical societies became Nazified. At the end of 1933, for example, Karl Fahrenhorst, then an Authority official, became the leader, with Herold officer Peter von Gebhardt, of the Working Group for German Family and Heraldry Societies.[78] Such Nazification occurred, as well, in at least some "second-tier" genealogical societies. In 1942, for example, the general advisory council for the Westfalia Genealogical Federation (established about 1920) included representatives of the Racial Policy Office, the SS, a Nazi agricultural organization (*Landesbauernschaft*), and the Nazi Teachers' Federation.[79]

Indeed, whether officially "Nazified" or not, both institutional and personal compliance by genealogists with the Genealogical Authority in particular and with the state's new racist orientation in general seems to have been the rule. In March 1937, for example, Oswald Spohr, owner of the Degener publishing house, which specialized in genealogically related works, agreed to an Authority request to stop printing his *Suchblatt für Familienforscher* (*Search Sheet for Genealogists*), a monthly circular that included information requests for genealogical research. This allowed the Authority to begin issuing its own replacement, the *General Search Sheet for Kinship Researchers*.[80] Prominent publishers of similar works also actively cooperated with the Authority. In January 1936, the Starke firm in Gorlitz allowed the Authority-controlled *Volk* Federation to take over its broadsheet *Practical Research Help*. The Alfred Metzner firm began publishing the Authority's *General Search Sheet*. And the civil registrars' publishing house became the first publisher of the Authority journal *Familie*,

Sippe, Volk, which initially appeared as an addendum to the civil registrars' own *Journal for Civil Registry Practice.*

General racist works also began appearing in genealogical publishers' catalogs. The title page to Starke's 1937 catalog, for example, added "Racial Studies [*Rassenkunde*]" to the earlier "Genealogy [*Sippenkunde*]" and "Heraldry [*Wappenkunde*]." The Alfred Metzner publishing house, too, began releasing new numbers of racist works.[81] The Zentralstelle also started publishing such books as *Family Studies and Racial Care,* which came with an introduction by Genealogical Authority director Mayer.[82] Further, while genealogical journals had already published lists of baptized Jews prior to 1933, this practice accelerated in the Third Reich. In 1937, for example, four articles in the Zentralstelle's journal *Family History Gazette* sought to elucidate the Jewish origins of nominally Christian families. In 1938, twelve articles did this, with two additional articles on Turks and one on Tatars. Another racist practice that began in genealogical journals after 1933 was the placing of index entries on Jews under the heading "Biology," thus supporting the Nazi assertion that "Jew" was a biological designation. This happened, for instance, in the *Family History Bibliography* in 1935, and the *Family History Gazette* in 1937. Other institutions involved in genealogical research, such as the German Foreign Institute's Main Office for Kinship Studies of Germans Abroad, in Stuttgart, assisted in carrying out Nazi racial policy by helping the Authority find documents regarding examinees' ancestors who lived outside of Germany.[83]

Many individual genealogists, both prominent and obscure, were likewise overtly willing to support the regime's racist policies. The role of professional genealogists in helping individuals make their ancestral proof has already been shown. But genealogists also assisted in the process in a variety of other ways. Many wrote works supporting it either directly or in its ideological underpinnings. As early as 1934, for example, Friedrich Wecken, already well known in the pre-Nazi period, published a work about using genealogical tables to prove one's "Aryan" ancestry. In a 1938 *Familie, Sippe, Volk* article, Wilfrid Euler gave detailed examples of Jewish converts whose descendants had married other persons with Jewish ancestry. This proved, wrote Euler, "that the blood and blood-related connections are stronger than the serious will to racial adaptation." In his *Sippenfibel,* Friedrich Hayn wrote: "As a consequence of the insights of genetics and racial science, we prohibit any mixture with Jewish and colored blood."[84] Less-eminent genealogists also wrote works promoting enforcement of racial policy.[85]

Genealogists frequently also donated, or at least offered to donate, their services in support of "racial purity" measures. As of January 1935, about ten members of the national genealogical association German Ancestral Community were voluntarily working in the Genealogical Authority's data division. Likewise, Hans von Bourcy, a professional genealogist in Vienna, volunteered his expertise to the Authority's local counterpart, the Gau Kinship Office Vienna. Genealogists also made suggestions for new and better ways to enforce racial policy. In a 1940 letter to the Education Ministry, for example, a self-described "kinship researcher" advocated the "founding of a private institute for study of German and similar names" to work in conjunction with university "racial-biological institutes."[86] Other genealogists actively sought to discover and report to the Genealogical Authority those responsible for falsification of documents, asked for jobs in the "racial enforcement field," or reported that their client was trying to disguise Jewish ancestry.[87]

The required applications for genealogical permits and "activity reports" to the Authority are a particularly rich source. These show evidence of numerous "ordinary genealogists" voluntarily assisting, or offering to assist, in the ancestral proof process. By way of example, a bookseller in Bautzen, Saxony, declared himself knowledgeable about "genealogy, racial questions and eugenics," and was ready "to place his abilities at the service of the state genealogical authority"; an unemployed Berlin man informed the Genealogical Authority that he was working on the "proof of Aryan ancestry" for two others; a Hamburg attorney noted that his chief research interest was "Jewish blood in Hamburg families"; a teacher from Silesia reported that his voluntary work for the civil registry kept him so busy working on soldiers' "ancestral relations" that he had no time for his personal research; the personnel office in Gau Berlin wrote that a permit holder, an engineer by profession, was working on "about three hundred Aryan proofs for political leaders in the local party district"; and an office worker in Merseburg sent the Authority a list of eight Jewish and one "Turkish" baptisms gleaned during his "research activities."[88] "I will continue to strive," wrote the latter, "to track down the marriages as well as the children and children's children of these baptized Jews."

Other permit applicants or holders expressed their approval of the regime's racial policies in other ways. In 1933, a university student in Chemnitz noted in her research permit application that she was an assistant to a professor of genetics. As such, she declared that she "helps find camouflaged Jews and descendants [*Stämmlinge*] of Jews in order to keep German blood pure."[89] Furthermore, while many permit holders did not overtly support racist policy, they nonetheless regularly reported on problems found in church books. These reports served to increase the efficiency in which genealogical research could be done and thus the efficiency with which "racially alien" persons could be identified.

However, the foregoing examples of enthusiasm for Nazi racial policy seem to represent the attitude of only a minority of those who received a Genealogical Authority permit. I looked at approximately 170 randomly chosen files of persons seeking such permits between 1934 and 1944. Only about 20 percent of them (36) indicated clearly in the application and/or correspondence that the permit seeker or holder was interested in assisting in the enforcement of racial policy. While some reasons for permit applications were ambiguous in this regard (e.g., to work on the organization of church books), the single most common reason was to research one's own family history.

On the other hand, racism was clearly endemic within genealogical practice in the Third Reich. No one doing such research could have had any doubt that the field constituted the primary tool for implementing the ancestral proof, and thus for supporting racist policies. Moreover, both of the national genealogical umbrella organizations—the Reich Association for Kinship Research and Heraldry, and the Volk Federation of German Kinship Studies Societies—had so-called "Aryan paragraphs." This meant that their members had to make an ancestral proof. By the late-1930s, virtually every genealogical society of note was a Volk Federation member.[90] Many regional genealogical societies and even some family groups also added "Aryan paragraphs" to their own membership qualifications.[91] Furthermore, every applicant for a genealogical research permit also had to sign a declaration that he or she was free from Jewish or other undesirable "racial admixture" and had to submit an ancestral table to verify it. Even to assist the Reich Institute for the History of the New Germany in its research efforts, interested persons needed to provide not only information regarding their expertise, but also an ancestral proof.[92] Yet the Genealogical Authority files evidence no discomfort by any genealogical practitioner with regard to the ancestral proof requirement in general, the particular institutionalization of racism in their field, or the use of the practice to support racist policies.

Whatever the reason for such failure to question racial policy, it was not because of a generalized fear of expressing dissatisfaction. To the contrary, the same files indicate that genealogists frequently complained to the Authority about a variety of subjects. They most frequently criticized a pastoral office, civil registrar, or regional kinship office for not sending requested documents or for sending them too slowly.[93] But they also remonstrated about the cost of research or certification fees; complained about the inefficient process for certifying an Ahnenpass; worried that a client was not paying; lamented the lack of access to church books (or noted their poor condition); griped that requested documents were in a foreign language; or even complained about the use of "uneducated women" in pastoral offices.[94] Indeed, in a rather unique complaint, in 1943 the professional genealogist Karl Unger, a retired administrative director in Berlin, grumbled that the Gestapo was repeatedly calling him in for questioning because they did not realize that his "collecting of Jewish documents . . . lay in the interest of the authorities and was not a 'representation of Jewish interests.'"[95] Again, however, none of this griping related to any aspect of racist ideology.

The Churches and the Ancestral Proof: Struggle for Control

> God created the races . . . that possession entrusted to us to improve
> and to pass on.
> —ACHIM GERCKE, 1933 [96]

At the Nazi assumption of power, Germany was divided into approximately 20,400 Protestant communal districts (*Kirchengemeinde*) and 9,900 Catholic parishes.[97] Most of these administrative districts had church books. These books recorded births, baptisms, marriages, deaths, and other genealogical information, and often dated back hundreds of years. Indeed church books constituted the primary repository of such data prior to 1875, the year the state civil registries were created. Thus, both churches controlled huge amounts of information of fundamental importance to the ancestral proof process.

Genealogical Authority documents verify this significance. The Authority was constantly corresponding with pastoral offices about the gathering, organizing, and evaluating of church books, as well as about obtaining genealogical information from them. Moreover, Authority files contain copies of, and Authority journals discuss, the numerous regulations issued by church authorities on the provision of such information. There was also much correspondence to the agency from other organizations and individuals about obtaining genealogical information from the churches. Finally, books, pamphlets, and articles on the ancestral proof also detail the fundamental consequence of church books in this process.

From the perspective of the leadership of both churches, the ancestral proof seems to have been a mixed blessing. On the one hand, control of the books gave churches a great deal of power within the state and the populace. They also constituted a large potential source of revenue. On the other hand, the churches and government authorities at times engaged in bitter conflict over control of these documents. Moreover, the potential income sometimes turned out to be a chimera, given the huge amount of work that the provision of genealogical data placed on the pastoral offices. This led to further conflict between church and state. Yet with regard to the ideology underlying the ancestral proof, racist eugenics, and to the related policy, both churches were essentially compliant.

Many of the Genealogical Authority documents dealing with church relations reveal ongoing dissatisfaction by the Authority, other governmental entities, and individuals, regarding not only the churches' care and control of the church books, but also relating to their inadequate provision of genealogical information. At least one historian has specifically noted that Protestant pastors sometimes refused to cooperate with Authority requests for parish registers.[98] This evidence could indicate covert church opposition to racism. Nevertheless, while individual motivation is extremely hard, and often impossible, to ascertain, a host of congruent factors support the view that problems relating to control of church books and church provision of genealogical information were, in most cases, not related to a disapproval of racist policies.

Most basically, the Genealogical Authority files show massive cooperation by both churches in the ancestral proof process. Throughout the Nazi period, the Authority, other institutions, and countless individuals asked for, and received, huge amounts of genealogical information from pastoral offices all over the Reich. Moreover, in addition to such large-scale church acquiescence, the Authority files show that many individual churchmen and church organizations went beyond the call of duty, providing more than just the basic genealogical information requested. Frequently, the pastoral offices provided this information on specially printed form documents stating "valid only for official use in the proof of Aryan ancestry." Moreover, church publishing houses printed "how-to" books for clergymen and church-book managers on providing documents for the ancestral proof.[99] Both activities indicated the institutionalization of and acquiescence in this racist enterprise. Church officials also frequently wrote to the Authority, asking it to help individual parishioners make the ancestral proof. Some pastors even recommended particular professional genealogists to assist their parishioners in the process.[100] These activities showed both the churches' familiarity with the ancestral proof obligation and the desire to see it properly implemented. And, although the Authority's attempt to gather church books was more often than not a point of friction, at least a few pastors voluntarily helped in this as well. Karl Themel, a leader of the German Christians, the Nazified movement within the Lutheran church, is one prominent example.[101]

Additionally, files from the Genealogical Authority show that the churches' leadership exerted pressure on the regime, not to force it to retreat from racist policy, but rather to lighten the related manpower pressure on the churches, or to increase church benefits from such policy. In 1935, for instance, responding to urging from church organizations to relieve the "burden on the church-book managers," the Interior Ministry allowed churches to charge a fee for each genealogical document they provided, even if it was only a copy of a previously furnished document. Later that year, it also raised the fee that the churches could charge for each document.[102] An Authority memorandum from January 1938 noted just how lucrative the provision of genealogical information could be for church officials. It complained that a sexton in Brandenburg was earning RM 250–300 per month selling genealogical information, but was doing nothing to organize or repair the church books, a case it cited as "typical." "It is therefore understandable," continued the memo, "if . . . church communities today place great value on retaining [for themselves] the work for the ancestral proof."[103] Correspondence from individual pastoral offices also supports the view that the monetary aspects of information provision were of great concern to them.[104]

While this evidence shows active participation by the churches in the ancestral proof process, and thus exhibits tacit approval of racist policies, at least some of the leadership of both churches *overtly* embraced such ideas. In 1934, for instance, Cardinal Michael von Faulhaber, Archbishop of Munich and Freising, wrote "there is no objection whatever to racial research and race culture," although "love of one's race should not lead to the hatred of other nations."[105] Similarly, an Evangelical Christian pamphlet, written in 1936, spoke out against "racial faith [*Rassenglauben*]," which it defined as "deification of race," but nevertheless accepted the idea of different races, each with "its naturally given character." It then declared: "We therefore understand our Volk's struggle to maintain the purity and health of its type and support it wholeheartedly."[106] A detailed guide for evangelical church workers in 1937 explained the fees that could be charged for the provision of genealogical information, noting that "[i]n view of the exceptional importance of the ancestral proof for the population-policy measures of the state as well as for the individual, it is the duty of the church-book offices and the ministers to carry out the investigation with the greatest feeling of responsibility." Specifically noted was the fact that agreement on this issue had been reached between the Genealogical Authority and "the highest authorities of both churches."[107]

This acceptance of racism was also reflected at the level of the individual pastoral office. The church-book office in Belleben, for example, a small town about thirty kilometers from Halle, printed a flyer containing parish news to accompany the provision of genealogical information. It began: "To our 'Aryans'!"[108] Even outspoken church opponents of the mistreatment of Jews did not dispute the allegation that Jews were racially different from "Germans," and thus comprised a hereditary threat. In 1936, for example, Cardinal Theodor Innitzer, the Archbishop of Vienna, condemned the denial to Jews of the "most elementary natural rights." He nevertheless stated that "[w]e will not be blind to [the need] for certain necessities [in regard to the Jews]."[109]

Other evidence also indicates the churches' comfort with racist eugenic ideas. While it is difficult to make an argument from silence, the Genealogical Authority files nevertheless show overt church hostility to other aspects of National Socialist policy and ideology, such as mass sterilization, euthanasia, and neopaganism. If there was also a hidden wellspring of church resistance to scientific-racist ideology, it seems likely that some evidence of this would, at some point, also have bubbled into the open. This simply does not occur in the Authority files. There is no indication, for example, of church discomfort on either an individual or institutional level with the Ministry for Church Affairs' 1938 order that church workers note all indications of Jewish ancestry that they encounter.[110] To the contrary, Authority files show various church officials voluntarily providing lists of baptized Jews, thus helping to identify their descendants.[111]

Moreover, while the churches for the most part remained silent regarding racist ideology, there was no shortage of confrontation between the churches and the government relating to other aspects of the ancestral proof process, especially regarding document provision and control of church books. These conflicts, if anything, further the view that the churches were comfortable with racist eugenics per se. One such area of friction revolved around some church authorities' professed reluctance to release documents containing embarrassing information, such as indications of illegitimacy, for fear they might be used for "family espionage," namely blackmail or humiliation. The Genealogical Authority took the position that such cases were so rare, and the need to prove ancestry so pressing, that these documents should as a rule be provided to persons requesting them.[112] Nevertheless, in 1940, the Reich Justice and Church Ministries jointly issued a decree designed to keep embarrassing facts regarding paternity from being made public. This indicates that the government officials viewed the churches' claim as having been made in good faith, not as veiled resistance to the ancestral proof.[113] Moreover, the only Authority correspondence I saw regarding this area of contention further supports this view. In 1941, a professional genealogist in Wolfenbüttel complained that, because he did not provide a release from the family in question, the Evangelical Lutheran pastoral office in Kindelbrück, Thuringia refused him a "church-book extract" for a relative born in 1732. When the *Landeskirchenamt* (provincial church administration) in Hanover defended this refusal as an effort to prevent "family espionage," the Authority countered that there can be no such thing regarding persons born more than two hundred years ago.[114] The Authority's Gerhard Kayser, the head of the Evangelical Church's Archive Hosemann, and a high church official (*Oberlandskirchenrat*) by the name of Dr. Lampe subsequently met to resolve this problem, but reached no decision. Yet the church representatives did agree that the Genealogical Authority would get all "Jew registers from Baden, and copies of all church-book pages dealing with Jews."[115] Clearly, in this case the church's concern was not to defend the "racially alien" from detection, but to protect "Aryans" from humiliation.

Frequently, in reply to document requests, pastoral offices claimed that they had no information, or sent incorrect information. These responses constituted a major source of complaints to the Genealogical Authority. The follow-up to such criticisms, however, also gives no indication that these problems were related to any church hostility to racism. In 1937, for example, when a Berlin engineer protested to the German Evangelical Church Chancellery that a pastor in the tiny town of Himmelpfort gave him incorrect information, causing him needless research and expense, the church office passed on the complaint to the Authority, which investigated.[116] The pastor in question responded that for more than three years, his wife had been responsible for addressing requests dealing with "Aryan ancestry" and that she did the best she could given the poor condition of the church books in question. This seems to have been a sufficient explanation. Similarly, when a professional genealogist in Kaukehmen, East Prussia, complained in 1938 about service from a particular pastoral office, the Evangelical Consistory in Königsberg took the offensive. Citing an article in the SS newspaper *The Black Corp (Das Schwarze Korp)* entitled "Expensive Genealogical Research," which criticized price gouging by professional genealogists, the Consistory alleged that the complaining genealogist did just this. The upshot, however, was that after the Consistory intervened, the genealogist received his document.[117]

Occasionally, a genealogist would allege that such provision problems were due to intentional lack of cooperation. In 1937, for instance, and again in 1941, a professional genealogist in Berlin complained that a Catholic and Evangelical pastoral office, respectively, were engaged in active "obstruction" by providing false information from church books. Similarly, in 1938, another professional genealogist in Baden-Baden complained that the civil registry was not certifying an Ahnenpass, and that this action constituted "a type of opposition to the rules" that he attributed to the fact that one of the civil registrars was a "good Catholic," while the other "was alleged to be a Freemason."[118] The files contain no information on the Genealogical Authority's response to these particular complaints. But the rarity of assertions of intentional noncompliance itself supports an understanding of general church cooperation.

Indeed, Authority officials themselves almost never understood a pastoral office's failure to provide documents as constituting veiled resistance to the ancestral proof process. Rather, they attributed this failure to other factors: their own request to the wrong parish office; lost or damaged church books; understaffing of the parish offices; laziness or indifference on the part of individual clergymen; or, at worst, a challenge to government control of such material. Indeed, the Authority files contain numerous Authority responses *defending* the churches against complaints from organizations and individuals regarding failure to provide documents.[119] This defense of the churches must also be viewed in light of the fact that at least some Authority officials were aware of and worried about the potential for church hostility to racist ideology. An Authority memorandum from January 1938, for example, claims that "the greatest portion of the church-book officials reject race notions," citing the difficulty in obtaining information.[120] Yet this concern appears in the last paragraph of an eight-page memo, the bulk of which concerns the churches' attempts to keep control of their books in order to reap the fees for provision of genealogical information for the ancestral proof. This would indicate that, to the contrary, the churches were not uncomfortable with racist thought. Moreover, this was the only instance I came across of such an allegation.

In reality, the accusation of church hostility to racism was probably wishful thinking on the part of a Genealogical Authority official. The Authority was constantly looking for information that would weaken the churches and thus their control over the church books. The foregoing Authority memorandum from January 1938 advised use of "combat measures" in this regard. Another Authority memorandum, from November of that year, described an effort between it and the SS to obtain material "on negligent and maliciously erroneous distribution of documents for the ancestral proof by the churches." As a result of this joint project, however, only eight cases were noted in the five and a half years since the ancestral proof process had begun. Moreover, only four of these cases directly indicated intent by a pastor or priest to hide Jewish ancestry in a genealogical document.[121]

The Genealogical Authority files document only one case (to my knowledge) in which any church authorities openly refused to provide it with documents for purposes of the ancestral proof. This occurred in 1938, under orders of the Evangelical Lutheran *Landeskirchenamt* in Kiel. Because of its singularity in this respect, and broad applicability in another—revolving as it did around the highly contested area of church-book control—it bears a detailed analysis.

In 1934, as a precursor to the creation of a planned Kreis Kinship Office (Genealogical Authority regional office), the Authority and the *Landeskirchenamt* in Kiel worked together to create an interim institution, a so-called *Sippenkanzlei,* in the towns of Heide and Bredstedt in the north German state of Schleswig-Holstein.

Duplicates of all regional church books were to be centralized in this Authority-controlled office for the purpose of providing information for the ancestral proof. Initially, church-state relations appear to have been cordial in this project. A *Landeskirchenamt* circular from December 1934, for example, commented that the foreseen Kreis Kinship Offices were necessary for the "distribution of documents for the proof of Aryan ancestry," and that these could only be created

> with the cooperation of the church authorities, which must put the church books, which are [the churches'] property, at [the civil authorities'] disposal. It is obvious that the church authorities most willingly place themselves at the disposal of these plans since, through the advancement of race and family research of the *Volk,* an important service is performed that will be meaningful for all the future.[122]

This *Landeskirchenamt* was openly embracing racist thought less than two years after the Nazis assumed power.

Nevertheless, not long afterwards, beginning in fall 1935, individual parish offices in Schleswig-Holstein began complaining about the two *Sippenkanzlei.* The basis of this hostility is revealed in later documents. A Genealogical Authority report to the Interior Ministry from May 1937 noted that a leading local pastor had claimed that the *Sippenkanzlei* in Heide and Bredstedt had violated the guidelines for filming church books and were furthermore "anti-Christian [*anti-christliche*]." Later complaints from fall 1937 maintained that the *Sippenkanzlei* did not return the church books that they had taken for copying or properly share the fees they received for documents with the local parish offices, and claimed that the head of the *Sippenkanzlei* in Heide did not belong to a "religious community." According to another report, at a meeting of the Workgroup for Landeskirche Archivists in Wittenberg in September 1937, a pastor had claimed that the *Sippenkanzlei* in Heide and Bredstedt were "nonentities" who should have no part in the organization of the church books. Moreover, all meeting participants agreed that the photocopying should be done by the churches, that other methods for organizing the church books were superior to those of the Genealogical Authority, and that there was abuse of the rules for obtaining cost-free copies of extracts, especially by "individual party-formations."

The heads of the two *Sippenkanzlei* in Schleswig-Holstein had their own set of complaints against the church, usually involving money. In the fall of 1935, the *Landeskirchenamt* in Kiel had begun asking for 15 percent of all fees coming into the *Sippenkanzlei,* apparently something never requested by any other *Landeskirchenamt.* Further, in a May 1937 letter to the Genealogical Authority, the head of the *Sippenkanzlei* in Heide protested that despite an April decree of the national Church Affairs Ministry, the local parish offices were not forwarding most genealogical inquiries to the *Sippenkanzlei.* Rather, they were attending to them on their own and collecting all the fees. The only inquiries forwarded, according to the *Sippenkanzlei,* were those that had to be provided at no charge. A letter of complaint from early 1938 summarized the view of the *Sippenkanzlei:* "these days the church authorities place the greatest value on retaining the arrangements for the ancestral proof. They see the possibility for financial gain in this. . . ."

Despite this conflict, both state and church seem to have sincerely tried to iron out their differences. In mid-December 1936, for example, a Genealogical Authority representative had met with officials from Schleswig-Holstein to discuss possible resolutions. Moreover, participants in the aforementioned *Landeskirche* archivists meeting in Wittenberg, despite their fiery rhetoric, also called for an end to friction and closer collaboration with state authorities. All eighteen of the participants who represented *Landeskirche* archives throughout the Reich expressed the "unanimous wish, that an organization of the church books be carried out (especially in regard to those related to the ancestral proof) with all emphasis . . . ," indicating that racist policy in itself was more than acceptable. Likewise, in October 1937, in another effort to settle differences, a joint meeting took place in the Interior Ministry between representatives of the Church Affairs Ministry, the Genealogical Authority, the Evangelical Church, and Hans Globke, a high-ranking Interior Ministry official. These joint efforts at reconciliation further indicate that the Evangelical Church authorities had no problem with the ancestral proof per se. None of these meetings, however, led to any resolution in Schleswig-Holstein.

The situation there came to a head in fall 1937. In October, the *Landeskirchenamt* in Kiel issued an order creating so-called provost church-book offices [*Propstei Kirchenbuchämter*] and proclaiming that the "handling of the work linked to the proof of German-bloodedness and kinship research is, as a matter of principle, the task of the provost church-book offices for the territory of their provost." It also ordered the parish administrators to forward, absent certain specific conditions, all inquiries related to the "proof of German-bloodedness" to a provost church-book office, and also to provide that office with copies of their church books. This order constituted a direct attack on the competencies of the *Sippenkanzlei*. In December 1937, the *Landeskirchenamt* in Kiel also ordered its own equipment for photocopying its church books. The Genealogical Authority complained that this, too, violated the rights of the *Sippenkanzlei*.

In order to sell this attempted usurpation of the *Sippenkanzlei's* functions to state authorities, church leaders argued that the change would lead to a more efficient organization of the church books and thus more effective provision of documents for the ancestral proof. This pitch did not work, however, and hostilities increased further. In late 1937 or early 1938, church administrators in the town of Eddelak filed a lawsuit against the head of the *Sippenkanzlei* in Heide for the return of two church books. In January 1938, Authority director Mayer complained to the Church Affairs Ministry that a genealogist with an Authority permit had been refused permission to look at the provost church-book office in Altona.

Finally, in the spring of 1938, a full "revolt" occurred. In May, *Sippenkanzlei* Heide reported to the Genealogical Authority that after a conference of pastors on the ninth of that month, local parish offices were no longer providing it with documents for the ancestral proof, causing it a loss of about RM 350 in that month alone. Moreover, the chief pastor's office in Heide would no longer stamp documents from the *Sippenkanzlei* with the church seal. *Sippenkanzlei* Bredstedt reported the same situation. A report of August 1938 to the Authority quoted the June newsletter of the local church administrators in the town of Hemme, which stated: "It is drawn to your attention that the documents for the proof of Aryan ancestry in Dithmarschen are now issued from the pastoral offices. The documents from the *Sippenkanzlei* in Heide have no legal validity since they bear no church seal and no church office signature." This report included similar statements from other local pastors.

Nazi authorities besides the Genealogical Authority were aware of what was happening in Schleswig-Holstein. None, however, viewed this Church recalcitrance as an attack on the ancestral proof process itself. When, for example, in early 1938 the Authority asked Dr. Kinder of the *Landeskirchenamt* to put pressure on the Eddelak administrators to withdraw their lawsuit, Kinder responded that the staff of the Office of Hitler's Deputy for Party Affairs in Munich—the highest party authorities—were aware of, and did not disapprove of, the suit. In October 1938, a local representative of the Propaganda Ministry, in a letter to the Interior Ministry, noted that church administrators in Schleswig-Holstein claimed that documents from the *Sippenkanzlei* were invalid, and simply asked for clarification in this regard. Indeed, in November 1938, someone from the Authority spoke with the deputy *Gauleiter* (head of the party administrative district) in Kiel to discuss whether the head of the *Sippenkanzlei* Heide should be removed.

While the documents are not clear regarding the subsequent course of events, the factions did eventually reach a modus vivendi. By November 1940, the Genealogical Authority reported to the Church Affairs Ministry that most of the differences between the local pastoral offices and the *Sippenkanzlei* had been resolved and that "the pastoral offices now increasingly deliver the requests that come to them to the *Sippenkanzlei*. . . . With this . . . it is to be reckoned that the changed attitude of the *Landeskirchenamt* gradually had a positive effect on the still somewhat resistant church-book managers." Thus, in the one case that I found of open refusal to provide documents to the Authority for the ancestral proof, this resistance clearly had nothing to do with hostility to the requirement itself. To the contrary, it appears to have been primarily the culmination of several years of conflict between heads of the local *Sippenkanzlei* and church authorities regarding responsibility for provision of cost-free genealogical information, as well as for primary control of the church books from which that information came. Rather than evidencing discomfort with racist policy, this story shows a church leadership comfortable enough with its position in the National Socialist state that it was willing openly to confront both the Interior Ministry and party organs in an effort to reap greater benefits from the ancestral proof requirement. Clearly, no one in the party perceived this as an attack on racist thought. Indeed, this challenge was launched with the full knowledge of the highest party authorities. The *Landeskirchenamt* in Kiel seems to have differed from the other church bodies vis-à-vis the ancestral proof requirement primarily in the degree to which it was willing to exert its own interests, which it apparently did not perceive as being impinged upon by racist ideology.[123]

8 | Other Means of Generating Acceptance of Racism

THE PRIMARY MEANS BY WHICH PROPONENTS OF RACIST POLICES in Nazi Germany made their ideas more palatable both to themselves and to other Germans was through racial-scientific ideology. Especially during the Third Reich, however, another important mechanism in generating acceptance for such policies, and for racial scientific ideology itself, was through a process of "familiarization." A state-mandated search for "racially alien" persons was something new to the Nazi era. But proponents of the ancestral proof process claimed a historical pedigree and created an institutional apparatus that they maintained had significant continuity with German history and culture. To a significant degree, this was true. Such constancy helped reduce any feelings of disjunction caused by racial policy, and reinforced the perception that the programs were "necessary" and "normal." Legal and genealogical-practice continuities also helped make institutionalized racism more agreeable to many Germans. For those uncomfortable with racism, those various nonracist social and cultural connections provided an opportunity to divert their attention elsewhere. Likewise, the complexity of the ancestral proof process allowed its administrators to concentrate on procedure, rather than on the idea underlying it. Finally, during the Nazi era, every major institution in Germany—academic, legal, governmental, and religious—cross-reinforced positive reception of the ancestral proof requirement: acceptance by one helped legitimize acceptance by the others.

Historical Continuities, Real and Imagined

> True nobility is grounded in the blood.
> —*THE GERMAN ROLAND*, 1925[1]

As the ancestral proof sought to reveal people with Jewish, "Gypsy," and other ostensibly "non-European" ancestry, it tied into long traditions of "nonscientific" xenophobia. The general European history of describing and treating Jews as essentially different from non-Jews, usually to the Jews' detriment, extends back to the Middle Ages. To some degree, this history of anti-Jewish (as well as anti-"Gypsy," anti-Slav, and anti-Black) sentiment also made the idea of seeking out and separating the "racially alien" more familiar, and thus more easily accepted: it made it easier to view persons so labeled as being somehow fundamentally different from, and inferior to, a "real German."[2]

Despite the ancestral proof's "scientific" rationalization, these traditions of contempt naturally enough also appeared in various aspects of the process. In 1937, the professional genealogist Hans von Bourcy, in Vienna, complaining in a letter to Genealogical Authority director Kurt Mayer about some of his clients' refusals to pay, closed with the seemingly unrelated "deduction" that the "big Jews must already be effectuating their black-market activities."[3] Moreover, despite the usually dispassionate language that Authority officials used in ancestral decisions, occasionally indications of loathing for Jews also crept in. Thus, in holding an examinee to be a "Jew" despite the man's claim that his true father was a "Prussian officer" with whom his mother once had sex, Mayer not only gave several reasons why he believed that this was untrue, but also asserted that the examinee's claim amounted to a smear on the Prussian Officer Corps. Without further information "regarding the person of the asserted, illegitimate father and his ancestry," wrote Mayer, "and the place, time, surroundings, and individual circumstances of the conception, the examinee must remain what he has been his entire life, namely a J-e-w."[4] Similarly, while the hereditary portion of a biological examination as opposed to the "racial-scientific" portion of the exam did not enter into the presence or absence of Jewish characteristics, antisemitism sometimes crept in. In their reports, for instance, scientists frequently labeled one putative father "the Jew."[5]

Actual continuity with traditional hatreds aside, proponents of the ancestral proof also expressly claimed historical constancy for various elements of institutionalized racism. Genealogical journals, for example, highlighted alleged early assertions of "racial" differences between "Jews" and "Germans."[6] Other genealogical works claimed deep historical roots for "racial thought" in general. An article in the May 1937 issue of the journal *Familie, Sippe, Volk,* for instance, recommended an exhibition on German racial unity put on by the city of Frankfurt am Main in conjunction with the Party's Racial Policy Office. According to the article, the exhibit began with a picture of Herman the Cherusker (victor over the Romans at the battle of the Teutoburger Forest in A.D. 9), "the first to have seen in a political sense the racial commonality of the German tribes." It ended with a picture of Hitler who, according to the journal, "after two thousand years . . . completed the German development."[7] Friedrich Knost's 1939 book on the ancestral proof argued that the idea of "*Volksgenossen* as all who are of the same blood . . . was self-evident in the time our *Volk* entered history."[8]

Claims of direct historical precedent for the racial laws were also common. In a 1935 book on medieval genealogical practice, the author, Andreas Veit, compared earlier and present prohibitions on Jews. Although the "fearful punishment for sins of lasciviousness between Jews and Christians," wrote Veit, as well as the "international dress codes [special clothes that identified one as a Jew] that were so embarrassing for the Jews" arose out of "non-racial considerations," they nevertheless show that "maintaining purity of the *Volk*-essence was highly important and profound. . . ."[9] In a March 1936 speech at the "Administrative Science Week for Civil Registrars" in Berlin, Mayer claimed that "the notion of selection, of blood-related solidarity . . . was so powerful, that, despite all confessional and other hostilities, it continued to exist in the German *Volk* until the period after the Middle Ages." Mayer went on to argue that knights, monasteries, and guilds all had racial purity requirements, and, as the Nuremberg Laws presently did, the church also forbade Jews from employing "German" female servants. These ideas were, according to Mayer, "indigenous and at home with our ancestors," and were lost primarily through the increasing predominance of "orientally influenced" Roman law after the thirteenth century. This state of affairs had led to the removal of notations on ancestry and religion in the civil registers after World War I.[10] In the 1938 *Familie, Sippe, Volk,* Schultze-Naumburg similarly claimed that "the demands formulated in our racial legislation are not without [earlier] example."[11] The genealogist Wilhelm Isenburg claimed that "[e]verywhere a strong sense of consanguinity [*Sippebewusstsein*] was found with the individual German tribes who structured their entire lives upon kinship principles and laws." Erich Wentscher, another genealogist, idealized the Middle Ages as a time when the "feudal and corporate state was based upon strong blood-ties of the individual and life was arranged according to blood."[12]

Proponents made the same claim of deep historical precedent for the ancestral proof specifically. The first page of Knost's book on the ancestral proof featured a fourteenth-century depiction of an *Ahnenprobe,* an ancestral proof of nobility. Likewise, in his aforementioned book Andreas Veit wrote that "the demand for the proof of German blood placed on the entire German *Volk* awakens memories. . . . Hundreds of German noble families formerly concentrated on the principle of acceptability into a monastic order [*Stiftsmäßigkeit*] . . . and thereby preserved themselves free from foreign blood . . . ."[13] The new "proof of German blood," however, rather than arising from "a church requirement," comes rather from "the self-will of the German essence." "For this," Veit declared, "all with a truly German sense know to thank the Führer." Similar claims of the deep historical roots of the ancestral proof appeared in genealogical literature throughout the Third Reich.[14]

Such claims of historical continuity for racist thought and policy actually preceded the Third Reich. In the 1920s, for example, one of the common names for the Nazi Party process for proving "pure Aryan descent" was *Ahnenprobe*. Likewise, an article in the 1931 *Journal for Civil Registry Practice* noted with satisfaction that "after the revolution [of 1918–1919], the nobility has once again remembered that its original merit lay in the racial purity of the family tree."[15]

There were in fact striking parallels between the medieval proofs of origin, and the new Nazi version. By the thirteenth century, contemporaries viewed a proof of noble ancestry as necessary for maintaining one's place in the aristocracy.[16] An 1873 *German Herald* article showed that an *Ahnenprobe* from 1446 consisted of two "genealogical trees [*Stammbäume*] in certified form" that served as a "proof of the eight ancestors" of a cathedral head in Cologne. An 1898 *German Herald* article also not-ed that one indispensable qualification for the *Ahnenprobe* of "the old German law" was proof that one was born into a "sovereign Christian house." Another imperative, partially anticipating the Nazi Blood Protection Law, stated that "non-Christian sov-ereign families do not have conjugal rights (connubium) with Europe's sovereign Christian houses."[17]

One problem, however, with such efforts to confer historical legitimacy on the ancestral proof by tying it to alleged medieval efforts at maintaining "purity" was that the *Ahnenprobe* seemed to apply almost entirely to the aristocracy. In order to "democratize" this history, some commentators sought to emphasize (or distort) the breadth of social strata that historically made the proof. Genealogical Authority offi-cial Christian Ulmenstein, for example, argued that from the fourteenth century on, such proofs had not been limited to the nobility, but were also commonly made by the handicraft professions (*Handwerkverstande*). Guildsmen, wrote Ulmenstein, were required to show *Echt und Recht:* legitimate birth and honorable position. But, according to him, the purpose of these earlier proofs of ancestry was not only to maintain the purity of the individual estates, but also to fulfill the "unconscious demand" of the German *Volk* to prevent mixing of German and foreign ("frequently Jewish") blood.[18]

Nevertheless, with regard to aristocracy, proponents of the racial laws often sought both to have their cake and eat it. While creating a "democratic" history for the ancestral proof, they also attempted to harness the cachet that still attached to the concept of "nobility." This was done by claiming that the new ancestral proof was part of a process of creating a "new nobility" transcending social strata. By this, they meant descent not from a specific noble lineage, but rather from a "racial nobility." According to the Nazi agricultural czar Walter Darré, for example: "In the German sense, nobility is nothing more than the unity of blood and soil encapsulated in the '*Sippe*'s hereditary farmstead [*Erbhof*]'. . . ."[19] Himmler similarly sought to create a new "German nobility of Nordic race."[20]

As with other claims of deep historical roots for racist thought, the concept of a "new nobility" defined by race also made its appearance in mainstream genea-logical journals prior to the Nazi period. A review in the 1929 *News of the Roland,* for example, noted that the *Iron Book of German Nobility of German Type* (*EDDA*), geared toward *völkisch* aristocrats was, in fact, not just for the blue-blooded: "[pure] German burgher and peasant blood is [also] . . . viewed as of full-value [in gaining acceptance]."[21] A 1931 *Journal for Civil Registry Practice* article similarly proclaimed: "Now, after the revolution [of 1919] . . . the nobility as a class [*Stand*] has been abol-ished . . . the concept of peerage as one understood it during the monarchy has thus become unimportant." But the nobility, continued the article, "on its own initiative" has placed the "concept of peerage on a new and more meaningful base . . . the pres-ence of pure Nordic blood." "Thus," continued the article, "there are many bour-geois family trees to be found in the *EDDA*. . . . The previous noblesse oblige is today faced with the obligation of racial purity!"[22] And again, apart from representing a continuity of the concept of a new "racial nobility" into the Nazi period, the overt racism of such pre-Nazi articles also served to underscore the more ambiguous racism inherent in other discussions of "Germanness" in contemporary articles.

Its proponents' claims to the contrary, however, the true progenitor of the ancestral proof appeared much later in German history, in the late nineteenth century, as the process by which a variety of German associations sought to insure the "racial purity" of their members. Since 1890, for instance, the statutes of the Middle-German Agricultural Society demanded that its members be both Christian and of "German ancestry." So did various other groups in the early decades of the twentieth century.[23] It was these modern "proofs," rather than the medieval *Ahnenprobe* (which, in fact, had little to do with "racial purity" in the sense meant by modern racist ideologues), that were the true progenitors of the ancestral proof requirement.

The ancestral proof's proponents also attempted to associate it with other lines of historical continuity. Although less directly related to the proof's fundamentally racist purpose, many of its supporters tied the associated genealogical research to an idyllic vision of earlier historical periods. Thus, for example, a genealogical table that the Bochum City Savings Bank distributed to its customers, in addition to extolling the value of honoring the blood line (and, of course, thrift), was filled with medieval, early modern, nineteenth-century and peasant iconography.[24] Similarly, a leaflet distributed by the church-book office in the small town of Belleben, along with genealogical information it provided for the ancestral proof, conveyed its greetings to "our 'Aryans'" from the "ancestors' *Heimat*" (loosely translated as "homeland") and featured a bucolic picture of a small town, "the source of the *Heimat*."[25] Genealogy was a powerful tool in this hearkening back to ages portrayed as more healthy and harmonious. Such efforts to develop a sense of historical continuity (or timelessness) around the ancestral proof also helped Germans more easily acquiesce in the institutionalization of racism.

Legal and Bureaucratic Continuities

> No kind of rule is endured so easily or accepted so gratefully as that of high-minded and highly educated civil servants. The German State is a State of the supremacy of officialdom—let us hope that it will remain so.
> —RECTOR, STRASBOURG UNIVERSITY, 1891[26]

Academics debated the continuity of the rule of law in Nazi Germany. They generally agreed that "the term *Volk* signaled the source and the specificity of the Nazi political order, and that the unit it constituted had supplanted the discord and confusion associated with the division of power in the 'liberal' state." Nonetheless, in many areas the traditional administrative procedures simply continued to function.

Moreover, the authorities adopted many other established concepts and processes to carry out new requirements.[27] This is particularly evident in regard to the ancestral proof. Its proponents familiarized the requirement by implementing it through the use of highly rational, tried-and-true legal and bureaucratic frameworks. The proof also displayed continuity with specific pre-Nazi aspects of German citizenship and family law. This also helped to confer a sense of reasonableness, constancy, and legitimacy.

The Genealogical Authority itself is a prime exemplar of the phenomenon: it developed both a detailed administrative apparatus and incorporated long-standing legal practices. In the best tradition of German bureaucracy, it generated official forms for all aspects of its ancestral decision-making procedures. The following, for example, was the method for initiating a request for a biological examination:

> Along with a short description of the facts, the applicant requests . . . forms X 104 (general instructions), X 106 (instructions on ancestral proof) for illegitimate birth, and X 253 (form for photograph certification). He then submits by use of forms X 105 and 253 the application for provision of a decision on ancestry.[28]

The Authority also had standard forms for, among other things, requesting information from church books, civil registries, and other government agencies; to obtain further data for purposes of the biological investigation; to request blood tests; to tell applicants to obtain an ancestral proof elsewhere; and to provide information on eased requirements for military marriages and the naturalization of ethnic Germans.[29] Such bureaucratic thoroughness was probably comforting for those carrying out the process, intimidating for those who had to undergo it, and legitimizing for both: it was highly "official."

Similarly, Genealogical Authority executives framed their decisions in precise legal language. Findings of "Jew," "*Mischling*," and "German or related blood" were all set forth (in a form document) in the exact language of the Blood Protection Law. The typical finding of "*Mischling* first degree," for example, stated that the examinee was a "Jewish *Mischling* with two racially full Jewish grandparents in the sense of the first regulation to the Reich Citizenship Law of November 14, 1935 (RGBl. I. S. 1933)." Other findings were written in the same fashion. When, for instance, the Genealogical Authority held that an examinee's "half-Jewish" grandparent was a member of a "Jewish religious community," it would typically state that "pursuant to §2, paragraph 2, sentence 2 of the first regulation to the Reich Citizenship Law, [for purpose of] the racial classification of the examinee, the grandparent is to be deemed as full-Jewish."[30] Fear of the regime aside, it was probably difficult for most people to take issue with such precise assertions of law.

Officials of the Genealogical Authority also frequently cited legal precedent in support of their decisions. For instance, in a request that the Interior Ministry uphold a finding of "Jewish *Mischling* First Degree" based on the reasoning in an ancestral decision that he wrote, Knost closed his letter by claiming: "The new jurisprudence takes these axioms [relied upon in the decision] into account (cf. judgment of the R.S.IV.Zivilsenat of 4/11/1940 published in the Journal for Civil Registry Work, 20th Volume 1940, p. 174)."[31] Likewise, Authority officials discussed the racial laws using traditional legal idioms. Knost, for example, used the Latin phrase *praesumptio juris et de jure* to describe the irrefutable presumption in the Blood Protection Law's regulations that a grandparent who was a member of a Jewish religious community was a "full racial Jew."[32] The Authority also observed traditional choice of law principles in rendering, for example, paternity decisions, or a determination of whether a conversion to Christianity was timely for "race-determination" purposes (i.e., before passage of the Nuremberg Laws). In regard to the latter issue, for example, in Prussia formal conversion sufficed as timely for "race determination." In Austria, however, a personal declaration before the "political authorities" was also necessary.[33]

The scientists, too, framed the results of their biological investigations in language designed to underscore their impartiality, methodicalness, and adhesion not just to scientific, but also to legal standards. Thus, for example, in a fairly typical report, the biological expert Otto Reche wrote that his decision that an examinee was a first-, not second-degree, *Mischling* was pursuant to his "expert conviction" which "is parallel to the expression 'judicial conviction' (compare "Decisions of the Reich Courts in Criminal Actions," vol. 66, no. 1, pp. 163–65)."[34] Similarly, an expert blood test stated: "It is assured that the guidelines of the RdErl. d. RuPrMdI. u. d. RJM. [general decree of the Reich and Prussian Interior Ministry and the Reich Justice Ministry] of 5.26.1937—IV B 12296/37/4396 and IV b 4042—were taken into account and the mandates of the work guidelines of the Reich Interior Ministry of 5.12.1940—IV f 2555/40/4398—were complied with. The investigation was carried out either by the expert himself or under his supervision."[35] This all seemed very proper indeed.

Not the least of the factors contributing to the ancestral proof's aura of legitimacy was the fact that the law relating to it was highly detailed, and was constantly being revised or reinforced by numerous decrees and ordinances. This very detail gave it a feeling of continuity, indicating a well thought-out process, executed by highly trained and skilled authorities who dealt with these intricate laws as with any others. In the Third Reich, for example, civil registrars debated such fine points as whether the Reich Treasury was required to compensate persons who, pursuant to law, had to obtain a biological investigation for a child.[36] Again, all of this tapping into traditional legal methods stressed the fundamental "legality" of the ancestral proof process.

The Genealogical Authority also incorporated familiar elements of due process within the ancestral decision procedure, most fundamentally the right of appeal. An examinee could seek to change a Genealogical Authority ancestral decision by providing further documentation showing that the decision was in error, and could also appeal directly to the Interior Minister.[37] In one Authority case, for example, a 41-year-old man in Vienna, who had been born out of wedlock and had received an ancestral decision of "Jew" from the Authority in April 1941, initiated an appeal in the Interior Ministry. Even after the authorities "evacuated" him to the east in August 1942, his "Aryan" stepmother continued to fight the ancestral decision. Indeed, the Gau Kinship Office Vienna helped her in this struggle, writing in November 1942 that "objections could be validly raised" to the ancestral decision, and inviting her into the office for a meeting. Ultimately, her struggle was futile. In April 1943, the Gau Kinship Office informed her that the Interior Minister had upheld the Reich Genealogical Authority's decision, and further denied a mercy request to give her stepson *Mischling* status.[38] Nonetheless, such cases helped to give the ancestral decision process an appearance of fairness. Furthermore, although the Genealogical Authority files indicate that most appeals were unsuccessful, there were exceptions that seemed to further legitimize the process.[39]

In another example of due process, while an examinee generally had to pay for his or her own biological investigation, "exceptions could be granted." At least ostensibly, the Authority would itself pay when "an overriding Reich interest in the ancestral proof existed" and both "the examinee and the person requiring the process [were] incapable of paying the cost."[40] If, in reality, the granting of such payment exceptions, as well as overall allowance of a biological investigation itself, seemed to have been almost entirely at the discretion of Authority officials, at least a semblance of fairness also existed in the process.

Genealogical Authority administrators themselves consistently maintained that they operated both fairly and within the letter of the law. In a speech to civil registrars in 1936, Mayer used an illustrative anecdote. A family had requested an ancestral decision for purposes of marriage. When the Authority did not provide it within four days, the (presumably well-connected) mother contacted the Reich Chancellery which, through the Interior Ministry, asked why this was so. Mayer said that he had replied that no special favors were available, for in the Authority "a principle of order and a principle of justice and equity towards all *Volksgenossen* prevails."[41] There was some truth to this. For example, in regard to a man who claimed to be a Karaite rather than a "racial Jew," Knost, honoring the "rule of law," wrote to the Dessau district court that although "[t]he examinee's appearance appears to me to speak against the assumption of [German or] related ancestry, this conclusion is nevertheless nonbinding since a biological judgment is based not only on the appearance of the examinee but also on his ancestors and the members of their extended family."[42]

There was, not surprisingly, some corruption. In a previously discussed case, for example, in September 1941 the Genealogical Authority gave an examinee an ancestral decision of "Jew." When, however, Winifried Wagner, the composer Richard Wagner's daughter, intervened on behalf of the examinee's full sister, the Authority issued the sister an ancestral decision of Jewish-*Mischling* first degree.[43] On a smaller scale, corruption sometimes also accompanied the previously discussed special services provided by Interior Ministry officials on behalf of well-connected examinees.

In one case, for example, Authority official Arthur Schultze-Naumburg thanked such an official for helping him to avoid a fine for running a stop sign in Weimar.[44] Nevertheless, such overt dishonesty, both large and small, in the Authority's practice appears to have been the exception rather than the rule. For the most part, the "rule of law" was truly the order of the day.

In addition to continuities in bureaucratic and legal concepts and processes, there were also important connections in distinct areas of law. Perhaps the most fundamental was that relating to the determination of German citizenship. Since unification, German citizenship had been based on *jus sanguinus,* meaning inheritance of the status from a German father or, in cases of illegitimacy, mother. This, in turn, required determining whether the grandfather in question had the "German attribute [*Deutscheneigenschaft*]," which obligated the making of the same determination for that man's father, and so on. In 1930, a commentator in the *Journal for Civil Registry Practice* noted that this practice could theoretically require "establishing nationality from Adam and Eve." Prior to German unification, however, most individual German states based citizenship on birth within the national territory (*jus soli*). Therefore, for the purposes of establishing citizenship, the "German attribute" was presumed on demonstrating that a direct male ancestor had lived in a German state prior to 1866.[45] This was, of course, very similar to the later procedure for determining who was a "Jew" for purposes of the racial laws: "Jewishness," like "Germanness," was biologically inherited, but was ultimately based on the legal status of a relatively recent ancestor.

The ancestral decision process also blended with preexisting legal methods for determining parentage. As early as 1898, the genealogist Stephan Kekule spoke of using a genealogical "proof of ancestry [*Abstammungsbeweis*]" for "proof of paternity and maternity" in legal proceedings.[46] During the Weimar period, the civil registrars' journal regularly featured articles on such topics as the use of blood tests and other medical examinations in order to determine paternity.[47] Moreover, these articles were replete with terms later used in the ancestral proof process: *Abstammung* (ancestry), *Blutuntersuchung* (blood test), *Gutachten* (expert report), and *körperlichen Merkmale* (physical characteristics). Prior to the Third Reich, genealogical societies also regularly purchased books on these subjects for their libraries.[48] And during the Third Reich, the Genealogical Authority leadership continued to keep abreast of the latest advances in the blood-testing field, lending an aura of both "modernity" and continuity to their work.[49]

As previously noted, before the Nazi era, in straightforward family law cases, German and Austrian courts had already begun using anthropological examinations that were virtually identical to the Nazi-era "biological investigation," minus the determination regarding "racial characteristics." This, too, helped to give the "biological examination" portion of the ancestral decision process an aura of familiarity and legitimacy in the Nazi period. Moreover, in the Third Reich, all of these procedures also continued to be used to determine paternity for traditional family law purposes as well as for "racial" decisions.[50] Indeed, there was so much overlap between the ancestral decision procedure and civil paternity lawsuits that individuals often instituted the latter in an attempt to gain a more favorable "racial" decision.

In 1937, the German Evangelical Church published a guidebook for its clergymen and church-book managers. This text, which dealt with the provision of genealogical information for the ancestral proof, provides insight into the role that legal and bureaucratic continuity played in gaining acceptance for institutionalized racism in German society. Written by an attorney commissioned by the Church Chancellery, the book was clearly designed to help enforce the racial laws. Nevertheless, it was entirely devoid of any explanation or rationalization of those laws. The fact that provision of such information was legally required was the sole justification for the detailed exposition of the related rules and regulations. Incorporating the ancestral proof process within the "rule of law" was thus another way in which its proponents made it, and racial policy in general, palatable to important German institutions, as well as to the German populace.

Genealogical Practice Continuities

Despite continued growth in interest in "scientific" genealogy during the Third Reich, traditional aspects of the practice by no means died out. Research and publications on established themes continued apace. Even in the Genealogical Authority, racist use of genealogy was tempered by concentration on nonracist topics (e.g., heraldry) or nonracist aspects of the ancestral decision process (e.g., collection, organization, and preservation of records). This helped to blunt the "sharp edge" of much Nazi racial policy. For those engaged in genealogical research, but uncomfortable to any degree with racism's more brutal aspects, there was sufficient opportunity to avert one's gaze.

Despite the genealogical society Herold's various Nazi ties, its *Vierteljahrschrift für Wappen-, Siegel- und Familienkunde* (*Quarterly for Study of Coats of Arms, Family Seals, and Families*) betrayed little evidence of the profound political and social changes that had occurred in Germany after 1933. The editions from 1939 to 1943, for example, give little or no indication that Germany was either a "racial state" or at war, but continued to center almost exclusively on heraldry and the history of notable families. Similarly, during the Third Reich, the primary concern of the Zentralstelle's journal, the *Family History Gazette,* also remained church books, gravestones, seals, coats of arms, noble and middle-class family histories, and other time-honored subjects. Various leading genealogical journals, such as the *News of the Roland* and *Journal for Civil Registry Practice,* also continued to publish a majority of essays on traditional and even Christian-related themes during the Third Reich.[51] Indeed, as of May 1941 the Herold's deputy director was a pastor.[52] Publishers also continued to issue numerous books on conventional genealogical subjects, such as on customary professional names, German first and family names, heraldry, and the nobility.[53]

The 1941 membership register of the Reich Association of Kinship Researchers and Heraldists, the later incarnation of the Nazi-era professional genealogists' organization, listed its members' areas of expertise. These, too, illustrated significant continuity in traditional genealogical practices. A few of the twenty-one indexed areas tied in directly with the new regime's racist eugenic interests, among them genetics, legal questions of kinship research, and paternity inquiries. Moreover, some, such as indexing and peasant kinship research, were ambiguous in this regard. But the majority lay in traditional fields, including nobility research, "house marks," and heraldry.[54]

Moreover, even as many genealogists increasingly promoted their practice as a tool of racist eugenics, the Genealogical Authority concurrently encouraged traditional genealogical research. It published or commissioned works on such noneugenic topics as genealogical sources in Mecklenburg and the Prussian army's military church books. It also purchased numerous traditional genealogical works to encourage such research, and administered the provision of money from the Interior Ministry to genealogical associations for publication of these works and the reordering of archives.[55] Much of the foregoing could, of course, also be put to "eugenic use." But such "dual use" cut both ways. Authority leaders, for example, foresaw their *Sippenkanzlei* as repositories not only for the genealogical information necessary for making the ancestral proof, but also for coats of arms, "house marks," and gravestones, genealogical sources less useful for racist eugenic purposes.[56] Likewise, the Authority's journal *Familie, Sippe, Volk*, despite its overtly racist bent, also published numerous articles on such traditional themes as heraldry and the study of professional groups. Each issue was also filled with illustrations depicting idyllic, traditional families, as well as quotations on family life from illustrious German literary figures such as Goethe, Hölderlin, and Schopenhauer.

There were, of course, limits to the regime's desire to promote traditional practice that had no eugenic application. In April 1935, for example, the Genealogical Authority agreed to pay a prominent genealogist RM 2,000 for his *Manuskriptes des Bandes I des Arlberger Bruderschaftsbuches* (*Manuscript of Volume I of the Arlberger Brotherhood Book*) relating to a monastic order. But the Interior Ministry balked. While, according to the ministry, the work might be valuable "from the standpoint of heraldry . . . [it] was not of such essential importance to the field of kinship research. . . ."[57] Yet in general, the two aspects of practice existed in tandem during the Third Reich.

In addition to this significant continuity in traditional genealogical practice, which allowed individuals to concentrate on areas other than racist eugenic applications, there is evidence that at various times a variety of individuals and institutions also actively sought to deemphasize the racist aspect of genealogical practice. The fact that the Genealogical Authority quickly dropped the word *race* from any permutation of its name is significant in this regard. That this soft-pedaling was conscious is revealed by correspondence in late 1934 in which Martin Bormann, then chief

Figure 9. Cover, *Familie, Sippe, Volk*, September 1942.
From the Library of Congress.

assistant to Deputy Führer Rudolf Hess, asked the Interior Minister, Wilhelm Frick, to change the name of the Genealogical Authority's civil branch from "Expert for *Racial* Research" to "Expert for *Kinship* Research." This would parallel the new name for the National Socialist Information Office, the Authority's Party branch, which was now the "Office for Kinship Research." In November 1934, Achim Gercke wrote Frick that he opposed the change. While he was a "kinship researcher," claimed Gercke, he used genealogical practice to make determinations of race and, therefore, the name change was inappropriate.[58] Despite this logical objection, the change occurred. The new stress on "kinship research" thus downplayed the Genealogical Authority's racist essence. It is also notable that in Nazi bureaucratic practice, the racial purity requirement was much more commonly referred to as the "ancestral proof" rather than the "Aryan proof," while the various regional and local genealogical authorities usually made "ancestral decisions" rather than "racial decisions."

A shift in emphasis from racism to traditional aspects of genealogical practice was also evident elsewhere. In 1937, for example, the Volk Federation of German Kinship Studies Societies, then the umbrella organization for all genealogical societies, informed readers of the Genealogical Authority broadsheet *General Search Sheet for Kinship Researchers* that it was a corporate member of the Reich Committee for Volk Health Services, and as such, had an important role to fill in the state's "selective measures" for hereditary and racial cultivation. Such "cultivation," the article continued, would primarily come through establishing the "ancestral communities" of famous Germans and the assembling of genealogical tables of talented kinship groups, such as doctors, musicians, politicians, and officers.[59] It did not mention the role of the ancestral proof—the key element—in this "racial cultivation." Similarly, in 1937 the Senate for Education in Bremen issued a decree on the teaching of genealogy that, while noting its importance for racial purity, particularly emphasized the study of regional culture, such as "Plattdeutsch [a northern German dialect] family names."[60] Likewise, influential genealogists praised the traditional benefits of the ancestral proof. According to Wilhelm Isenburg, for instance, the regime's insistence on an "Aryan proof" had the salutary effect of leading many Germans to learn about their ancestors.[61]

The ancestral proof also served to revive an older civil registry practice whose loss had been lamented by some "traditionalists." In 1875, Prussia issued unified civil registry regulations under a civil code (*Personstandsgesetz*) that became effective for the entire Reich on January 1, 1876. These required civil registrars to record all births, marriages, and deaths, which always included a notation of each person's religion. In June 1920, however, the German National Assembly approved a new civil code that no longer required the listing of religion in the civil registry records. A 1925 *Journal for Civil Registry Practice* article complained that these changes made it more difficult not only for genealogists, but also for "everyone who needed to prove his ancestry for whatever reason."[62] The Nazi regime, for obvious reasons, was sympathetic to this argument and reinstated the former practice of recording religion in the civil registries.

In his 1939 work *Introduction to Practical Genealogy,* the genealogist Erich Wentscher noted that, depending on individual genealogists' proclivities, each study will tend either to genetics or to historical and sociological research.[63] Because of continuity in the latter two areas in the Third Reich, many individuals could view the making of the ancestral proof as part of a more intellectually and emotionally tolerable tradition. This, too, helps to account for the racial laws' wide acceptance in Nazi Germany.

Cross-Institutional Support for Racist-Eugenic Thought and Policy

As shown throughout this study, all major institutions in Nazi Germany—government, business, academia, the professions, and the churches—accepted and incorporated racist eugenic ideas. All of the disparate factors discussed in this study were important in this process. In addition, however, a "snowball effect" also likely took place: acceptance by one institution was an additional factor contributing to assent by others, as well as by the general populace. In reciprocal fashion, one acceptance legitimized another. As the one institution with the clout to dispute the claimed scientific validity of racist ideology, academia played the key role in this regard. But in any event, this cross-institutional reinforcement also contributed to an aura of "correctness" around the implementation of racist policy in Germany, and thus to Germans' wholesale acquiescence.[64]

The *Journal for Civil Registry Practice* gives many examples of this cross-fertilization in the fields of administrative, legislative, and legal practice. The 1941 volume, for example, published approximately 250 laws, regulations, and decrees from the national and state governments, as well as from the General Government in occupied Poland, and other areas under administrative control of the Reich. Of these laws, only twelve dealt specifically with the ancestral proof. These included when and how it had to be made (five), the obtaining of genealogical documents specifically for that purpose (two), the Ahnenpass (two), use of the biological investigation (one), and Kreis Kinship Offices (two). These relatively small numbers, however, underrate the infiltration of the ancestral proof into German bureaucratic life. Five additional regulations published in the *Journal* dealt with implementation of the Nuremberg Laws; six with determination of Jewish or "Gypsy" ancestry; and three more with the application of certain laws to Jews in particular. All of these entries indirectly implicated the use of an ancestral proof. Furthermore, dozens of the additional listed laws dealt with marriage, name change, and nationality issues, many of which also directly or indirectly demanded use of the ancestral proof.

Likewise, most issues of the *Journal for Civil Registry Practice* also contained copies or abstracts of court decisions of import to civil registrars. The 1941 edition contained some thirty-three of them. Only three dealt specifically with the ancestral proof—determining ancestry for "racial" purposes.[65] Yet some of the other decisions still indicated the obligation's presence. Thus, a case involving a dispute over a marriage between a 45-year-old and a 22-year-old referred to the Blood Protection Law without reference to its racial application. Another, involving paternity, specifically discussed the significance of a "hereditary investigation" when neither the "racial composition" nor hereditary health of the parties involved was in question. Still another dealt with the necessity of a biological investigation under Austrian law in a paternity case that again did not deal with racial composition of any of the parties involved.[66] Even in the Third Reich, racist eugenics was not the center of civil registry or family law practice. But it had deeply permeated both, using much of the same language and concepts. This likely occurred in other fields as well, cross-fertilizing the acceptance of racist ideology and policies in German society.

9 | Racial Scientific Ideology and the Holocaust

> I must ask you only to listen and never to speak about what I am telling you in this intimate circle. We had to answer the question: What about the women and children? Here, too, I had made up my mind, find a clear-cut solution. I did not feel I had the right to exterminate the men—that is to murder them, or to have them murdered—and then allow their children to grow into avengers, threatening our sons and grandchildren. A fateful decision had to be made: This people had to vanish from the earth.
>
> —Heinrich Himmler,
> Posen, Poland, October 8, 1943 [1]

The virulent antisemitism of the Nazi era is rightly regarded as one of its hallmarks. No one who studies the Third Reich is unfamiliar with the regime's widely promoted propaganda images: hook-nosed or frog-faced Jews engaged in conspiracies to dominate the world; killing "Aryan" children; destroying European culture through Bolshevism, "money" capitalism, parliamentarianism, and race-mixing; or at the very minimum, engaged in, and being the source of, every villainous activity known to modern German or indeed Western society. This type of antisemitism clearly played a causal role in the development and execution of the Holocaust: without it, the decision to hunt down and destroy every "Jew" within the German sphere of influence is inexplicable.

Yet, as this study has shown, at the same time that the Nazi regime advocated this virulent antisemitism, it also concurrently engaged in the massive promotion of a much more subtle form of antisemitic propaganda: one carefully framed within a specific racial scientific ideology, institutionalized through the myriad of so-called racial laws, and touching the everyday lives of most Germans through, among other things, the demand for an ancestral proof. Such propaganda was usually unaccompanied by antisemitic caricature, and was often quite measured, and even apologetic, in tone. What role, if any, did this "dispassionate" antisemitism play in the perpetration of the Holocaust?

Before addressing this question, it is worth reemphasizing just how "neutrally" pitched much of the antisemitic discourse was in Nazi Germany. The various racial laws, for example, contained no overtly antisemitic rhetoric. Indeed, they initially distinguished only between "Aryans" and "non-Aryans." The word *Jew* appeared only in the implementing regulations. Proponents of the ancestral proof, too, almost invariably justified it in "neutral" terms. A standard work on the process from 1941, for example, defined it only as a "proof of German or related lineage or, respectively, of the grade of foreign admixture of blood."[2] Explanatory information in various versions of the Ahnenpass also usually emphasized only the "scientific necessity" undergirding the racial laws. A very popular version, justifying what it called the "racial axiom," stated: "The belief rooted in National Socialist thought, that it is the highest duty of a *Volk* to maintain the purity of its blood from foreign influences and to further extirpate influxes of admixtures of foreign blood, is based on the scientific insight of hereditary science and racial research."[3] The word *Jew* was absent. Likewise, the introduction to Genealogical Authority director Achim Gercke's 1933 bibliography of racist works (*Die Rasse*) noted the importance of "racist thought" to the Nazi worldview, but did not mention Jews in particular. In the early years of the Third Reich, the *Journal for Civil Registry Practice*, while printing much about the racial laws, had virtually no specific references to Jews. And the Genealogical Authority broadsheet *General Search Sheet for Kinship Researchers* contained few if any antisemitic canards.

The direct implication was that the racial laws were based on objective, value-neutral, scientific findings, not on the fiendish antisemitic stereotypes concurrently promoted by the regime. Thus, according to this propaganda, anti-Jewish measures were necessary not because Jews were "evil world conspirators," criminals, Bolshevists, and so forth, but because "Jews" were "racially-alien," and mixing with them caused hereditary and cultural damage.

Indeed, some explanations for the racial laws were quite apologetic in tone. Thus, for example, while one of the leading commentaries on the Nuremberg Laws could claim in 1935 that the legislation was based on the "fundamental recognition of the inequality of the human races," another could assert the next year that "there is no absolute hierarchy between the races. . . ."[4] Similarly, at the same time that anti-Jewish rhetoric and policy were becoming increasingly strident in many quarters, a widely sold version of the Ahnenpass could still assert that "National Socialist thought . . . grants full equity to every other *Volk* and, moreover never speaks of superior or inferior, but rather only of alien racial admixture." In January 1936, a Stuttgart newspaper went so far as to claim that the Nuremberg Laws would actually lead to a decrease in hatred of the Jews since, once "the Jewish guest *Volk* . . . are . . . separated from the German *Volk* politically, culturally, and above all biologically," they will live "according to their own type of life" and this will "serve as a guarantee for acceptable joint living in the same national space."[5] Thus, according to this paper, in the long run anti-Jewish policy, being scientifically grounded, was really in the Jews' best interests as well. Even in the 1942 edition of a major commentary on the Nuremberg Laws, published after mass killings of Jews in the East were well under way, Wilhelm Stuckart, State Secretary in the Interior Ministry and a participant in the Wannsee Conference, explained:

> A mixture of blood between members of unrelated races leads . . . to . . . [a meeting] of capacities that are not compatible with each other. As a consequence of this, inner tensions arise in the carriers of these capacities, which rob them of their full abilities. Because of the aforementioned internal rupture[, race-mixing] may appear less desirable for the generality despite possible talents in individuals.[6]

Again, the racial laws were said to be necessary to protect the hereditary capacities of the *Volk,* and not because "the Jews" were ontologically evil. Indeed, the work even acknowledged that in individual cases, "mixed-race" individuals (presumably also including mixtures between "Jews" and "Aryans") could exhibit considerable "talents."

What connection, if any, did this widespread "dispassionate" form of antisemitism have to the Final Solution? It was certainly not the underlying ideological force. Of course the basic premise of racist eugenic ideology in Nazi Germany, no matter how gently phrased, was that in order to save German society, Jews, being "racial aliens," must be removed. Given the alleged importance of racial purity, the death of a few of the "racially innocent" or even the mass death of the "racially guilty" did not, in itself, contradict this underlying logic. Moreover, even if some of those adversely affected because of alleged "Jewish ancestry" were not, in fact, "racially alien," their destruction could still be logically justified on the basis that it was too much work to identify the specific "racial background" of each and every person with three or more grandparents who were members of a Jewish religious community. One cannot, after all, make an omelet without breaking a few eggs. Indeed, this policy fit in well with the Nazi conception of *Volksgemeinschaft:* sometimes innocent individuals had to suffer for the greater good of the *Volk.* Moreover, the actual physical destruction of the racially alien was a rational if cruel means to a clear racist eugenic end: racial purification of the *Volk.* If there were no racially alien persons present, there was no danger of "race-mixing."

But the policy of intentional destruction of all "Jews," everywhere, made no sense in this regard. One can prohibit interbreeding between populations without resorting to genocide. This was, after all, the German policy in regard to other "racially alien" ethnic groups. Complete exploitation and removal of such persons from German *Lebensraum* ("living space"), even if mass death might be a by-product, did not *require* their utter annihilation wherever they might be in the world. Moreover, if one is going to remove the "racial threat" through a policy of physical destruction, it makes no sense to destroy only one particular "racially alien" group. Yet the Nazi extermination policy was primarily directed only against "Jews." Finally, even if one is only killing off one "racially threatening" group, it is not necessary to engage in sustained and deliberate brutality in the process. Such brutality, however, was in fact built into the destruction process of the Jews. Thus racist eugenic ideology could not, in reality, have been the fundamental rationale for the Nazi's genocidal policy against Jews. Clearly, the actual justification for the genocide was the other widespread allegation about Jews in Nazi Germany: that they were ontologically evil entities.

Yet, while not the ideological engine of the Holocaust, racist eugenic ideology was still an indispensable factor in creating the social conditions necessary for its perpetration. First, the ideology was vital to building a social consensus in Germany allowing for mistreatment of Jews. Hitler and many other Nazi ideologues obviously preferred virulent to dispassionate antisemitism. Demonic images of Jews were rampant in their speeches, in party papers such as the *Völkischer Beobachter* and *Der Stürmer,* and in Propaganda Ministry films like *Der ewige Jude* (*The Eternal Jew*) and *Jud Süss* (*The Jew Süss*). Well-developed racial scientific rationalizations, on the other hand, were usually absent. Yet the regime almost invariably justified the racial laws and the ancestral proof on the alleged need to maintain racial purity, not prevent Jewish perfidy. Why?

The most plausible explanation is that the Nazi leadership recognized that many in Germany felt uncomfortable with the more intemperate forms of antisemitism. With regard to Kristallnacht, the government-orchestrated pogrom against Jews in 1938, for example, the historian Marion Kaplan notes that "many [Germans] disapproved of the open barbarism." Yet, Kaplan also writes that "most approved of, or went along with, 'moderate' antisemitism."[7] Racist eugenic ideology provided as "moderate" an antisemitism as could be desired: it was not directed at Jews qua Jews but, rather, at all individuals with "threatening" racial characteristics, many of whom "happened" to be Jewish. By creating the impression that Jews comprised an actual health threat to the German *Volksgemeinschaft,* such propaganda allowed many Germans who found it difficult to embrace the more acerbic aspects of antisemitic ideology nevertheless to view harsh exclusionary measures against Jews as morally justified, or even, in the long run, in the Jews' own "best interests."

Such propaganda was also more acceptable outside of Germany. In distinction to its virulent antisemitic caricature, the regime never felt the need to stem the flow of racial scientific propaganda to placate foreign opinion. Thus, for example, when the regime was backpedaling on dissemination of virulent antisemitism, as for example in the consolidating years of 1933 and 1934, and in the period prior to the 1936 Olympics in Berlin, this much more subtle form of antisemitic propaganda proceeded at full steam, and on a massive and ever-increasing scale.[8]

While such propaganda was superficially "neutral," however, it was not so neutral as to stymie the regime's goal of defaming "Jews." Thus, despite the fact that the racial laws were, for the most part, rationalized with colorless language, there can be no doubt that virtually everyone in Germany was aware that in both theory and practice the laws' proponents clearly had Jews uppermost in mind in both drafting and applying the legislation. The first implementing regulation of the Civil Service Law, the initial "racial law," for example, defined a "non-Aryan" as one "who is descended from non-Aryan, especially Jewish parents or grandparents. This premise especially obtains if one parent or grandparent was of Jewish faith."[9] The Nuremberg Laws of September 15, 1935 more strongly emphasized that Jews were the primary racial-hygienic threat to the German *Volk*. Unlike the earlier racial laws that, at least on their face, differentiated only between "Aryans" and "non-Aryans," the Nuremberg Laws expressly distinguished between persons of "German or related blood" and "Jews."

Indeed, lest there be any doubt, after explaining the "value-free" basis for the racial laws, their spokespersons usually then pointed out that Jews and persons of Jewish ancestry were the main threats in this regard. Yet even this direct implication of Jews was often framed in such a way as to make it seem as if Jews were not being arbitrarily singled out. In December 1936, for example, the mayor of Cologne provided city employees with an instructional pamphlet on the ancestral proof process, which included information on how to make genealogical tables and obtain and evaluate documents.[10] The brochure also contained the usual justification for the requirement: "Each member of the racial community must keep his blood pure of foreign influences" because "unrestrained penetration of foreign essence" leads to the "ruin of the *Volk*." Then, however, the mayor specifically noted that the "foreign blood" to be identified included not only that of "Jews," but also "Gypsies," as well as "the Asiatic and African races, [and] the indigenous inhabitants of Australia and America . . . in short, every admixture of blood of a colored person." This, again, was ostensibly neutral: not directed at Jews in particular; any other person of "colored race" was also to be subjected to these laws. Nevertheless, neutral application supported racist policies whose predominant targets were clearly persons with Jewish ancestry. In other words, the ideology stigmatized Jews as the primary carriers of "racially damaging" hereditary characteristics in the Reich.

This "neutral" propaganda thus rationalized persecution of Jews in a more widely acceptable way than through the attribution of demonic characteristics. To again quote Marion Kaplan: "[t]he social death of Jews and German indifference to their increasingly horrific plight were absolute prerequisites for the 'Final Solution.'"[11] Racial scientific propaganda, precisely because of its superficial "neutrality," created a climate in which anti-Jewish policy could flourish. In the Third Reich, the core ideas that there were different races, some of which should not mix, and that *Jew* was a racial concept, were not to be questioned. But between the poles of demonic and racial scientific antisemitism, one could choose the style with which one felt most comfortable. This was key to building the consensus for anti-Jewish policies, and for helping to create an atmosphere in which physical atrocities against Jews could become, at the least, conceivable.

In addition to helping build a consensus for the mistreatment of Jews, racial-scientific ideology also constituted another necessary "ingredient" for the Holocaust. Widespread compliance with the racial laws that it helped to develop, in turn, acted as a "signal" to the regime that its antisemitic ideology need not be internally consistent in order to be acceptable to large numbers of Germans. This, in turn, emboldened the leadership to undertake ever more radical policies based on increasingly far-fetched ideas.

The ancestral proof requirement is a case in point. As shown, its theoretical foundation was logically flawed. Apart from the fact that most of the broader assumptions underlying racist eugenic ideology were unsupported by empirical evidence, *Jew* itself did not constitute a racial category according to any extant scientific definition. All attempts to find a "biological marker" for Jews had failed. Thus, during the Nazi period, a powerful ideological tool existed to *resist* the ancestral proof requirement and, more broadly, antisemitic policy. Why did a tall, blond, blue-eyed "Jew" constitute a greater racial threat to the German *Volk* than a short, swarthy "Aryan?" Yet even as anti-Jewish policy became increasingly brutal, and increasingly unrelated to the ostensible theoretical basis for the racial laws, apparently no individual or institution in the Reich ever publicly mentioned this discrepancy, or questioned the necessity of making an ancestral proof.

This utter lack of resistance to the requirement sent a message to the regime that the irrational basis for racial policy—a policy that virtually everyone in Germany knew led to severe consequences for the "racially alien"—was not a fundamental issue for the vast majority of Germans. Every time a German made an ancestral proof, whatever his or her actual feelings about racism and Jews, he or she implicitly endorsed racism and anti-Jewish policy, and encouraged the regime in its racist policies. These policies, again, became increasingly violent and increasingly disassociated from racist eugenic thought. By the early 1940s, such "feedback" from the German populace helped the Nazi leadership feel empowered to implement a policy to identify and kill all Jews, wherever they were located. A complete lack of resistance to racism in principle helped embolden the Nazi leadership to undertake genocidal policies (and not just against Jews), which were based on "irrational" rather than "scientific" racist ideology.[12]

Despite the role of racial science in helping gain the German population's compliance with racist policy, it is nevertheless important not to overestimate the power of the foregoing "signaling function." Evidence indicates that Nazi proponents of demonic antisemitic views never felt entirely sure of the degree to which the German public would accept policies based primarily on those ideas, as opposed to more clearly racial scientific rationalizations. This becomes especially clear with regard to a third function of racial science in relation to the "Final Solution": as a tool for disguising the blatantly irrational character of the ideology that actually fueled the Holocaust.

The widespread allegation in Nazi Germany that Jews were ontologically evil entities was problematic from a racial scientific perspective. There was an inherent logic (within a racial-scientific context) of finding Jewish ancestry as a reasonable marker for "racially alien" characteristics: Jews were supposedly predominantly "racially Asiatic." But the idea of a "racial Jew" who carried "Jewish racial characteristics" was another matter. This concept directly contradicted the oft-repeated idea that Jews were, like "Germans," a "*Volk*" (that is, a mixture of "compatible" races sharing a common culture) and not a "race." And if Jews were a *Volk,* and even if each and every individual "Jew" was entirely composed of the most "racially alien elements" imaginable and thus posed an unquestionable racial-hygienic threat to the German *Volk,* it was nevertheless still difficult to reconcile such threat with the ferocity of the regime's hatred of Jews, and especially with the horrific propaganda images of "the Jew," the heart of all evil in the world. *Racially alien* encompassed so many persons, both "Jewish" and "non-Jewish," and *diabolical* was so outside of ordinary experience, that the equation of the two was a hard sell indeed.[13]

Given, however, the widespread desire in Germany to view anti-Jewish policy as "rational," how was one to reconcile the "racial-scientific" and demonic notions of "Jew"? The answer was to elide the differences by treating "Jewish" as indicating the presence of specific, immutable racial characteristics rather than generally "racially alien" qualities. In fact, in Nazi Germany, despite the concurrent denial of such, many persons engaged in a concerted effort to make it appear as if there were specific "Jewish" racial characteristics. Thus, for example, each Genealogical Authority ancestral decision was a determination as to how many "*racially* Jewish," as opposed to "Jewish" or "racially alien" grandparents, an examinee had. Again, this made no "racial-scientific sense," as Jews were supposedly a *Volk,* not a race. Similarly, one task of the Genealogical Authority's biological experts was to determine whether an examinee exhibited "Jewish," as opposed to "alien-type," "racial characteristics." Despite acknowledgments by leading racial scientists that there actually were no specifically "Jewish" physical characteristics, those seeking to find Jews continued to act as if there were. At the same time, racial scientists devised no tests for determining whether an individual exhibited "Jewish" mental characteristics. And high-ranking officials, including Genealogical Authority officials who must have known better, repeatedly referred to "the Jewish race" in their communications.[14]

Other agencies also contributed to this conceptual blurring. The Party's Racial Policy Office's efforts to determine whether the "Mountain Jews of the Caucuses," Krimchaks, and other "Judaized sects" were racially distinct from other "Jews," for example, otherwise made no sense.[15] If both Krimchaks and "regular" Jews were, in any event, of "alien-type" race, there was no reason for this effort other than to try to emphasize the alleged existence of particularly "Jewish" racial characteristics. For this purpose as well, an Interior Ministry report, outlining the basis for the Nuremberg Laws, stated that any mixture between "German-blooded" persons and "Jews" would lead to an influx of "Jewish characteristics" rather than "racially alien" characteristics. Moreover, that report operated under the assumption that "full-Jews" were 100 percent endowed with "Jewish characteristics," "half-Jews" carried 50 percent "Jewish characteristics," and so on.[16] This was also senseless from a racial-scientific perspective. Likewise, when deciding on whether a marriage between a "half-Jew" and a "German-blooded person" would be allowed, the report stated that each individual "half-Jew" would have to be judged on his or her "outer appearance . . . character and intellectual and other abilities," and thus by how "Jewish" they were. Why, then, couldn't a "full-Jew" also be judged on his or her outer appearance, character, and intellectual and other abilities, since, per standard racial scientific rhetoric any individual "Jew" could be composed of a variety of "racial types"?

In fact, the attempt to conflate the racial-scientific view of Jews as bearers of "racially alien" characteristics, and the preferred Nazi view that Jews were a "race," permeated the Third Reich. Soldiers, for example, had to take an oath stating that "to the best of my knowledge, none of my parents or grandparents belonged to the Jewish race as a full-Jew or *Mischling*."[17] This widespread conceptual smudging helped to legitimize the other widespread portrayal of "Jews" in Nazi Germany: as inherently evil entities. Erasing the distinction between the idea of Jews as carriers of "racially alien" characteristics and Jews as bearers of "Jewish racial characteristics" helped undergird the view of "Jew" as a racial entity unto itself. This, in turn, provided a scientific sheen to long-standing, primitive beliefs about the alleged diabolical attributes of "Jews." Only a "pure Jewish race," not a racially mixed "Jewish *Volk*," could exhibit particularly "Jewish racial characteristics." And it was the vibrancy of *this* particular set of beliefs in Nazi Germany, legitimized in great part by association with racist eugenic thought, that both caused, and allowed, the government to sanction, encourage, and implement a policy of murdering every "Jew" on the face of the earth.

Conclusion

THE CASE OF ALICE G. AND MARGARETTE K., discussed in chapter 6, illustrates the uneasy nature of the effort in Nazi Germany to provide a rational gloss over the irrational Jew hatred that fueled the Holocaust. Margarette, it will be remembered, claimed to the Genealogical Authority that her biological father was an "Aryan." With only ambiguous documentary and testimonial evidence available, however, and after a succession of inconclusive biological investigations, in September 1941 the Authority decreed her to be a "Jewess." Yet subsequently, a Vienna district court, in a parallel case involving "racial shame," ordered another biological investigation of Margarette. Genealogical Authority official Schultze-Naumburg then wrote the Central Agency for Jewish Emigration in Vienna, the SS office responsible for the "evacuation" of Viennese Jews, that it should temporarily stop any efforts to deport Margarette.

In September 1942, however, SS Captain Brunner (probably Alois, 1912–?) responded: "the Jewess was already evacuated to the occupied Eastern Territory on 8/31/1942 and communication with her is no longer possible." Margarette, Brunner claimed, had instituted an "ancestral swindle in the court." The alleged "Aryan" ancestry of the father, he wrote, was obviously false, since "out of instinct a full-Jewess [i.e., Margarette's mother] in the known Jew-city Laupheim in Würtemberg would not marry an Aryan."[1] Brunner was clearly less worried than the Authority about maintaining a scientific façade for anti-Jewish activities. Also, as previously noted, after the intervention of Richard Wagner's daughter Winifried on behalf of Margarette's sister Alice, the Genealogical Authority, based on the same evidence, issued an ancestral decision of "Jewish-*Mischling* first degree" for Alice. When, however, the Vienna district court reasonably asked the Authority to change the ancestral decision of the now deported Margarette (the "racial-shame" case against the "Aryan" man involved was still pending), the Authority refused, saying it would seek yet another biological investigation. Even in Nazi Germany, it would not have been difficult to ascertain that racial scientific ideology was fundamentally a series of unproven assertions expressed in scientific verbiage, while the idea of the inherently evil "Jew" transcended the bounds of even the tenuous support of racial science.

To date, few scholars have analyzed the process by which such ideas nevertheless became central ideological pillars in a highly sophisticated society. The probable reason for this lack of scholarly interest is that despite ideological inconsistencies, the regime was still able to implement all of its anti-Jewish policies, including the Final Solution. Yet the failure to elucidate these contradictions distorts our understanding of the historical processes involved in producing the destruction of the Jews. In an influential work, for example, Götz Aly and Susan Heim discuss the Nazi policy of euthanizing the severely "hereditarily ill"—the "Action T4." They claim that its significance

> as predecessor to the gas chambers of Belzec or Auschwitz does not lie so much in the development of specific camouflage or killing techniques, but rather in the indisputable political success: in the open or silent acceptance of the murder of marginalized, defenseless humans by the vast majority of all social strata of the master *Volk*. It is hardly surprising, that as a consequence of this the state leadership derived the confidence that the Germans would quietly accept the acceleration of their policy of annihilation.[2]

While this argument does emphasize an important connection between the two types of mass murder, it is nevertheless problematic. Not only does it overstate the social consensus behind euthanasia (there was, in fact, outspoken condemnation of "Action T4"), but it also mistakenly implies that the killing of the "hereditarily ill" and the killing of Jews were based on essentially the same social consensus. In fact, the murderous progression—from the killing of allegedly physically or mentally ill persons to persons with no other disease than "Jewishness"—is not self-evident. Clearly, there must have been a different motivation for the murder of tens of thousands of so-called useless eaters and millions of work-capable adults. Indeed, the destruction of the "hereditarily ill" was based on widely discussed eugenic policy, often calling for exceedingly harsh measures, which significantly predated the Third Reich. On the other hand, prior to 1933 there was little public call for sterilization of Jews, much less their physical destruction.

Similarly, in a recent work, Claudia Koonz states that Nazi ideology, the key component of which she calls "ethnic righteousness," "may well have facilitated the clear consciences of those who robbed, tormented, and murdered their helpless victims."[3] This work supports that argument. Yet Koonz also writes that this ethnic righteousness extended to "the Aryan community, as defined by what racial scientists believed to be the most advanced biological knowledge of the day."[4] This is incorrect with regard to the Final Solution. Whatever racial scientists may have believed, it was certainly not that science had proven that Jews were hereditarily evil. The policy to destroy all Jews went well beyond the internal logic of racial science.

Indeed, the success of the Final Solution, despite the fact that it was motivated by a complete fantasy, is one of its most important facets. In the first third of the twentieth century, Germany was among the most advanced Western societies in terms of industrialization, public education, and other forms of "modernity." Many Germans of the time were perfectly capable of making an informed assessment of the reasonableness of the claim of inherent Jewish evil. That such a society was nevertheless capable of producing a massive genocide based on this absurd idea raises the question of the degree to which modern Western civilization rests upon reasoned discourse. How susceptible, in fact, are Western societies to movements motivated by fundamentally irrational beliefs?

In *The Holocaust in American Life,* Peter Novick argues against the idea of deriving "lessons [from] the Holocaust" because, inter alia, the Holocaust is "too extreme." He states that there are "more important lessons about how easily we become victimizers to be drawn from the behavior of normal Americans in normal times than from the behavior of the SS in wartime."[5] What this study emphasizes, however, is that it was also the behavior of "normal" Germans in "normal" times, not just the SS in wartime, that played a key role in creating the conditions for the Final Solution. Both individual Germans, and German institutions, had powerful motivations—positive (material and psychic benefit) and negative (avoidance of the wrath of neighbors and the regime)—to avoid seeing certain things. First, that the racial-scientific rationalization for exploiting others was, in direct contrast to the oft-repeated claims that it was based on empirical science, actually a faith-based belief. Second, that their government was engaged in a policy of genocide driven in large part by an untenable idea. It was unnecessary for all, or even a majority, of Germans to embrace an "eliminationist antisemitism" in order for the regime to implement the Final Solution.[6] All that was needed was a widespread disinclination to question and an acceptable rationalization for that failure.

Essentially, this study has been about important historical factors that both caused this disinclination and created such justification. But in a sense, it is also an indictment of an entire society. Although racist eugenics was less logically coherent than hereditary health eugenics, greater numbers of "racially acceptable" Germans appear to have been willing to accept racist eugenic doctrine in order to come to terms with their own failure to act in the face of their neighbors' suffering. In other words, such doctrine was "an indicator of what people sincerely hoped to be true."[7] Thus, while during the Third Reich "historic social groups" in Germany "continued their conflicts like men wrestling under a blanket," and there may well have been substantial "fracturing or atomization of opinion," this did not apply to the institutionalization of racism.[8] While, for example, many Germans made known their distaste for the most brutal actions that they witnessed—public humiliations, looting, beatings, and killings—there is on the other hand almost no indication of any questioning, at any time, of the necessity for the regime's fundamental policies of segregating, isolating, impoverishing, and then, finally, deporting the Jews.[9] Indeed, of all aspects of the regime's anti-Jewish policy, it only attempted to keep the mass murder secret. Overt Nazi racial policy was based in important part on consensus between government and governed.[10]

The extent to which German society was corrupted in the process of institutionalizing racism has been difficult for many to accept. After World War II, for example, some of the genealogists who are a central concern of this study expressed their distress over the conduct of their profession during the Nazi regime. A 1950 work by Klocke, for example, asked the question: How did genealogy become "perverted" into the service of racist thought, and ultimately the Nazi regime? His answer was that genealogy's failing was due to the attempt to incorporate "science" into an unscientific field, and that the vast majority of genealogists were not competent to apply biological concepts to their work.

This explanation says more about Klocke than about the "perversion" of genealogy. In fact, genealogists simply embraced a prevalent ideological strain that claimed science had justified racism. Thus, the racist assumptions were not primarily the result of genealogists going beyond their field of competence. They resulted, rather, from genealogists' acceptance of a worldview promoted not just by a few scientists, but by many segments of German society.[11] Genealogists had their own specific motivations for accepting this worldview. But they were only one group of many in Germany that uncritically embraced what amounted to a new faith. This faith provided a satisfactory means for many Germans to maintain the perception of their own integrity while promoting or acquiescing in the brutal policies leading to the Final Solution and other atrocities.

Notes

Introduction

1. For the purposes of this work, *genealogical practice* includes traditional research on ancestry—both amateur and professional—as well as civil registry work, the most closely related profession.

2. For a discussion of such attitudes in the higher levels of the civil service, see Caplan, *Government,* 62–64.

3. MacMaster, *Racism,* 151.

4. Hitler quoted in Kershaw, *Hitler,* 176; Müller, "Unternehmen Barbarossa," 125–57 (magnitude of exploitation). A recent estimate of Soviet deaths in World War II is 25 million, 17 million of whom were civilians. See Overy, *Russia's War,* 288. Moreover, of the approximately 8 million Soviet military dead, almost 3.5 million died in German captivity from exposure and starvation, that is, due to the withholding of material resources. See Streit, "Behandlung," 159–83. A plausible estimate of the number of Polish Christian dead is approximately 3 million. See Lukas, *Forgotten Holocaust,* 38–39.

1. Racial Science

1. See, e.g., Wecken, *Ahnentafel,* 3 ("the experience of modern racial research has shown that . . . [German or] similar blood can be exterminated by the intrusion of alien blood with racially inferior or dissimilar hereditary properties"); Wilhelm Frick, "Bedeutung der Nürnberger Gesetze," *Westdeutscher Beobachter,* 2/13/36, NS20/143-3 ("if a Volk does not maintain the purity of its blood, but rather absorbs into itself blood of a different kind, the necessary consequence is that a rupture arises in its unity and . . . its nature perishes . . ."); Stuckart, *Rassen- und Erbpflege,* 6 ("A mixture of blood between members of unrelated races leads . . . to . . . [a meeting] of capacities that are not compatible with each other"); Stuckart, *Rassengesetzgebung,* 135 ("there are . . . crosses of alien-type races that are racially pernicious and damaging to the Volk").

2. See, e.g., Frick, *Westdeutscher Beobachter,* 2/13/36, and Lösener, *Nürnburger,* 19 (Jewish problem is a race problem); Report by Abteilung Volksgesundheit des Reichs- und Preußischen Ministeriums des Innern, 9/35, Rep. 320/513:33–39, and Rundschreiben Nr. 117/43, Leiter der Partei-Kanzlei, 8/22/43, NS6/342:50–52 (Jewish characteristics are hereditary).

3. *Der Ahnenpaß* (Berlin: Verlag für Standesamtswesen, nd.), 3.

4. Koonz, *Nazi Conscience,* 9.

5. Quoted in Arnd, "Horse Breeder's Perspective," 376.

6. Baur, *Human Heredity,* 499.

7. Heilbron, *Dilemmas,* 180.

8. Macrakis, *Surviving the Swastika,* 3, 45–46.

9. See, e.g., Walker, *Nazi Science,* 87; Mehrtens, "Social System," 299.

10. Proctor, *Racial Hygiene,* 37–38. This was in the context of the debate over the heritability of acquired characteristics. Proponents of "nature" over "nurture," which included Nazi ideologues, actually had the better of the scientific debate in this regard.

11. Verschuer, "Volkstum und Rasse," *Zeitschrift für Volksaufartung und Erbkunde* 1 (1926): 128–29.

12. Bauer, *Human Heredity,* 663–66. See also Hutton, *Race.*

13. See, e.g., Verschuer, *Rasse,* 4 ("we are still determining the present cultural abilities of the races through inductive means").

14. Langmuir, "Prolegomena," 136–38; Zmarzlik, "Social Darwinism," 13. Indeed, Verschuer seemed to disdain the need for actual scientific verification in this regard, writing: "Is any proof actually necessary that the mind of a Negro and a European is so very different that all the arts of the world cannot make them equivalent?" Verschuer, *Rasse,* 6.

15. On claims of the dangers of race-mixing see, e.g., Günther, *Racial Elements,* 2–3, 51–52, 167; Baur, *Human Heredity,* 177–78, 181, 193, 624–25, 682, 692–93; Eugen Fischer, "Spezielle Anthropologie: Rassenlehre," in G. Schwalbe/E. Fischer (Hrsg.), *Die Kultur die Gegenwart,* 167; Friedlander, *Origins,* 11.

16. On the widespread confusion in this regard in the late nineteenth and early twentieth centuries, see, e.g., Kiefer, *Problem;* Lilienthal, "Rassenmerkmale," 173.

17. Mazumdar, "Blood and Soil," 200–202.

18. Fishberg, *Rassenmerkmale,* vi, 256–62.

19. See Gould, *Mismeasure of Man.*

20. Ehrenreich, *Anti-Semitism,* 29–33.

21. Richard Eckstein, "Rassenforschung, Rassenglaube, Rassenlegende," *Zeitenwende* 4 (1928): 289–99, quoted in Weiss, "Vorgeschichte," 507. For similar criticism, see also "Rassenwissenschaft und Rassenwahn," *Die Gesellschaft,* 4 (1927): 97–114.

22. See, e.g., Reuter, *Race Mixture;* Dover, *Half-Caste;* Jennings, *Scientific Aspects of the Race Problem.* For a contemporary analysis, see Barkan, *Retreat of Scientific Racism.*

23. S. Wellisch, "1. Anthropologische Rassenanalyse," *Zeitschrift für Rassenkunde* 5 (1937): 152.

24. Verschuer, "Erbanlage als Schicksal und Aufgabe," *Preussische Akademie der Wissenschaften Vorträge und Schriften,* 18 (Berlin: de Gruyter, 1944), 13, 17–18, 24. Despite this, Verschuer insisted on the truth of the basic racist premise: notwithstanding the great physical and mental variability within each race, the "average" abilities of each race "show differences" between the races. These "racial differences" are the primary reason for differences in culture, and "racial degeneration" leads to cultural degeneration. Ibid., 15.

25. Verschuer, "Rassenbiologie der Juden," *Forschungen zur Judenfrage,* 3 (1938): 137–51.

26. Eugen Fischer, "Rassenentstehung und älteste Rassengeschichte der Hebräer," *Forschungen zur Judenfrage* 3 (1938): 136.

27. The entire 1937 edition of the *Zeitschrift für Rassenkunde,* for example, discusses the racial characteristics of, inter alia, Nordics, Alpines, Mediterraneans, Dinarics, East Europeans, Uzbeks, Kirgisiens, Armenians, Turks, Arabs, Sardinians, Laps, Westfinns, Eastfinns, Chinese, Malaysians, and indigenous Australians. There was, however, seemingly nothing on Jews. Likewise, the journal *Rasse,* a "Monthly for the Nordic Movement" published between 1934 and 1944, contained numerous articles with detailed studies on the "Nordic race" in all its physical and cultural attributes. Despite frequent mention of Jews, their physical attributes were rarely discussed, and their cultural attributes were always bad. See also Schultze-Naumburg's review

of Dr. Fritz Arlt's *Volksbiologische Untersuchungen über die Juden in Leipzig* (Leipzig: S. Hirzel, 1937) in *FSV* 4 (1938): 60 (noting general lack of research on Jews).

28. Dr. Elfriede Fliethmann, "Vorläufiger Bericht über Anthropologische Aufnahmen an Judenfamilien in Tarnow," *Deutsche Forschung im Osten* 2 (1942): 92–111. For more on this study, see Schafft, *From Racism to Genocide,* 15–36.

29. Gesetz zur Widerherstellung des Berufsbeamtentums (RGBl. I S. 175).

30. Erste Verordnung zur Durchführung des Gesetzes zur Widerherstellung des Berufsbeamtentums. Vom 11. April 1933 (RGBl. I S. 195).

31. Ulmenstein, *Abstammungsnachweis,* 103–104; Knost, *Feststellung,* 4–7.

32. Memo, Deutsches Generalkonsulat Istanbul (Toepke) to Auswärtige Amt, 5/16/38, R39/152.

33. Rundschreiben Nr. 124/43, Der Leiter der Partei-Kanzlei, 9/2/43 ("Zugehörigkeit von Parteigenossen zum Islam"), NS6/342:64.

34. Seel to Gercke, 7/31/33, R39/1.

35. Gercke to Frick, 8/1/33, R39/1.

36. Reichs Erbhofgesetz vom 29.9.1933 (RGBl. I S. 685).

37. See, e.g., Ulmenstein, *Abstammungsnachweis,* 12.

38. Ulmenstein claimed that the term *Aryan* was dropped in legal usage because it referred to linguistic groups and the races who initially spoke those languages. Now, however, wrote Ulmenstein, many non-Aryan races speak Aryan languages while many Aryan races now speak non-Aryan languages. Since no Volk is of pure race, it is more accurate to seek out "German or related blood." Ulmenstein, *Abstammungsnachweis,* 11–13. Yet in the same work, Ulmenstein wrote that "Negroes and gypsies," in addition to Jews, were "non-Aryan." Ibid., 105.

39. "Einbürgerung des Bela N. in Dresden. Zu Nr. 399 c V vom 22. August 1934," 10/3/34, R39/1.

40. Wecken, *Ahnentafel, 3.*

41. Lösener, *Nürnburger,* 18.

42. S. Wellisch, "Rassendiagnose der Ungarn," *Zeitschrift für Rassenkunde* 1 (1938): 33. The two major "schools of thought" were either that "pure Hungarians" were predominantly Asiatic or predominantly "Alpine," i.e., of "European race." Ibid., 33–34.

43. See, Rundschreiben Nr. 184/42, Partei-Kanzlei, "Heiraten von Wehrmachtangehörigen mit Angehörigen der artverwandten germanischen Nachbarvölker," NS6/338:239.

44. Gross to Mayer, 9/7/43, and subsequent correspondence, R39/29. The agencies were the GSA-W, the Reich Genealogical Authority, the RPA, and the Auslands-Organisation.

45. Knost, *Feststellung, 4.*

46. "Einbürgerung des Bela N. in Dresden. Zu Nr. 399 c V vom 22. August 1934," 10/3/34, R39/1.

47. Verfügung V 10/40 (Hess), 23/11/40, NS6/333:50.

48. Ulmenstein, *Abstammungsnachweis,* 11–13.

49. Knost, *Feststellung, 4.*

50. Fishberg, *Rassenmerkmale,* vi, 256–62.

51. Prof. Dr. Felix Jentzsch, "Wie erforscht man die Grösse und Art der deutschjüdischen Vermischung (Bastardierung) am Besten?" (n/d, but under cover of 4/1/36 letter to Günther), R39/2.

52. Günther to RfS, 4/9/36; Mayer to Günther, 4/27/36. Both in R39/2. On this concern, see also E. H. Schulz, "Der jüdische Blutstrom. Schon eine Million Menschen in Deutschland erfaßt?" *Ziel und Weg* (1938), 213–16.

53. Jentzsch, "Wie erforscht man?" R39/2.
54. Mayer to Günther, 4/27/36, R39/2.
55. Jentzsch, "Wie erforscht man?" R39/2.
56. "Rußland-Institut der Auslandhochschule Berlin, 19.5.1938," contained in memo, Ulmenstein to RMdI, 6/17/38, R39/152.
57. Gutachten, Prof. Dr. Lothar Loeffler, Rassenbiologischen Instituts der Universität Königsberg/Pr, 11/2/39, R39/152.
58. N/d, NS20/143-5.
59. All of the following reports were enclosures, under cover of Dr. Gross, Hauptamtslieter, to Partei-Kanzlei, München, Führerbau, 3/22/45, R39/152.

2. The Origins of Racist Eugenics in Imperial Germany

1. Definition of socioeconomic classes is highly specialized. This study uses those of Michael Kater in his social profile of Nazi Party members. Kater, *Nazi Party,* 5. While Kater's definitions apply to the Weimar and Nazi eras, for the purposes of this work—essentially to show the extent to which interest in genealogical research spread across socioeconomic strata—these broad definitions are also sufficiently accurate for the years 1870–1914.
2. For a more detailed description of these historical interactions, see Weiss, *Race Hygiene,* 7–14.
3. Kelly, *Descent of Darwin;* Gasman, *Scientific Origins of National Socialism.*
4. On the growth of eugenics in Germany, see Weiss, "Race Hygiene Movement," 8–68.
5. V. S. Naipaul, *Beyond Belief: Islamic Excursions Among the Converted Peoples* (New York: Random House, 1998), xii.
6. Klocke, *Entwicklung,* 15; Dr. Heinrich Butte, Dresden, Ratsarchivar, "Über Familienforschung" *StAZ* 4 (1924), 261–64.
7. See, e.g., Mommsen, *Imperial Germany,* 120; Blackbourn, *History of Germany,* 276–78, 310, 314–16.
8. See Ribbe, *Taschenbuch,* 625. In 1911, the series' name changed to the *German Book of Lineages (deutsches Geschlechterbuch).*
9. Ibid., 623.
10. Klocke, *Entwicklung,* 23.
11. Klocke, *Entwicklung,* 17–18, 44. On the founding of the Zentralstelle, see Schupp, "Der Weg der Zentralstelle," 91–110. For a Nazi-era evaluation of the "Leipziger circle," see *FSV* 4 (1938): 8.
12. Ribbe, *Taschenbuch,* 344–46, 623. In 1872, the Herold also began producing a quarterly, the *Vierteljahrschrift für Wappen-, Siegel- und Familienkunde,* which continued to appear until 1943.
13. Ibid., 346–49.
14. Ibid., 628.
15. Klocke, *Entwicklung,* 25–26. See also, e.g., "Vermischtes," *DH* 41 (1910): 34 (describing the course "Introduction to Genealogy" at Albertus University, Königsberg).
16. "Vermischtes," *DH* 41 (1910): 62; Ein neuer Kursus über "Familienforschung und Vererbungslehre," *DH* 42 (1911): 233.
17. See, e.g., Devrient, *Familienforschung;* Heydenreich, *Familiengeschichtliche Quellenkunde.*
18. Arthur Czellitzer, "Zum Geleit," *Judischer Familienforschung* 1 (1925): 2.
19. Weiss, "Vorgeschichte," 432–36.

20. In its very first edition, the *FB* promised its potential subscribers that it would deal not only with north and central, but also southern Germany. *FB* 1 (1903): 2.

21. See, e.g., *FB* 13 (1915): 3–4, 65–66; *FB* 16 (1918): 25–26, 97–98.

22. Weiss, "Vorgeschichte," 497.

23. C. U. Knab, *FB* 13 (1915): 97–100.

24. On the jubilant nationalism that spread throughout Germany at the outbreak of World War I, irrespective of class, politics, or religion, see, e.g., Craig, *Germany*, 339–40. On the essential "conservatism of the cult of the fallen," see Mosse, *Fallen Soldiers*, 103.

25. N/a, "Ueber Familien-Chroniken," *DH* 24 (1893): 32.

26. O. frh. v. u. z. Aufsetz, "Mitteilungen aus einem Vortrage . . . ," *DH* 19 (1888): 102; Esaias Tegner, *FB* 1 (1903): 1.

27. Edith Zerbin-Rüdin, "Genetische Familienforschung," in Ribbe, *Taschenbuch*, 104.

28. Klocke, *Entwicklung*, 23.

29. Ibid., 27.

30. Devrient, *Familienforschung*, 90; Klocke, *Entwicklung*, 28.

31. Wentscher, *Einführung*, 164. Cf. Isenburg, *Sippen*, 57 (Lorenz established genealogy as the "bridge" between history and natural science).

32. Klocke, *Entwicklung*, 27. A table that traced all descendents of a couple, both male and female, was called a "descendants table [*Nachfahrentafel*]." A "kinship table [*Sippschafts-tafel*]" showed the relationship of a person to all of the descendants of his grandparents. Lothar Stengel v. Rutkowski, "Historische Genealogie oder züchterische Familienkunde," *Volk und Rasse* II (1935): 40–49.

33. Isenburg, *Sippen*, 7. In the Nazi era, of course, the *Ahnentafel* became the preferred method for making the ancestral proof. See, e.g., Achim Gercke, "Wir treiben Sippenfor-schung," *FSV* 1 (1935): 19–23.

34. Klocke, *Entwicklung*, 29.

35. Kekule, "Ziel und Aufgaben der wissenschaftlichen Genealogie," *Vierteljahrsschrift für Wappen-, Siegel- und Familienkunde*, Jg. 31 (1900); Arnim Tille, "Genealogie als Wissen-schaft," *MdZ* 2 (1906): 32; Arnim Tille, "Die sozialwissenschaftliche Bedeutung der Genealo-gie," *MdZ* 6 (1910): 1.

36. "Geburtskoeffizient," *DH* 43 (1912): 260; Dr. med. Ed. Krauß, "Ueber Vererbung und Familienforschung," *MdR* 1 (1916): 42, 50, *MdR* 2 (1917): 2; Dr. Hans Meyer, *Zur Biolo-gie der Zwillinge* (Stuttgart: Union, 1917), reviewed in *DH* 48 (1917): 79–80.

37. Kekule, "Ein Institut für Vererbungsforschung," *DH* 45 (1914): 127; Gruber und Rüdin, "Uebersicht über die wichtigsten vererblichen Mißbildungen, krankhaften Anlagen und Krankheiten des Menschen," *MdR* 1 (1916): 5; Valentin Haecker, *Die Erblichkeit im Mannesstamm und der vaterrechtliche Familienbegriff* (Jena: Gustav Fischer, 1917), reviewed in *FB* 17 (1919): 39.

38. Professor Dr. Sommer, "Ein Kursus über Familienforschung und Vererbungslehre," *DH* 39 (1908): 82–83; Kekule, "Bericht über den Kursus über Familienforschung und Ver-erbungslehre . . . in Gießen," ibid., 168–69.

39. J. Grober, "Die Bedeutung der Ahnentafel für die biologische Erblichkeitsfor-schung," *AfRuG*, 1 (1904): 664–81. See also *DH* 43 (1912): 259 (same article).

40. See, e.g., Wilhelm Strohmayer, "Über den Wert genealogischer Betrach-tungsweise in der psychiatrischen Erblichkeitslehre," *Monatschrift für Psychiatrie und Neurologie* 22 (1907): 115; Robert Sommer," Genealogie und Vererbungslehre vom psychiatrischen Standpunkt," *Deutsche medizinische Wochenschrift* 38 (1911): 1733; Prof. Dr. Walter Scheidt, *Einführung in die naturwissenschaftliche Familienkunde (Familienanthropologie)* (München: Lehmann, 1923); Ribbe, *Taschenbuch*, 627.

41. Isenburg, *Sippen,* 8.

42. See, e.g., Walter Pfeilsticker, "Die Dauerbarkeit des Stammestypus und die Verwertbarkeit des Bildnisses zur Vererbungsforschung," *FB* 17 (1919): 27; Max Grünwald, "Über Blutgruppenzugehöörigkeit, insbesondere bei unehelicher Vaterschaft," *FB* 26 (1928): 252–53.

43. "Die Feier des dreißigjährigen Bestehens des 'Roland'," *MdR* 17 (1932): 14.

44. Weingart, *Rasse,* 199–205.

45. C. v. Bardeleben, "Der Kongreß für Eugenik in London vom 24. bis 30. Juli 1912," *DH* 43 (1912): 193.

46. Kekule, "Die Genealogie auf der Internationalen Hygiene-Ausstellung zu Dresden," *FB* 10 (1912): 3–4, 19–20, 39–40.

47. Weiss, "Vorgeschichte," 432.

48. Dr. Moriz Wertner, "Die Entwicklung des genealogischen Begriffes," *DH* 17 (1886): 12. The idea also appeared in more subtle forms. For example, Lorenz's classic 1887 work, *Manual of Complete Scientific Genealogy,* later appeared under the title *Mystery of the Blood,* which, at a minimum, implied that heredity was a very important factor in determining individual destiny. Klocke, *Entwicklung,* 10.

49. Dr. med. et. phil. Robert Sommer, *Friedrich der Große vom Standpunkt der Vererbungslehre* (no publication information), reviewed in *DH* 48 (1917): 111.

50. C. v. Bardeleben, "Der Kongreß für Eugenik in London vom 24. bis 30. Juli 1912," *DH* 43 (1912): 194; "Bericht über den Kongreß für Familienforschung, Vererbungs- und Regenerationslehre vom 11. bis 13. April 1912," ibid., 127–31.

51. Fredrickson, *Racism,* 24–25, 67.

52. See, e.g., Chickering, *We Men,* 244.

53. Devrient, *Familienforschung,* 97–98.

54. "Referat über die Vorträge . . . ," *DH* 29 (1898): 17.

55. Dr. Theodore Arldt, *Die Stammesgeschichte der Primaten und die Entwicklung der Menschenrassen* (Berlin: Hirschwald, 1915), reviewed in *FB* 13 (1915): 183.

56. v. Lenthe, "Der Neger Peters des Großen," *DH* 48 (1917): 87.

57. "Türkentaufe," *DH* 47 (1916): 127; "Vermischtes," *DH* 49 (1918): 7; "Vermischtes," *DH* 49 (1918): 15. See, e.g., Wilhelm Bandau, "Eine Prenzlauer Mohrentaufe," *ArchfS* 8 (1931): 219; Walther van Hees, "Eine Negertaufe 1823 im Kb. Mülheim a. Rh.," ibid., 362.

58. See, e.g., Benz, *Vorurteil;* Goldhagen, *Executioners;* Tal, *Christians and Jews;* Katz, *Prejudice;* Volkov, "Antisemitism."

59. Ernst Moritz Arndt, *Ein Blick aus der Zeit auf die Zeit* (1814), quoted in Lilienthal, "Rassenmerkmale," 173.

60. For in-depth studies of these parties, see Pulzer, *Rise of Political Anti-Semitism;* Levy, *Downfall of the Anti-Semitic Political Parties;* Massing, *Rehearsal for Destruction.*

61. Mosse, *Toward the Final Solution,* 120–21, 176–77; Katz, *Prejudice,* 304–307.

62. Guido List, *Der Bilderschrift der Ario-Germanen* (Leipzig: Steinacker, 1910), reviewed in *DH* 41 (1910): 187.

63. *Geadelte jüdische Familien.* 3. Auflage. (Salzburg: Kyffhäuser, 1891), reviewed in *DH* 24 (1893): 35.

64. *Geadelte jüdische Familien, Sonder-Abdruck aus der deutsch-nationalen Wochenschrift "Der Kyffhäuser,"* (Salzburg; Kyffhäuser, 1889), reviewed in *DH* 20 (1889): 114–19.

65. Werner Sombart et al., *Judentaufen* (München: Müller, 1912), reviewed in *FB* 10 (1912): 86–87.

66. Grolle, "Deutsches Geschlechterbuch," 316–17.

67. Marcelli Janecki, "Die ältesten Juden-Nobilitirungen in Litauen," *DH* 21 (1890): 97–99.

68. Koerner, "Jüdische Familiennamen," *DH* 38 (1907): 28–31; Vibrans, "Jüdische Familiennamen im Braunschweigischen," ibid., 157.

69. Pfarrer O. Fischer, "Familienkunde in Zeitungen," *DH* 48 (1917): 34.

70. Ibid.

71. Ph. Stauff, *Deutsche Judennamen* (Deutsch-völkischen Schriftsteller-Verbandes, 1912), reviewed in *FB* 10 (1912): 195.

72. P. v. Gebhardt, "Taufe einer Jüdin in Pesterwitz im Jahre 1706," *FB* 13 (1915): 307.

73. See, e.g., *DH* 42 (1911): 214; "Das unberechtigte 'von'," *DH* 48 (1918): 39.

74. Koerner, however, was not elected to the Zentralstelle's board the following year. Weiss, "Vorgeschichte," 497, 500.

3. The Spread of Racist Eugenics in Weimar

1. See, e.g., Laqueur, *Weimar,* 31–32.

2. Isenburg, *Sippen,* 59; Klocke, *Entwicklung,* 42–43.

3. Bürgermeister Dr. Ritter, "Zur Namen- und Familienkunde," *StAZ* 4 (1924): 102; Ribbe, *Taschenbuch,* 344–49, 629.

4. Denkschrift, Umlauft, 9/15/43, 5, R1509/5.

5. Wilhelm Hussong, *Familienkunde, ihre Bedeutung und ihre Ziele* (Leipzig: Reclam, 1928), reviewed in *DH* 59 (1928): 111–12.

6. See, e.g., Theodore Müller, *Baurliche Familienforschung: Ein Beitrag zur Fami-lien-geschichtlichen Quellenkunde Niedersachsens* (Leipzig: Degener, 1930), discussed in *FB* 29 (1931): 82; *ArchfS* 7 (1930): 226–38; "Bäuerliche Familienforschung," *StAZ* 11 (1931): 382–83; Ribbe, *Taschenbuch,* 631.

7. Hertz, "Genealogy Bureaucracy," 54, 63–64.

8. See, e.g., Fritz Curschmann, "Zwei Ahnentafeln Kaiser Friedrichs I., u. Heinrichs des Löwen," *MdZ* 27 (1921); Isenburg, *Die Ahnen der deutschen Kaiser und Könige und ihrer Gemahlinnen* (Görlitz: Starke, 1932).

9. Contributors' professions were listed until 1927. The title *von* or *Freiherr* usually indicated noble lineage.

10. For a brief history of the Roland, see "Aus der Vereinsgeschichte des 'Roland'," *MdR* 12 (1927): 1–3.

11. Walter Schneider, "Schwartz-rot-gold," *DH* 50 (1919): 60; A. Cloß, "Ist schwarz-rot-gold als alte Reichsfarbe zu betrachten?" *DH* 57 (1926): 25; Bürgermeister Baumgarten, Feital/Sa., "Die Aufgaben des Standesbeamten im neuen Staat," *StAZ* 10 (1930): 334.

12. Gercke to unidentified correspondent, 3/16/34, Rep. 309/280.

13. Wecken, *Taschenbuch,* 141.

14. Kurd v. Strantz, "Bücherschau. Elster, Sozialbiologie . . . ," *DH* 55 (1924): 49; Pfarrer i. R. D. Franz Blanckmeister, "Der innere Wert der Familienforschung," *MdR* 17 (1932): 15.

15. Hohlfeld, "Neue Bücher zu Rassenkunde und Familienpolitik," *FB* 26 (1928): 142.

16. See, e.g., Stern, *Cultural Despair.* In 1932, the *FB* changed the table of contents heading from *Ständische* Genealogy to *Sociological* Genealogy. In 1935, it switched back to the original format.

17. Dr. Freiherrn Eric v. Born, "Das Absterben der Adesgeschlechter in Nordeuropa," *FB* 26 (1928): 25–32.

18. v. Strantz, "Bücherschau. Elster, Sozialbiologie . . . ," *DH* 55 (1924): 49.

19. Kekule, "Familienforschung in Volks- und Freistaaten," *DH* 50 (1919): 10; Standes-beamten Lehrer Georg Meilahn, "Sinn und Zweck der Familienforschung," *StAZ* 9 (1929): 236.

20. *FB* 26 (1928): 260–62.

21. Standesamtsdirektor Wlochatz, "Familienforschung und Standesamt," *StAZ* 7 (1927): 74–76. For similar claims, see also *FB* 26 (1928): 260–62; *Deutsches Einheits-Familienstammbuch* (Reichsbund der Standesbeamten Deutschlands e.V., 1928), reviewed in *DH* 6 (1930): 55–56; Pfarrer i. R. D. Franz Blanckmeister, "Der innere Wert der Familienforschung," *MdR* 17 (1932): 15.

22. *DH* 51 (1920): 34; "Zum neuen Jahre!" *FB* 18 (1920): 2; Standesbeamten Max Sachsenröder, "Der Standesbeamte im Dienste der Heimatpflege," *StAZ* 6 (1926): 268–69; "Die Feier des dreißigjährigen Bestehens des 'Roland'," *MdR* 17 (1932): 14.

23. Standesamtsdirektor Wlochatz, "Standesamt und Namengebung," *StAZ* 7 (1927): 213–14.

24. Staatsoberarchivar Dr. Fürst, "Grundlagen der Familienforschung," *StAZ* 2 (1922): 278.

25. Wundt, *Volk, Volkstum, Volkheit*, 14.

26. Karl Förster, "Deutsche Ahnengemeinschaft (DA). Ein Aufruf," *Thüringer Heimatspiegel* 8 (1931): 226–28.

27. See, e.g., Kekule, "Festrede zum Gedenktage des fünfzigjährigen Bestehens des Herold," *DH* 51 (1920): 5–10; Dr. med. R. Fetscher, "Familienforschung und Erbbiologie," *MdR* 13 (1928): 24–25; Dr. med. Roesler, "Zwischen Naturwissenschaft und Geschichte," *FB* 26 (1928): 343.

28. See, e.g., Dr. phil. Arthur Heller, "Über vererbliche Kurzfingerigkeit," *FB* 20 (1922): 33–38; Wecken, "Zur Geschichte des Vererbungsproblems," *DH* 61 (1930): 45; *ArchfS* 9 (1932): 236 (reviewing book *Vererbung und Krebsforschung*).

29. "Bezugs-Einladung," *ArchfS* 1(1928): 2.

30. Weiss, "Vorgeschichte," 615; Prof. Dr. Kuhn, "Vererbung und Gattenwahl," *MdR* 8 (1923): 28; Dr. med. Kaufmann, "Menschliche Erblichkeitsgesetze," ibid. 24; *FB* 23 (1925): 272 (course for hereditary research and social hygiene).

31. *FB* 23 (1925): 340–42.

32. Breymann, "Genealogie und Vererbungslehre," *FB* 20 (1922): 193–96. See also, e.g., Dr. Scheumann, "Eheberatung und Standesamt," *StAZ* 10 (1930): 345–48; Dr. Konrad Dürre, "Eugenik Politik. Eine brennende Tagesfrage," *StAZ* 11 (1931): 248.

33. Scheidt, *Familienbuch. Anleitung und Vordrucke zur Herstellung einer Familiengeschichte* (München: Lehmann, 1924), reviewed in *DH* 57 (1926): 15. See also, e.g., Fritz Lenz, *Über die biologischen Grundlagen der Erziehung* (München: Lehmann, 1925), reviewed in *StAZ* 6 (1926): 144; Dr. jur., Dr. med. H. C. Carl F. L. v. Behr-Pinnow, *Menschheitsdämmerung? Eine Darst. d. menschl. Vererbung u. ihrer Bedeutung f. d. Volkswohl* (Berlin: Stilke, 1929), reviewed in *StAZ* 10 (1930): 32, 64.

34. Weiss, "Vorgeschichte," 430–31. This institute was the basis for the later Kaiser Wilhelm Institute for Anthropology.

35. Noted in *StAZ* 10 (1930): 64. See also Weindling, *Health*, 406; Weingart, *Rasse*, 252–53; Weiss, "Race Hygiene Movement," 34–35.

36. See, e.g., Sachsenröder, "Mehr Familien-, Heimat- und Volkssinn!" *StAZ* 5 (1925): 151–53.

37. "Fachwissenschaftliche Woche für Standesbeamte," *StAZ* 5 (1925): 165 (advertisement); "Bericht über die Verhandlungen des 4. Bundestages des Reichsbunds der Standesbeamten Deutschlands E.V.," *StAZ* 5 (1925): 305–307.

38. Bundesdirektor Krutina, "Ein für Standesbeamte unentbehrliches Werk über Volksaufartung und Erbkunde," *StAZ* 5 (1925): 174–75.

39. "Vermischtes," *DH* 48 (1917): 101.

40. Klocke, "Familienkunde und Familienpolitik," *MdR* 14 (1929): 22.

41. Stadtschularzt Dr. Th. Fürst, "Der Standesbeamte als Förderer der biologischen Familienkunde," *StAZ* 11 (1931): 27. For earlier examples see, e.g., Georg Hänel, "Pflege der Ahnen- und Familienforschung in ihrer Bedeutung für die Zukunft des deutschen Volkes," *MdR* 6 (1921): 4, 33; Preußische Minister für Volkswohlfahrt, Stölzel, "Ehebartungstellen und Gesundheitszeugnisse," *StAZ* 6 (1926): 113–16.

42. Krutina, "Rundfunkvortrag, gehalten über die Deutsche Welle am 21. September 1932, 'Standesamt und Eugenik'," *StAZ* 12 (1932): 413.

43. Report by Abteilung Volksgesundheit des Reichs- und Preußischen Ministeriums des Innern, Rep. 320/513:33–39.

44. See, e.g., Ed. Krauß, "Über Vererbung und Familienforschung," *MdR* 9 (1924): 2 ("heredity is the red thread that goes through everything, what life means . . . our mental and physical attributes are first and foremost founded on our genes which lie in the nucleus of the germ cells").

45. Dr. Ludwig Finckh, "Neues von der Ahnenkunde," *MdR* 8 (1923): 21.

46. Behr-Pinnow, "Vererbung—Erziehung und Unterricht," *StAZ* 8 (1928): 107; Dürre, "Eugenik Politik. Eine brennende Tagesfrage," *StAZ* 11 (1931): 248.

47. Alexander Elster, *Sozialbiologie* (Berlin, Leipzig: de Gruyter, 1923), reviewed in *DH* 55 (1924): 49; Dr. Jacob Graf, *Vererbungslehre und Erbgesundheitspflege. Einführung nach methodischen Grundsätzen* (München: Lehmann, 1930), reviewed in *FB* 28 (1930): 360–61.

48. Schultze-Naumburg, "Rassenkunde und Sippenforschung," *FSV* 4 (1938): 3.

49. Sachsenröder, "Familienregister, Stamm- und Heimatbuch, Gesundheitspaß," *MdR* 10 (1925): 37.

50. Sachsenröder, "Die förderung biologischer Aufzeichnungen beim Standesamte durch Gesundheitspässe und -bogen," ibid., 62 (article noted that a "circle of family and locality [*Heimat*] researchers" greeted with "full understanding" the author's proposal for the "preservation of the health and regeneration of the Volk"); Krutina, "Der Standesbeamte in Dienste der Allgemeinheit," *StAZ* 8 (1928): 125; Max Kätzbacher, Wissenschaftlicher Mitarbeiter der Anthropologischen Abteilung des Anatomischen Instituts der Universität Heidelberg, "Gesundheitskataster," *StAZ* 10 (1930): 59–61.

51. See, e.g., Satzung des Reichsbundes der Standesbeamten Deutschlands E.V., *StAZ* 6 (1926): 110; Standesbeamter Wilh. Braeger, "Das Familienstammbuch," *StAZ* 10 (1930): 25.

52. Standesbeamten Leib, "Familienstammbuch und Wiederaufbau," *StAZ* 2 (1922): 80–81; v. Wrangel, "Bevölkerungspolitik und Eheberatung," *StAZ* 9 (1929): 358; "Bäuerliche Familienforschung," *StAZ* 11 (1931): 382–83.

53. Krutina, "Der Standesbeamte in Dienste der Allgemeinheit," *StAZ* 8 (1928): 125.

54. N/a, "Ausbau der Standesämter zu 'Ehe- und Familien-Aemtern'," *StAZ* 12 (1932): 417.

55. Standesbeamten Hans Wander, "Eine neue Aufgabe des Standesbeamten," *StAZ* 12 (1932): 145; ibid. (1932) (advertisement, cover sheet, 2); Sachsen. Urkundenbuch der Kinderheit. (Ministerium des Innern, 11. 6. 1932 . . .), ibid., 221; Braunschweig. Urkundenbuch der Kindheit. Der Braunschweigische Minister des Innern . . . 8. Juli 1932, in ibid., 261–62; Ibid. (advertisement, back cover sheet, 2).

56. Standesamtsobersekretär Müller, "Das Gesundheits Merkblatt," *StAZ* 2 (1922): 267.

57. Wecken, *Taschenbuch* (1919), 150; see, e.g., Dr. med. R. Neubert, "Bevölkerungspolitik und Eheberatung," *StAZ* 7 (1927): 273–74.

58. v. Wrangel, "Bevölkerungspolitik und Eheberatung," *StAZ* 9 (1929): 358. See also Krutina, "Ueber die Zukunft der deutschen Personenstandsregisterführung," *StAZ* 11 (1931): 5; Fälle aus der Praxis, Ibid., 61; Dürre, "Eugenik Politik. Eine brennende Tagesfrage," ibid., 248.

59. Dr. med. Karl Nissen, "Der Verhütung lebensunwerten Lebens," *FB* 23 (1925): 175.

60. Wilhelm Karl Prinz von Isenburg, *Genealogie als Lehrfach. Zugleich Einführung in ihre Probleme* (Leipzig: Degener, 1928), quoted in Burghardt, *Familienforschung,* 202.

61. See, e.g., Dr. Leo Francke, "Stand und Kinderzahl," *FSV* 2 (1936): 7–8; Dürre, "Die Vererbung überdurchschnittlicher Begabung," ibid., 9.

62. Arthur Czellitzer, "Leitsätze der Deutschen Gesellschaft für Eugenik," *Jüdische Familienforschung* 8 (1932): 430. This journal lasted from 1925 to 1938.

63. "Was will der Deutsche Bund für Volksaufartung und Erbkunde," *Zeitschrift für Volksaufartung und Erbkunde* 1 (1926): 3.

64. Wecken, *Taschenbuch,* 144–45.

65. Standesbeamten Georg Müller, "Was Bezweckt die Aushändigung der Gesundheitsmerkblätter bei Aufgebotsantragen und Einforderung ärztlicher Eheatteste," *StAZ* 3 (1923): 100.

66. Büchersprechung, *StAZ* 7 (1927): 64.

67. G. von Hoffmann, *Rassenhygiene und Fortpflanzungshygiene (Eugenic)* (no publication information), reviewed in *DH* 48 (1917): 52; Scheidt, *Einführung* (München: Lehmann, 1923)," reviewed in *DH* 55 (1924): 25.

68. Dürre, "Wie sind die eugenischen Abteilungen auf den Standesämtern zu organisieren?" *StAZ* 5 (1925): 24–25; Sachsenröder, "Der Standesbeamte im Dienste der Heimatpflege," *StAZ* 6 (1926): 268–69.

69. v. Wrangel, "Die Mitarbeit der Standesbeamten an der Familiengeschichte," *StAZ* 6 (1926): 78; "Bevölkerungspolitik und Eheberatung," *StAZ* 9 (1929): 358.

70. Finckh, "Neues von der Ahnenkunde," *MdR* 8 (1923): 21.

71. Fritz Kern, *Stammbaum und Artbild der Deutschen. Ein Kultur- und Rassengeschichtlicher Versuch* (München: Lehmann, 1927), reviewed in *MdR* 13 (1928): 6.

72. K. Saller, *Die Fehmaraner. Eine anthropologische Untersuchung aus Ostholstein* (Jena: Gustav Fischer, 1930), reviewed in *FB* 28 (1930): 424.

73. Wilh. Klenck und Walter Scheidt, *Niedersächsische Bauern I* (Jena: Gustav Fischer, 1929), reviewed in *MdR* 16 (1931): 19–20; Scheidt, *Nidersächsische Bauern* (Jena: Gustav Fischer, 1932), reviewed in *MdR* 17 (1932): 38.

74. Dr. Med. Gottfried Roesler, "Die Mischung genealogischer Gruppen," *FB* 30 (1932): 249.

75. "Aus der Vereinsgeschichte des 'Roland'," *MdR* 12 (1927): 2; Finckh, "Familienforschung vor dem Standesamt," *StAZ* 7 (1927): 283–86.

76. Standesbeamten Leib, "Familienstammbuch und Wiederaufbau," *StAZ* 2 (1922): 80–81; Butte, *Das Geheimnis des Blutes* (Wien, Leipzig: Reinhold, 1932), reviewed in *MdR* 17 (1932): 38.

77. See, e.g., Dr. Rothenfelder, "Gedanken zur Rassenpsychologie," *MdR* 10 (1925): 30; Dr. Koch, "Aus meiner Bildermappe zur Familien- und Rassenkunde," ibid., 8; "Werkbund für Deutsche Volkstums- und Rassenforschung," *MdR* 11 (1926): 50. Both the *FB* and *MdR* wrote on the *AfRuG*.

78. Dr. med. Focke, "Ueber das Zussamenarbeiten der Familienkunde mit der Anthropologie in Rassefragen," *FB* 24 (1927): 119–24. See also, e.g., Oberstleutnant a. D. Max Petiscus, "Subjektiv und objektiv Familienkunde," *MdR* 12 (1928): 1; Selle, "Die Feier des dreißigjährigen Bestehens des 'Roland'," *MdR* 17 (1932): 14.

79. Standesbeamten Gluck, "Ebenbürtigkeit," *StAZ* 11 (1931): 249–50.

80. Bürgermeister Dr. Ritter, "Zur Namen- und Familienkunde," *StAZ* 4 (1924): 102; Standesbeamten Hans Haehnel, "Findet der Standesbeamte in seinem Berufe Gelegenheit zur förderung deutschen Ansehens im Auslande?" *StAZ* 6 (1926): 127.

81. Ministerialrat Dr. Brandis, Reichsjustizministerium, "Zum Kapitel: Verehelichung deutscher Frauen mit Ausländern," *StAZ* 7 (1927): 199–200.

82. Verlagsbuchhändler Carl Berkhan, "Vererbung des Familientypus," *FB* 17 (1919): 165–66; Behr-Pinnow, *Zukunft* (1925 ed.), reviewed in *MdR* 11 (1926): 32; Finckh, "Familienforschung vor dem Standesamt," *StAZ* 7 (1927): 283–86. See also, e.g., Matthias Mieses, *Zur Rassenfrage. Eine stammes- und kulturgeschichtlicher Untersuchung* (Wien, Leipzig: Braumüller, 1919), reviewed in *FB* 20 (1922): 22 (negative review of book that says race-mixing is fruitful for culture); Otto Hauser, *Rassezucht* (Braunschweig, Hamburg: Westermann, 1924), reviewed in *MdR* 9 (1924): 43 (positive review of book calling for increasing Nordic, and "exterminating" "dark blood").

83. W. His, *Über die natürliche Ungleichheit der Menschen* (Rektoratsrede, Berlin, 1928).

84. See, e.g., Sanitätsrat Dr. Alfred Seeliger, "Das Standesamt im Dienste der Volksaufartung," *StAZ* 5 (1925): 172–73 (exhorting Germans "to make our blood healthy and pure," as a "strong influx of foreign blood" has led to an influx of "foreign ideas" into German Volk); Dr. Hübschmann, "Eheschließung weißer Mädchen mit fremdrassigen Männern," *StAZ* 8 (1928): 53–54 (warning "women of white race and culture" to avoid men of "foreign race," for mixed-race children "according to experience, exhibited all the bad characteristics of both races. . . ."); Standesbeamten Gluck, "Ebenbürtigkeit," *StAZ* 11 (1931): 249–50 (claiming "racial mixing" had "ominous" effect on German noble families which, while initially "chiefly composed of the Nordic race," had, through "race-mixing" become "foreign to the Volk in thought and feeling"); Sachsenröder, "Archive für familiengeschichtliche und biologische Aufzeichnungen bei den Standesämtern," *MdR* 11 (1926): 20 (claiming "unfavorable changes in our Volk's life" due not only to war and population mobility, but also to the "mixing of our Volksgenossen with foreign Volk, causing destruction of much valuable hereditary material . . ."); Hans Günther, *Rassenkunde Europas* (München: Lehmann, 1925), reviewed in *MdR* 12 (1927): 33 (praising book for "bringing to light the races as living building stones . . . which in their single heredity [*Einzelvererbung*] build the nations and determine their fate in accordance to which admixture wins the upper hand . . ."); Dr. med. Gottfried Roesler, "Die Mischung genealogischer Gruppen," *FB* 30 (1932): 249 (referring to *Rehoboeter Bastarde,* anthropologist Eugen Fischer's famous work on "race-mixing" in German Southwest Africa).

85. *FB* 25 (1927): 22. See also, e.g., *FB* 26 (1928): 253–54 (listing "Turkish" baptisms); Wilhelm Bandau, "Eine Prenzlauer Mohrentaufe," *ArchfS* 8 (1931): 219; Walther van Hees, "Eine Negertaufe 1823 im Kb. Mülheim a. Rh.," *ArchfS* 8 (1931): 362.

86. Dürre, "Wie sind die eugenischen Abteilungen auf den Standesämtern zu organisieren?" *StAZ* 5 (1925): 24–25.

87. Standesbeamten Gluck, "Ebenbürtigkeit," *StAZ* 11 (1931): 249–50.

88. Fr. Siebert, *Der völkische Gehalt der Rassenhygiene* (München: Lehmann, 1917), reviewed in *FB* 17 (1919): 244–45. "Unfortunately," wrote Wecken in his book review, "in reality [such a law] would never happen."

89. *Der Weltkrieg im Lichte naturwissenschaftlicher Geschichtsauffassung. Leiengedanken eines Berufsoffiziers* (Verlag Georg Bath, 1920), reviewed in *DH* 53 (1920): 14–15.

90. Geh. Oberregierungsrat Dr. Grahl, Dresden, "Betrachtungen über das Personenstandsgesetz" [footnote omitted] Vortrag, gehalten auf dem 3. Bundestag des Reichsbundes der Standesbeamten Deutschlands E.V., *StAZ* 4 (1924): 216–17; Butte, "Familienforschung und Rassenkunde," *MdR* 9 (1924): 19–20; Günther, *Rasse und Stil* (München: Lehmann, 1926), reviewed in *FB* 25 (1927): 92–93; *Ausgewählte Ahnentafeln der Edda* (Gotha: Justus Perthes, 1925 ff.), reviewed in *MdR* 14 (1929): 5; Dr. Med. Gottfried Roesler, "Die Mischung genealogischer Gruppen," *FB* 30 (1932): 249.

91. *FB* 29 (1931): 275–82, 297–308. See also, e.g., *FB* 20 (1922): 53–55; *FB* 26 (1928): 16; Kleine Mitteilungen, "Judentaufen in Jüterbog. Handschriftliche Chronik von Joh. Glob. Schulze (Rothlauf)," *MdR* 7 (1922): 43; "Zwei Judentaufen," *ArchfS* 8 (1931): 324; "Judentaufen in Belzig (Mark)," *DH* 56 (1925): 74.

92. v. Arnswaldt, "Judentaufen," *FB* 17 (1919): 134.

93. Pfarrer Otto Fischer, "Evangelische Pfarrer jüdischer Abkunft," *DH* 59 (1928): 23–24.

94. Achim Gercke, *Der jüdische Einfluß und den Deutschen Hohen Schulen. Ein familienkundlicher Nachweis über die jüdischen und verjudeten Universitäts und Hochschulprofessoren* (1928–1932).

95. Dr. med. Walter Pfeilsticker, *FB* 23 (1925): 271–72. Story repeated in *FSV* 4 (1938): 9.

96. See, e.g., *MdR* 14 (1929): 5; *MdR* 15 (1930): 16–17; *ArchfS* 8 (1931): 36–37.

97. Klocke, *Entwicklung,* 28.

98. Quoted in Brigette Hamann, "Einer von Ganz Unten," *Der Spiegel* 28/2001, 134.

99. Klocke, *Entwicklung,* 21, n. 32; Ribbe, *Taschenbuch,* 628–29. This particular trend increased, of course, most markedly after the Nazi assumption of power.

100. G. von Hoffman, *Rassenhygiene und Fortpflanzungshygiene (Eugenic)* (no publication information), reviewed in *DH* 48 (1917): 52; Dürre, "Der Standesbeamte im Dienste der Rassenhygiene," *StAZ* 4 (1924): 279–81; Sachsenröder, "Archiv für familiengeschichtliche und biologische Aufzeichnungen beim Standesamte," *StAZ* 5 (1925): 93–95. See also, e.g., R. Fetscher, L. R. Grote, and J. Hohlfeld, *Zwischen Naturwissenschaft und Geschichte* (Leipzig: Selbstverlag, 1928), reviewed in *FB* 12 (1928): 343; *MdR* 13 (1928): 54.

101. "Vererbungs and Rassenlehre; Biologie," *MdR* 12 (1927): 68. At least one work was anti-racist to some degree: Fritz Merkenschlager, *Götter, Helden und Günther. Eine Abwehr der Günterischen Rassenkunde* (Nürnberg: Spindler, 1927). For further implicit equation of the validity of racial science and other natural sciences, see, e.g., Butte, "Über Familienforschung," *StAZ* 4 (1924): 261–64; Sommer, *Familienforschung, Vererbungs- und Rassenlehre* (Leipzig: Barth, 1927), reviewed in *DH* 58 (1927): 95–96.

102. See, Weiss, "Vorgeschichte," 618, 622; DZfG file 25.

103. Prowe, "Köpfe deutscher Sippenforscher," *FSV* 3 (1937): 45.

104. *Zeitschrift für Volksaufartung und Erbkunde* 5 (1927): 57.

105. Weiss, "Vorgeschichte," 497, 500.

106. "Der Standesbeamte und die Familienforschung," *StAZ* 2 (1922): 1–2. The other five were the Roland, the Herold, the *Hessische Chronik,* the *Westdeutsche Gesellschaft für Familienkunde,* and the *Niedersächsischer Landesverein für Familienkunde.*

107. *Das Deutsche Geschlechterbuch* (Görlitz: Starke, 1926), reviewed in *MdR* 12 (1927): 32.

108. See, e.g., *StAZ* 11 (1931): 304; v. Wrangel, "Wie triebt man Familienforschung?" *StAZ* 12 (1932): 156.

109. "Aus der Vereins Geschichte des 'Roland'," *MdR* 12 (1927): 3. See also, e.g., Ludwig Finckh, *Das Vogelnest. Geschichten aus der Ahnenschau* (München: G. Franz, 1928), reviewed in *MdR* 14 (1929): 5; Bundestag 1927 in Stuttgart des Reichsbundes der Standesbeamten Deutschlands E.V. *StAZ* 7 (1927): 177–79 (Finckh is one of five speakers).

110. See, e.g., Prof. Franz Schütz, "Familienforschung und Rassenhygiene," *Zeitschrift für Volksaufartung und Erbkunde* 1 (1926): 37, 39.

111. *Ahnentafel der Edda* (Gotha: Justus Perthes, 1926), reviewed in *DH* 56 (1925): 79–80; *Die Ahnentafeln der EDDA* (Gotha: Justus Pertha, 1925), reviewed in *MdR* 12 (1927): 32.

112. *Ausgewählte Ahnentafeln der Edda II. Band* (Gotha: Justus Perthes, 1929), reviewed in *DH* 60 (1929): 95; *Ausgewählte Ahnentafeln der Edda* (Gotha: Justus Perthes, 1925 ff.), discussed in *MdR* 14 (1929): 5, 34.

113. See, e.g., Hans F. K. Günther, *Rassenkunde des deutschen Volkes,* 8. Auflage (München: Lehmann, 1925), reviewed in *DH* 57 (1926): 14; Günther, E. Fischer, *Deutsche Köpfe nordischer Rasse* (München: Lehmann, 1927); Günther, *Adel und Rasse* (München: Lehmann, 1926); Günther, *Rasse und Stil* (München: Lehmann, 1926), reviewed in *MdR* 12 (1927): 81–82; *MdR* 13 (1928): 25–26; Sommer, *Familienforschung, Vererbungs- und Rassenlehre* (Leipzig: Johann Ambrosius Barth, 1927), reviewed in *DH* 58 (1927): 95–96; *MdR* 15 (1930): 23.

114. Roland member and senior medical advisor (*Sanitätsrat*) Dr. med. Voelsch, "Rassenkunde d. dtsch Volkes," *MdR* 9 (1924): 39. See also, e.g., Ed. Krauß, "Familienforschung und Vererbung," ibid., 13; Dr. med. Kuhn, "Vererbung und Gattenwahl," ibid., 1; *FB* 26 (1928): 188.

115. *MdR* 16 (1931): 14.

116. On the Baur-Fischer-Lenz, see, e.g., Erwin Baur, Eugen Fischer, Fritz Lenz, *Grundriß der menschlichen Erblichkeitslehre und Rassenhygiene* (München: Lehmann, 1923), reviewed in *DH* 56 (1925): 47–48; *DH* 60 (1929): 19; *MdR* 12 (1927): 63. On the Lehmann publishing house, see, e.g., *MdR* 13 (1928): 6; "Vierzig Jahre Dienst am Deutschtum, 1830 bis 1930. Den Mitarbeitern und Freunden gewidm. von J. F. Lehmanns Verlag, München," *MdR* 15 (1930): 36.

117. Butte, "Hakenkreuz und Runen," *MdR* 6 (1921): 87; Klocke quoted in Weiss, "Vorgeschichte," 498–99; Butte, "Flugschriften der Zentralstelle für deutsche Personen- und Familiengeschichte. H. 1–3," *MdR* 8 (1923): 23; Fritz Lenz, *Menschliche Auslese und Rassenhygiene* (München: Lehmann, 1931), reviewed in *MdR* 16 (1931): 26.

118. W. Schmidt, *Rasse und Volk* (München: J. Kösel u. Fr. Pustet, 1925), reviewed in *MdR* 14 (1929): 35.

119. Quoted in Weiss, "Vorgeschichte," 502.

120. Reinhard Hederich, "Sippenforschung als Wissenschaft und Politik," *Mitteilungen des Deutschen Roland* 18 (1925): 574–76, quoted in Weiss, "Vorgeschichte," 502.

121. Heinrich Kurtzig, *Ostdeutsches Judentum. Tradition einer Familie,* 2nd ed. (Leipzig: Engel, 1930), reviewed in *FB* 28 (1930): 359.

122. Hohlfeld, "Zur biologischen Familienforschung," *FB* 28 (1930): 53–55.

123. Hohlfeld, "Nachwort," *FB* 37 (1939): 71. See Gerhard Kessler, "Judentaufen und judenchristliche Familien in Ostpreussen," *FB* 36 (1939): 201–32, 261–72, 297–306.

124. By law, after 1935 the term *Mischehe* could only refer to a marriage between an "Aryan" and "non-Aryan." Knost, *Feststellung,* 128.

125. *MdR* 14 (1929): 34. This was certainly not a concern limited to the genealogical community. Cf. Hitler's *Mein Kampf* (Boston: Houghton Mifflin, 1943), trans. Ralph Manheim, 52, 54 (worried about "irrational" appearance of most antisemitism).

126. *Meyers Lexikon,* 7th ed., s.v. "Juden."

127. *FB* 42 (1944): 128.

4. Making the Ancestral Proof in Nazi Germany

1. Walk, *Sonderrecht für Juden.* In addition, so-called Aryan paragraphs appeared "in the articles of organizations, associations and clubs from all conceivable areas of life." Lösener, *Nürnburger,* 22.

2. Knost, *Feststellung,* 140.

3. Satzung der N.S.D.A.P. für den Handgebrauch der Parteigerichte in der Fassung vom 1.1.34, §3.

4. See, Ulmenstein, *Abstammungsnachweis,* 25.

5. Benz, *Enzyklopädie,* s.v. "Nationalsozialistische Deutsche Arbetierpartei."

6. Ulmenstein, *Abstammungsnachweis,* 129.

7. Benz, *Enzyklopädie,* s.v. "Sturmabteilungen."

8. Caplan, *Government,* 143–44, 268.

9. Verlag für Sozialpolitik, "Volks-, Berufs- und Betriebszählung," 1/2–1/3.

10. See, e.g., RfS Umlauf, 5/8/35, R39/3.

11. Wehrgesetzes vom 21. Mai 1935, §15(1) and (2) (RGBl. I S. 609); 31.5.1941, Heiratsordnung für die Dauer des besonderen Einsatzes der Wehrmacht, §4, R39/163 (soldiers' wives); Herbst, "Deutschland im Krieg," 69 (draftee numbers).

12. Gesetz zum Schutze des deutschen Blutes und der deutschen Ehre vom 15. September 1935 (RGBl. I S. 1146).

13. Erste Verordnung zur Ausführung des Gesetzes zum Schutze des deutschen Blutes und der deutschen Ehre vom 14.11.1935, §§6, 7 (RGBl. I S. 1334).

14. Länderrat, *Statistisches,* 47.

15. Reichsarbeitsdienstgesetz in der Fassung des Gesetzes vom 19. März 1937, §7 (RGBl. I S. 325).

16. Gesetz gegen die Uberfüllung deutscher Schulen und Hochschulen vom 25.4.1933 (RGBl. I S. 225); Länderrat, *Statistisches,* 622.

17. Gesetz über die Zulassung zur Rechtsanwaltschaft vom 7.4.1933 (RGBl. I S. 168); Gesetz betreffend die Zulassung zur Patentanwaltschaft und zur Rechtsanwaltschaft vom 22.4.1933 (RGBl. I S. 217); Gesetz über die Zulassung von Steuerberatern vom 6.5.1933 (RGBl. I S. 257); Erste Verordnung zur Durchführung des Gesetzes über Ehrenämter in der sozialen Versicherung und der Reichsversorgung vom 19.5.1933 (RGBl. I S. 283); Zweite Verordnung zur Durchführung des Gesetzes über Ehrenämter in der sozialen Versicherung und der Reichsversorgung vom 23.6.1933 (RGBl. I S. 397); Gesetz zur Änderung einiger Vorschriften der Rechtsanwaltsordnung der Zivilprozeßordnung und des Arbeitsgerichtsgesetzes vom 20.7.1933 (RGBl. I S. 522); RdErl. d. RuPrMdI. v. 26.10.1933 (betreffend Vergebung von Apothenkonzessionen); Schriftleitergesetz vom 4.10.1933 (RGBl. I S. 713); Verordnung über die Zulassung von Ärzten zur Tätigkeit bei den Krankenkassen vom 17.5.1934 (RGBl. I S. 390).

18. RdErl. d. RuPrMdI. v. 23.6.1937 (Abstammungsnachweis beim Nachsuchen von Ehestandsdarlehen); Erste Durchführungsbestimmungen zur Verordnung über die Gewährung von Kinderbeihilfen an kinderreiche Familien vom 31.8.1937 (RGBl. I S. 989); RdErl. d. RuPrMdI. v. 6.8.1937 (Kindesannahmeverfahren); Gesetzes über die Aenderung und Ergänzung familienrechtlicher Vorschriften und über der Rechtstellung der Staatenlosen v. 12.4.1938 (RGBl. I S. 380) § 5; RdErl. d. RuPrMdI. v. 8.1.1938 (name change).

19. For relevant laws, see Knost, *Feststellung,* 94; Ulmenstein, *Abstammungsnachweis,* 219–33.

20. See, e.g., RdErl. d. RMdI. v. 29.3.1939 (Deutsche Volkszugehörigkeit).

21. See, e.g., Zweite Verordnung zur Durchführung des Gesetzes über die Änderung der Familien- und Vornamen vom 17.8.1938; RdErl. d. RMdI. v. 18.8.1938, betreffend Vornamen, Afs. A(5); RdErl. d. RuPrMdI. v. 23.3.1938 (Widerruf von Namensänderungen) §7.

22. Ministerialrat Dr. Strutz, Vizepräsident der Regierung Koblenz, "Quellen und Methoden der Sippenforschung," *FSV* 2 (1936): 25; R43II/721:28 (1938 advertisement); *StAZ* 21 (1941): 64 (quoting Lösener).

23. Feldscher, *Rassen,* 154.

24. Speech at Verwaltungswissenschaftlichen Woche für Standesbeamte zu Berlin, March 1936, *FSV* 2 (1936): 13–18.

25. RfS Geschäftsvertiefungsplan, I. Abteilung: Abstammungsbescheid, 2000–2017, R39/20.

26. *ASS* 1 (1937): 35–36.

27. Weiss, "Vorgeschichte," 623. Satzung der NSDAP, §3. For the term *arische Blutbe-kenntnis*, see, e.g., Wecken, *Ahnentafel,* 3.

28. Wecken, *Ahnentafel,* 3.

29. Ribbe, "Genealogie," 75.

30. Wecken, *Ahnentafel,* 4.

31. This year may be an inaccurate reference to the Napoleonic Kingdom of Westphalia (established in 1807) and the resulting emancipation of the Jews in 1808.

32. *ASS* 1 (1937): 11. This read: "The [named person], born in . . . , residing in . . . , is free from an alien type blood admixture [*artfremden Bluteinschlag*] in the sense of the conditions of acceptance to the National Socialist German Workers Party." Ibid.

33. Knost, *Feststellung,* 64–65. On SS requirements, see, e.g., "SS-Ahnentafel," n/d, and memo on "Einrichtung des Sippenbuches." Both in R1509/95.

34. Various information sheets for personnel in civil service offices in ZB II 3175, 3259, 3700, 4038, 4130, 4170.

35. Memo Gercke, 1/8/35, R39/2.

36. *ASS* 1 (1937): 23 (large proof); Knost, *Feststellung,* 56–57 (small proof).

37. Hayn, *Sippenfibel,* 22.

38. Dr. Haagen to Ministerialrat Stäglisch, Rechnungshof des Deutschen Reichs, Präsidialabteilung, 8/22/34, R39/1.

39. Erl. d. RuPrMfWEuV v. 23.3.1935.

40. *ASS* 1 (1937): 22; Reichshaushalts- und Besoldungsblatt vom 14.7.39, Nr. 24, 10.7.1939, Nr. 3165, Arischer Nachweis der nichtbeamteten Gefolgschaftsmitglieder, R39/10.

41. RdErl. d. RuPrMdI. v. 26.11.1935.

42. RdErl. d. RuPrMdI. v. 10.10.1935, §4 (Gebührenfreiheit bei der Ausstellung von Urkunden zum Nachweis der arischen Abstammung).

43. Ulmenstein, *Abstammungsnachweis,* 105. See also, e.g., Decision of Acceptability, R1509/50 (Paul D.).

44. Order, RuPrMdI, 20.8.1936; RdErl. d. RuPrMfWEuV v. 29.12.1936 (Nachweis der Abstammung der Beamten und Lehrer und ihrer Ehefrauen); Nachweis der Abstammung. RdErl. D. RFSSuChdDtPol. im RMDI. v. 24. 5. 1937.

45. In ZA VI 4027 A.12 (note dated 9/6/37).

46. RdErl. d. RMdI. v. 25.9.1939 (Einstellung der Behandlung von Einbürgerungsanträgen und Einbürgerung von Kriegsfreiwilligen).

47. See, e.g., RdErl. d. ? v. 11.1.40, cited in Genealogical Authority form X306, R39/163.

48. RdErl. d. RMdI. v. 4.3.1941; "Abstammungsnachweis in Kriege," *KfRuF,* 7/29/43, 3–4; RdErl. d. RMdI. v. 11.7.1944 ("Nachweis der deutschblütigen Abstammung bei der Zulassung zu den medizinischen Prüfungen").

49. See, e.g., Anordnung der Parteikanzlei vom 26.9.1941 (A 43/41 Betrifft: Anforderung und Prüfung des Nachweises der deutschblütigen Abstammung von Parteigenossen und Politischen Leitern und deren Ehefrauen . . .).

50. "Abstammungsnachweis in Kriege," *KfRuF,* 7/29/43, 3–4.

51. *ASS* 1 (1937): 35–36.

52. Pursuant to the Civil Status Law of February 2, 1875, beginning on January 1, 1876, the newly created civil registry offices began to record all births, marriages, and deaths. Prior to this, church books were the primary repositories of this information. Johannes Bücher, "Die geschichtliche Entwicklung der Personenstandsregister," *FSV* 3 (1937): 40–43, 51–54.

53. For an extensive list of such offices and types of documents, see R1509/98:8–12.

54. RdErl. d. RMdI. v. 13.3.1939, R39/10 (Übersetzung fremdsprachiger Urkunden für den Abstammungsnachweis); Knost, *Feststellung,* 131–33, 142–49 (certification of documents, access to civil registries, and fees for documents).

55. Erl. d. RMdI. v. 18.6.1934; excerpt, BfdK, Breslau to RfS, 12/2/1936, R39/565 (complaining of increased workload for pastoral office, and civil registrars having individuals go to pastoral offices for Ahnenpass certification); Knost, *Feststellung,* 97.

56. Rundschreiben 67/35, Der Stellvertreter des Führers, Stabsleiter, 4/15/35, NS6/218: 121–22.

57. Genealogical Authority internal memo, n/a, "Kirche, Kirchenbücher, Abstammungsnachweis und Gebührenfragen," 1/25/38, R39/541.

58. See, e.g., Knost, *Feststellung,* 107–18; RdErl. d. RMdI. v. 10.4.1938 (regulations governing access to, and fees charged for, information from police registers).

59. RdErl. d. RuPrMdI. v. 24.9.1935 (Beschaffung von Urkunden zum Nachweise der arischen Abstammung aus dem Auslande).

60. See, e.g., Knost, *Feststellung,* 122–24; RdErl. d. RuPrMdI. v. 27.11.1936 (Verwendung von Auszügen aus dem Schweizerischen Familienregister bei Eheschließungen); Ulmenstein, *Abstammungsnachweis,* 62 (RMdI decree on Protectorate). See also, e.g., Chemist Otto Jatzlau, Berlin to Deutsche Generalkonsulat, Posen, 6/18/38, R1509/76 (seeking foreign documents).

61. Knost, *Feststellung,* 123; Anordnung Nr. 7/39, 1/4/39, NS6/232–13.

62. Anordnung A 35/40, 3/18/40, "Anforderung von Urkunden für den Abstammungsnachweis aus den Gauen Danzig–Westpreußen und Wartheland," NS6/820:76–7.

63. See, e.g., RSA to Frau v. Ehrenkrook, Breslau, 11/20/42; RSA to Ministerialrat Willfort, Berlin, 12/8/42. Both in R39/814, "Aufstellung von Kirchenbuchurkunden," Archivamt der Deutschen Evangelischen Kirchenkanzlei. K.K. V. 359, Berlin, 6/8/43, R39/815; "Abstammungsnachweis in Kriege," *KfRuF* (7/29/43): 3–4.

64. RdErl. d. RMdI u. RMdF. v. 31.10.1934.

65. See, e.g., RdErl. d. RMdI. v. 25.6.1938 (Nachweis über die rassische Einordnung) (regularly certified Genealogical Authority ancestral decision fully valid as ancestral proof); RdErl. d. RMdI. v. 9.9.1940 (Nachweis deutschblütiger Abstammung) (reminder that regulation from previous month had been issued to explain how to reduce redundancy).

66. Quoted in *StAZ* 21 (1941): 64.

67. Knost, *Feststellung,* 88; RdErl. d. RuPrMdI. v. 4.3.1935; RdErl. d. RuPrMdI. v. 24.4.1936; Oberkommando des Heeres 24.6.1936 (P.A.2); Rundschreiben Nr. 87/36, 7/6/36, Der Stellvertreter des Führers (Hess), NS6/223:48.

68. RdErl. d. RuPrMdJ. v. 5.4.1937, Ulmenstein, *Abstammungsnachweis,* 94; RdErl. d. RuPrMdI. v. 26.1.1935; RdErl. d. RuPrMdI. v. 19.3.1936; Knost, *Feststellung,* 90.

69. See, e.g., RdErl. d. RuPrMdI. v. 19.6.1936 (Ahnenpass may be used to meet racial requirements for granting of pharmacist concession); RdErl. d. RuPrMdI. v. 16.2.1937 (properly certified Ahnenpass suffices for "proof of German blooded ancestry" for "civil servants, clerks and workers in public service"); RdErl. d. RMdI. v. 19.8.1942 (special Ahnenpass designed specifically for "German Volks-group in Romania" to be accepted as any other).

70. Offices listed in Schulle, *Reichssippenamt,* 302–304. On the chaotic nature of GSA competencies, see ibid., 285–90.

71. See, e.g., *FSV* 4 (1938): 22 (on creation of "Sippenauskunft der NSDAP" in Kreisleitung Strehlen); "Rundschreiben Nr. 1," 5/2/38, "Sippenforschungsstelle Schlesien," R39/792 (one of its tasks is gathering all genealogical material for Ratibor and Breslau).

72. See, e.g., Mitteilungsblätter der Gaues Köln-Aachen der NSDAP, 20. November 1935, 19–20, and 20. Dezember 1935, 14–15 (including information on "Helpful Sources for

Proof of Aryan Ancestry" and an "Index of Church Books Based in the Church Archive of the Bonn district court").

73. Archiv des Ministeriums des Innern der Protektoratesregierung, Abstellung für Beschaffung von Abstammungsnachweisen, Prag. Bekanntgabe B 25/40, "Betr: Urkundenbeschaffungen aus dem Protektorate Böhmen und Mähren," 5/8/40, NS6/820:101 (Office of Hitler's Deputy for Party Affairs decries "increasing cases in which Party members and racial comrades are turning to the various [Czech] agencies in the Protectorate of Bohemia and Moravia in order to obtain documents" rather than the Ministry agency); A-E Abel-Alma A6/1 (Herbert A.) (referring to Kraków); Speer to Kayser, 4/7/43, R39/832 ("administrative card file for the Eastern Territory [Ostlandes] . . . now exists . . .").

74. Schulle, *Reichssippenamt,* 302–304.

75. *FSV* 4 (1938): 57.

76. See, e.g., A-E Abel-Alma A6/1 (Herbert A.).

77. Listed in Schulle, *Reichssippenamt,* 302–304.

78. As late as 1943, a documentary ancestral proof was still required for "naturalization, acceptance into the German *Volkslist,* marriage and a few other cases." "Abstammungsnachweis in Kriege," *KfRuF,* 7/29/43, 3–4. See also, e.g., Meldung als Wehrmachtshelferin for RSA employee Irma Strathoff (geb. 18.10.20), 12/18/44, R1509/23:141.

79. Dortmund, n/d, R39/573.

80. Metzner Verlag, *50 Jahre,* 97–99; Starke Verlag, *Wegweiser* (240 pages); Engemann, *Wegweiser* (480 pages).

81. See, e.g., Karl Endler-Albrecht, *Mecklenburgs Familiengeschichtliche Quellen* (Hamburg: Hermes, 1936); Eduard Grigoleit, *Verzeichnis der Ostpreußischen und Danziger Kirchenbücher sowie der Dissidenten- und Judenregister* (Görlitz: Starke, 1939).

82. *ABC für Sippenforscher, Familiengeschichtsforschung in Stichworten* (Leipzig: Spohr, 1936); *ASS* 1 (1937): 63, 64, 76 ("Die Heraldische Bibliographie").

83. See, e.g., "Die urkundlichen Feststellungen der unehelichen Vaterschaft," *Stuttgarter NS.-Kurier,* 6/19/41, R1509:147.

84. Wecken, *Ahnentafel,* 3. In 1940, another version of this work sold as *Die Ahnentafel, der Nachweis der Abstammung. Veränderte Aufl.* (Berlin: Reichsbund Dt. Familie, Abt. Propaganda, 1940), 30 pages. *FamB* VII, 17.

85. Heinz-Eberhardt Denckler, *Wie finde ich meine Ahnen? Anleitung, wie man schnell seine arische Abstammung nachweist* (Berlin: Denkler, 1936); Friedrich A. Knost, *Festlegung u. Nachweis der Abstammung. Systematische Darstellung* (Berlin: Vahlen, 1939). See also, e.g., Ulmenstein, *Abstammungsnachweis,* 1936 [1st and 2d editions], 1937 [3d edition], 1938 [4th ed.], 1941 [5th ed.]; Fritz Zeller, *Ratgeber zum Abstammungsnachweis. Für die Standesbeämter und Kirchenämter* (München: Verlag für Verwaltungspraxis, 1936); ibid., *Ratgeber zum Abstammungsnachweis. Für das Land Österreich bearab* (München: Verlag für Verwaltungspraxis, 1938); *Wie beschaffe ich meinen Abstammungsnachweis?* (München: Franz Rehm, 1938); Hans-Bogislaw Graf v. Schwerin, *Die Erstellung des Ahnenpasses* (München: Eher, 1939 [2nd ed.], 1941).

86. See, e.g., Oswald Spohr, *Familienkunde, eine der Voraussetzungen des neuen Staates.* 6th ed. (Leipzig: Degener, 1938).

87. Dr. jur. Hans Bogislav Graf v. Schwerin, "Was ist mit dem Ahnenpaß?," *KfRuF* (12/5/39): 1–3.

88. Alfred Eydt, *Der Rasse- und Gesundheitspaß als Nachweis erblicher Gesundheit und rassischer Vollwertigkeit* (Leipzig: Degener, 1933).

89. See *FamB* (1934): 23, 336; ibid. (1935): 5; ibid. (1936/7): 5–7; ibid. (1938/45): 5–6, 8–9, 16.

90. *Wegweiser* (1937 ed.), 260.

91. RSA Rechnung, 8/2/43, R1509/29:3–4.

92. Advertisement, *FSV* 4 (1938): end page; VfS Advertisement, n/d but 1936 or later, R43II/721:36. See also *FSV* 3:2 (1937): endsheet (advertisement for VfS *Bilder-Ahnentafel* noting it allows for "racial-scientific and hereditary registration").

93. Advertisement for *Zentralverlag der NSDAP*'s *Ahnenpaß*, in Schwerin, *Die Erstellung*, end pages.

94. National-Verlag "Westfalia," to RfS, 4/29/41 and 10/22/41, R39/573.

95. All correspondence in R43II/721:20–36.

96. Ribbe, *Taschenbuch*, 629.

97. See, e.g., contract with genealogist Unger, 2/13/42, A-E Alt-Antretter A6/2 (Erika A.) (RM 200 advance for procurement of documents for small ancestral proof, scheduling paternity application by Genealogical Authority, and further representation); A-E Abel-Alma A6/1 (over RM 200 for research).

98. Bill, "Instytut Heraldyczny," Warsaw, by Graf Ludgard Grocholski, to Consul Willy Eisenbach, 5/14/37, R1509/70. This work was primarily for the purposes of determining any Jewish ancestry.

99. See, e.g., Kurt Kraushaar to Dr. K. Strache, 10/22/40, R1509/88 (dentist pays RM 28.39 for provision of paternal grandparents' marriage certificate, a paternal great-grandfather's birth and death certificates, and marriage certificates of two paternal great-great-grandparents); Schram-Steiner to Barbaß, 10/1/44, A-E Balla-Bauer Josef A6/5 (soldier charged RM 59.79 for services including fifteen document requests to various offices).

100. Regierungsbaumeister a. D. Friedrich Bludau, Hannover to Staszewski, 2/1/38 and 5/31/38; Staszewski to Heinrich v. Cosel, Landsberg a.W., 4/30/38; Hans Doennig cand. mach, Schönberg to Staszewski, 3/14/39; Paul B., Zollbetriebsassistent, Karlsruhe to Kurt v. Staszewski, 3/34/39, 4/26/39 and 5/11/39; Staszewski to Paul B., 6/10/39; Staszewski to Besch, 5/22/38. All in DZfG 27 RSA.

101. Verein für Familienforschung in Ost-u. Westpreußen e. V., Auskunftsstelle to Evangel. Pfarramt Germau, 5/20/39, and to Superintendentur, Fischhausen, 5/31/39. Both in DZfG 27 RSA; RSA to Kustos Dr. Josef Wastl, 5/6/43, R39/244; GSA-W-B (Maximilian Israel B.) (genealogist Plattensteiner's unsuccessful request for Genealogical Authority reconsideration); A-E Baader-Balko-Kastaly A6/4 (Plattensteiner makes successful appeal).

102. Löcker to GAfS, 3/23/40, A-E Alt-Antretter A6/2; Familien-Forschungs Institut to RSW, 11/24/39, R1509/67; Arbeitsplatz für sudetendeutsch Familienforschung to VSV, 10/19/39, R1509/7; Auswärtige Amt to RfS, 10/20/37, R39/244; ZB II 5181 A.3.

103. Röttinger, Bamberg to RSA, 9/4/42, R1509/123. "VBS" was the Union of Professional Kinship Researchers and "RSH" was the later Reich Association of Kinship Researchers and Heraldists. See also, e.g., Ernst Bähreke's letterhead, R39/566; *ASS* 1 (1937): 528–29 (genealogists' advertisements); "Deutscher Berufssippenforscher," Repke to Landsippenstelle Posen, 12/8/44, R39/815; "Sippenforscher (RSH)," Dr. Mudretzkyj to Catholic Pastoral Office Ustron, 7/10/41, A-E Abel-Alma A6/1; "Sippenforscher, Mitglied (409) des Reichsverbandes der Sippenforscher und Heraldiker," Schram letterhead, R39/165.

104. Fromm, *Blood and Banquets*, 170.

105. A-E Abel-Alma A6/1, 1706; N/d, R39/574.

106. See, e.g., A-E Alt-Antretter A6/2, 04138 ("application" and "authorization" of retired Viennese administrator).

107. Themal, *Berufssippenforscher*.

108. See, e.g., SfR to Riechers, 10/8/34, ZB II 4375 A.17 ("even today the outlook for a professional genealogist is extraordinarily unfavorable"); RfS to Jürges, 3/37, ZB II 3475 A.17 ("Your application for admission into the V.B.S. has not been allowed . . . the area is already overcrowded. . . . "); VBS to Landrat Mayerhoffer, Biberach an der Riß, 6/17/37, R1509/37 (he cannot open an "Advisory Office for Ancestral Research," because VBS no longer issues permits for professional genealogists); RfS or VBS to Frau Brülle, Berlin, 1/20/39 (prohibition still in place because Berlin already has too many genealogists); RfS or VBS to Arndt, Leipzig, 7/9/37 (no present admission to VBS allowed). Both in R39/244.

109. Themal, *Berufssippenforscher,* foreword.

110. RuPrMdI (Stuckart) to Reichsstatthalter, außerpreußischen Landesregierungen, Reichskommissar für das Saarland, Oberpräsidenten in Preußen, Stadtpräsidenten der Reichshauptstadt Berlin, Oberbürgermeister der Reichshauptstadt Berlin, 3/24/37, R43II/721:8–9.

111. Deutscher Sparkassenverlag G.m.b.H., Berlin, n/d, R39/574.

112. Both in R39/574.

113. In ZB II 4375–18 (publisher obscured in copy, n.d).

114. See, Stadtische Sparkasse Bochum and Allianz und Stuttgarter Lebensversicherungsbank, AG, tables. Both in R39/574.

115. Mayer to RuPrMdI, 10/28/36, R39/574; RuPrMdI (Stuckart) to Reichsstatthalter, außerpreußischen Landesregierungen, Reichskommissar für das Saarland, Oberpräsidenten in Preußen, Stadtpräsidenten der Reichshauptstadt Berlin, Oberbürgermeister der Reichshauptstadt Berlin, 3/24/37, R43II/721:8–9.

5. The Reich Genealogical Authority and Its Tasks

1. See, e.g., Kurt Mayer article in *Ziel und Weg* (1938), quoted in *KfRuF,* 10/18/38, R39/813; Wilhelm Jahn, "Standesamt und Sippenforschung," *FSV* 2 (1936): 3.

2. Wilhelm Jahn, "Standesamt und Sippenforschung," *FSV* 1 (1935): 25. In actual practice, the various genealogical authorities dealt with Jewish and non-Jewish "racial aliens" in virtually the same way. Knost, *Feststellung,* 10. See also, e.g., GSA-W-Benisch (Amalia B.) (potential Javanese ancestry).

3. See, e.g., Achim Gercke, "Die Reichssippenkartei," *StAZ* 17 (1934): 297–300.

4. Müller, *Beamtentum,* 36–37.

5. Ministerialblatt für die Preußische innere Verwaltung, §3 (MbliV. 1933, S. 887), R39/Findbuch:I.

6. In May 1938, the Interior Ministry also ordered establishment of a Genealogical Authority branch office in Vienna. "Geschäftsbericht," Otto Jahnke to RMdI, 6/17/38, R39/8. This so-called Zweigstelle-Wien operated only until May 1940. See R1509/24. Technically, the party office's area of responsibility extended to "all applications for ancestral examinations in the sense of the acceptance requirements of the NSDAP" as well as its "various groups . . . affiliated formations . . . [and] various similar . . . formations . . ." as well as "all enquiries from *party* offices on the racial makeup [*Rassezugehörigkeit*] of both the living and dead." Abstammungsprüfungen durch das Amt für Sippenforschung der NSDAP, 6.7.1939, R39/10 (emphasis in original).

7. Verfügung des Stellvertreters des Führers Nr. 21, vom 15. Oktober 1934; RdErl. d. RuPrMdI. v. 5.3.1935; Bekanntmachung des RMdI. v. 12.11.1940; Ulmenstein, *Abstammungsnachweis,* 14.

8. Ulmenstein, *Abstammungsnachweis,* 13.

9. Gercke to SS Gruppenführers Schmauser, SS.-Oberabschnitt Süd, München, 1/7/35, R39/2.

10. See, e.g., July 1933 correspondence between Gercke and Prussian Interior Minister, R39/1 (Gercke insists that non-application of Aryan provisions in case of civil servant engaged to woman who previously had a child by a non-Aryan would only lead to "further penetration of non-Aryan blood into German families . . ."); Gercke to Frick, 8/16/33 and 12/1/33, R39/1 (conversion from Judaism should in no way be equated with being an Aryan).

11. BDC, Gercke.

12. R39/Findbuch; R39/7, 57.

13. Schulle, *Reichssippenamt,* 82. For state and party branch divisions in October 1936, see Geschäftsverteilungsplan der RfS and AfS der NSDAP, 10/1/36, R39/20.

14. Division I of the AfS differed from Divisions I and II of the RfS primarily in that the former was limited to the more rigorous party ancestral decision. In April 1936, the Genealogical Authority also established a "Decision Board [*Spruchkammer*]." This was made up of Mayer, the heads of the Research, Hereditary, and Racial Scientific (Forschungs-, Erb- und Rassenkundlichen) Divisions, and the AfS. Its purpose was to decide on racial origin in doubtful cases, or cases lacking sufficient documentation, based on a quorum and, in large part, on input from the Hereditary and Racial Scientific Division. Mayer, memo, 4/15/36, R39/3. The Genealogical Authority files, however, contain little evidence of how or to what degree this board functioned.

15. R1509/9:27–28.

16. See "1.5.41 Geschäftsplan des Reichssippenamtes," R39/20; "Geschäftsplan des Reichssippenamtes, 15. Januar 1943" and "Geschäftsplan des Reichssippenamtes, 1. September 1943," R1509/9.

17. Geschäftsverteilungsplan der RfS und AfS der NSDAP, 10/1/36, R39/20.

18. Ulmenstein, *Abstammungsnachweis,* 13. In September 1936, the Interior Ministry changed the designation "certification" (*Gutachten*) to "decision on ancestry [*Abstammungsbescheid*]." RdErl. d. RuPrMdI. v. 21.9.1936.

19. Verordnung über die Zulassung von Ärzten zur Tätigkeit bei den Krankenkassen vom 17.5.1934 (RGBl. I S. 390); RdErl. d. RuPrMdI. v. 18.4.1935; Ausführungsbestimmungen zum Reichsbürgergesetz v. 14.9.1935; RdErl. d. RuPrMdI. v. 6.8.1937 (Kindesannahmeverfahren); RdErl. d. RuPrMdI. v. 23.3.1938 (Widerruf von Namensänderungen); (Reichsbürgergesetz, Reichserbhofgesetz) Abstammungsprüfungen durch das Amt für Sippenforschung der NSDAP, 6.7.1939, R39/10. On military matters, see, e.g., RuPrMdI to Reichskriegsminister und Oberfehlshaber der Wehrmacht, 6/18/36, R1509/36:30.

20. Ulmenstein, *Abstammungsnachweis,* 17.

21. See, e.g., the decree of July 6, 1939, above, which repeats the Genealogical Authority's power in relation to the Nuremberg Laws.

22. See, e.g., R39/229 (Lina Sara B. geb. H.) (examinee's daughter institutes civil lawsuit to establish paternity of Aryan man); R1509/87 (Heinrich S.) (RSA arranges biological investigation on behalf of Landau district court in civil case where "Aryan" man seeks to renounce paternity); A-E Abel-Alma A6/1 (Hedwig A.) (examinee institutes civil suit after GSA-W finding of Jewish-Mischling first degree); R1509/5 (Melanie T.) (examinee's children institute civil suit in Vienna district court after RSA finding of "Jewess").

23. See, e.g., memo, n/d (1942 or later), R1509:20:12–24. The Genealogical Authority also became involved in determining "race" in cases of "racial shame." See, e.g., R39/227 (Margarette K.) (Vienna district court seeks expert report on ancestry as part of action against "Franz K[.] and others concerning §2 of the Blood Shame Law [*Blutschandegesetz (sic)*] . . .").

24. See, e.g., A-E Alt-Antretter A6/2 (Erika A.) (after several years, Berlin district court decides it has no jurisdiction and RSA is responsible authority, but lawyers' correspondence indicates continued confusion).

25. RMdI (Seel) to RMfWEuV, 4/25/41, R4901/11861.

26. "Jahresrechnung 1937 des Reichsmin. Des Innern (Reichsstelle für Sippenforschung)," Rechnungshof des Deutschen Reichs (Müller) to RuPrMdI, 6/28/38, R1509/26:6; "Vereinfachter Haushaltsplan für das Rechnungsjahr 1944, Reichssippenamt, Ausgaben [und] Einnahmen," R1509/31.

27. See, e.g., Abweisender Bescheid für einen Zurückstellungsantrag, 3/1/41, R39/11; R1509/23 (correspondence with Generalbevollmächtigten für die Reichsverwaltung). For most of the foregoing numbers, see Schulle, *Reichssippenamt,* 168. For December 1936, see circulation sheet, R39/3. For September 1943, see "Geschäftsplan des Reichssippenamtes, 1. September 1943," R1509/9:27. For January 1945, see R1509/9:51. All of these numbers are for the civil office only.

28. The "Alphabetic list of associates" (Card catalog, R1509) contains cards for 362 employees. It is unclear whether this also includes AfS employees.

29. Gercke to Frick, 8/15/33, R39/1; Internal SfR Memo, 9/27/34, R39/3.

30. RdErl. d. RMdI. v. 26.10.1934 (betreffend Gutachten über arische Abstammung).

31. Mayer to [Interior Minister?], n/d, R39/2.

32. Speech published in *FSV* 2 (1936): 15, 17.

33. RdErl. d. RuPrMdI. v. 6.7.1936.

34. See, e.g., R39/Findbuch:IV; Ulmenstein, *Abstammungsnachweis,* 14–16; *ASS* 1 (1937): 11; Rundschreiben Nr. 88/38 Der Stellvertreter des Führers, Stabsleiter, 8/16/38, NS6/230:67; RfS to RPA, 6/17/35, R39/29 (regarding determination of German ancestry of Russian returnees for naturalization purposes, Authority's competency limited to assessing "*Aryan ancestry* in individual cases"; determination of "*German ancestry* in naturalization processes" is Reich Office for Emigration's [Reichsstelle für das Auswanderungswesen] jurisdiction); Office of Hitler's Deputy for Party Affairs to Gauleitung Berlin, 1/13/38, R39/13; AV. d. RJM. v. 10.2.1939 (Beteiligung der Reichsstelle für Sippenforschung bei erb- und rassenkundliche Untersuchungen), Ulmenstein, *Abstammungsnachweis,* 122; Landgerichtsrat Wien to GSA-W, 1/14/43, A-E Balla-Bauer Josef A6/5 (asking for any information on whether a 5-year-old child whose legal father is Jewish, is "*Mischling* or . . . German-blooded"); Schircks to Auslandbriefprüfstelle Berlin bei der Abwehrstelle im Wehrkreis III, 10/31/42 (date probable), R39/163.

35. Kayser to Kern, 1/28/44, R39/832.

36. Kayser to Grenadier Dr. Heinrich Blank, 5/4/44, R39/832; Examinee's Lawyer to RSA, 4/10/45, R1509/92 (appealing ancestral decision).

37. According to the German Federal Archive, some animosity developed between the Genealogical Authority and the Interior Ministry due to the Ministry's overturning numerous negative decisions of ancestry (R39/21; R39/Findbuch:IV). There is no indication, however, that these decisions were overturned on the basis of hostility to the process itself.

38. Speech to civil registry officials, March 1936, *FSV* 2 (1936): 17.

39. Gercke to RuPrMdI, 4/7/33, R39/1:7–8.

40. RdErl. d. RMdI. v. 18.7.1933, R39/1; Erl. d. RuPrMdI. v. 31.7.1935, *ASS* 1 (1937): 2; RdErl. d. RuPrMdI. v. 12.2.1936 (VI A 1648/1890).

41. Gercke to RuPrMdI, 4/7/33, R39/1:7–8.

42. Ulmenstein, *Abstammungsnachweis,* 19; Erl. d. RMJ. v. 29.5.1936 (photocopying church books); "Fotografische Vervielfältigung von Kirchenbüchern," *FSV* 2 (1936): 38–39.

43. See, e.g., Bekanntgabe B 46/40, 7/12/40, NS6/820:136 (Betr. Sicherstellung und Zusammenziehung der Kirchenbücher).

44. Dr. W. Lampe to Kayser, 5/25/44, R39/808. See also Weiss, "Auseinandersetzungen zwischen Reichsnährstand und Reichssippenamt," 1–17.

45. See, e.g., Dr. Fritz Voss, "Leiter des Stadtarchivs in Neuwied" to RfS, 10/22/37, R1509/131 (compendium of church books in Evangelical Synod Wied and Catholic deanship [Dekanat] Engers).

46. See, e.g., Erl. d. RMdI. v. 17.7.39 (ordering contribution of RM 4,000 for this task); R1509/28 (numerous documents showing amounts paid to both Catholic and Protestant churches for this purpose); Oberpräsident, Provinz Ostpreußen (Angestellte Bessel) to RSA, 12/27/44, R1509/100:8 (report regarding sites in four districts indicated that population evacuated in several districts, church books were packed and in some cases also evacuated).

47. See, e.g. RfS Aktenvermerk, Kayser, 2/8/39, R39/470 (obtaining Einwohnermeldekarten); Reichsmeldeordnung of 1938; R39/381 (1941 correspondence on church books and military registers). On obtaining private genealogical collections, see, e.g., various correspondence in R1509/97:18–24, 47–56. On Gestapo help, see, e.g., Gestapo to RfS, 2/22/38, R1509/97:30 (informing RfS that retired teacher Wilhelm G. has important genealogical material which, because he is a political opponent of the regime, he intends to have burned after his death).

48. See, e.g., "Niederschrift über die Besprechung wegen der Sicherung des Baltendeutschen Archivgutes im Reichsministerium des Innern," 12/8/39, R39/381; RSA to Volksdeutsche Mittelstelle, 3/5/41; RSA to SfoR, 3/11/41. Both in R39/772.

49. See #3063, handwritten memo, n/d, R39/22RSA (organizational chart with totals of "districts [*Kreise*]" per "Bezirk, Provinz and Staat").

50. *ASS* 1 (1937): 12. In December 1938, however, the Authority returned it. Jahnke to RMdI, 12/3/38, R39/20.

51. In R39/2.

52. R39/Findbuch:IV–V.

53. See, e.g., Kummer to Generaldirektor der staatl. Archiv Bayerns, 7/6/33 R1509/40:30 ("Subject: Sources for the history of the Jews in Germany . . . especially for the eighteenth and nineteenth centuries . . .); R1509/158 for hundreds of responses, ca. July through December 1933, from towns and cities starting with letters A through F.

54. *Der Archivar,* 13 (1960): 287–88.

55. RdErl. d. RMdI. v. 18.7.1933 (granting SfR regulatory power); RdErl. d. RMdI. v. 14.8.1933 (restricting civil registry access). Both in R39/1.

56. Achim Gercke, "Die Sippenforscher und Seine Familie," *FSV* 1 (1935): 8.

57. In ZB II 3146 A.5. In 1941, Hitler allowed him to remain in the party despite being a "1/16 Jew." Ibid.

58. Rühle, *Dritte Reich,* 266; *FSV* 1 (1935): 30, endsheet.

59. The RSW dissolved itself in November 1935. *FSV* 2 (1936): 10. On Genealogical Authority subsidies to VSV, see, correspondence, RfS and VSV, 3/31/39, 3/8/41, 5/6/41, R1509/7:272–74.

60. *ASS* 1 (1937): 24; *FSV* 2 (1936): 46; "An unsere Leser," *FSV* 3 (1937): 1; Hans v. Bourcy to Mayer, 8/11/38, R39/22 (Vienna).

61. *FSV* 2 (1936): 22; *ASS* 1 (1937): 4; VBS to potential applicant, 12/23/38, R39/244 (citing requirements).

62. Isenburg, *Sippen,* 59. Themal was also director of the evangelical (Lutheran) church-book office in Berlin (Kirchenbuchstelle Alt-Berlin).

63. *ASS* 1 (1937): 77.

64. See, e.g., Ackermann, Lehrer, Konstanz and VBS, 8/28/37, 9/4/37(asking whether Alfred Kopf is licensed genealogist); VBS to Bönig, Kassel, 3/22/38 (advising that Hermann Schütze is not VBS member); Deutsches Auslands-Institut, Stuttgart and VBS, 8/5/38, 8/31/38 (asking for information on "Sippenforschungs-Institutes Haro"). All in R39/244.

65. v. Behrens to Mayer, 6/14/37, R1509/37:86–96.

66. See, e.g., Correspondence, Auswärtige Amt to RfS, 10/20/37, 10/22/37, R39/244 (in response to Foreign Office request, RfS recommends German consulate in Geneva cease using firm "Forschungshilfe" in Berlin-Dahlem; proprietors "politically" and "criminally" unreliable); Correspondence, 2/16/37 through 4/15/37, R1509/37 (Genealogical Authority threatens genealogist Dr. Jur. Schindler with legal action due to client's complaint Schindler has done nothing despite repeated requests); Correspondence, R1509/123 (1942 revocation of professional genealogist Ernst Zapf's permit for failing to provide contracted services to client); RSA memo, "Vorgänge . . . des Sippenforschers Karl Friedrich Reimer," 6/13/42, R39/12 (legal action against genealogist); GAfS (v. Schoen) to Gestapo, 6/43, GSA-W-Benisch (Maximillian Israel B.) (claiming woman cheated by professional genealogist who charged her RM 140 for minimal work after her step-son already "evacuated," and asking Gestapo to see she gets refund).

67. See, e.g., ZB II 3800 A.16 (in spring 1936, Authority reprimands Munich civil servant for using stamp on his "Aryan proof" work saying he is registered as "Sippenforscher by the SfR in the RMdI").

68. All of the following is in ZB II 5181 A.3.

69. See, e.g., numerous disbursements in R1509/28 (providing money to private genealogists pursuant to measures for acquisition and evaluation of genealogical archives and collections of Baltic German returnees); Friedrich Lauer to RfS, 11/23/39, R39/10 (asking RM 100 for delivery of documents identifying Jewish baptisms); various correspondence, RfS and professional genealogist Ernst Zapf, 1936, R1509/123 (regarding purchase of Zapf's work *Judentaufen in Südthüringen und ihre Nachkommen,* as well as his work identifying baptized Negroes, Turks, Janissaries, and "Gypsies"); correspondence, Fritz Schütz, Gumbinnen and Genealogical Authority, 1934–1943, R1509/122 (regarding Schütz's work for Authority); Edgar v. Brackel (Sippenforscher RSH) to RfS, n/d, R39/152 (expert report on Karaites).

70. See, e.g., v. Kotze to VBS, 12/18/36, R1509/37 (ancestral proof in doubtful cases); RSA to Dr. Fritz Zschaeck, Sippenforscher, Frankfurt a.M., n/d, R39/163 (obtaining foreign documents).

71. Knost, *Feststellung,* 55; Ulmenstein, *Abstammungsnachweis,* 59, 119; R. Scholl, "Praktische Winke für die Sippenforschung im Ausland," *FSV* 10 (1937): 109.

72. See, e.g., Blochwitz, Breslau and VBS, 6/7/37 and 12/17/37; VBS and Mayor of Deutschneudorf, Erzgebire, 7/10/37 and 7/14/37; Baron Julius B., Budapest and VBS, 6/30/37 and 7/5/37. All in R39/244. RfS to Gaupersonalamt Baden, 12/15/37; RfS to Gaupersonalamt Kurmark, 12/21/37; RfS to Gauleitung München-Oberbayern, 6/24/38. All in R39/13. RfS to Bade, Spandau, 12/14/37; RfS to Fäger, 1/10/38; RfS or VBS to inquirent, 1/29/38; RfS to Ev. luth. Pfar. Wredenhagen, 2/22/38; RfS to Buddensieg, Langensalze, Thür., 4/12/38; VBS to Rechtsanwalt Feldmüller, 5/31/38; RfS to Lt. Col. van den Berg, Montreal, Canada, 8/23/38; RfS to Dürner, Vienna, 7/16/38; RfS to Dr. med. H. Boehm, Alt-Rehse/Meckl., 4/29/40; all in R39/244.

73. See, e.g., Butte to Mayer, 4/9/45, R1509/8.

74. Rosenhainer and RfS, 7/31/41, 8/4/41, R39/11.

75. See, e.g., RSA to Schütz, 3/1/43, R1509/122:2.

76. Advertisement on tearsheet, R1509/49.

77. The number of issues published each month ranged from about 22,000 (March 1937) to 17,500 (August 1939). As of September 1939, the *ASS* no longer noted the number of each issue that was printed. It appears to have stopped publication in December 1942.

78. *ASS* 1 (1937): 10.

79. "An unsere Leser," *FSV* 2 (1936): 49.

80. Achim Gercke and Rudolf Kummer, *Die Rasse in Schrifttum. Ein Wegweiser durch das rassenkundliche Schrifttum* (Berlin: Metzner, 1933). Kummer later wrote *Rasputin. Ein Werkzeug der Juden* (Nürnberg: Der Stürmer, 1939).

81. BA, Abt. III (BDC), SS-HO 1063, 1064.

82. Ruttke to RfS, 11/18/35, R39/29.

83. Rifat Bey to RuPrMdI, 10/14/33 (Turks); RuPrMdI to Gercke, 12/7/33 (Samoans); RuPrMdI to Gercke, 3/22/34 (Dutch/Indian). All in R39/1.

84. See, e.g., RfS to RPA 4/9/35, 9/22/36, R39/29.

85. Gross to Mayer, 5/10/35, R39/29; RPA to RfS, 6/22/35, R39/29 (civil registrar); Gaubeauftragten für Sachsen des Rassenpolitischen Amtes der NSDAP an SfR (Sächsisches Hauptstaatarchiv Dresden, Aussenministerium Nr. 8329), 8/15/34, R39/1 (Rumanian woman).

86. On Sippenkanzlei, see, e.g., Erl. d. RuPrMdI. v. 13.5.1935; "Vorläufige Richtlinien für der Errichtung und die Amtsführung von Sippenkanzleien," n/d (probably 1935), R39/778; Erl. d. RuPrMdI. v. 17.4.1936; Erl. d. RuPrMdI. v. 7.5.1936; Erl. d. RuPrMdI. v. 1.7.1937. On other supervisory and advisory tasks, see, e.g., *ASS* 1 (1937): 23 (Ahnenpass); RSA to Landessippenstelle, Sippenamt für ostdeutsche Rückwanderer, 12/2/42, and extensive other correspondence, R39/772 (advising which documents necessary for making ancestral decision in particular case, and where to locate them); Chef der Zivilverwaltung für den Bezirk Bialystok to RSA, 6/30/44, R1509/22; Utikal, Chef der Einsatzstabes to Kayser, 10/24/42, 1/19/43, R39/830 (Authority official Gerhard Kayser heads a Reich Kinship Office in Alfred Rosenberg's Operational Staff for the Occupied Territories).

87. See various drafts in R39/1.

88. Denkschrift Gercke, n/d, R39/44.

89. R 39/44 contains three undated drafts, R39/22 six, and R1509/35 one.

90. In *FSV* 2 (1936): 18.

91. RGBl. I. S. 119, 5.11.1937, discussed in *FSV* 3 (1937): 103–104. The law also required the "racial classification" of spouses.

92. See, e.g., RSA to Bürgermeisteramt, Der Standesbeamte, in Altkirch i.Elf., 3/20/42 (proper procedures for provision of Ahnenpass on sworn declaration); RSA to Reichshauptmann des Kreises Warschau-Land Amt für Innere Verwaltung—Das Deutsches Standesamt, Warschau, 3/23/42 (Ahnenpass regulations); Knost to Gefr. Christian Polster, and RSA to Unteroffizier Willi Röder, 9/12/42 (advising on marriage process under military jurisdiction). All in R39/163. Oberkirchenrat to Gercke, 11/14/34, Gercke to RuPrMdI, 11/16/34, R39/1 (church official needs advice regarding man alleging his career chances hurt by failure to receive quick ancestral proof and threatening to make church responsible for damages).

93. See, e.g., Bähreke, Potsdam to RfS, 8/24/37, R39/566 (trying to obtain documents for SS man who wants to get married); Oberst a.D. Haardt, Landeshut to Evangelische Zentralarchiv, Breslau, n/d, R39/815 (needs early-eighteenth-century documents for an SS Gruppenführer).

94. Some cities, however, are proportionally underrepresented, e.g., Vienna (8) and Munich (7).

95. See, e.g., Riebicke and SfR, 1/21/35, 1/24/35, ZB II 4375 A.10 (explaining gene-alogical research permit is not substitute for actual ancestral proof); Kurt Beurer, Baden and RfS, 5/31/37, 6/16/37, R39/244 (discussing proof of "Aryan ancestry" for purposes of NSKK Formation); Knost to Fräulein Marianne Zappen, Duingen, 8/11/42 (how to make genealogical table supporting Ahnenpass); RSA to Alexander Döring, 3/19/42 (advis-ing "Fanny" is unacceptable name for Jewess). All in R39/163. Kurt Beurer, Emmedin-gen/Baden and RfS, 3/13/37, 6/16/37 (finding paternal grandfather for ancestral proof); Biagosch, Leipzig, to VSV, 4/14/37 (placing advertisement in *ASS*); Baron Julius B., Buda-pest and VBS, 6/30/37 and 7/5/37 (getting genealogical documents for citizenship applica-tion); Behning, Neukloster to RfS, 8/11/37 (seeking town location); RfS or VBS to Engel-mann (seeking town location); Fäger to VBS (seeking information on cost of Ahnentafel); RfS to Böhme, 8/13/37 (providing address of Reich Committee for Volk Health Service); Engelmann, Danzig to VBS, 1/10/38 (requesting town information); Bollendorf to VBS, 10/12/38 (seeking help with heraldry research); Alma Bahlke, Cincinnati, Ohio and RfS, 5/18/37, 5/31/37 (seeking help with genealogical research); Joanna Downes, Downes and Downes Law Office, Chicago and RfS, 5/14/37, 6/17/37 (seeking town location); RfS or VBS to Andre, Verdohl i.W., n/d (requesting translation of Dutch documents). All in R39/244.

96. Brack, Stabsleiter des Reichsgeschäftsführers to Gercke, 9/18/34, R39/1.

97. Correspondence, 1/26/37 and 4/6/37, R1509/37. See also Letter to VSV, 10/19/39, R1509/7.

98. Gerrit Schuster (stud. agr.) to RMfWEuV, 5/8/38, MPG 1 Abt. 2399 Rep. 0001A, 122a.

99. Margarette Strauß, "Die Aufgaben der Frau in Sippenkunde und Sippenpflege," *FSV* 4 (1938): 74.

6. The Reich Genealogical Authority and the Ancestral Proof

1. German courts also frequently made decisions on race during the Nazi period, often in paternity suits. A Genealogical Authority ancestral decision, however, was at least theoreti-cally better for an examinee. It had legal validity as a determination of race beyond the parties to the lawsuit. Knost, *Feststellung*, 77.

2. "Beispiele zur Abfassung von Abstammungsbescheiden," 2/1/37, R1509/42:127–31.

3. See, e.g., Abstammungsnachweis 8/13/43, R1509/82 (Kurt M.); GAfS (v. Schoen) "Pfrüngsergebnis" 10/12/44, A-E Alt-Antretter A6/2 (Kurt A.).

4. See, e.g., GSA-W (v. Schoen) to Gestapo, 8/16/44, A-E Baader-Balko-Kastaly A6/4 (informing Gestapo that examinee is Jewish-Mischling first degree); GSA-W (Sellner) to vari-ous authorities, 1/30/45, ibid., (Dr. Oskar B.); Gollmer (RSA) to Reichsstatthalter Darmstadt, 5/24/41, R1509/77. After issuing an ancestral decision, the genealogical authorities informed examinees that they must also indicate this racial status in response "to all inquiries." See, e.g., GAfS to Amalia B., 11/3/42, GSA-W-Benisch.

5. On government employees, see, e.g., Paul B., Zollbetriebsassistent, Karlsruhe to Staszewski, 3/34/39 and 4/26/39, DZfG 27 RSA (wife's "proof of Aryan ancestry" demanded by Badenese government official). On military referrals, see, e.g., R1509/82 (Kurt M. and brothers, from Wehrbezirkskommando Wien) and ZA I 12238 A.1. On naturalization and marriage, see, e.g., "Jahresrechnung 1937," 6/28/38, R1509/26:8–9 (of 8,387 ancestral deci-sion applications in last six months of 1937, almost 32% [2,652] for naturalization and 8% [672] for marriages).

6. See, e.g., ZA I 12238 A.9 (Karl W.) (probably Reichsmusikkammer) and A.5 (Walter P.) (probably Reichstheatrekammer); Schmitz-Berning, *Vokabular,* 4–5 (Prussian Art Academy)

7. See, e.g., RfS to RPA, 5/14/35, R39/29; Föhl to Amt für Volkswohlfahrt, Kreis Leipzig, 2/6/37, R39/13; Gemeindeverwaltung Reichsgaues Wien to RfS, 4/9/40, ZA I 12238 A.9 (Karl W.).

8. R1501/5246:F.4 (Adolf F.); Otto Jatzlau to Evangelische Pfarrämter, Blindow Krs. Prenzlau, and Schweinrich b/Wittstock a.D., 6/17/39, R1509/76; Wilhelm Eulberg to RfS, 3/6/38, ZA I 12238 A.7.

9. Rektor der Albertus-Universität, Königsberg, Gerullis, to RfS, 6/26/35; Reichsausschuß für Volksgesundheitsdienst to RfS, 8/3/35. Both in R1509/91.

10. Gercke (probable) to Ministerialdirektor Dr. Schütze, RuPrMdI, 9/1/34, R39/1.

11. Quote in R39/1.

12. All in R39/1.

13. R39/228 (Frieda D.).

14. RdErl. d. RuPrMdI. v. 4.3.1935: RdErl. d. RuPrMdI. v. 10.10.1935.

15. For courts, see, e.g., R39/243 (Wolfgang B.) (district courts in Breslau and Hannover). For foreign office, see, e.g., ZA I 12238 A.8 (Kraków); postcard, 11/8/39, R1509/66 (Budapest); A-E A6 4 Baader-Balko-Kastaly (Zagreb, Sarajevo); A-E Abel-Alma A6/1 (Pressburg); A-E Alt-Antretter A6/2 (Kaschau, Constantinople). For occupation authorities, see, e.g., Memos, 8/14/41, 8/28/41, R39/11 (Abteilung für die Beschaffung von Abstammungsnachweisen beim Ministerium des Innern); postcards from October 1939 from Reich Protectorate (Urkundenbeschaffungsstelle, Der Reichsprotektor in Böhmen und Mähren) to RfS, R1509/66.

16. List of "Dienststellen der Reichsadoptionsstelle," in MbliV vom 6/10/42, Nr. 23, R39/165. See also, e.g., Red Cross to AfS-Wien, 11/26/38, ZA I 12238 A.6.

17. The 1937 increase consisted of the organization of 59,475 "ancestral cards [*Ahnenkarten*]" and 69,620 "Jewish registers and sources." Graf Reyferlingk, Arbeitsbericht der Abteilung IV/1 für das Jahr 1937, R39/15; Ulmenstein, *Abstammungsnachweis,* 66.

18. See, e.g., R39/228 (Frieda D.).

19. Quoted in *FSV* 2 (1936): 16.

20. See, e.g., Kriminaltechnisches Institut der Sicherheitspolizei-Beim Reichskriminalpolizeiamt, Gutachten Nr. Tgb. 1911/42, 7/10/42, R39/557 (expert report on various documents finding all to have been tampered with); correspondence SfR and Katholische Pfarramt Potsdam (8/34), SfR and Evangelisch-lutherisches Landeskirchenamt Sachsens (8–9/34), RfS and Regierungspräsidenten in Aachen (8/36), Karl M., Kriminalamt Eschweiler and AfS (11/36), R39/557 (all on investigation of possible tamperer, Karl M.); A-E A6 4 Baader-Balko-Kastaly (Stephanie v. B.) (GSA-W contacts Viennese criminal police requesting investigation of document falsification).

21. RfS Umlauf, 7/30/35, R39/3.

22. "Revolutionskalender," R1509/42:203.

23.

	1935	4 (0.8/11)	1941	42 (8.4/7.6)
	1936	6 (1.2/15.3)	1942	46 (9.2/8.3)
	1937	17 (3.4/10.8)	1943	29 (5.8/10.6)
	1938	56 (11.2/11.2)	1944	31 (6.2/na)
	1939	173 (34.7/12.9)	1945	7 (1.4/na)
	1940	87 (17.5/6.3)		

Parenthetical numbers correspond to percentage of files this represents from sample versus actual percentage of Genealogical Authority files opened. For the GSA-W, I had no data on total numbers of files actually opened per year.

24. RfS memo, n/d (probably 8/35), R39/3.
25. Mayer, memo, 6/15/36, R39/3.
26. Erl. d. RMdI. v. 4.12.1942.
27. R1509/51 (Paula L.).
28. Lawyer to RSA, 3/29/40, R1509/77.
29. R39/228 (Frieda D.).
30. Noted in "Material zur Lösung der Halbjudenfrage," RuPrMdI (Dr. Lösener), 10/11/35. Rep. 320/51:141. See also Kaplan, *Dignity,* 98–99 (similar anecdotes regarding schoolchildren).
31. A-E Abel-Alma A6/1 (Johanna A.).
32. Hahm to Oberst und Kommandeur Wallon, Wehrbezirkskommando I, 12/14/43; Obergemeinschaftsleiter der NSDAP, Wagner, Rassenpolitisches Amt, Gausippenstelle, Gauleitung Niederschlesien to RSA, 5/23/44. Both in R39/243.
33. A-E Abel-Alma A6/1 (Katharina A.).
34. Ulmenstein, *Abstammungsnachweis,* 107.
35. See, e.g., A-E Abel-Alma A6/1 (Jacob Karl Israel A.) (GAfS asks Gestapo to send 67-year-old noncompliant examinee and his wife to General Government in order to prevent their "uncontrolled drifting about in Niederdonau").
36. Correspondence in R39/228 (Frieda D.).
37. In R1509/20:12–24.
38. Until 1938, because of the child's interest in legitimacy only the husband could rebut the presumption, and only in a legal proceeding brought within one year of the child's birth (*Anfechtung der Ehelichkeit*). In 1938, however, the law was changed to allow the husband to rebut the presumption from the time he gained knowledge of circumstances of the child's illegitimacy, and also allowed the state's attorney to bring such process when it lay "in the public interest." The reason for the change was the new regime's "superseding interest" in determining the child's "racial" and hereditary health characteristics. Knost, *Feststellung,* 18–20.
39. Ibid., 34–35.
40. Ulmenstein, *Abstammungsnachweis,* 102.
41. Abstammungsnachweis, 1/11/43, R39/243 (Wolfgang B.).
42. Ulmenstein, *Abstammungsnachweis,* 103–104.
43. Abstammungsnachweis, 12/8/41, R39/838 (Gustav M.). The Authority nevertheless held the examinee to be a "Jew" because of his membership in a Jewish religious community. Ibid. "Racial shame" was the popular designation for violation of the antimiscegenation provisions of the Nuremberg Laws.
44. Knost, *Feststellung,* 76.
45. Abstammungsbescheid, 7/2/41, R39/837 (Margarete E.).
46. R39/268 (Peter M.). He received an ancestral decision of "German or related blood."
47. A-E Alt-Antretter A6/2 (Margarethe A.).
48. A-E Balla-Bauer Josef A6/5 (Bernhard B.). On 2/2/44, the GSA-W (Sellner) informed the RPA that "Bernhard B. is a Geltungsjude (legally a 'Jew' for reasons besides ancestry)." Ibid.
49. R39/838 (Agnes E.). See also, e.g., R39/231 (Brothers Karl and Johannes O.—real grandfather was an Irishman); R1501/5246:F.5–6 (Lydia H.—mother had affair with Aryan man); R1509/77 (Lisolette K.—mother had affair with Aryan man); A-E Alt-Antretter A6/2 (Erika A.—Aryan rather than Jewish man is examinee's maternal grandfather).
50. See, Knost, *Feststellung,* 34–35, 73–74.
51. Sturm to RMdI, 11/6/41, R1509/77 (Lisolette K.).

52. R1509/77 (Lisolette K.); Frieda D. to RfS, 10/27/39, R39/228; Hahm to RSA, 3/8/42, R39/243.

53. R1501/5246:F.2–3 (Hilde B.).

54. BDC Paul Anton R.

55. Abstammungsbescheid, R39/838 (Hans Jacob A.).

56. Ulmenstein, *Abstammungsnachweis,* 110.

57. Mayer to RMdI, 11/4/41, R39/838. This does seem to have been a fairly common claim. See, e.g., Abstammungsnachweis R39/838 (Walter Israel B.—real father was Prussian officer); Melanie T. to RSA, 1/18/41, R1509/5 (real father was "deceased lieutenant field Marshall").

58. Rundschreiben Nr. 91/42, Partei-Kanzlei, "Beurteilung jüdischer Mischlinge durch die Partei," NS6/338:4–5.

59. Ulmenstein, *Abstammungsnachweis,* 110.

60. Abstammungsnachweis, 8/22/42, R39/229:3–4 (Lina B.).

61. R39/838 (Sidonie M.).

62. Kreisleitung Weimar to RSA, 5/31/43, R39/163.

63. Thoma to RSA, 3/22/44, R1509/50.

64. Rechtsanwalt and Notar Hermann Kahl, Halle-Salle, to RSA, 2/7/45.

65. See, Knost, *Feststellung,* 4–10. Sometimes, as with Jewish sects such as Karaites and Krimchaks, the religious determination was viewed as insufficient for the "racial determination." See, e.g., Memo, "*Betrifft:* Feststellung der Konfession 'Krimtschatzki,' RfS to RMdI, 6/17/38, R39/152. For dark-skinned people, religious affiliation also played little role.

66. Verordnung über die Zulassung von Nichtariern zum aktiven Wehrdienst v. 25.7.1935 §1[2]) (RGBl. I S. 1047).

67. Jellinek to RfS, 11/7/35, 11/15/35, and note dated 1/3/35, R1509/91. On Jellinek's legal career, see Heinrichs, *Deutsche Juristen,* 181–82.

68. Abstammungsnachweis, 10/28/41, R1509/42 (Moschka G.).

69. Report, Rußland-Institut der Auslandhochschule Berlin, 5/19/38, contained in memo, Ulmenstein to RMdI, 6/17/38, R39/152.

70. RMdI (Hering) to RfS, 12/22/38, R39/152.

71. Gestapo (Heller) Berlin to RfS, 3/29/39; RfS to Gestapo Berlin, 4/3/39. Both in R39/152.

72. RfS (Knost) to Landgericht Dessau, 1/6/40, R39/152.

73. Gutachten on M., Prof. Dr. Lothar Loeffler, Rassenbiologischen Instituts der Universität Königsberg/Pr, 11/2/39, R39/152.

74. See, e.g., RSA to Wirtschaftskammer Pommern, 9/8/41, R39/152.

75. GSA to Gau-Wirtschaftskammer Wien, 9/22/44, A-E Bella-Bauer Josef (M. Bartel).

76. Knost, *Feststellung,* 6.

77. Abstammungsbescheid, 6/11/40, R39/838 (Sidonie M.).

78. Abstammungsbescheid, 8/22/42, R39/229:3–4 (Lina B.).

79. Abstammungsbescheid, 6/18/41, R39/838 (Alice P.).

80. GSA-W-Benisch (Amalia B.) ("Sareh"); ZB II 5181 A.12 ("Goldhorn").

81. In ZB II 4043 A.12. The Genealogical Authority granted Mendel a permit. Unfortunately for him, in 1937 the Authority discovered he had been a Freemason until 1932 and revoked his permit. Ibid.

82. Vfg., Knost to "Leiter der Abt. I," 10/1/40, R39/11.

83. All in A-E Balla-Bauer Josef A6/5, file 02628.

84. R1501/5065 (Elly M.-R., 1936); Klara S. to RSA, 2/17/41, R1509/77; notarized statement of Ludwig M., 6/17/38, R29/227.

85. Melanie T. to RSA, 1/18/41, R1509/5.

86. Jellinek to RuPrMfWEuV, 12/2/35, R1509/91 ("Also my father's thinking was not Jewish-disreputable [*jüdisch-rabulistisch*] or Jewish-corrosive [*jüdisch-zersetzend*]").

87. Hirschwald to RSA, 9/30/40; Frieda D. to RfS, 10/27/39; Frieda D. to Abel (probable), 5/5/44. All in R39/228.

88. BDC Paul Anton R.

89. Gercke to Hess, 8/11/33 (year probable), R39/1.

90. RfS Umlauf, 5/9/35, R39/3. The Authority used both the Gestapo and SS Security Service to obtain photographs. See, e.g., Schircks to Breslau Gestapo, 9/16/42; Der Befehlshaber der Sicherheitspolizei und des SD, Zentralamt für die Regelung der Judenfrage in Böhmen und Mähren to RSA, 11/7/42. Both in R39/243.

91. Abstammungsbescheid, 4/9/41, GSA-W-Benisch (Maximillian B.).

92. R39/228 (Frieda D.).

93. Frieda D. to Lösener, 5/23/40; Hirschwald to RSA, 12/2/41 (approx.). Both in R39/228; notarized statement, 6/17/38, R29/227 (Johann K.).

94. Hubertus Alois T. to RSA, 2/22/44, R1509/50; statement of Heinrich Zindel, n/d, R29/227; R1501/5065 (Elly M.-R., 1936).

95. RMdI to RSA, 9/18/41, R1509/42 (Eduard S.).

96. Jellinek to Genealogical Authority, 1/3/35, R1509/91; R1501/5065 (Elly M.-R., 1936); R1501/5246:F.2–3 (Hilde B., 1937).

97. Dr. Gustav Klein-Doppler, Vienna to RSA, 8/4/41, R39/227.

98. Unger to Regierungsrat Dr. Dubitscher, Oberarzt, Berlin Poliklinik, 6/23/42, 7/14/42, A-E Alt-Antretter A6/2. The client was sent to Theresienstadt. Ibid.

99. Clara B. to RSA, 4/2/43, R1509/58. In response to this request, the NSDAP Obergemeinschaftsleiter in Niederschlesien requested that the Genealogical Authority not change its designations. The file does not indicate what ultimately happened.

100. Hahm to RSA, 7/15/42, R39/243; Frieda D. to Prowe, 4/6/44, R39/228; A-E A6 4 Baader-Balko-Kastaly (Stephanie v. B., 9/1942).

101. In one of Jellinek's memoranda, for example, an Authority official (probably Mayer) wrote "fantasy" and "nonsense" next to Jellinek's discussion of the non-Jewish origin of his family.

102. Ulmenstein to RuPrMdI, 11/14/36, R1509/91.

103. For the "small ancestral proof," a grandparent who was not part of a Jewish religious community would only be classified as "non-Aryan" if both of his or her parents were "non-Aryan." See, e.g., *Deutsche Zeitung*, 18.1.34, Nr. 15, R39/1.

104. R39/228 (Frieda D.).

105. R1501/5065 (Elly M.-R. and Erich G.).

106. R1501/5246:F.2–3) (Hilde B., 1937).

107. Lösener, RMdI, to Steinkopff, 5/8/39, R1501/5246:F.3–4 (Oskar C.).

108. R1501/5246:F.5–6 (Lydia H.).

109. The file is R1509/80.

7. Three Beneficiaries of the Ancestral Proof

1. Quoted in Cohn, *Europe's Inner Demons*, 24.

2. Ulmenstein, *Abstammungsnachweis*, 106; RdErl. d. RMdI. v. 24.4.1934. Other non-documentary methods, such as graphological investigations, were also investigated. See, e.g., Schultze-Naumburg to Steinkopff, 11/28/39, R1501/5246:F.4.

3. At a March 23, 1939 professional meeting of leading anthropologists at the University of Munich's Anthropological Institute, the participants concluded that up to that point, halfway through the Third Reich, 2,800 biological investigations had been made, only 370 of which were for the Genealogical Authority. A further 500 or so were in the process of being performed. Kramp, "erbbiologische," 383.

4. See, e.g. Mollison, Expert Report, 2/21/42, R1509/80:134–41 (Minni V., Beate K.); Eickstedt, Expert Report, 12/22/42, R39/243:65 (Wolfgang B.); Weinert, Expert Report, 12/8/42, R39/226:35 (Horst K.); Dubitscher, Expert Report, 9/29/42, R39/231:2 (Karl O.).

5. Ulmenstein, *Abstammungsnachweis,* 114–15.

6. Gutachten, Institut für gerichtliche Medizin, Heidelberg, 8/28/40, R1509/77 (Lisolette K.).

7. See, e.g., Kramp, "erbbiologische"; Schultz, "Erbbiologisches Gutachten," 3/20/40, R39/229:21–25 (Martha J.); Wastl, "Anthropologischen Gutachten," 7/10/40, R39/227:91–98 (Alice G.); Dr. phil. Karl Tuppa, "Bericht, Befund und Gutachten," 12/16/41, R39/227:72–84 (Margarette K.); Eickstedt, Expert Report, 12/22/42, R39/243:65–80 (Wolfgang B.); Tuppa, "Gutachten," 3/17/43, R39/224:79–103 (H. twins).

8. Verschuer, Expert Report, 4/5/41, R1509/77:89–100 (Lisolette K.).

9. Eickstedt, Expert Report, 12/22/42, R39/243:65–80 (Wolfgang B.); Boehm, "Abstammungsgutachten," 8/13/43, R39/225:32 (Gerda S.).

10. Knost to RMdI, 10/14/41, R39/838 (appeal of Carolina B.).

11. Verschuer, Expert Report, 4/5/41, R1509/77:89–100 (Lisolette K.).

12. Kramp, "erbbiologische," 382.

13. See, e.g., Wastl, "Anthropologisches Gutachten," 7/10/40. R39/227:97 (Alice G.).

14. See, e.g., Tuppa, "Bericht, Befund und Gutachten," 3/26/43, R39/224:100; Geyer, "Bericht, Befund and Gutachten," 4/14/39, R39/224:51 (Ludwig Z.); Tuppa, "Bericht Befund und Gutachten," 12/16/40, R39/227:84 (Alice G.); Wastl, "Anthropologisches-erbbiologisches Gutachten," 6/21/43, R39/224:11 (Lisbeth W.); letter, Kranz to RSA, 8/26/43, R39/224:60.

15. Reche, Expert Report, 4/20/40, R39/231:15–16, 18 (Johannes O.).

16. Mollison, Expert Report, 2/21/42, R1509/80:141 (Minni V. and Beate K.).

17. Weinert, "Abstammung" decision, 8/12/42, R39/226:30 (Horst K.).

18. Dubitscher, Expert Report, 9/29/42, R39/231:10–13 (Karl O.)

19. "Ergebnis der rassenkundlichen Untersuchung" in A-E Balla-Bauer Josef A6/5 (Aristidou B.) and GSA-W-Benisch.

20. On use of photos, see also, e.g., Schultze-Naumburg to Steinkopff, 11/28/39, R1501/5246: F.4; Reche, Expert Report, 4/20/40, R39/231:14–19 (Johannes O.); Dubitscher, Expert Report, 9/29/42, R39/231:10–13 (Karl O.); Abstammungsnachweis, 7/2/41, R39/837 (Margarete E.).

21. See, e.g., Reche, Expert Report, 4/20/40 (Johannes O. is Jewish Mischling first degree; Genealogical Authority issued ancestral decision accordingly); Dubitscher, Expert Report, 9/29/42 (Karl O., Johannes O.'s full brother is Jewish Mischling second degree). In October 1942, the Authority requested that Dr. Abel at the Kaiser Wilhelm Institute for Anthropology make a third examination to reconcile this discrepancy. Reich Genealogical Authority Aktenvermerk, 10/19/42. All in R39/231:2–20. The file does not indicate whether this requested reexamination took place.

22. Weinert, Expert Report, 12/9/41, R39/838 (B.).

23. GSA-W Aktenvermerk, "Ferndmündliche Äusserung Dr. Pendls," 9/1/44, A-E Balla-Bauer Josef A6/5 (Gertrude B.).

24. Schircks to RMdI, 7/8/40, R39/838 (re: Agnes E.); Ulmenstein, *Abstammungsnachweis,* 111.

25. See, e.g., Abstammungsnachweis, 10/28/41, R1509/42 (Moschka G.).

26. Weinert, Expert Report, 12/9/41, R39/838 (B.).

27. Weinert, "Abstammung" decision, 8/12/42, R39/226:35 (Horst Julius K.).

28. Mollison, Expert Report, 2/21/42, R1509/80:136.

29. Abstammungsnachweis, 6/25/42, R1509/80.

30. Verschuer, Expert Report, 4/5/41, R1509/77:89–100 (Lisolette K.).

31. Abstammungsnachweis, 4/25/41, R1509/77:137 (Lisolette K.).

32. Dubitscher, Expert Report, 9/29/42, R39/231:3, 8, 10 (Karl O.).

33. Eickstedt, Expert Report, 12/22/42, R39/243:65, 69 (Wolfgang B.).

34. "Der Wert des erbbiologischen Abstammungsnachweises. Eine amtliche Stellungnahme," *Informationsdienst Rassenpolitisches Amt der NSDAP, Reichsleitung,* 10.September 1939—Nr. 93, BDC Otto Reche.

35. Form X 162/35, R1509/42:125–26.

36. Ulmenstein, *Abstammungsnachweis,* 117–18.

37. Reichsstatthalter Thüringen to DdRfS, 7/20/40, R1509/42.

38. On increased prestige and resources for racial scientists in the Third Reich, see Proctor, *Racial Hygiene,* 42–45; Burleigh, *Racial State,* 51–55; Weindling, *Health,* 495, 525; Weingart, *Rasse,* 389–92.

39. Gering to RuPrMfWEuV, 6/22/36, MPG 1 Abt. 2399 Rep. 0001A; Ulmenstein, *Abstammungsnachweis,* 121; Memo, RMdI to RMdF, 3/21/41, R4901/965.

40. Fischer to RMdI, 11/29/38, R4901/965.

41. See, e.g., Boehm to RMfWEuV, 12/16/37; Prof. Dr. Martin Staemmler to RMf-WEuV; Schnellbrief, RMfWEuV (Groh), 6/20/39. All in R4901/965. Verschuer to Generalverwaltung der Kaiser Wilhelm Institute, 5/6/43, MPG 1 Abt. 2409 Rep. 0001A.

42. Reche to Leiter des Sächsischen Ministeriums für Volksbildung, 9/23/40, R4901/965.

43. Loeffler to Curator of the Albertus-Universität, 2/23/39, R4901/965.

44. Knost, *Feststellung,* 87.

45. See, e.g., Erl. d. RMdI. v. 13.3.1941 (Universitäts-Institut für gerichtliche und soziale Medizin, Wien); (R39/165); RdErl. d. RMdI. u. RJM. v. 21.4.1942 (supplemental listing of "recognized experts"); Erl. d. RMdI. v. 6.5.1942 (Weimar: Thüringisches Landesamt für Rassewesen).

46. See R39/165 (108 doctors in 1941).

47. Felbor, *Rassenbiologie,* 100–101.

48. E.g., Pendl in Vienna. See also "Expert Report" by Dr. I. Schreckeis in Zagreb, NS19/971:36 (photographs of examinee's immediate ancestors show "no signs that are typical of belonging to the Jewish race").

49. Grant, *Untergang,* 5, 6.

50. Fischer, Tätigkeitsbericht (vom 1. April 1935 bis 31. März 1936), in MPG 1 Abt. 2399 Rep. 0001A.

51. Carl Sterzel, "Über der Abänderung des Personenstandsgesetzes," *StAZ* 20 (1921): 168.

52. Schultze-Naumburg, "Rassenkunde und Sippenforschung," *FSV* 4 (1938): 3.

53. *Völkischer Beobachter,* Nr. 95/31. 10. 1920/S. 5.

54. See, e.g., Knost, *Feststellung,* 92–94; Emil Jörns, *Meine Sippe, ein Arbeitsheft für de rassebewußte deutsche Jugend* (Görlitz: Starke, 1934); Bruno Manger, *Erste Familienkunde für deutsche Jungen und Mädel* (Langensalza/Berlin/Leipzig: Beltz, 1934); Ernst Reinstorf, *Familiengeschichte und Sippenkunde in der Schule* (Stade: W. Heimberg, 1934); Gerhard Steiner, *Lebendige Familienforschung und Familiengeschichte in der Schule* (Osterwieck am Harz, Berlin: A.W. Zickfeldt, 1935).

55. Klocke, *Entwicklung,* 25–26; Isenburg, *Sippen,* 60–61.

56. See, e.g., Rutkowski, "Historische," 40–49; Alfred Eydt, "Rassenpolitische Erziehung des Handarbeiters durch Sippenpflege," *Volk und Rasse* 12 (1937): 200.

57. Ribbe, *Taschenbuch,* 631.

58. Klocke, *Entwicklung,* 49–50. After 1940, the war effort put an end to this work. Ibid.

59. Ibid., 57.

60. Werner Gebler, "Sieldung des Blutes," *FSV* 2 (1936): 3.

61. Bock, *Zwangssterilisation,* 189, 212, 329.

62. Wentscher, *Einführung,* 1–2.

63. Werner Gebler, "Sieldung des Blutes," *FSV* 2 (1936): 29; Margarete Strutz, "Die Aufgaben der Frau in Sippenkunde und Sippenpflege," *FSV* 4 (1938): 91.

64. *FSV* 2 (1936): 14.

65. Discussed in *KfRuF,* 10/18/38, R39/813.

66. Wentscher, *Einführung,* 170.

67. Karl Valerius Herberger, *Familienforschung als Wegweiser zur Volksgemeinschaft* (Schwarzenberg i. Erzg.: Glückauf, 1935).

68. N/a, *Begründung zum Entwurf einem Sippenamtsgesetz,* I A . . . 617/5018, n/d (but no later than 1934), R39/44.

69. Personenstandsgesetz v. 3.11.1937, Ch. 2, §4.

70. Dr. Franz Josef Umlauft, "Sippenkunde als Mittel zu Gemeinschaftsbildung," 11, R1509/5.

71. Klocke, *Entwicklung,* 45–47.

72. See, e.g., *StAZ* 17 (1937): 381–94; Maruhn, *Staatsdiener,* 80, 101.

73. Dr. Georg Meyer-Erlach, Direktor, Familiengeschichtliche Arbeitsgemeinschaft am Staatsarchiv Würzburg, "Eine Anstalt für Sippenforschung" (1936), R1509/96.

74. Wentscher, *Einführung,* 164; "Bericht über die Tagung des Reichsbundes der deutschen Standesbeamten," 2/16/36, R39/778; *FSV* 2 (1936): 18.

75. "Protokoll der Vorstandssitzung vom 19.3.1934, Bericht Hohlfeldt," in DZfG, Nr. 22.

76. Lorenz to Gercke, 3/9/34, Rep. 309/280.

77. Sitzung des Vereins "Deutscher Roland" v. 14.5.35, R39/2; *ASS* 1 (1937): 24.

78. *ArchfS,* 10 (1933): 336.

79. RSA "Aktenvermerk," 7/10/42, R39/381.

80. Spohr to Kayser, 3/17/37, R1509/7.

81. See, e.g., Prof. Dr. Herman Lundborg, *Bevölkerungsfragen, Bauerntum und Rassenhygiene* (Berlin: Metzner, 1934); Prof. Dr. Friedrich Burgdörfer, *Volks- und Wehrkraft, Krieg und Rasse* (Berlin: Metzner, 1936); Dr. Heinrich Banniza v. Bazan, *Das Deutsche Blut im Deutschen Raum, sippenkundliche Grundzüge des deutschen Bevölkerungswandels in der Neuzeit* (Berlin: Metzner, 1937).

82. Karl Bamberger, *Familienkunde und Rassenpflege* (Leipzig: Zentralstelle für Deutsche Personen- und Familiengeschichte, 1935).

83. RfS to Deutsche Auslands-Institut, Hauptstelle für auslandsdeutsche Sippenkunde, 11/16/37, R39/268.

84. Wecken, *Ahnentafel;* Wilfrid Euler, "Die Rassische Ruckkreuzung des Judenmischlings," *FSV* 4 (1938): 6; Hayn, *Sippenfibel,* 22.

85. See, e.g., Josef Schram-Steiner, "Die jüdischen Matriken der Ostmark," *FSV* 6 (1940): 86.

86. "Jahresbericht der Deutschen Ahnengemeinschaft (D.A.) e.V. Sitz Dresden," *FSV* 1 (1935): 24; Bourcy correspondence in R1509/91; Walter Haines to RMfWEuV, 12/4/40, R4901/933.

87. See, e.g., Adelheid v. Livonius to RfS, 11/7/40, R39/567; Berrufssippenforscher, Finkernagel to Sippenkanzlei, 4/17/36, R39/778; R1509/59 (Margarete L.)

88. ZB II 4043 A.12 (bookseller, 1933); ZA VI 4022 A.19 (unemployed man's RSW application, 1934); ZB II 3125 A.7 (Hamburg attorney, 1934); ZB II 5210 A.9 (teacher, 1936); ZB II 4675 A.11 (NSDAP Gauleitung, Personaldienststelle to Genealogical Authority, 1937); ZA VI 4101 A.3 (Merseburg office worker, 1937).

89. In ZB II 3146 A.21.

90. Ulmenstein, *Abstammungsnachweis,* 20–23.

91. On regional groups, see, e.g., Rep. 309/285 (containing articles for four different groups), Rep. 309/280 (Reichsverein für Sippenforschung und Wappenkunde, e.V., Berlin); R1509/7 (Verein für Sippenforschung für den Gau Niederdonau, Wien). On family groups, see, e.g., Max Prowe, "Köpfe deutsche Sippenforscher," *FSV 3* (1937): 35.

92. *ASS* 1 (1937): 95.

93. See, e.g., Letter to Genealogical Authority, 1934, ZB VI 4100 A.2; Treichel, Kosslin/Pom to VBS, 4/8/37; Fritz Schulz to RfS, 1/12/39. All in R1509/568. Studienrat i.R. Gg. Dittrich, Berlin to Reichsführer SS, 10/7/37, R39/470; Schwartz to RfS, 4/5/38, R39/566a; Hellman, Glogau to RSH, 1/24/41; Dr. Scheiber, Vienna to Genealogical Authority, 7/22/42; Unger to RSA, 8/28/42. All in R39/746. Leist, Magdeburg to RfS, 7/1/39, R39/778; v. Ehrenkrook, Breslau to RfS, 11/6/42, R39/814.

94. Regarding cost, see, e.g., Bährecke, Potsdam to RfS, 3/10/38, R39/570; v. Blumencron, Linz, to RfS, 4/11/38, R39/573. Regarding inefficiency of Ahnenpass certification, see, e.g., v. Livonius to Genealogical Authority, 6/28/37, ZB II 3750 A.17; Röttinger to RfS, 3/4/39, R39/573. Regarding client's failure to pay, see, e.g., Dr. Hans Macco, Berlin to VBS, 11/7/37; v. Brackel, Berlin to VBS, 3/30/37. Both in R1509/37. Regarding church-book problems, see, e.g., Zapf, Berufssippenforscher, Hildburghausen to SfR, 3/21/34, R1509/123; Dr. jur. Steinbok, Thomaswaldau u. Bunzlau to RfS, 1/5/37, R39/565a. See also Bähreke, Potsdam to RfS, 4/24/39 (documents in Czech); Oberst a. D. v. Hohenhorst, Innsbruck to RfS, 7/19/41 (use of uneducated women). Both in R39/565.

95. Unger to Mayer, 10/22/43, R1509/5.

96. "Die Erziehung zu rassischem Denken," radio address, 7/17/33, R39/49.

97. "Zusammenstellung der evangelischen Pfarrämter," n/d, R39/534; "Zusammenstellung der katholischen Pfarrämter," n/d, R39/535.

98. Hertz, "Genealogy Bureaucracy," 61.

99. See, e.g., *Richtlinien für die Verkartung der Kirchenbücher. Ausgestellt vom Sachverständigen für Rasseforschung beim Reichsministerium des Innern* (Berlin: Evangel. Konsistorium der Mark Brandenburg, 1934); Erzbischöfl. Generalvikariat in Paderborn (ed.), *Fragen der Urkundenbe-schaffung zum Nachweis der arischen Abstammung und des Schutzes kirchlicher Archivalien. Amtliche Erlasse u. Richtlinien* (Paderborn: Bonifacius-Druckerei, 1935); Kurt Kronenberg, *Kirchenbuch Urkunden für Sippenforschung und deutschblütigen Abstammungsnachweis. Ein Wegweiser für Pfarrer u. Kbführer in die geltenden Best. Erlasse u. Gebührenordnungen* (Berlin: Ev. Preßverband, 1937).

100. See, e.g., Luth. Pfar. Wredenhagen to VBS, 2/14/38, R39/244; Staszewski to Heinrich v. Cosel, Landsberg a.W., 4/30/38; Hans Doennig cand. mach, Schönberg to Staszewski, 3/14/39. Both in DZfG 27 RSA.

101. Gailus, "Beihilfe zur Ausgrenzung," 255.

102. RdErl. d. RuPrMdI. v. 4.3.1935, 10.5.1935 and 10.10.1935.

103. N/a, "Kirche, Kirchenbücher, Abstammungsnachweis und Gebührenfragen," 1/25/38, R39/541.

104. See, e.g., Pastor, evangelische Pfarramt Spremberg to Otto Jetzlau, 2/6/34, R1509/76.

105. Faulhaber, *Judaism, Christianity and Germany,* 107.

106. Quoted in *Pressebericht des Rassenpolitisches Amtes RL der NSDAP,* Nr. 192/36, 1/28/36, NS20/143-3.

107. Knost, *Feststellung,* 107–18.

108. In R39/565.

109. Rorschacher Zeitung, 2/15/36, quoted in *Pressebericht des Rassenpolitischen Amtes RL der NSDAP,* 191/36, 2/27/36, in NS20/143-3. See also Norden, "Evangelische Kirche," 103 (1935 Evangelical document decrying brutal treatment of Jews, entitled "On the Position of the German non-Aryans"); ibid., 104, 106, 108 (Protestant leaders describing people of Jewish ancestry who converted to Christianity as "Christian non-Aryans" or "racially Jewish Christians").

110. Knost, *Feststellung,* 119.

111. See, e.g., Braunschweigische ev.-luth. Landeskirche to Braunschweig. Ministerpräsidenten, 8/11/38, R1509/130; Generalvikar, Bischöfliches Ordinariat Augsburg to RSA, 11/10/41, R39/381. While the Evangelical Church initially balked at applying the "Aryan paragraph" to its own clergymen, this did not entail a criticism of racism, but rather a plea for an exception. See, e.g., Gutteridge, *German Evangelical Church,* esp. 91–138; Gordon, *Hitler,* 261.

112. Karl Schofeld, "Urkunden über uneheliche Kinder beim Nachweis der arischen Abstammung," *FSV* 2 (1936): 56.

113. Ulmenstein, *Abstammungsnachweis,* 135–37.

114. There were 28 *Landeskirchenamt* on the Nazi assumption of power. Helmreich, *German Churches,* 123.

115. Correspondence in R39/566a (re: v. S. family).

116. Correspondence, Fuhst, Dipl. Ing., BfdK and RfS, 1/8/37 et seq., R39/565a.

117. Correspondence, Grigoleit, RfS, Ev. Konsistorium Königsberg, 6/14/38 et seq., R39/565a.

118. Reimer to ?, 1/2/37, R39/566; Reimer to RSA, 6/9/41, R39/567; Arnold to RfS, 11/4/38, R39/570.

119. See, e.g., Correspondence, Dittrich, BfdK and RfS, 7/38 to 11/38; Correspondence, genealogist Bähreke, Potsdam and RfS, 8/24/37 et seq. All in R39/566. Correspondence, Kapitanleutnant a. D. Treichel, Köslin/Pom, VBS and RfS, n/d, R39/568.

120. Internal memo, "Kirche, Kirchenbücher," n/a, 1/25/38, R39/541.

121. RfS Aktenvermerk, n/a, 11/29/38, R39/565. The other four cases involved incorrect provision of information with no indication that a Jewish ancestor was involved.

122. This and all other documents relating to the case are in R39/541.

123. A 1938 Genealogical Authority memorandum noted that the Catholic Church was more compliant than the Protestant churches with regard to state control over provision of genealogical information. Internal Memo, "Kirche, Kirchenbücher," n/a, 1/25/38, R39/541.

8. Other Means of Generating Acceptance of Racism

1. Quoted in Weiss, "Vorgeschichte," 501.

2. See, e.g., Fredrickson, *Racism,* 123.

3. v. Bourcy to Mayer, 11/1/37, R39/244.

4. Abstammungsnachweis, R39/838 (? B.) (emphasis in original).

5. See, e.g., Schultz, "Erbbiologisches Gutachten," 3/20/40, R39/229:21 (Martha J.); Verschuer, Expert Report, 4/5/41, R1509/77:89–100 (Lisolette K.); Kranz to RSA, 8/26/43, R39/224:54–60.

6. See, e.g., Karlwerner Klüber, "Wie drei Brüder Klüber vor über hundert Jahren zur Judenfrage Stellung nahmen," *FSV* 2 (1936): 43.

7. *FSV* 3 (1937): 35.

8. Knost, *Feststellung*, 1.

9. Veit, *stiftsmäßige*, 3, 4, 20, 30.

10. *FSV* 2 (1936): 13–14.

11. Schultze-Naumburg, "Rassenkunde und Sippenforschung," *FSV* 4 (1938): 3.

12. Isenburg, *Sippen*, 50; Wentscher, *Einführung*, 2.

13. Veit, *stiftsmäßige*, 3, 4, 20, 30.

14. See, e.g., *MdR* 20 (1935): 28 (reviewing Veit's book); Klocke, "Die Gestaltung der deutschen Ahnenprobe im 13., 14. und 15. Jahrhundert," *FSV* 4 (1938): 133; Hohlfeld, "Von der Genealogie zur Sippenkunde. Ein geistesgeschichtlicher Wandel in Deutschland," *FB* 42 (1944): 1–8.

15. Weiss, "Vorgeschichte," 623; Standesbeamten Gluck, "Ebenbürtigkeit," *StAZ* 11 (1931): 249.

16. Wentscher, *Einführung*, 2–3; Isenburg, *Sippen*, 50–55.

17. C. Chl. Frhr. v. R., "Ahnenproben alter Zeit," *DH* 4 (1873): 34; "Referat über die Vorträge des Dr. Stephan Kekule v. Stradonitz . . . betreffend die Genealogie als Wissenschaft," *DH* 29 (1898): 16–19.

18. Ulmenstein, *Abstammungsnachweis*, 9–11.

19. Darré quoted in Schmitz-Berning, *Vokabular*, 575. Note also the titles of Walther Darrés's *Neuadel aus Blut und Boden* (München: Lehmann, 1930) and Hans F. K. Günther's *Füheradel durch Sippenpflege* (München: Lehmann, 1936).

20. Aronson, *Heydrich*, 76.

21. *Ausgewählte Ahnentafeln der Edda* (Gotha: Justus Perthes, 1925), reviewed in *MdR* 14 (1929): 5.

22. Standesbeamten Gluck, "Ebenbürtigkeit," *StAZ* 11 (1931): 249–50.

23. Weiss, "Vorgeschichte," 427–28, 436, 621–22; Goldstein, "Anti-Semitism," 73. These groups included the genealogical organizations the German Roland and the German Nobles Cooperative (Deutsche Adelsgenossenschaft).

24. In R30/574.

25. In R39/565.

26. Quoted in Caplan, *Government*, 10.

27. Ibid., 197–98 (quote), 201–203.

28. Ulmenstein, *Abstammungsnachweis*, 118.

29. RuPrMdI (Hering) to RfS, 7/29/35, R39/565a; RfS Form X 230, R1509/41; Form X 257/2./42/500; X 305/12/41/500. All in R39/163. Blank SfR form, R39/18. For blood tests, the Genealogical Authority used forms X 324, X 322 and X 164. All in R1509/41:6–7, 16.

30. See, e.g., R39/838 (Wolfgang D.).

31. Knost to RMdI, n/d, R39/838 (re: Carolina B.).

32. Knost, *Feststellung*, 6.

33. Ulmenstein, *Abstammungsnachweis*, 38.

34. Expert Report by Reche, 4/20/40, R39/231:19 (Johannes O.).

35. Dr. Blumenberg to Genealogical Authority, 10/20/42, R39/243.

36. E. Peters, "Besteht eine Entschädigungspflicht der Reichskasse gegenüber Personen, die im Rechtsstreit erb- und rassenkundlich untersucht werden?" *StAZ* 21 (1941): 38–39.

37. Ulmenstein, *Abstammungsnachweis,* 14. The Nazi Party statutes also provided, at least ostensibly, the right to appeal to the Genealogical Authority for verification of Party ancestral decisions. Satzung der NSDAP für Handgebrauch der Parteigerichte vom 1.1. 1934, Sec. 3, Anmerkung 2.

38. All in GSA-W-Benisch (Maximillian Israel B.).

39. See, e.g., A-E Baader-Balko-Kastaly A6/4 (Rosalie B.) (ancestral decision changed from "Jewess" to "First-Degree Mischling").

40. Knost, *Feststellung,* 72.

41. *FSV* 2 (1936): 16.

42. RfS (Knost) to Landgericht Dessau, 1/6/40, R39/152.

43. Abstammungsbescheid, 9/22/41, R39/227 (Margarette K.); Abstammungsbescheid, 2/2/43. R39/227:103–105 (Alice G.).

44. Schultze-Naumburg to Steinkopff, 11/28/39, R1501/5246:F.4.

45. Oberverwaltungsgerichtsrat Dr. Ernst Isay, "Die Feststellung der Staatsangehörigkeit," *StAZ* 10 (1930): 213.

46. "Referat über die Vorträge des Dr. Stephan Kekule v. Stradonitz . . . betreffend die Genealogie als Wissenschaft," *DH* 29 (1898): 16–19.

47. See, e.g., "Kann nach dem heutigen Stande der Forschung durch Blutuntersuchung der . . . vorgesehene Nachweis offenbarer Unmöglichkeit der Emfängnis geführt werden?" *StAZ* 8 (1928): 51; "Unehelichkeitserklärung auf Grund eines ärztlichen Gutachtens," ibid., 231–32.

48. See, e.g., Max Henke's "Blutprobe und Vaterschaftsbeweise" (München: Gmelin, 1928), listed in the Roland's new library acquisitions for 1928. *MdR* 13 (1928): 43.

49. See, e.g., Erl. d. RMdI., "Betr: Blutgruppenbestimmungen zur Vaterschaftsfeststellung," citing the most recent works in the field, and Mayer's comments thereto, 10/1/42, R1509/53; Ulmenstein, *Abstammungsnachweis,* 117; *Deutsches Recht* 25/26 (1943): 713–14.

50. See, e.g. "Beweiswert der Blutgruppenuntersuchung," *StAZ* 21 (1941): 251.

51. See, e.g., Ulmenstein, "Bilderahnentafeln," *StAZ* 21 (1941): 7–8; Ulmenstein, "Hausmarken als Sippenzeichen," ibid., 35–38; "Das Wappen Christi," *Herold* 3 (1943): 89–108.

52. Mayer to Fischer, 5/15/41, Rep309/809.

53. See, e.g., *ASS* 2 (1938): 157–60; *Gothaische Genealogische Taschenbücher* (nobles).

54. Themal, *Berufssippenforscher,* 169.

55. See, e.g., Dr. C. U. Endler und Kirchenregierungsrat Edm. Albrecht, *Mecklenburgs familiengeschichtliche Quellen* (Hamburg: Richard Hermes Verlag, 1937); Alexander v. Lyncker, *Die Altpreußische Armee 1741–1806 und ihre Militärkirchenbücher* (Berlin: VfS, 1937); Lynker, *Die preussische Armee 1807–1867 und ihre sippenkundliche Quellen* (Berlin: VfS, 1939). On provision of money, see, e.g., Receipts, R1509/29 11–17; Mayer to Bayerischen Landesverein für Familienkunde, e.V., 4/29/4; Dr. med. et rer. pol. Ernst Peust, Stadtarzt-Nervenarzt, Magdeburg to Mayer, 2/15/41; Correspondence with Verband der Angehörigen des Kurländischen Stammadels, e.V., 1939–40. All in R39/381.

56. "Vorläufige Richtlinien für der Errichtung und die Amtsführung von Sippenkanzleien," n/d (probably 1935), R39/778.

57. Mayer to Professor Otto Hupp, Schleißheim b./München, 4/5/35; RuPrMdI (Hering) to RfS, 1/2/36. Both in R39/6.

58. Bormann to Frick, 10/9/34; Gercke to Interior Minister, 11/3/34. Both in R39/1.

59. *ASS* 1 (1937): 52. A *Sippentafel* represented all persons related to an individual by blood. See Ulmenstein, *Abstammungsnachweis,* 6.

60. Knost, *Feststellung,* 92–94.

61. Isenburg, *Sippen,* 2.

62. Amtsgerichtsrat Dr. Thost, "Familienregister und Archiv für familiengeschichtliche Aufzeichnungen," *StAZ* 5 (1925): 129.

63. Wentscher, *Einführung,* 166.

64. See, e.g., Barnett, *Bystanders,* 41–43 (institutional complicity with Nazi regime created veneer of legitimacy, compartmentalization of responsibility, and "illusion of normality").

65. "Die blutmäßige Abstammung eines in einer Ehe geborenen Kindes . . . ," *StAZ* 21 (1941): 4–5; "Zugehörigkeit zur jüdischen Religionsgemeinschaft," *StAZ* 21 (1941): 17–18; "Zum Begriff 'Jude'," *StAZ* 21 (1941): 96.

66. "Feststellung der Nicht-Abstammung und Unterhaltsurteil," *StAZ* (1941): 5–6; "Eheverbot des Altersunterschiedes," ibid., 49; "Notwendigkeit erb- und rassenkundlicher Untersuchung nach österreichischem Recht," ibid., 139.

9. Racial Scientific Ideology and the Holocaust

1. Quoted in Mendes-Flohr, *Jew in the Modern World,* 684–85.

2. Ulmenstein, *Abstammungsnachweis,* 5.

3. Berlin: VfS, n/d (1937 or later).

4. Bernhard Lösener: "Die Hauptprobleme der Nürnberger Grundgesetze und ihrer 1. Ausführungsverordnung," RVerwBl. (1935), S. 929; Stuckart, *Rassengesetzgebung,* 135.

5. *Ahnenpaß* (n/d, but later than 2/37), 3; *Stuttgarter Neues Tagblatt* v. 3.1.36, quoted in *Pressebericht des Rassenpolitischen Amtes RL des NSDAP* 174/36 9.1.36, NS20/143-3.

6. Stuckart, *Rassen- und Erbpflege,* 6.

7. Kaplan, *Dignity,* 124.

8. Gellately, *Backing,* 25.

9. Erste Verordnung zur Durchführung des Gesetzes zur Wiederherstellung des Berufsbeamtentums. Vom 11. April 1933 (RGBl. I S. 195).

10. *Verwaltungsblatt der Hansestadt Köln,* Nr. 42, 12. December 1936, 195–96, NS20/143-2.

11. Kaplan, *Dignity,* 229.

12. On the Nazis' careful monitoring of public opinion, see, e.g., Gellately, *Backing,* 257, 259, 262; Kershaw, *Hitler Myth,* 257.

13. Even in 1943, Himmler complained to fellow SS leaders of the German public's inability to understand the necessity for the then ongoing slaughter of the Jews: "And then they come along, the worthy eighty million Germans, and each one of them produces his decent Jew. It's clear the others are swine, but this one is a fine Jew." Secret speech to SS leaders, Posen, 10/4/43. Translated in Noakes, *Nazism,* 1199–1200.

14. See, e.g., Schultze-Naumburg book review, *FSV* 4 (1938): 60; Knost, *Feststellung,* 75; Ulmenstein, *Abstammungsnachweis,* 104.

15. See, "Anlage zu meinem Bericht über die Karaimen-Frage," covered by Dr. Gross, Hauptamtslieter, to Partei-Kanzlei, München, Führerbau, 3/22/45, R39/152.

16. Report by Abteilung Volksgesundheit des Reichs- und Preußischen Ministeriums des Innern (possibly Lösener), n/d, Rep. 320/513:33–39.

17. See, e.g., Erklärung Ogfr. Karl Gellersen, 11/22/43, R1509/58.

Conclusion

1. Brunner to RSA, 9/30/42, R39/227.

2. Aly, *Vordenker,* 280.

3. Koonz, *Nazi Conscience,* 3.

4. Ibid., 6.

5. Novick, *Holocaust in American Life,* 13.

6. This is Daniel Goldhagen's term from *Hitler's Willing Executioners.* This work, however, takes issue with Goldhagen's claim regarding the extent of such antisemitism in German society both prior to and during the Third Reich.

7. Kettenacker, "Sozialpsychologische Aspekte," 131.

8. Schoenbaum, *Hitler's Social Revolution,* 286.

9. See, e.g., Grunberger, *Social History,* 459; Bankier, *Germans,* 155.

10. See, Gellately, *Backing,* 261.

11. On the incorporation of racist ideology into various academic and professional disciplines, see, e.g., Michael Burleigh, *Germany Turns Eastward: A Study of Ostforschung in the Third Reich* (Cambridge: Cambridge University Press, 1988); Hanjost Lixfeld, *Folklore and Fascism: The Reich Institute for German Volkskunde* (Bloomington: Indiana University Press, 1994); Maruhn, *Staatsdiener;* Proctor, *Racial Hygiene;* Redaktion Kritische Justiz (ed.), *Der Unrechts-Staat: Recht und Justiz im Nationalsozialismus* (Baden-Baden: Nomos, 1983); Alan Steinweis, *Studying the Jew: Scholarly Antisemitism in Nazi Germany* (Cambridge: Harvard University Press, 2006).

Bibliography

Archival

Bundesarchiv Berlin-Lichterfelde West
 R36 (Deutsche Gemeindetag)
 R43II (Reichskanzlei)
 R1509/alt R39 (Reichssippenamt)
 R1501/alt/Rep. 320 (Reichsministerium des Innern)
 R1001 (Reichskolonialamt)
 R4901 (Reichsministerium für Wissenschaft, Erziehung und Volksbildung)
 NS 6 (Partei-Kanzlei der NSDAP)
 NS 20 (Kleine Erwerbungen NSDAP)
 NS 22 (Reichsorganisationsleiter der NSDAP)
Bundesarchiv Dahlwitz-Hoppegarten
 ZA IV, ZB II
Geheimes Staatsarchiv Preußischer Kulturbesitz Berlin-Dahlem
 Rep. 309 (Reichssippenamt)
Bundesarchiv, Berlin Document Center, Personalakten, SS-Hauptorganisation
Archiv zur Geschichte der Max Planck Gesellschaft
 1 Abt. 2399 Rep. 0001A
 1 Abt. 2400 Rep. 0001A
 1 Abt. 2409 Rep. 0001A
Deutsche Zentralstelle für Genealogie, Leipzig
 25, 26, 28 Mitglieder-Verzeichnis der Zentralstelle für Personen-u.
 Familiengeschichte
 27 RSA
Wiener Stadt- und Landes Archiv
 Abstammungs-Erhebungen Abel-Alma A6/1
 Abstammungs-Erhebungen Alt-Antretter A6/2
 Abstammungs-Erhebungen Baader-Balko-Kastaly A6/4
 Abstammungs-Erhebungen Balla-Bauer Josef A6/5

Pre-1946 Journals and Newspapers

Allgemeines Suchblatt für Sippenforscher
Archiv für Rassen- und Gesellschaftsbiologie
Archiv für Sippenforschung und alle verwandten Gebiete
Deutsche Forschung im Osten
Der Deutsche Herold
Deutsche medizinische Wochenschrift
Deutsches Recht
Deutsche Zeitung
Familie, Sippe, Volk
Familiengeschichtliche Blätter
Familiengeschichtliche Quellen
Forschungen zur Judenfrage
Jüdischer Familienforschung
Korrespondenz für Rasseforschung und Familienkunde
Mitteilungen der Zentralstelle für deutsche Personen- und Familiengeschichte
Mitteilungen des Deutschen Roland
Mitteilungen des Roland
Monatschrift für Psychiatrie und Neurologie
Stuttgarter NS.-Kurier
Thüringer Heimatspiegel
Vierteljahrschrift für Wappen-, Siegel- u. Familienkunde
Völkischer Beobachter
Volk und Rasse
Westdeutscher Beobachter
Zeitschrift für Rassenkunde
Zeitschrift für Standesamtswesen
Zeitschrift für Volksaufartung und Erbkunde
Ziel und Weg

Books, Articles, and Other Published Works

Aly, Goetz, and Susanne Heim. *Vordenker der Vernichtung: Auschwitz und die deutschen Pläne für eine neue europäische Ordnung.* Hamburg: Hoffmann und Campe, 1991.

Aronson, Shlomo. *Heydrich und die Anfänge des SD und der Gestapo (1931–1935).* Berlin: Ernst-Reuter-Ges, 1967.

Bankier, David. *The Germans and the Final Solution: Public Opinion Under Nazism.* Oxford: Blackwell, 1992.

Barkan, Elazar. *The Retreat of Scientific Racism: Changing Concepts of Race in Britain and the United States between the World Wars.* Cambridge: Cambridge University Press, 1992.

Barnett, Victoria. *Bystanders: Conscience and Complicity During the Holocaust.* Westport, Conn.: Greenwood, 1999.

Baur, Erwin, Eugen Fischer, and Fritz Lenz. *Human Heredity,* trans. Eden and Cedar Paul. New York: Macmillan, 1931.

Benz, Wolfgang, and Werner Bergmann, eds. *Vorurteil und Volkermord: Entwicklungslinien des Antisemitismus.* Freiburg, Basel, Wien: Herder, 1997.

Benz, Wolfgang, Hermann Graml, and Hermann Weiß, eds. *Enzyklopädie des Nationalsozialismus.* Stuttgart: Klett-Kotta, 1997.

Blackbourn, David. *History of Germany, 1780–1918: The Long Nineteenth Century.* Malden, Mass.: Blackwell, 2003.

Bock, Gisela. *Zwangssterilisation im Nationalsozialismus: Studien zur Rassenpolitik und Frauenpolitik.* Berlin: Westdeutscher, 1986.

Burghardt, Franz Josef. *Familienforschung. Hobby und Wissenschaft.* Meschede: Thomas, 1995.

Burleigh, Michael. *Germany Turns Eastward: A Study of Ostforschung in the Third Reich.* Cambridge: Cambridge University Press, 1988.

Burleigh, Michael, and Wolfgang Wipperman. *The Racial State: Germany 1933–1945.* Cambridge: Cambridge University Press, 1991.

Caplan, Jane. *Government without Administration: State and Civil Service in Weimar and Nazi Germany.* Oxford: Clarendon, 1988.

Chickering, Roger. *We Men Who Feel Most German: A Cultural Study of the Pan-German League, 1886–1914.* Boston: Allen & Unwin, 1984.

Cohn, Norman. *Europe's Inner Demons.* New York: Meridian, 1975.

Craig, Gordon. *Germany 1866–1945.* New York, Oxford: Oxford University Press, 1978.

Devrient, Ernst. *Familienforschung.* Leipzig: Teubner, 1911.

Dover, Cedric. *Half-Caste.* London: Martin Seeker and Warburg, 1937.

Ehrenreich, Eric. "Anti-Semitism as Applied Biology: Nazi Ideology, Racial Science and the 'Jewish Question.' Masters Thesis, University of Wisconsin–Madison, 1998.

Engemann, Friedrich, et al. *Wegweiser durch das sippen-, rassen- und wappenkundliche Schrifttum des Fachverlages C.A. Starke in Görlitz.* Görlitz: Starke, 1937.

Faulhaber, Michael von. *Judaism, Christianity and Germany.* New York: Macmillan, 1934.

Felbor, Ute. *Rassenbiologie und Vererbungswissenschaft in der Medizinischen Fakultät der Universität Würzburg, 1937–1945.* Würzburg: Königshausen und Neumann, 1995.

Feldscher, Werner. *Rassen- und Erbpflege in deutschen Recht.* Berlin, Leipzig, Wien: Deutscher Rechtsverlag, 1943.

Fishberg, Maurice. *Die Rassenmerkmale der Juden.* München: Reinhardt, 1913.

Fredrickson, George. *Racism: A Short History.* Princeton, N.J.: Princeton University Press, 2002.

Friedlander, Henry. *The Origins of Nazi Genocide: From Euthanasia to the Final Solution.* Chapel Hill: University of North Carolina Press, 1995.

Friedrichs, Heinz, ed. *Familiengeschichtliche Bibliographie.* Band XI, Jahrgänge 1960. Neustadt an der Aisch: Verlag Degener & Co., 1961.

Fromm, Bella. *Blood and Banquets: A Berlin Social Diary.* London: G. Bles, 1942.

Gailus, Manfried. "Beihilfe zur Ausgrenzung. Die "Kirchenbuchstelle Alt-Berlin in den Jahren 1936 bis 1945." *Jahrbuch für Antisemitismusforschung* 2 (1993): 255–80.

Gasman, Daniel. *The Scientific Origins of National Socialism: Social Darwinism in Ernst Haeckel and the German Monist League.* New York: American Elsevier, 1971.

Gellately, Robert. *Backing Hitler: Consent and Coercion in Nazi Germany.* New York, Oxford: Oxford University Press, 2001.

Goldhagen, Daniel. *Hitler's Willing Executioners.* New York: Vintage Books, 1997.

Goldstein, Jeffrey. "Anti-Semitism in Occultism and Nazism." In Michael Marrus, ed., *The Nazi Holocaust: Historical Articles on the Destruction of European Jews.* Vol. 2, *The Origins of the Holocaust.* Westport, Conn. and London: Meckler, 1989.

Gordon, Sarah. *Hitler, Germans and the "Jewish Question."* Princeton: Princeton University Press, 1984.

Gould, Stephen Jay. *The Mismeasure of Man.* New York and London: Norton, 1981.

Grant, Madison. *Der Untergang der großen Rasse. Die Rassen als Grundlage der Geschichte Europas,* trans. Rudolf Polland. München: Lehmann, 1925.

Grolle, Joist. "Deutsches Geschlechterbuch: Ahnenkult und Rassenwahn." *Zeitschrift für Niederdeutsche Familienkunde* 4 (1999): 311–26.

Grunberger, Richard. *A Social History of the Third Reich.* London: Weidenfeld and Nicolson, 1971.

Günther, Hans F. K. *The Racial Elements of European History.* Port Washington, N.Y.: Kennikat, 1970.

———. *Rassenkunde des deutschen Volkes.* München: Lehmann, 1930.

Gutteridge, Richard. *The German Evangelical Church and the Jews, 1879–1950.* New York: Barnes & Noble, 1976.

Hayn, Friedrich. *Sippenfibel.* Berlin: Offene Worte, 1936.

Heilbron, J. L. *Dilemmas of an Upright Man: Max Planck and the Fortunes of German Science.* Cambridge: Harvard University Press, 2000.

Heinrichs, Helmut, Harald Franzki, Klaus Schmalz, and Michael Stolleis. *Deutsche Juristen Jüdischer Herkunft.* München: Beck'sche, 1993.

Helmreich, Ernst Christian. *The German Churches under Hitler: Background, Struggle, and Epilogue.* Detroit: Wayne State University, 1979.

Herbst, Ludolf. "Deutschland im Krieg 1939–1945." In Martin Broszat, ed., *Das Dritte Reich im Überblick.* München: Piper, 1990.

Hertz, Deborah. "The Genealogy Bureaucracy in the Third Reich." *Jewish History* 11 (1997): 53–78.

Heydenreich, Eduard. *Familiengeschichtliche Quellenkunde.* Leipzig: Degener, 1909.

Hohlfeld, Johannes, ed. *Familiengeschichtliche Bibliographie,* Band III–VII. Leipzig: Zentralstelle für Deutsche Personen- und Familiengeschichte, 1931–1951.

Hutton, Christopher. *Race and the Third Reich: Linguistics, Racial Anthropology and Genetics in the Dialectic of the Volk.* Cambridge: Polity, 2005.

Isenburg, Wilhelm Karl Prinz von. *Genealogie als Lehrfach. Zugleich Einführung in ihre Probleme.* Leipzig: Degener, 1928.

———. *Sippen- und Familienforschung.* Heidelberg: Carl Winter Universitätsverlag, 1943.

Jennings, Herbert Spencer, et al. *The Scientific Aspects of the Race Problem.* London, New York, Toronto: Catholic University Press, 1941.

Kaplan, Marion. *Between Dignity and Despair: Jewish Life in Nazi Germany.* New York, Oxford: Oxford University Press, 1998.

Kater, Michael. *The Nazi Party: A Social Profile of Members and Leaders, 1919–1945.* Cambridge: Harvard University Press, 1983.

Katz, Jacob. *From Prejudice to Destruction: Antisemitism, 1700–1933.* Cambridge: Harvard University, 1982.

Kelly, Alfred. *The Descent of Darwin: The Popularization of Darwinism in Germany, 1860–1914.* Chapel Hill: University of North Carolina Press, 1981.

Kershaw, Ian. *Hitler, 1936–1945: Nemesis.* New York: Norton, 2001.

———. *The "Hitler Myth."* Oxford: Clarendon, 1987.

Kettenacker, Lothar. "Sozialpsychologische Aspekte der Führer-Herrschaft." In Gerhard Hirschfeld and Lothar Kettenacker, eds., *Der "Führerstaat": Mythos und Realität. Studien zur Struktur und Politik des Dritten Reiches.* Stuttgart: Klett-Cotta, 1981.

Kiefer, Annegret Kiefer. *Das Problem einer "jüdischen Rasse": eine Diskussion zwischen Wissenschaft und Ideologie, 1870–1930.* Frankfurt a.M., New York: Lang, 1991.

Klocke, Friedrich von. *Die Entwicklung der Genealogie vom Ende des 19. bis zur Mitte des 20. Jahrhunderts: Prolegomena zu einem Lehrbuch der Genealogie.* Schellenberg bei Berchtesgaden: Degener, 1950.

Knost, Friedrich. *Feststellung und Nachweis der Abstammung.* Berlin: Vahlen, 1939.

Koonz, Claudia. *The Nazi Conscience.* Cambridge: Harvard University Press, 2003.

Kramp, P. "Der erbbiologische Abstammungsnachweis." *Der Biologe* 12 (1939): 383–94.

Krüger, Arnd. "A Horse Breeder's Perspective: Scientific Racism in Germany, 1870–1933." In Norbert Finzsch and Dietmar Schirmer, eds., *Identity and Intolerance: Nationalism, Racism and Xenophobia in Germany and the United States.* Cambridge: Cambridge University Press, 1998.

Länderrat des Amerikanischen Besatzungsgebiets, ed. *Statistisches Handbuch von Deutschland, 1928–1944.* München: Ehrenwirth, 1949.

Langmuir, Gavin. "Prolegomena to Any Present Analysis of Hostility against Jews." In Michael Marrus, ed. *The Nazi Holocaust: Historical Articles on the Destruction of European Jews*. Vol. 2, *The Origins of the Holocaust*. Westport, Conn. and London: Meckler, 1989.

Laqueur, Walter. *Weimar: A Cultural History, 1918–1933*. New York: G. P. Putnam's Sons, 1974.

Levy, Richard. *The Downfall of the Anti-Semitic Political Parties in Imperial Germany*. New Haven: Yale University Press, 1975.

Lilienthal, Georg. "Die jüdischen 'Rassenmerkmale': zur Geschichte der Anthropologie der Juden." *Medizinhistorisches Journal* 28 (1993): 172–98.

Lorenz, Ottokar. *Lehrbuch der gesammten wissenschaftlichen Genealogie: Stammbaum und Ahnentafel in ihrer geschichtlichen, sociologischen und naturwissenschaftlichen Bedeutung*. Berlin: Hertz, 1898.

Lösener, Bernard, and Friedrich A. Knost. *Die Nürnburger Gesetze*. 2nd ed. Berlin: Vahlen, 1937.

Lukas, Richard. *The Forgotten Holocaust: The Poles under German Occupation, 1939–44*. New York: Hippocrene, 1997.

MacMaster, Neil. *Racism in Europe, 1870–2000*. New York: Palgrave, 2001.

Macrakis, Kristie. *Surviving the Swastika: Scientific Research in Nazi Germany*. New York, Oxford: Oxford University Press, 1993.

Maruhn, Siegfried. *Staatsdiener im Unrechtsstaat: Die deutschen Standesbeamten und ihr Verband unter dem Nationalsozialismus*. Frankfurt a.M., Berlin: Verlag für Standesamtswesen, 2002.

Massing, Paul. *Rehearsal for Destruction: A Study of Political Anti-Semitism in Imperial Germany*. New York: Harper, 1949.

Mazumdar, Pauline. "Blood and Soil: The Serology of the Aryan Racial State." *Bulletin of the History of Medicine* 64 (1990): 187–219.

Mehrtens, Herbert. "The Social System of Mathematics and National Socialism: A Survey." In Monika Renneberg and Mark Walker, eds., *Science, Technology and National Socialism*. Cambridge: Cambridge University Press, 1994.

Mendes-Flohr, Paul, and Jehuda Reinharz, eds. *The Jew in the Modern World: A Documentary Reader*. New York, Oxford: Oxford University Press, 1995.

Metzner Verlag. *50 Jahre Alfred Metzner Verlag*. Frankfurt a.M., Berlin: Metzner, 1959.

Mommsen, Wolfgang. *Imperial Germany, 1867–1918: Politics, Culture, and Society in an Authoritarian State*. London: Arnold, 1995.

Mosse, George. *Fallen Soldiers: Reshaping the Memory of the World Wars*. New York, Oxford: Oxford University Press, 1990.

———. *Toward the Final Solution: A History of European Racism*. London: Dent, 1978.

Müller, H. *Beamtentum und Nationalsozialismus*. Munich: Eher, 1931.

Müller, Rolf-Dieter. "Das 'Unternehmen Barbarossa' als wirtschaftlicher Raubkrieg." In Gerd Ueberschär and Wolfram Wette, eds., *Der Deutsche Überfall auf die Sowjetunion*. Frankfurt a.M.: Fischer, 1999.

Noakes, Jeremy, and J. G. Pridham, eds. *Nazism: A Documentary Reader.* Vol. 3, *Foreign Policy, War and Racial Extermination.* Exeter: University of Exeter Press, 1984.

Norden, Günther van. "Die Evangelische Kirche und die Juden im 'Dritten Reich'." In Günter Brakelmann and Martin Rosowski, eds., *Antisemitismus. Von religiöser Judenfeindschaft zur Rassenideologie.* Göttingen: Vandenhoeck & Ruprecht, 1989.

Novick, Peter. *The Holocaust in American Life.* Boston, New York: Houghton Mifflin, 1999.

Overy, Richard. *Russia's War: A History of the Soviet War Effort, 1941–45.* New York: Penguin, 1998.

Proctor, Robert. *Racial Hygiene: Medicine under the Nazis.* Cambridge: Harvard University Press, 1988.

Pulzer, Peter. *The Rise of Political Anti-Semitism in Germany and Austria.* Cambridge: Harvard University Press, 1988.

Reuter, Edward. *Race Mixture: Studies in Intermarriage and Miscegenation.* New York: McGraw Hill, 1931.

Ribbe, Wolfgang. "Genealogie und Zeitgeschichte: Studien zur Institutionalisierung der nationalsozialistischen Arierpolitik." *Harold-Jahrbuch* 3 (1998): 73–108.

Ribbe, Wolfgang, and Eckart Henning. *Taschenbuch für Familiengeschichtsforschung.* Neustadt/A: Degener, 1995.

Rühle, Gerd. *Das Dritte Reich. Dokumentarische Darstellung des Aufbaus der Nation. Das erste Jahr 1933.* 2nd ed. Berlin: Hummel, 1934.

Schafft, Gretchen. *From Racism to Genocide: Anthropology in the Third Reich.* Urbana and Chicago: University of Illinois Press, 2004.

Schmitz-Berning, Cornelia. *Vokabular des Nationalsozialismus.* Berlin, New York: de Gruyter, 1998.

Schoenbaum, David. *Hitler's Social Revolution: Class and Status in Nazi Germany 1933–39.* New York: Doubleday, 1966.

Schulle, Diane. *Das Reichssippenamt: Eine Institutionen nationalsozialistischer Rassenpolitik.* Berlin: Logos, 2001.

Schupp, Waldemar. "Der Weg der Zentralstelle für deutsche Personen- und Familiengeschichte in Leipzig." *Herold-Studien* 5 (2000): 91–110.

Schwerin, Hans Bogislav Graf von. *Die Erstellung des Ahnenpasses.* Berlin: Eher, 1939.

Starke Verlag. *Wegweiser nebst Anwendungs-hinweisen für das sippen- und wappenkundliches Schrifttum des Fachverlages C. A. Starke, Görlitz.* Görlitz: Starke, 1933.

Steinweis, Alan. *Studying the Jew: Scholarly Antisemitism in Nazi Germany.* Cambridge: Harvard University Press, 2006.

Stern, Fritz. *The Politics of Cultural Despair: A Study in the Rise of the Germanic Ideology.* Berkeley: University of California Press, 1963.

Streit, Christian. "Die Behandlung der sowjetischen Kreigsgefangenen und völker-
  rechtliche Probleme des Krieges gegen die Sowjetunion." In Gerd Ueberschär
  and Wolfram Wette, eds., *Der Deutsche Überfall auf die Sowjetunion*. Frankfurt
  a.M.: Fischer, 1999.
Stuckart, Wilhelm, and Hans Globke. *Kommentar zur deutschen Rassengesetzgebung,*
  Bd. I, Reichsbürgergesetz, Blutschutzgesetz, Ehegesundheitsgesetz. München, Berlin:
  Beck, 1936.
Stuckart, Wilhelm, and Rolf Schiedermair. *Rassen- und Erbpflege in der Gesetzgebung*
  des Reiches. Leipzig: Kohlhammer, 1942.
Tal, Uriel. *Christians and Jews in Germany: Religion, Politics, and Ideology in the*
  Second Reich. Ithaca, N.Y.: Cornell University Press, 1975.
Themal, Karl, and Bernhard Freudenberg. *Die Deutschen Berufssippenforscher:*
  Mitgliedverzeichnis des Reichsverbandes der Sippenforscher und Heraldiker e.V.
  (R.S.H.). Berlin: Selbstverlag des Reichsverbandes der Sippenforscher und
  Heraldiker e.V., 1941.
Ulmenstein, Christian Ulrich Freiherr von. *Der Abstammungsnachweis*. Berlin:
  Verlag für Standesamtswesen, 1941.
Veit, Andreas Ludwig. *Der stiftsmässige deutsche Adel im Bilde seiner Ahnenproben*.
  Freiburg im Breisgau: Fr. Wagnersche Universitätsbuchhandlung, 1935.
Verlag für Sozialpolitik, Wirtschaft und Statistik. "Volks-, Berufs- und Betriebs-
  zählung vom 17. Mai 1939." In *Statistik des Deutschen Reichs*. Berlin: Verlag für
  Sozialpolitik, Wirtschaft und Statistik, Paul Schmidt, 1942. Band 556, Heft 1.
Verschuer, Otmar Freiherr von. "Erbanlage als Schicksal und Aufgabe." In *Preussische*
  Akademie der Wissenschaften Vorträge und Schriften, vol. 18. Berlin: de Gruyter,
  1944.
———. *Rasse*. Frankfurt a.M.: Englert & Schlosser, 1924.
Volkov, Shulamit. "Antisemitism as Cultural Code." In *Yearbook of the Leo Baeck*
  Institute 23 (1978): 25–45.
Walk, Joseph, ed. *Das Sonderrecht für Juden im NS-Staat*. Heidelberg, Karlsruhe:
  Müller Juristischer Verlag, 1981.
Walker, Mark. *Nazi Science: Myth, Truth, and the German Atomic Bomb*. Cambridge,
  Mass.: Perseus, 1995.
Wecken, Friedrich. *Die Ahnentafel als Nachweis deutscher Abstammung: "Der ari-*
  sche Nachweis" eine nationalsozialistische Bedingung für die Erwerbung des
  Staatsburgerrechtes. 7th ed. Leipzig: Degener, 1934.
———, ed. *Familiengeschichtliche Bibliographie*, Band VI, Jahrgänge 1920–1926.
  Leipzig: Zentralstelle für Deutsche Personen- und Familiengeschichte, 1928
  and 1932.
———. *Taschenbuch für Familiengeschichtsforschung*. Leipzig: Degener, 1919, 1922,
  1924, and 1937.

Weindling, Paul. *Health, Race and German Politics between National Unification and Nazism, 1870–1945.* Cambridge: Cambridge University Press, 1989.

Weingart, Peter, Jürgen Kroll, and Kurt Bayertz. *Rasse, Blut und Gene: Geschichte der Eugenik und Rassenhygiene in Deutschland.* Frankfurt a.M.: Suhrkamp, 1988.

Weiss, Sheila Faith. "The Race Hygiene Movement in Germany." In Mark Adams, ed., *The Wellborn Science: Eugenics in Germany, France, Brazil, and Russia.* New York, Oxford: Oxford University Press, 1990, 8–68.

———. *Race Hygiene and National Efficiency.* Berkeley, Los Angeles, London: University of California Press, 1987.

Weiss, Volkmar. "Die Auseinandersetzungen zwischen Reichsnährstand und Reichssippenamt um die Kirchenbuchverkartung." *Genealogie* 1/2 (2000): 1–17.

———. "Die Vorgeschichte des arischen Ahnenpasses." *Genealogie* 1/2 (2001): 417–36.

Wentscher, Erich. *Einführung in die praktische Genealogie.* 3rd ed. Görlitz: Starke, 1939.

Wundt, Max. *Volk, Volkstum, Volkheit.* Langensalza: Beyer, 1927.

Zmarzlik, Hans-Günter. "Social Darwinism in Germany." In Michael Marrus, ed., *The Nazi Holocaust: Historical Articles on the Destruction of European Jews.* Vol. 2,

Index

Page numbers in italics refer to illustrations.

Final Solution and, xvi–xvii, 165–72, 174–75; genealogical practice and, 16, 23–24, 32, 39, 41–42, 134–40, 159–63, 176; historical continuities and, xii, 42, 51, 57, 150–54; legal/bureaucratic continuities and, 42–44, 154–59; scientists and, xii–xiii, 130, 132–33; as unifying doctrine, xiii–xv, 135–36
racial shame (*rassenschande*), 196n23, 203n43
racial superiority/purity, xii, 28, 33, 45–49, 78, 166
"racially alien" persons, xiv, xvi, 41–42, 58, 66, 125–27. *See also specific groups*
Ranke, Leopold von, 18
Rasse (journal), 178n27
Reche, Otto, 124–26, 129, 131, 156
Reclams Universal-Bibliotech, 34
Red Cross, 97
Reich Adoption Office, 97
Reich Association of Kinship Researchers and Heraldists, 76, 87, 90, 137, 140, 160
Reich Citizenship Law (1935), 64, 103, 155. *See also* Nuremberg Laws (1935)
Reich Federation of German Civil Registrars, 34, 36, 40–41, 43, 53, 68; publishing house of, 34, 71, 73–74, 137. *See also Journal for Civil Registry Practice*
Reich Genealogical Authority, xv; advice/education and, 78, 89, 90–93; ancestors, determining of, by, 103–107; appeals of decisions and, 75, 82, 103, 156–57; corruption and, 157–58; cross-institutional support and, 91; documentation, gathering/preserving/evaluation of, and, 78, 81, 84–86, 97–98, 139, 141, 160; employee proof requirements of, 63; examinees, profile of, considered by, 98–103; genealogists as volunteers for, 138–39; history of, 51, 78–84; jurisdictions of, 79, 81–84, 86; legal/bureaucratic continuity claims of, 155–58; personal characteristics in decisions of, 111–16, 126; processes of, 96, 97, 100–101, 103, 155; racial determinations and, 80–82, 94, 108–10,

129–30, 171; regulation/promotion of genealogical practice and, 77, 78, 86–90, 137; tasks of, 78, 84–93. *See also* ancestral decisions; *Familie, Sippe, Volk*
Reich Institute for the History of the New Germany, 140
Reich Kinship Office, 79
Reich Office for Kinship Research, 79
Reich Union of Jews in Germany (*Reichsvereinigung der Juden in Deutschland*), 86
Reich Work Law (1939), 60
Reichsnährstand (agricultural organization), 85
Reichsverband der Sippenforscher und Heraldiker. See Reich Association of Kinship Researchers and Heraldists
Richard Wagner Yearbook, 55
RNK Papier- und Schreibwaren, 73–74
Rodde, Freiherr von, 19
Roland, 17, 19–20, 34, 35, 38, 49, 53–54. *See also News of the Roland*
Rosenhainer, Otto, 89–90
Russian ancestral decisions, 82
Ruttke, Falk, 53, 91

SA (*Sturmabteilungen*), 59
Saller, K., 47
Sardinians, 178n27
Scheidt, Walter, 25, 40, 46, 53
Schircks, Eberhard, 127
Schmidt, Wilhelm, 55
Schönberg, Adolf, Freiherr von, 20
Schultze-Naumburg, Arthur, 42, 88–89, 152, 158, 173
Schütz, Franz, 53
scientists: as beneficiaries of racist policies, xiv, xv, 130–33; biological investigations and, 121–33; costs of ancestral proofs and, 131–32; as genealogy promoters, 25; legal/bureaucratic continuities and, 156; racial scientific ideology and, xii–xiii, 130, 132–33
Security Police, 86
Seel, Hans, 9
Seidlinger (genealogist), 89
Semigotha, 31, 57, 90
Siebert, Friedrich, 49

Eric Ehrenreich holds a law degree from the University of California, Davis, and a Ph.D. in History from the University of Wisconsin–Madison. Dr. Ehrenreich has received numerous academic honors, including a Fulbright fellowship, a Berlin Program for Advanced German and European Studies fellowship, a George L. Mosse Wisconsin Distinguished Graduate Fellowship, and the Douglas and Carol Cohen Postdoctoral Fellowship at the U.S. Holocaust Memorial Museum's Center for Advanced Holocaust Studies. He has lectured on Nazi racial policy throughout the United States and has also taught courses on racism and Nazi science at the University of Wisconsin and George Mason University. He presently practices law in Washington, D.C.